NAVIGATING THROUGH ADOLESCENCE:
EUROPEAN PERSPECTIVES

NAVIGATING THROUGH ADOLESCENCE: EUROPEAN PERSPECTIVES

EDITED BY JARI-ERIK NURMI

Routledge Falmer
New York & London
2001

Published in 2001 by
RoutledgeFalmer
29 West 35th Street
New York, NY 10001

Published in Great Britain by
RoutledgeFalmer
11 New Fetter Lane
London EC4P 4EE

RoutledgeFalmer is an imprint of the Taylor & Francis Group.

Printed in the United States of America on acid-free paper.

Library of Congress Cataloging-in-Publication Data

Navigating through adolescence : European perspectives / edited by Jari-Erik Nurmi.
p. cm. - (Michigan State University series on children, youth, and families ; v. 8)
Includes bibliographical references and index.

ISBN 0-8153-3703-5 (alk. paper) ✓
1. Identity (Psychology) in adolescence. 2. Adolescent psychology.
I. Nurmi, Jari-Erik. II. Series

BF724.3.I3 N38 2001
155.5'18—dc21
00-046012

CONTENTS

Navigating Through Adolescence:
Introduction

Jari-Erik Nurmi

CHAPTER 1

Navigating Through Adolescence: Introduction

JARI-ERIK NURMI

Adolescence is a journey to adulthood. There are several destinations, a diversity of routes, many means of transportation, and a variety of companions. As in any journey, maps and advice are important, still choices have to be made. Most paths lead somewhere: some to the grand avenues of famous historic sites, others to the narrow streets of darkness. Indeed one does learn from new places—but, more importantly, from oneself. This book will focus on how individuals navigate through adolescence.[1] Twelve chapters will conceptualize, present data, and discuss the kinds of values, goals, beliefs, strategies, explorations, and commitments adolescents construct as tools with which to direct their lives across the diversity of routes they find available in their developmental environments as pathways to adulthood, and the kinds of self-definitions and identities they develop during this process. In many of the chapters, the role of interpersonal contexts—the traveling companions—is investigated and discussed.

The notion of the second and the third decades of life as a period of navigating through adolescence has its basis in two major features of adolescent development. On the one hand, rapid changes occur during this period in the navigational tools young people deploy: the ways in which they perceive and understand the world around them, and themselves as part of it; the ways in which this world seems to appeal to them in terms of valuing different behaviors and activities, and becoming interested in adult roles and related options; and the extent to which they have developed different means to deal with the various challenges they face during this life period (Nurmi 1993). Such changes are evidenced in the values, goals, planning, strategies, explorations, commitments, decision making, and self-identities individuals develop during their adolescent years. A variety of psychological developments during late childhood and early adolescence provide the basis for such changes in individuals navigational tools: For example, adolescents reach a level of thinking that is qualitatively different from their earlier cognitive skills (Markstrom-Adams 1992). They also face a variety of physiological changes, such as puberty and physical growth (Brooks-Gunn & Reiter 1990), which are reflected in the ways in which they perceive themselves and the world around them, and the ways in which others perceive them.

On the other hand, during the second and third decades of their lives individuals have to deal with a number of developmental transitions, normative demands and related decisions in their developmental environments that is greater than at any other life-period (Caspi, in press). These include decisions about future education, career, interpersonal commitments, and future family. By these decisions and choices, and related behaviors and commitments, adolescents create their developmental trajectories into adulthood. For example, school achievement and related investments, educational decisions, and choices of leisure activities all provide a basis for the kind of adult roles into which adolescents will grow (Nurmi 1991). Moreover, during their adolescent years individuals exercise and explore a variety of alternative activities and build up interpersonal relationships, which then provide a basis for their future social skills, gender role identity and interpersonal commitments. This development is partly enhanced by the fact that adolescents acquire a growing amount of autonomy in their interpersonal life. Parents, for example, provide increasing independence for their growing children.

This book will focus on dealing with the ways in which individuals navigate through adolescence: what kinds of psychological tools they deploy, with whom they negotiate and interact, what alternative developmental pathways exist, and, finally, what consequences this process has for their later lives and well-being.

Navigational Tools

An increasing amount of research has been carried out during the past decades on the ways in which adolescents navigate into adulthood. Some of this research, conceptualized as future orientation, has focused on investigating the kinds of future-related maps, views, and interests adolescents have. Some other studies have focused on investigating the ways in which adolescents attempt to deal with future challenges, such as explorations of future opportunities, planning for the future, coping with new demands, decision making and other related commitments. There is also a long tradition of examining the ways in which adolescents construct a conceptualization of themselves as a consequence of this process, such as research on identity formation.

Future-orientation

A number of studies have been carried out during the past fifty years on young adults' thinking about the future (Nurmi 1991). One of the earliest extensive studies in this field was carried out by Gillispie and Alport (1955) who compared students outlook of the future in ten countries in the early 1950s. Interestingly, in one of the most recent publications in this field, Nurmi, Liceanu and Liberska (1999) investigated adolescents' future interests in eleven European countries and the United States as a part of the large EURONET study (Alsaker & Flammer 1999). Some of the major findings in this research field can be summarized as follows.

A majority of adolescents seem to be interested in the future, when asked about hopes and goals (e.g., Nurmi 1989; Nurmi 1991). Even adolescents who have shown substantial amounts of problem behavior report a variety of hopes and goals concerning their future lives (Salmela-Aro, Nurmi & Ruotsalainen 1995). Young people are also optimistic about their personal future (e.g., Nurmi 1989; Poole & Cooney 1987). This optimism is reflected in the ways in which they anticipate future events: they do not, for example, consider negative life-events, such as divorce, to be likely in their own future lives (Blinn & Pike 1989). Adolescents also tend to report that personal crises and negative life events, such as unemployment, are more likely to happen to other people rather than themselves.

When adolescents are asked about their future hopes, interests, and expectations, they typically report topics that focus on their personal lives, such as future education, occupation, family, leisure activities, travel, and self-related issues (Nurmi, Seginer & Poole 1995; Salmela-Aro, in this volume). Interestingly, there seems to be only little variation across societies and cultures in such hopes and interests (Nurmi & al. 1999; Solantaus 1987; for a review see Nurmi 1991). However, when adolescents are asked about their fears or worries concerning the future, a substantial proportion of them deal with societal and even global issues. Furthermore, considerable cross-cultural variety and change across historical time is found in such fears and concerns (Solantaus 1987). These differences seem to reflect the topics that are discussed in the mass media and in public during a particular era (Nurmi 1991; Solantaus, Rimpelä, & Taipale 1984).

There is, however, a great deal of individual variation in the future-oriented goals young people report, which seems also to predict their subsequent life-paths, such as family transitions and life events (Salmela-Aro & Nurmi 1997a). Moreover, the kinds of future-oriented goals young people have are reflected in their well-being. Interpersonal and family-related goals, for example, are associated with high well-being (Emmons 1991; Salmela-Aro-Nurmi 1997). Although it has been suggested that working with identity is one of the major developmental tasks during adolescence (Erikson 1959; Marcia 1980), self-focused, existential kinds of goals, particularly if associated with concerns and negative emotions, seem to be associated with low well-being among young adults (Salmela-Aro & Nurmi 1997b).

Decision Making, Planning, and Cognitive Strategies

In the course of navigating into adulthood, adolescents have to make a variety of decisions, choose between a number of alternative routes, plan their behavior, and construct a variety of strategies to deal with the new demands and challenges they are facing. A variety of conceptualizations has been used to describe this process. For example, many studies have focused on investigating adolescents' decision making in a variety of contexts, such as education (Klaczynski & Reese 1991) and future career (Blustein et al. 1989). Similarly, a substantial amount of research has examined the ways in which adolescents plan their lives (Malmberg 1996; Nurmi 1989). This research seems to show that during their adolescent years individuals begin to deploy increasingly complex plans and decision making as a means of directing their lives into adulthood (Nurmi 1989).

A substantial amount of research has also focused on investigating the kinds of tools adolescents develop in order to cope with the demands they meet during the transition into adulthood, and the consequences these have for their success in dealing with these demands. For example, several studies have shown that the deployment of adaptive achievement strategies, typified by optimism, task-focused behavior and high effort, lead to high achievement at school and related adjustment, whereas the use of maladaptive strategies, characterized by failure expectations, self-handicapping and helplessness, lead to low achievement and poor adjustment (Aunola, Stattin, & Nurmi, 1999; Midgley, Arunkumar, & Urdan 1996; Nurmi, Onatsu, & Haavisto 1995). Similarly, the deployment of task-focused coping efforts, such as developing a plan of action, utilizing social resources, discussing problems, and engaging in scholastic activities, has been found to be associated with adolescents' optimal adjustment, whereas stress palliation coping, like daydreaming, listening to music, and blaming others for one's problems, is related to less optimal adjustment (Jorgensen & Dusek 1990). Berzonsky (1988) has described individual differences in the social-cognitive processes young people use to deal with their identity issues in terms of identity styles. His findings have shown that utilization of informational and normative identity styles is associated with heightened self-esteem, whereas reliance on diffuse, avoidance identity styles is associated with lowered self-esteem and various problem behaviors (Berzonsky & Kinney 1994b).

Identity Explorations and Commitments

In the course of their adolescent years, individuals develop a relatively stable and coherent sense of themselves, described as self-identity (Erikson 1959). It has been suggested that this identity formation, consists of a series of crises and decisions in several life domains focusing on individuals' entry into major adult roles. A lot of research on identity formation has relied on Marcia's (1966, 1980) identity status paradigm, in which four identity statuses are defined in terms of the presence and absence of self-exploratory crises and commitment: identity diffusion (no current crisis or commitment), moratorium (current crisis, no commitment), foreclosure (commitment, no apparent former crisis), and identity achievement (commitment, previous crisis resolved). The main idea of Marcia's original theory was that adolescents proceed from less advanced identity statuses to more advanced ones. However, there is an increasing body of evidence suggesting that adolescents' identity development is a less linear and more complex process than was assumed in Marcia's original theory: in many cases there seem to be transitions from more advanced to less advanced identity statuses (Adams & Jones 1983; Waterman 1982), identity formation seems to follow different patterns in different life domains (Kroger 1988), and a considerable amount of identity development seems to occur beyond the years of adolescence (Pulkkinen, Nurmi, & Kokko, in press).

This body of evidence has lead to the construction of a new, process-oriented approach to identity development (Bosma 1995; Grotevant 1987; Marcia 1988). Underlying this process-oriented approach is the idea that during adolescence individuals end up engaging in a variety of explorational activities and related commitments that reflect their personal values and needs and the variety of opportunities offered by society (Bosma 1985; Grotevant 1987). According to Kroger (1988), for example, identity is not a unitary structure but rather a sequence of distinct psychosocial resolutions involved in the definition of self. The findings reported in research using this process-oriented approach resemble those found in the field of future-orientation. For example, school, occupation, leisure activities, friendship, and parents have been found to be the most important topics related to identity exploration and commitment, and the focus on these topics has been found to increase with age (Bosma 1985; Kalakoski & Nurmi 1998). The majority of the research on adolescents' identity formation thus far has focused on investigating the process of identity formation. One complementary approach in the field, however, has been to investigate the antecedents and the consequences of identity formation. For example, Blustein, Devenis, and Kidney (1989) found that exploratory activities in vocational domains were positively associated with moratorium and achievement identity statuses and negatively with diffusion status.

Navigation into Adulthood: Routes and Destinations

During adolescence and young adulthood, people are frequently faced with a variety of developmental transitions, new challenges and new opportunities in several life domains. Such transitions have been described using a variety of concepts, such as developmental tasks (Havighurst 1948), role transitions (Elder 1985) and institutional careers (Klaczynski & Reese 1991). Such cultural, societal and institutional structures not only define the routes to adulthood that are available to adolescents but also provide a basis for the kinds of decisions, choices, and actions they can take concerning their future.

The Role of Age-graded Developmental Tasks and Transitions

There is a substantial amount of evidence suggesting that the age-graded transitions, normative demands, and institutional tracks individuals face provide a basis for the ways in which they navigate through adolescence. For example, a substantial proportion of adolescents' future hopes and interests have been found to focus on the major developmental tasks of this age period, such as future education, occupation, interpersonal relationships and family (For a review, Nurmi 1991; Nurmi et al. 1995; Poole & Cooney 1987). It has also been shown that adolescents become increasingly interested in such topics with age (Nurmi 1989; Nurmi, Poole, and Kalakoski 1994). Young people have also been found to be continuously changing their goals in accordance with the major changes, demands, and challenges they are faced with during a certain transition, such as the transition from school to work (Nurmi & Salmela-Aro 2000) and the transition to parenthood (Salmela-Aro, Nurmi, Saisto, & Halmesmäki, in press). The future time perspective of adolescents' thinking has also been shown to reflect the normative life course pattern, mainly focusing on events expected to occur in the early twenties (Nurmi 1989).

Similarly, it has been shown that the major topics of adolescents' identity work deal with the major age-graded developmental tasks and transitions. For example, Bosma (1985) found that school, occupation, and friendship were among the most important topics of adolescents' identity explorations and commitments. Moreover, Kalakoski and Nurmi (1998) showed recently that adolescents' identity explorations and commitments seem to reflect the institutional transitions they are currently facing. They found, for example, that young peoples' identity explorations and commitments related to future education increased before the transition from junior to senior high school.

Cross-cultural and Cross-national Diversity

Although the key themes of the developmental tasks and normative transitions adolescents face during the process of navigating into adulthood are similar across societies and cultures, there is a substantial amount of variation in the timing and sequencing of such transitions (Hurrelmann 1994; Nurmi, Seginer, & Poole 1995). In many European countries streaming in education based on academic achievement begins relatively early, at the age of ten in Germany, for example, and continues later in several more stages (Hurrelmann & Settertobulte 1994). By contrast, Scandinavian adolescents receive comprehensive education until the age of fifteen without any streaming, and only after then do they have to make their first educational choices (Nurmi & Siurala 1994). These differences in educational transition are coincident with those of occupational life. In Scandinavia, for example, the majority of adolescents continue their schooling up to the age of eighteen (Roe, Bjuström, & Fornäs 1994), whereas in Switzerland a substantial proportion serve apprenticeships after the age of fifteen (Buchmann 1994). Similar differences are also evident in the transitions related to interpersonal life. In Northern Europe, Sweden for example, the mean age of first marriage is about twenty-eight (Roe et al. 1994), whereas in Southern Europe, such as in Spain, marriage takes place on average between twenty-three and twenty-five years of age (Martinez, de Miguel, & Fernandez 1994). Such cross-national and cross-cultural differences in the timing and sequencing of the major developmental transitions are important because they create cross-national diversity in the routes which adolescents may take when they navigate into adulthood.

Interestingly, the cross-cultural and cross-national differences in the timing and sequencing of the major developmental and institutional transitions have also been found to be reflected in adolescents' future-oriented goals and identity explorations and commitments. For example, Nurmi, Seginer, and Poole (1995) found that, due to earlier and shorter educational transitions, Australian adolescents showed a higher level of exploration and commitment, both in the domain of future education and work, compared with their Israeli and Finnish counterparts. They also expected their goals and hopes related to future education and work to be realized earlier in their lives than did young Finns and Israelis. Other differences, such as urban versus rural living environments and related differences in the opportunity structures, have also been shown to be reflected in the changes in young people's future-oriented goals during adolescence (Nurmi et al. 1994).

Co-navigation

Navigating through adolescence does not only consist of individual planning, decision making and exploration, but is often influenced by significant others, such as parents, peers, and siblings. In many cases, there are good reasons for describing this process as co-navigation into adulthood rather than seeing it as a purely individual adventure.

Parents influence the ways in which their children navigate through adolescence in three ways at least: first, by communicating expectations and setting normative standards, they direct the development of their children's interests, goals, and values; second, by acting as role models and providing tutoring, they influence the ways in which their adolescent child deals with the various developmental demands they face; and, finally, by providing support and feedback, they contribute to the ways in which adolescents evaluate their success in dealing with these demands (Nurmi 1991). A number of studies have also shown that family relations contribute to the ways in which adolescents explore their future options, and make related commitments, as a part of their identity formation

(Grotevant & Cooper 1986). For example, foreclosures have been shown to have the closest relationships with their parents, whereas adolescents in the moratorium and achievement identity categories are more critical toward their parents (for a review, see Waterman 1982). However, the parent-adolescent relationship consists of mutual interactions. In many cases, the ways in which adolescents deal with their future in terms of explorations, commitments, and choices influence their parental relationships. For example, adolescents' efforts to become independent in their decision making may create conflicts or at least increase parents' motivation in becoming involved in their children's future-planning. Moreover, problems in dealing with the key developmental demands, such as low school achievement, may increase parents' efforts to control and monitor their children's behavior. It has also been shown that the role of parents in their children's decision making concerning the future varies to a great extent across cultures (Poole, Sundberg, & Tyler 1982).

Aside from parents, peers, friends, and siblings might be assumed to be involved in the ways in which adolescents navigate into adulthood. Adolescents spend a substantial amount of time with their peers (Larson 2000), which creates a natural context for the negotiation of topics they consider to be important for their future lives. Peer groups also provide a natural setting for social comparisons, which might be assumed to influence the ways in which adolescents evaluate their success in dealing with the major developmental demands (Nurmi in this volume). Also, other factors in society, such as the mass media, may be influential in adolescents' goal-construction and decision making, for example, by providing information about the opportunities available in the society of the future, as well as alternative adult roles.

Contents of this Book

The aim of this book is to contribute to our understanding of the ways in which individuals navigate through adolescence. In consequence, contributors were invited from ten European research groups whose work has dealt with a variety of related topics, such as adolescents' values, goals, future-orientation, cognitive-motivational strategies, identity explorations and commitments, and decision making. The book is divided into four parts. The first part presents research on the development of the major psychological tools young people deploy in navigating through adolescence; the second part examines the deployment of these tools in two particular life domains, future education and occupation; the third part focuses on the role of family in this process; and the fourth part introduces a few recent theoretical advancements in European research on the topic of navigating through adolescence.

The Role of Values, Goals and Strategies during Adolescence and Young Adulthood

Part I consists of three chapters that focus on investigating the developmental dynamics of some of the major motivational and cognitive processes involved in navigation from adolescence to young and middle adulthood. In the second chapter, Stattin and Kerr discuss adolescents' values as an important organizing principle for how they feel, think, behave, and relate to others. By using data from two studies among Swedish adolescents, they investigate the associations between adolescents' values and their everyday activities, family relationships, personality, and subsequent life-span development. Their results show that adolescents who have self-focused values differ in a variety of ways from their age-mates with other-focused values, for example, in the terms of their everyday activities, relationships with their peers and parents, norm-breaking behavior, school adjustment, and partner relationships in adulthood.

In the third chapter, Salmela-Aro presents data on the kinds of personal goals young adults report when they are facing the transition from school to work. One of her particular tasks is to identify homogeneous groups of young adults who show different goal patterns, and then to investigate the extent to which these groups differ in terms of their well-being and success in dealing with this particular transition. The results of a cross-lagged longitudinal study among Finnish young adults show that the kinds of goal patterns young adults show, i.e., whether these are focused on dealing with major normative demands, achievement-related topics, interpersonal relationships, material aspects of life, or existential self-related issues, have a variety of consequences for their well-being and success in dealing with the transition from school to work.

In the fourth chapter, Eronen focuses on investigating the kinds of cognitive-motivational strategies young people deploy in two major developmental environments, i.e. academic and interpersonal settings, and what the major antecedents and consequences are for the use of such strategies. The results of three studies among young Finns show that the kinds of strategies young people deploy contribute to their success in dealing with a variety of demands and challenges in both settings. Moreover, individuals' success in dealing with such demands and challenges seems to provide a basis for the kinds of strategies they later deploy.

Future-planning and Career Explorations in Educational and Vocational Settings

Part II consists of two chapters that focus on investigating adolescents' future-orientation and identity explorations in two particular domains of life, i.e. education and occupation. In the fifth chapter, Malmberg investigates the extent to which adolescents' future-planning and related information gathering should be described as an individual cognitive activity or as an interpersonal negotiation process. His results, based on two studies among Swedish-speaking Finnish adolescents, show that peers and parents seem to play an important role in young people's future planning. Apart from these, adolescents report also the mass media to be an important source of future-related information.

In the sixth chapter, Kracke and Schmitt-Rodermund present findings on the antecedents and consequences of adolescents' exploration and information-gathering concerning future work and careers. Using data from a number of studies among German adolescents, they show that a high level of occupational exploration is influenced by child-centered parenting and adaptive personality characteristics, such as self-efficacy and openness to experience, rather than a lack of previous information on this particular topic.

Future-orientation and Decision-making in the Family Context

Part III consists of two chapters which deal with the role of the family in adolescents' future-orientation and decision-making. In the seventh chapter, Lanz, Rosnati, Marta, and Scabini investigate the kinds of hopes and fears adolescents' parents have about their children's future and compare these to the views of the adolescents themselves. The results found in an Italian sample show that the parents are optimistic about their children's future, as are the adolescents about their own future. Moreover, parents' hopes for their children's future lives seem also to reflect the normative life-span development, i.e., age-graded developmental tasks and institutional transitions. This result was also in accordance with how adolescents perceive their own future.

In the eighth chapter, Zani, Bosma, Zijsling, and Honess examine adolescents' efforts to search for autonomy and the extent to which negotiations of this issue lead to conflicts in family relationships. They investigated this in three countries (Italy, Wales, and the Netherlands) with a particular emphasis on gender differences. The results show that, overall, adolescents and their parents perceive the norms related to a variety of issues concerning autonomy in similar ways. For example, there seems to be an increase in autonomy during the years of adolescence, as perceived by both the adolescents and their parents. However, although there were also discrepancies in their views, they mainly seem to concern the timing of the acquisition of autonomy.

Theoretical Advances in Adolescents' Self-direction

Part IV contains three chapters that aim at introducing recent theoretical and methodological advances in research into the ways in which individuals navigate through adolescence, and the kinds of self definitions they construct during this process. In the ninth chapter, Nurmi discusses a theoretical model in which navigating through adolescence is described in terms of two processes: self-direction and self-definition. A particular emphasis is on describing how these two processes function on the one hand, in the context of changing age-graded sociocultural environments, and, on the other, in interpersonal contexts such as family and peer groups.

In the tenth chapter, Kunnen, Bosma, and van Geert introduce a dynamic systems theory as a tool with which to investigate and model adolescent development. By using a recent theory on adolescents' identity formation, they construct a model which includes identity commitments, the tendency to assimilate or accommodate, and positive and negative life-events faced by adolescents, as major parameters of the model. Then, on the basis of formulating this theory according to specific variables, and after defining their relation as mathematical formula, they test several hypotheses raised recently in research into adolescents' identity formation by performing a number of simulations based on the mathematical model.

In the eleventh chapter, Guichard introduces a theoretical analysis of various processes that are involved in adolescents' identity development and describes future projects that have not been typically discussed in research on adolescent development. He expands the previous conceptualization of identity by introducing some recent European sociological theories. These theories focus on the key mechanisms by which educational institutions and related practices, social position and related beliefs, behaviors, tastes, values, and habits, and the ways of speaking of oneself in social situations contribute to the development of adolescents' identity and future projects.

As an effort to understand the ways in which individuals navigate through adolescence, this volume is European in at least three respects. First, the findings are reported from a variety of societies across Western Europe. This not only provides an opportunity to understand the cultural and institutional diversity that young people face, but also to search for more general laws governing adolescent development across a variety of sociocultural contexts. Second, the book devotes more space to theoretical issues than is typical of similar texts in the United States. Such a focus on theory has a long tradition in European psychology in general, and in adolescent research in particular. Third, a variety of theoretical viewpoints on adolescent development are introduced. Such diversity of theoretical ideas is typical not only of adolescent research in Europe, but of any discussion and argumentation in this part of the world. It is seen here as important to pursue this diversity in the ideas and the methodologies applied.

References

Adams, G. R. & Jones, M. (1983). Female adolescents' identity development: Age comparisons and perceived child-rearing experience. *Developmental Psychology, 19,* 249–256.

Alsaker, F. D. & Flammer, A. (Eds., 1999). *The adolescent experience. European and American adolescents in the 1990s.* Mahwah, N.J.: Lawrence Erlbaum.

Aunola, K., Stattin, H., & Nurmi, J. B E. (1999). Parenting styles and adolescents'achievement strategies. *Journal of Adolescence, 29,* 289–306

Berzonsky, M. D. (1988). Self-theorists, identity status and social cognition. In D. K. Lapsley & F.C. Power (Eds.). *Self, ego, and identity: Integrative approaches* (pp. 243–262). New York: Springer.

Berzonsky, M. D. & Kinney, A. (1994b). *Identity processing orientation, need for structure, depressive reactions, and attributional styles.* Unpublished data. State University of New York, Department of Psychology, Cortland, NY 13045.

Blinn, L. M. & Pike, G. (1989). Future time perspective: Adolescents' predictions of their interpersonal lives in the future. *Adolescence, 24,* 289–301.

Blustein, D. L., Devenis, L. E., & Kidney, B. A. (1989). Relationship between the identity formation process and career development. *Journal of Counseling Psychology, 36,* 196–202.

Bosma, H. A. (1985). Identity development in adolescence. Coping with commitments. Groningen: Rijksuniversiteit Te Groningen.

Bosma, H. A. (1995). Identity and identity process: What are we talking about? In A. Oosterwegel & R. A. Wicklund (Eds.). *The self in European and North American culture: Development and processes,* (pp. 5–17). Amsterdam: Kluwer Academic Publishers.

Brooks-Gunn, J. & Reiter, E. O. (1990). The role of pubertal processes. In S. S. Feldman and G. R. Elliott (eds.). *At the threshold: The developing adolescent* (pp. 16–53). Cambridge, MA: Harvard University Press.

Buchmann, M. (1994). Switzerland. In K. Hurrelmann (Ed.) *International handbook of adolescence.* Westport: Greenwood Press.

Caspi, A. (in press). Social selection, social causation and developmental pathways: Empirical strategies for better understanding how individuals and environments are linked across the life course. In L. Pulkkinen & A. Caspi (Eds.), *Successful development.*

Elder, G H., Jr. (1985). Perspective on the life course. In G. H. Elder, Jr. (Ed.) *Life course dynamics* (pp. 23–49). Ithaca, NY: Cornell University Press.

Emmons, R. A. (1991). Personal strivings, daily life events and psychological and physical well-being. *Journal of Personality, 59,* 455–472.

Erikson, E. H. (1959). *Identity and the life cycle.* New York: International Universities Press.

Gillispie, J. M. & Allport, G. W. (1955). *Youth's outlook on the future (a cross-national study)*. New York: Doubleday & Company.

Grotevant, H. D. & Cooper, C. R. (1986). Individuation in family relationships. A perspective on individual differences in the development of identity and role-taking skills in adolescence. *Human Development, 29*, 82–100.

Grotevant, H. D. (1987). Towards a process model of identity formation. *Journal of Adolescent Research, 2*, 203–222.

Havighurst, R. J. (1948). Developmental tasks and education. New York: McKay.

Hurrelmann, K. (Ed., 1994). *International handbook of adolescence*. Westport: Greenwood Press.

Hurrelmann, K. & Settertobulte, W. (1994). Germany. In K. Hurrelmann (Ed.). *International handbook of adolescence*. Westport: Greenwood Press.

Jorgensen, R. S. & Dusek, J. B. (1990). Adolescent adjustment and coping strategies. *Journal of Personality, 58*, 503–513.

Kalakoski, V. & Nurmi, J.-E. (1998). Identity and educational transitions: Age differences in adolescent exploration and commitment related to education occupation and family. *Journal of Research on Adolescence, 8*, 29–47.

Klaczynski, P. A. & Reese, H. W. (1991). Educational trajectory and action orientation: Grade and track differences. *Journal of Youth and Adolescence, 20*, 441–462.

Kroger, J. (1988). A longitudinal study of ego identity status interview domains. *Journal of Adolescence, 11*, 49–64.

Larson, R. W. (2000). Toward a psychology of positive youth development. *American Psychologist, 55*, 170–183.

Malmberg, L.-E. (1996). How do Finnish students prepare for their future in three school types? The relation between content of plans, information gathering and self-evaluations. *British Journal of Educational Psychology, 66*, 457–469.

Marcia, J. E. (1966). Development and validation of ego identity status. *Journal of Personality and Social Psychology, 3*, 551–558.

Marcia, J. E. (1980). Identity in adolescence. In J. Adelson (Ed.), *Handbook of adolescent psychology*. New York: Wiley, pp. 159–187.

Marcia, J. E. (1988). Common processes underlying ego identity, cognitive/moral development, and individuation. In D. K. Lapsley & F. C. Power (Eds.), *Ego, self, and identity: Intergrative approaches* (pp. 211–225). New York: Springer.

Markstrom-Adams, C. (1992). A consideration of intervening factors in adolescent identity formation. In G. A. Adams, T. P. Gullotta, & R. Montemayor (Eds.). *Adolescent identity formation* (pp. 173–192). Newbury Park, CA: Sage Publications.

Martínez, R.-A., de Miguel, M., & Fernández, S. (1994). Spain. In K. Hurrelmann (Ed.). *International handbook of adolescence*. Westport: Greenwood Press.

Midgley, C., Arunkumar, R., & Urban, T. C. (1996). "If I don't do well tomorrow, there's a reason:' Predictors of adolescents' use of academic self-handicapping strategies. *Journal of Educational Psychology, 88*, 423–434.

Nurmi, J.-E. (1989a). Adolescents' orientation to the future: Development of interests and plans, and related attributions and affects, in the life-span context. *Commentationes Scientiarum Socialium, 39*. Helsinki: The Finnish Society for Sciences and Letters.

Nurmi, J.-E. (1991). How do adolescents see their future? A review of the development of future orientation and planning. *Developmental Review, 11*, 1–59.

Nurmi, J.-E. (1993). Adolescent development in an age-graded context: The role of personal beliefs, goals and strategies in the tackling of developmental tasks and standards. *International Journal of Behavioral Development, 16*, 169–189.

Nurmi, J.-E., Liiceanu, A., & Liberska, H. (1999). In F. D. Alsaker, & A. Flammer (Eds.). *The adolescent experience. European and American adolescents in the 1990s*. Mahwah N J: Lawrence Erlbaum.

Nurmi, J.-E., Poole, M. E., & Kalakoski, V. (1994). Age differences in adolescent future-oriented goals, concerns, and related temporal extension in different sociocultural contexts. *Journal of Youth and Adolescence, 23*, 471–487.

Nurmi, J.-E. & Salmela-Aro, K. (in press). Goal construction, reconstruction and depressive symptomatology in a life-span context: The transition from school to work. *Journal of Personality*.

Nurmi, J.- E., Seginer, R., & Poole, M. E. (1995). Searching for the future in different environments: A comparison of Australian, Finnish and Israeli adolescents' future orientations, explorations and commitments. In P. Noack, M. Hofer, & J. Youniss (Eds.) (pp. 219–237) *Psychological responses to social change. Human development in changing environments*. Berlin: Walter de Gruyter.

Nurmi, J.-E. & Siurala, L. (1994). Finland. In K. Hurrelmann (Ed.). *International handbook of adolescence*. Westport: Greenwood Press.

Nurmi, J.- E., Onatsu, T., & Haavisto, T. (1995). Underachievers' cognitive and behavioral strategies—Self-handicapping at school. *Contemporary Educational Psychology, 20*, 188–200.

Poole, M. E. & Cooney, G. H. (1987). Orientations to the future: A comparison of adolescents in Australia and Singapore. *Journal of Youth and Adolescence, 16*, 129–151.

Poole, M. E. & Sundberg, N. D., & Tyler, L. E. (1982). Adolescents' perception of family decision-making and autonomy in India, Australia, and the United States. *Journal of Comparative Family Studies, 18*, 349–357.

Pulkkinen, L., Nurmi, J.-E., & Kokko, K. (in press). Individual differences in personal goals in the thirties. In L. Pulkkinen, & A. Caspi (Eds.) *Paths to successful development: Personality in the life course*. Cambridge, U K: Cambridge University Press.

Roe, K., Bjurström, E., & Fornäs, J. (1994). Sweden. In K. Hurrelmann (Ed.). *International handbook of adolescence*. Westport: Greenwood Press.

Salmela-Aro, K., Nurmi, J.-E., & Ruotsalainen, H. (1995). Personal goals of young social drop-outs. *Perceptual and Motor Skills, 80,* 1184–1186.

Salmela-Aro, K. & Nurmi, J.-E. (1997a). Goal contents, well-being and life context during transition to university: A longitudinal study. *International Journal of Behavioral Development, 20,* 471–491.

Salmela-Aro, K. & Nurmi, J.-E. (1997b). Positive and negative self-related goals and subjective well-being: A prospective study. *Journal of Adult Development, 4,* 179–188.

Salmela-Aro, K., Nurmi, J.-E., Saisto, T., & Halmesmäki, E. (2000). Women's and men's personal goals and concerns during the transition to parenthood. *Journal of Family Psychology, 14,* 171–186.

Solantaus, T. (1987). Hopes and worries of young people in three European countries, *Health Promotion, 2,* 19–27.

Solantaus, T., Rimpelä, M., & Taipale, V. (1984). The threat of war in the minds of 12- to 18-year-olds in Finland. *Lancet, 8380,* 784–785.

Waterman, A. S. (1982). Identity development from adolescence to adulthood: An extension of theory and a review of research. *Developmental Psychology, 18,* 341–358.

Notes

1. This concept of 'navigating through adolescence' was first mooted by Professor Gisela Trommsdorf when she acted as a discussant in the symposium 'Future time perspective and motivation: A cross-cultural and developmental approach,' organized by W. Lens and T. Shirai, at the XIVth Biennial Meetings of ISSBD, Quebec City, Canada.

Part One

The Role of Values, Goals, and Strategies
During Adolescence and Young Adulthood

CHAPTER 2

Adolescents' Values Matter

HÅKAN STATTIN AND MARGARET KERR

Values and Socialization

One could argue that the fundamental goal of socialization is to teach children to place the good of others and society above their own pleasures. Many of the basic values that parents try to instill in their children deal with concern for the good of others: respecting life, refusing to discriminate, embracing democratic and human rights, treating others with respect and dignity, and serving others. Values concerning interpersonal relations are part of the cultural, social, and religious macrosystems, as well. Most religions have variants of the golden rule: do to others as you expect them to do to you. In many dictionaries, the word "good," when it refers to a person, is defined as someone who willingly tries to help and do what is best for others. Of course, this would be especially true in collectivist cultures, but even in the most individualistic cultures living within the law often requires people to place the good of the whole and the rights of others above their own desires. Thinking and caring about others, then, is fundamental to the socialization of children and adolescents.

Nonetheless, many adults in Western Europe and North America seem to expect adolescents to be self-absorbed. People think of adolescence as a pleasure-seeking phase in the life cycle rather than as a time of serving other people. Teenagers have so much free time and we seem to assume that they will spend a lot of it on their own amusement and entertainment. We should, perhaps, not be surprised to find adolescents being self-centered, not caring particularly about, or committing themselves to, the welfare of the surrounding community; nor should we be surprised to find that materialistic values become more dominant from childhood to adolescence (Cohen & Cohen 1996).

On the other hand, values should be very important in adolescence, because this is the time when important life decisions are being made. By late adolescence, people develop complex and abstract self-concepts that include philosophies of life, beliefs, principles, and moral standards—general value orientations (Damon & Hart 1988; Montemayor & Eisen 1977). It has been proposed that adolescents set goals for the future based on their values and motives, and then they plan specific activities to reach their goals (Nurmi 1991; 1993a). If this is so, then values should matter in adolescence. Moreover, it should be this very contrast between the values that parents and society have been trying to neutralize—concern for only personal satisfaction and enjoyment—and the values that parents and society have been trying to inculcate—concern for others' well-being and the common good—that should form a basis for adolescents' future decisions and relationships with others.

Two broad value orientations that reflect this distinction have often been identified in research (Braithwaite & Law 1985; Crosby et al. 1990; Rokeach 1973; Schwartz 1992; 1994). Different labels have been attached. They have been called hedonistic versus humanistic, materialistic versus altruistic, and, to some extent, individualistic versus collectivistic values. But overall, across studies and regardless of labels, there is a basic distinction between what we shall call self-focused and other-focused values. By self-focused values we mean a focus on one's own needs and enjoyment. By other-focused values we mean a focus on people, relationships, and the common good. Other-focused values are what parents try to socialize in children and are approved by the broader society. Self-focused values are not approved by parents and society. This should have important implications for life in adolescence and adulthood.

The existing literature offers hints that these types of values may have differential consequences for behavior in diverse domains. One comes from a study in which materialistic/hedonistic values were linked to high involvement with peers and with antisocial behavior (Cohen & Cohen 1996; see also Bear & Rys 1994). The other comes indirectly from studies on moral reasoning (Carlo, et al. 1996; Eisenberg 1986; Eisenberg, Lennon, & Roth 1983; Eisenberg, et al. 1995; Miller & Eisenberg 1988). Across studies, hedonistic reasoning has been found to be negatively related to prosocial behavior and needs-oriented reasoning has been positively related. Moreover, hedonistic reasoning has been linked to acting-out behavior and low sociometric status in elementary school (Bear & Rys 1994). Whitbeck, Simons, Conger, and Lorenz (1989) reported that adolescents with altruistic values had less involvement with deviant friends relative to those with success and affluence values.

In this chapter, we argue that adolescents' life values are organizing principles that guide, and are reinforced by, activities and interests. Thus, we expect a coherent pattern of activities, behaviors, interpersonal relations, and personalities for adolescents with certain types of value orientations. We argue that these life values are likely to be intimately linked to how people pass through the adolescent years and should have consequences for adult life and well-being. Specifically, we argue that adolescent values: are reflected in adolescents' everyday activities and lifestyles, are related to personality, and have long-term implications for adult life because future well-being depends, in part, on whether goals that are related to these adolescent values are attained.

An Organized System

Development is a holistic affair that involves biological, psychological, and socio-environmental influences that become fused over ontogeny. Single aspects of development—biological, behavioral, or environmental—gain meaning through their functional relations with one another and with the individual's developmental history. The way an individual functions in one domain is lawfully linked to how he or she functions in others, and the broader picture of interrelations can be described as an organized person-environment system (Cairns 1979; Magnusson & Stattin 1998): "A modern interactionist view emphasizes an approach to the individual and the person-environment system as organized wholes, functioning as totalities and characterized by the patterning of relevant aspects of structures and processes, in the individual and in the environment. The totality derives its characteristic features and properties from the interaction among the elements involved, not from the effect of each isolated part on the totality. Each aspect of the structures and processes that are operating (perceptions, plans, values, goals, motives, biological factors, conduct, etc.), as well as each aspect of the environment, takes on meaning from the role it plays in the total functioning of the individual" (Magnusson & Stattin 1998). If one takes this holistic perspective seriously, then particular aspects of development must be analyzed in terms of their relations to the whole person-environment system. Individual patterns at one point in time can provide an entry point into the developmental process from which developmental trajectories can be studied (Magnusson 1988). Presently, we have limited knowledge about the interrelations among diverse aspects of adolescent functioning. Models that integrate several domains are scarce, the work of Jessor and Jessor (1977) being a notable exception. But values offer a way of doing this.

Values as Organizers of Adolescent Life

Values, according to our argument, play an important role in organizing the adolescent behavior-environment system. The conceptual definition of values that most scholars agree on reveals why. Scholars agree, among other things, that values are beliefs about what is desirable, they determine which behaviors generalize across situations, and they underlie important decisions such as with whom we associate, how we behave, and what we do (Crosby, Bitner, & Gil 1990; Rokeach 1973; Schwartz 1994). Values are thought to underlie and determine the short-term and long-term goals that direct people's thoughts and behaviors (Pervin 1983). They are considered meta-goals that encompass more specific goals such as personal projects (Little 1983) and life tasks (Cantor & Kihlstrom 1987). Despite this conceptual agreement, there are only a few studies that directly have tested the idea that values guide people's thoughts and actions. In a couple of studies, people made choices that were consistent with their values (Durgee, O'Connor, & Veryzer 1996; Lindberg, Gärling, & Montgomery 1989), and in another, they rated everyday activities as important if they were related to important life values (c.f., Gärling, Lindberg, Montgomery, & Waara 1985). These studies suggest, tentatively, that values should provide a general framework for organizing the mental, behavioral, and social aspects of adolescent life.

How would these mental, behavioral, and social aspects of life be organized for adolescents with self-focused values? These are the values of which parents and society do not directly approve and, in fact, away from which have tried to socialize children. We should expect this chasm between the adolescent and conventional society to be evident in the organization of many aspects of life. If parents do not approve of the basic values guiding their adolescents' behavior and, by extension, the here-and-now, pleasure-seeking, self-focused behavior itself, then adolescents should stay away from home more and become more heavily involved with peers who have similar values and are engaged in desired behaviors. This might mean spending time out on the streets in the evening and being exposed to, and involved in, behaviors such as drinking alcohol, taking drugs, vandalizing property and other delinquent acts, skipping school, and early or risky sexuality. These adolescents are likely to have few hobbies and interests that would keep them at home in the evening and few household responsibilities. Thus, an overinvolvement in peer culture might be the hallmark of a self-focused adolescent lifestyle. Cohen and Cohen (1996) ended their investigation of the impact of life values on children's and adolescents' mental health by concluding: "Perhaps the most significant of the findings is the fact that children who spend more time with peers are more likely to endorse the more self-focused and deviant ideals and goals" (p. 155).

Adolescents with self-focused values will not want to tell their parents much about their activities or thoughts and feelings. Parents will have limited knowledge about where these adolescents are, what they are doing, with whom they are spending time, or how they are thinking and feeling. Parents are likely to be worried and distrustful because their adolescents are away from home unsupervised at times of the day when they may put themselves in risky situations and expose themselves to negative influences.

Compared to others of their age, adolescents with self-focused values will press harder for parental permission to spend time out with their friends. This is a high priority for them, so they will be persistent, and probably succeed in getting permission to spend time away from home. But, even though they are out more than their peers, they may complain that their parents try to control them too much. This peer-oriented lifestyle, will also involve being up late in the evening, being tired in the morning, and being late for school, behaviors of which parents do not normally approve. They are likely to have many conflicts with parents over these issues. Furthermore, because their parents are quite distrustful, they might respond more negatively than other parents do. Parent-child relationships will be relatively poor and common family activities rare.

Planning for and commitment to the future are integral parts of society's values, but they are not consistent with self-focused values. Adolescents with self-focused values should be more absorbed in short-term than long-term pursuits, avoiding responsibilities and withdrawing from tasks that demand persistence. When faced with demanding tasks such as schoolwork, they may exhibit what has been called task irrelevant behavior (Nurmi 1993b, 1997), which can include escaping and seeking more pleasurable activities. They are likely to achieve less, and adjust less well to school, than other adolescents.

In short, adolescents with self-focused values are likely to regard hanging out with friends as particularly pleasurable, amusing and exciting, and highly important in their lives. Hence, many of the everyday and leisure time activities of adolescents with self-focused values are likely to be outside of the home, in the company of peers, and protected from their parents' insights.

A different organization of activities and priorities can be expected for adolescents with other-focused values. These are the values that are approved by parents and society, and we should see that reflected in more conventional activities and long-term planning. Most fundamentally, adolescents with other-focused values should be more home-centered and involved in family activities. Like others their age, they will be involved in evening activities with their friends. The activities, however, will be structured, organized activities such as sports, music, and hobbies, rather than unstructured activities such as being out on the streets. Adolescents with other-focused values are likely to tell their parents about their activities and inner feelings. As a result, their parents will have relatively few worries and high levels of trust. These adolescents are likely to feel that they have a great deal of freedom. They will seldom have conflicts with their parents about getting up in the morning, getting to school on time, doing homework, or being home before curfew. They will have affectionate relationships with their parents and join in family activities. Finally, compared with those who have self-focused values, adolescents with other-focused values will be more task and future oriented. They should get along well at school and have good relations with their teachers.

In summary, we propose that self-focused and other-focused values can be seen in the organization of everyday behaviors. We have made a number of specific propositions about how adolescents with self-focused values should differ from those with other-focused values, and we have tested these propositions using data from a large sample of Swedish adolescents and their parents. The propositions are as follows.

Social context of everyday activities

We expect adolescents with other-focused values to spend more time doing daily activities at home, whereas adolescents with self-focused values will spend more time away from home, with like-minded peers.

Risky behavior

We expect that adolescents with self-focused values will be exposed to more normbreaking than will those with other-focused values because they will be spending a lot of unsupervised time with their peers late in the evening. As a result, they will be more tolerant of normbreaking and more likely to engage in it themselves. Peer groups tend to form because of shared interests and values. Children and adolescents tend to affiliate with similar others (e.g., Kandel 1978). Consequently, we expect that adolescents with self-focused values will have more norm-violating peers in their circles of friends than those with other-focused values.

Sleep-wake patterns

We propose that adolescents with self- and other-focused values will have distinct sleep-wake patterns that reflect the time of day when they want to be most alert. Adolescents with self-focused values spend time with their friends in the evening, often late in the evening. Subsequently, they will go to bed late, will be difficult to awaken in the morning, and will not feel fresh and alert when school begins. By contrast, adolescents with other-focused values will have an earlier activity peak, will go to bed earlier, and will arise alert and refreshed in the morning.

Long-term commitments

We propose that adolescents with self-focused values are interested in here-and-now activities and uninterested in long-term commitments. They value academic achievement less and are less success oriented than adolescents with other-focused values. They would rather focus on things that are not related to school achievement. Hence, they will more often fail to concentrate on demanding tasks at home or at school and do more pleasurable things instead. As described by Nurmi's (1993b, 1997) "failure-trap" model, when school work becomes difficult, instead of concentrating, they day dream or find excuses to do other things.

Hiding thoughts and actions from adults

One basic premise for our argument is that adolescents with self-focused values will avoid parental supervision and control to pursue their preferred activities (of which parents do not approve). They are likely to be secretive about their activities and thoughts. Adolescents with other-focused values, by contrast, will have an open dialogue with their parents about their daily activities, thoughts, and feelings. Consequently, parents of adolescents with self-focused values will have less information and will be more worried and distrustful than will parents of adolescents with other-focused values.

Affective relationships to parents

Research has not supported the old idea that adolescents, in general, experience a tug of war between parent and peer influences (Bandura 1972; Offer 1969; Offer & Offer 1975). This might be true for some adolescents, however (Kandel & Davies 1982). We expect that adolescents with self-focused values will experience this conflict. For them, relationships with parents will be strained, and they will have more conflicts with their parents about leisure time activities, curfews, going to bed and getting up on time, getting to school on time, and other school-related issues. Generally, adolescents with self-focused values will have less close relationships with their mothers and fathers than those with other-focused values.

Personality

We propose that, when compared with each other, adolescents with self-focused values will have relatively more adventurous, unconventional personalities, whereas adolescents with other-focused values will have relatively more conventional personalities.

Method
Subjects and material

A list of twelve different values (self-focused: "looking good," "the opposite sex," "having fun with my friends," "having a lot of free time," "having the freedom to do what I want," and "having a lot of money" and other-focused: "developing deep relationships with others," "helping others," "a peaceful world," and "working with others for a better society," plus two filler items) was presented to fourteen-year-old adolescents living in Örebro, the fifth largest city in Sweden. There were thirteen schools in the town and 1,288 adolescents in grade eight. One thousand and one hundred twenty-six adolescents were tested with different instruments (Stattin & Kerr 1999; Kerr & Stattin 1999; Kerr, Stattin, & Trost 1999). Information on values could not be collected in all classes because of time constraints, but it was collected in the majority of the schools (totally 844 subjects).

We asked the subjects to rank the twelve values according to priority. As our list of values is constrained and contains basically two types of value orientations, if the respective value orientations are homogeneous, then adolescents who score high on one type are forced to score low on the other. Our two value orientations were also found to be largely bipolar using the rank order procedure described. We made an index of the six self-focused values and another aggregated measure of the four other-focused values. The correlation between them was -.86 (p < .001). For the separate items, "Having fun with my friends" was rated as the most important (mean = 8.9 on a scale from 1 [least important] to 12 [most important]), followed by "A peaceful world" (M = 7.0), "Looking good" (M = 6.9), "The opposite sex" (M = 6.7), "Having a lot of free time" (M = 6.3), "Having the freedom to do what I want" (M = 5.9), "Having a lot of money" (M = 5.5), "Helping others" (M = 5.4), "Developing deep relationships with others" (M = 4.2), and "Working with others for a better society" (M = 3.4).

The subjects responded to the value instrument and other questionnaires (see below) during the regular school hours, and they were assured that their answers would be confidential. Teachers were not present. The administration of the questionnaires was done by research assistants. The study was approved by the county ethics committee.

Parents also participated in the study. They were asked to fill out and return a questionnaire by mail. Of the parents of the 844 adolescents with data on life values, 725 parents, or 86 percent, responded. In most cases, it was the mother in the family who responded to the questionnaire.

Other measures
Social context of everyday activities

We asked the subjects "How many times per week do you spend the whole evening at home?", "Do you often hang out in the city at night without doing anything special?", "In the group you belong to, how many people (that you know of) are often out in the city during the evenings?", "Do you have a curfew on weekdays (fixed time)?", "If yes, what time?", "Do you have a curfew on Saturday night (fixed time)?", "If yes, what time?", "Which of the following activities do you go to in your free time (where there is a leader, and you meet at least once a week at a set time): sports, music, theater, hobby, church, scouts, politics, other?", "How many nights per week do you usually: socialize with peers, play a musical instrument (not as part of an organized activity), read a book (not homework), work on a hobby (not as part of an organized activity), draw, paint, or do other artistic work (not as part of an organized activity), clean, do chores or run errands?", and "Are you responsible for any chores in the following areas: meals, housekeeping, laundry?"

Parents were asked "How many times per week does the child spend the whole evening at home?", "Does the child have a curfew on weekdays (fixed time)?", "If yes, what time?", "Does the child have a curfew on Saturday night (fixed time)?", "If yes, what time?", "Is the child regularly responsible for any chores in the following areas: meals; housekeeping; laundry?"

Risky behavior

We used normbreaking as our measure of risky behavior. Fourteen items comprised a normbreaking scale: "Have you taken items from a mall, store, or newsstand without paying?", "Have you gotten caught by the police for anything you have done?", "Have you purposely vandalized or taken part in vandalizing something that did not belong to you such as a window display, car, telephone booth, bench, or garden?", "At home, have you taken money that did not belong to you?", "Have you been part of scribbling, vandalizing with graffiti, or writing something with ink or paint somewhere, such as on a wall?", "Have you taken part in breaking into a house, store, newsstand, storage, or any other building intending to steal something?", "Have you bought or sold something that you knew or suspected was stolen?", "Have you taken a bike without permission?", "Have you been part of a physical fight in the city?", "Have you carried a weapon in school or in the city?", "Have you been part of taking a car without permission?", "Have you taken a moped or motor cycle without permission?", "Have you smoked hashish?", and "Have you used any drugs other than hashish?" The alpha reliability was 0.84 for this scale. The subjects were also asked "Have you had sexual intercourse?", "Do you smoke?", and "Have you drunk beer, liquor, or wine to the point of feeling drunk?"

The parents were asked if they knew that their son or daughter had done any of the seventeen behaviors in the normbreaking index just described. The items were worded similarly. The alpha reliability was 0.58 for the normbreaking scale, the low value is likely to be attributed to skewed distributions of the items involved. Parents were also asked if they knew if their son or daughter had had sexual intercourse, smoked, or had been drunk.

Sleep-wake patterns

To assess the youths' sleep-wake patterns, the adolescents were asked "If you consider how you feel at night, at what time in the evening do you start to feel tired and feel like going to bed?", "If you could choose by yourself, what time would you want to go to bed at night?", "Do you have a certain time to go to bed on weekdays?, "If so, what time?", "How easy is it to get up in the morning?", "How alert do you feel?", "How tired do you feel?", "If you could choose by yourself, what time would you want to get up in the morning?", "Sometimes people talk about 'morning' and 'evening' (night-owl) types of people. Which one of these types do you think you are?", "Think about how you feel when you have just awoken in the morning. To what extent do you feel: grouchy, talkative, happy."

The parents were asked "Does the child have a certain time to go to bed on weekdays?, "If yes, what time?", "How does the child function in the morning, and how does he/she feel the first half hour?", "How easy is it to get up?", "How alert does he/she feel?", "How tired does he/she feel?", and "You sometimes hear about 'morning' and 'evening' types of people. Which of these types do you consider your child to be?"

Long-term commitments

School adjustment was used as one indicator of long-term commitments and short-term pleasures. This measure comprised five items: "Do you like school?", "Do you try your best at school?", "Does school feel like a prison to you?" (rev.), "How would you describe the relationship between school and you," and "Are you satisfied with your schoolwork?" The alpha reliability was 0.80 of this scale. Subjects were also asked "How satisfied are you with your school grades?", "Have you skipped school this semester (been gone from school the whole day)?" and "In the group to which you belong, how many do well in school?"

Our aggregated measure of task-irrelevant behavior contained eight items: "If something starts going badly with school work, I find reasons to withdraw from it," "It is very easy for me to think about other things, daydream, or get lost in my own thoughts when I really should be concentrating on more important things," "I often find other things to do when I should be solving a difficult problem," "If a difficult problem comes up, I usually quickly decide to do something else", "I am a person that chooses to do something else if a problem is not solved quickly," "If I think that a school assignment is boring, I choose to do something else instead," "Even if there are other things to do that are more fun, I always finish the work that I am doing first" (reversed), and "I begin many different things, but it is difficult for me to finish them." Alpha reliability was 0.81 for the scale. Subjects were also asked "How many nights per week do you do homework (study on your own)?"

Parents answered the same questions about the child's school adjustment and about the child's task irrelevant behavior with only slight changes in wording where necessary. Alpha reliabilities were 0.83 and 0.88 for these scales. They were also asked "Has the child ever skipped school or cut class this semester?"

Parents' knowledge, trust, and worries

Five indices measured parents' knowledge about the child and their trust and worry. Six items composed our measure of adolescents' spontaneous disclosure of leisure time and school information: "Do you keep a lot of secrets about what happens during your free time?", "Do you hide a lot from your parents about what you do during the evening and on weekends?", "Do you usually tell how school was when you get home (how you did on different exams, your relationships with teachers, etc.)?", "When you get home from being out at night, do you tell what you have done that evening?", and "Do you often spontaneously talk at home about how you are doing in the different subjects in school?" The alpha reliability was 0.78 for the scale.

Seven questions made up a scale of the subjects' spontaneous disclosure of their thoughts and intimate matters: "Do you tell your mom or dad how you really feel inside?", "If you are worried about something, do you talk with one of your parents?", "Do you talk to your mom or dad about intimate things (e.g., your boyfriend or girlfriend)?", "Can you talk freely, for the most part, with your parents like you do with your friends?", "If something bothers you, do you want your parents to know about it?", "Do you talk with your parents about what is really important to you?", and "Do you tell your parents if something happens, even if you are embarrassed about it (feel ashamed about it)?" The alpha reliability was 0.87 for the scale.

Parents' knowledge of the adolescent's whereabouts was measured by nine items: "Do your parents know what you are doing during your free time?", "Do your parents know which friends you hang out with during your free time?", "Do your parents usually know what you have for homework?", "Do your parents know how you spend your money?", "Do your parents usually know when you have an exam or deadline for school?", "Do your parents know how you are doing in your different subjects at school?", "Do your parents know where you go (your hangouts) when you are out with your friends in the evening?", "In the last month, has there been a time when your parents did not have any idea where you were during the evening?", and "Do your parents usually know where you are and what you are doing in the afternoon directly after school?" The alpha reliability was 0.85 for the scale.

The subjects perception of being controlled by parents was measured with the following five items: "Do you think that your parents give you enough freedom to do what you want during your free time?", "Do you feel that your parents demand to know everything?", "Do you think that your parents control everything in your life?", "Do you think your parents are too involved in what you do during your free time?", and "Do you feel as though you can keep nothing to yourself because your parents want to know everything?" The alpha reliability was 0.75 for the scale.

The perception of parents' worries was measured with a scale including: "Are your parents worried that you will start using narcotics; get into trouble with the police; get into bad company; begin to abuse alcohol; or fail to finish school?" and "Are they worried about what you do with your friends at night and on weekends?" The alpha reliability was 0.90 for the scale.

The perception of parents' trust was a scale involving six items: "Do your parents trust that you will not hang out with bad people?", "Do your parents trust that you will watch your money (not be in debt, not buy useless things)?", "Do you feel that your parents are completely trusting of you and allow you to take responsibility over your free time?", "Do your parents trust that you will do your best in school?", "Do your parents trust that you will not do anything dumb during your free time?", and "Do your parents trust what you say that you are going to do on a Saturday night is true?" Alpha reliability was 0.82 for this scale.

For four of the aggregated measures, parents answered the same questions as the adolescents. The alpha reliabilities were 0.80 for the adolescent's disclosure of information about free time and school, 0.82 for parental knowledge, 0.88 for parents' worries, and 0.81 for parents' trust in the adolescent.

Relationships with parents and teachers

Four specific questions asked about everyday life conflicts with the mother: "How often do conflicts arise between you and your mother: about when you get up in the morning, about staying out late in the evenings, because you are late getting off to school in the morning, because you have forgotten to do your homework, or have put it off until the last minute?"

A scale measuring the affective mother relations contained the items: "Do you and your mother fight and argue with each other?" (rev.), "How often do you feel disappointed with your mother?"(rev.), "How often do you feel proud of your mother?", "How often do you think that you and your mother understand each other?", "Do you wish your mother was different?" (rev.), "Do you accept your mother the way she is?", How often do you feel angry or irritated with your mother? (rev.), and "Does your mother usually support and encourage you?" The alpha reliability was 0.87 for this scale. The same items, with the word father instead of mother, formed a measure of affective father relations. The alpha reliability was 0.88 for this scale.

A scale measuring common activities in the family contained the items: "On an average weekend (Saturday and Sunday), how much time do you and your parents spend together (playing a game, going out to a film or theater, going together to workout or do something else—but not watching TV together)?", "How often do you do something fun with your whole family?", "How often do your parents take the time to plan something for the whole family to participate in?", "Is it important in the family to do things together, or do family members (you and your parents) usually satisfy their separate interests individually?", and "How often does the whole family visit neighbors, relatives, or friends together?" Alpha reliability was 0.76 for the scale.

Parents' negative reactions to the adolescent's communications was measured with the items: "Has it happened that you told your parents things, and you later regretted that you did?", "How often have you regretted that you told your parents too much about yourself, your friends, and your free time?", "Have you been punished for something that you spontaneously told your parents?", "Has it ever happened that your parents have used what you told them against you", "Do your parents bring up things that you told them in confidence again and again?", and "Has it happened that your parents have made fun of things you've told them about yourself and your life?" The alpha reliability was 0.81 for this scale.

A teacher relations scale contained the following seven questions: "Do you like your teachers?", "Do you think that your teachers are fair with you?", "Do you usually talk back to your teachers?" (rev.), "Do you feel defiant against your teachers?" (rev.), "Do you think that your teachers like you?", and "If you have a problem in school, can you talk with your teachers about it?" Alpha reliability was 0.85 for the teacher relations scale. Also, the adolescents rated their satisfaction with their teachers on a 7-point Libert-type scale anchored with "very unsatisfied" and "very satisfied."

Parents were asked three questions about daily conflicts: "How often do conflicts arise between you and your child: over getting up in the morning, because he/she does not get off to school on time in the morning, because he/she forgets to do homework or has put it off until the last minute?" Parents also answered the same questions that the children answered concerning family activities. The alpha reliability was 0.76 for that scale.

Personality

Adolescents' personality styles were measured with Cattell's High School Personality questionnaire (HSPQ, Form A, Cattell 1962). The instrument includes thirteen personality scales of relevance for the present study: Reserved vs. Outgoing, Affected by feelings vs. Emotionally stable, Phlegmatic vs. Excitable, Obedient vs. Assertive, Sober vs. Happy-go-lucky, Disregards rules vs. Conscientious, Shy vs. Venturesome, Tough-minded vs. Tender-minded,

Table 2: Stepwise multiple regression predicting self-focused and other-focusd value orientation from the HSPQ (n=158)

Variables in the equation	Beta	t	p<
Other-focused value orientation[1]			
Less Intelligent—More Intelligent	.15	2.05	.04
Obedient—Assertive	-.18	-2.08	.05
Tough-minded—Tender-minded	.22	3.52	.001
Self-focused value orientation[2]			
Affected by feelings—Emotionally stable	-.17	-2.54	.05
Obedient—Assertive	.23	3.36	.001
Sober—Happy-go-lucky	.14	2.07	.05
Disregards rules—Conscientious	-.21	-2.33	.05
Tough-minded—Tender-minded	-.10	-2.14	.05
Self-assured—Apprehensive	-.15	-2.28	.05

[1] Model $R^2 = .14$, $F = 12.26$, $p<.0001$
[2] Model $R^2 = .26$, $F = 8.77$, $p<.0001$
* $p<.05$ *** $p<.001$
From Stattin and Kerr (in press). Reprinted by permission of the British Psychological Society.

Vigorous vs. Doubting, Self-assured vs. Apprehensive, Group-dependent vs. Self-sufficient, Casual vs. Controlled, and Relaxed vs. Tense. This questionnaire was not administered to the present cross-sectional sample, but to adolescents in a longitudinal study. Further descriptions are presented later in the chapter.

Results
Social context of everyday activities

The first two columns in Table 1 report correlations between various measures of home and away-from-home activities and self- and other-focused values. Also, we calculated a dichotomized self-focused versus other-focused measure (SF vs. OF). We selected as adolescents with self-focused values those who were above the median on the aggregated self-focused value measure and below the median on the aggregated other-focused value measure (n = 337), and as adolescents with other-focused values those who scored below the median on the aggregated self-focused value measure and above the median on the aggregated other-focused value measure (n = 380). This dichotomized measure includes 85 percent of the total sample (717 out of 844). T-tests of the differences between these two groups are presented in the third column in Table 1. All analyses were conducted with one-sided tests, and we report only significance levels below p < .01. Unless stated otherwise, our discussion of the results includes only the findings using the dichotomized measure.

As reported in Table 1, adolescents with self-focused values spent more evenings away from home, were more often out on the streets in the evening, and had more friends who were often out on the streets in the evening. There was no relation between values and having a fixed time to be at home on weekdays or a fixed time to be at home on Saturdays. In agreement with our proposition, the adolescents with self-focused values who *had* fixed times were allowed to stay out later on Saturdays than the adolescents with self-focused values. Adolescents with self-focused values were less likely to be involved in structured evening activities (sports, music, hobbies).

Evening activities for the adolescents with self-focused values often meant being together with peers. Adolescents with other-focused values were more often at home in the evening reading a book, playing an instrument, or painting than were adolescents with self-focused values. Finally, more of the adolescents with other-focused values had household responsibilities such as making meals, cleaning, shopping, or helping in other ways. Altogether, adolescents with self-focused values seemed to have more away-from-home activities, to be more involved in peer activities, to have fewer household responsibilities, and to have fewer regular activities at home.

Do parents' reports agree with these adolescents' views? Parents reported on

Table 1: Differences in everyday lifestyles between adolescents with self- and other-focused value orientations

	t-test of Self-Focused vs. Other-Focuses
Social context of everyday activities	
Number of evenings spent home	3.18*
Often out in the streets doing nothing	-3.10*
Have peers who often are out in the streets	-3.27*
Time be home weekdays	-2.35**
Time be home Saturdays	-3.91**
Structured leisure activities (scale)	3.38**
Evenings activities: together with my peers	-3.84*
play an intrument	3.19*
read a book	4.25**
work with a hobby	-0.28**
paint, art	3.82**
clean, help, buy	5.77**
Home resposibilities: making meals	5.35**
cleaning	4.15**
washing	1.89
Risky behavior	
Normbreaking behavior (scale)	-3.93**
Delinquent friends	-2.41*
Sexual intercourse	-1.78
Smoking	-1.91*
Drinking	-4.66**
Sleep-wake patterns	
Time when you start to feel tired	-3.16*
Own choice of time to go to bed	-5.47**
Time for going to sleep	-1.78*
How easy it is to get up in the morning	2.80**
How alert in the morning	3.40**
How tired in the morning	-2.42*
Own choice of time when going up	-2.87*
Perception of oneself as lark versus owl	-2.96*
Grouchy in the morning	-2.97*
Talkative in the morning	1.16
Happy in the morning	1.96
Long-term commitments	
School adjustment (scale)	5.75**
Satisfaction: My school achievement	2.92*
Truancy	-3.40**
Have peers who are good at school	2.64*
Task-irrelevant behavior (scale)	-4.72**
Evening activities: doing homework	2.85*
Hiding thoughts and actions from adults	
Disclosure leisure time information to parents (scale)	8.95**
Disclosure personal things to partnets (scale)	7.53**
Parental knowledge (scale)	7.19**
Perception of being controlled by parents (scale)	-4.60**
Parental worries (scale)	-4.25**
Parental trust (scale)	5.99**
Affective relationships to adults	
Conflicts with mother: about getting up in the morning	-1.79*
about curfew times	-4.72**
about time to go to school	-2.46
about forgetting to do homework	-2.19*
Affective mother relations (scale)	5.52**
Affective father relations (scale)	4.16**
Family activities (scale)	6.90**
Perents' negative reactions (scale)	-2.63*
Teacher relations (scale)	6.71**
Satisfaction with teachers	5.22**

*P<.01   **P<.001

some of the measures covering time and home responsibilities. Only for time to be home on Saturdays did we find significant differences. The parents of the adolescents with self-focused values reported that the child was allowed to stay out later than did the parents of the adolescents with other-focused values.

Engagement in risky behavior

We compared the two groups of adolescents on the broad measure of norm-breaking behavior. As expected, the adolescents with self-focused values were more engaged in many types of normbreaking than were the adolescents with other-focused values. Significant differences between the two groups were also found for drinking. Furthermore, there were significant correlations between the self-focused orientation and all five measures of risky behavior: normbreaking, delinquent friends, sexual intercourse, smoking, and drinking.

Again, no significant differences were obtained between the two groups of parents with respect to the adolescents' engagement in risky behavior. However, significant positive correlations were found between self-focused values and parents' awareness of normbreaking, sexual intercourse, and smoking.

Sleep-wake patterns

Adolescents with self-focused values were more likely to be night-owls than larks. They started to feel tired later and, if they could choose, they would go to bed later than those with other-focused values. The two groups of adolescents did not differ on having a fixed time to go to sleep but among those who had fixed times there was a positive correlation between self-focused values and going to bed late. The adolescents with self-focused values also had a harder time getting up in the morning. They reported that it was more troublesome for them to get up, they did not feel as alert as the adolescents with other-focused values, they were more tired, and if they could choose freely they would choose a later time. The adolescents with other-focused values were more likely to label themselves as larks than were the adolescents with self-focused values.

As for their feelings in mornings, the adolescents with self-focused values reported that they felt more grouchy. There was also a negative correlation between the self-focused value orientation and being happy in the morning. Altogether, our findings support the notion that adolescents with self-focused values differed in sleep-wake patterns from adolescents with other-focused values. They were more alert in the evening and more tired in the morning.

As we have seen in earlier sections, few differences could be detected between the two groups of parents. On the questions about sleep-wake patterns, the only significant difference was in the time the child was allowed to stay up in the evening. Bedtime was later for the adolescents with self-focused values than for the adolescents with other-focused values.

Long-term commitments versus short-term pleasures

For the school adjustment scale, the adolescents with self-focused values scored considerably lower than the adolescents with other-focused values. The adolescents with self-focused values were also less satisfied with their school achievement and more often skipped school. In their circle of peers, they were less likely to have friends who were good at school.

As we had proposed, when they encountered demands, the adolescents with self-focused values were more likely to do other, more pleasant things instead. On a broad measure of "task-irrelevant behavior," the two groups of adolescents differed considerably. The adolescents with self-focused values also spent less time doing homework in the evening.

Of the three parent-reported measures, differences between the two groups existed for two. The parents of the adolescents with self-focused values reported poorer school adjustment for their youths and more task-irrelevant behavior than did the parents of adolescents with other-focused values. For all three measures, parents with adolescents who had a high self-focused value orientation reported poorer school adjustment on the part of the son or daughter, more truancy, and more task-irrelevant behavior, than parents of adolescents with low self-focused values.

Hiding thoughts and actions

As we predicted, the adolescents with self-focused values reported that they told their parents less about their leisure time activities, thoughts, and feelings than did those with other-focused values. They also reported that their parents knew less about their leisure time activities (what they did when they were out, where they went, and with whom). As reported earlier, the adolescents with self-focused values were allowed to be out later than were the adolescents with other-focused values and they had fewer responsibilities at home. Despite this, the adolescents with self-focused values felt more controlled by their parents than did those with other-focused values. Finally, compared with adolescents with other-focused values, those with self-focused values perceived their parents as more worried and less trusting.

For four of these measures we also have parents' reports, and for all four there are significant associations with self-focused values. Self-focused values are linked to parents' reports of less adolescent disclosure, less general knowledge about activities away from home, more worries, and less trust. For two of the measures, adolescent disclosure and parental trust, there are significant differences for the dichotomized SF versus OF measure. Overall, then, according to parents and the adolescents themselves, adolescents with self-focused values disclosed less to their parents, and their parents were more distrustful.

Relationships with adults

On all of the ten measures of adult relationships, the stronger the self-focused values, the poorer the parent and teacher relations. Furthermore, for the majority of measures, other-focused values were linked to better parent and teacher relations. Compared with the adolescents with other-focused values, the adolescents with self-focused values reported more conflicts with their mothers about curfew times, poorer mother relations, poorer father relations, fewer family activities, and more negative responses from parents. The adolescents with self-focused values also reported poorer teacher relations and expressed less satisfaction with their teachers.

No significant differences existed for parents' reports of daily conflicts or family activities. However, the stronger the adolescents' self-focused values, the more likely parents were to report having conflicts about forgetting to do homework and doing few family activities.

Personality

We expect adolescents with self-focused values to have relatively more adventurous and unconventional personalities, and adolescents with other-focused values to have more conventional personalities. For the adolescents that we have been talking about, we do not have personality measures. However, for our longitudinal sample (described below), Cattell's High School Personality Questionnaire (HSPQ, Form A, Cattell 1962) was administered when the subjects were fifteen years old. The instrument includes thirteen personality scales. Each scale comprises ten items.

To discover what personality characteristics typify adolescents with self- and other-focused values, we performed multiple regression analyses with backward elimination of non-significant variables, predicting other- and then self-focused values from the HSPQ variables. Table 2 shows the variables that were retained in these equations. These results were reported elsewhere (Stattin & Kerr, in press).

As shown in the table, other-focused values are associated with being less assertive and tender-minded rather than tough-minded. This model explains a significant proportion of the variance in other-focused values, $R^2 = .14$, $F = 12.26$, $p < .0001$. Self-focused values are associated with being less emotionally stable, more assertive, more happy-go-lucky, more willing to disregard rules, tough- rather than tender-minded, and more self-assured. This model explains a significant proportion of the variance in the self-focused values, $R^2 = .26$, $F =$

8.77, p < .0001. Furthermore, in a discriminant analysis using the HSPQ variables to classify adolescents as having self-focused or other-focused values (the groups were formed as described previously), 82 percent of subjects could be correctly classified (84 percent of the adolescents with other-focused values and 79 percent of the adolescents with self-focused values). Adolescents with different value orientations, then, do tend to have the distinctive personality characteristics that we predicted.

A summary of adolescent value orientations and their associations to behavior, leisure time, interpersonal relations, and personality

The findings reported confirm our propositions about differences in lifestyles and personality between adolescents with self- and other-focused value orientations. As was predicted, adolescents with self-focused values spent much of their time with peers away from home, and they were often involved in unstructured leisure time activities. They were less likely to take responsibility for household activities. These adolescents were also more involved in normbreaking activities. We suggested that because they are out late in the evening, these adolescents are likely to adopt the evening-type characterization of getting to bed late, being tired in the morning, and being less prepared for school. This was also found to be true. Most of the measures of sleep-wake patterns confirmed that they were more likely to be night-owls than morning-larks. They were tired in the morning and preferred to stay up late in the evening. The reverse picture, with a stronger home orientation, engagement in more structured afternoon and evening activities, having more home responsibilities, being less engaged in normbreaking behavior, and feeling tired in the evening and alert in the morning, characterized the adolescents with other-focused values.

Most of the measures in the three domains briefly reviewed—the social context of everyday life activities, engagement in risky behavior, and sleep-wake patterns—differed significantly between the adolescents with self- and other-focused values, and/or correlated significantly with either or both of the two value orientations.

Are the reports of the adolescents in these domains matched by the reports of their parents? No. With few exceptions, parents of adolescents with self-focused values did not report that their sons or daughters were more often out in the evenings or had fewer home responsibilities. Neither did parents of adolescents with self-focused values report more normbreaking behavior on part of their sons and daughters, compared with parents of adolescents with other-focused values, nor did they report other sleep-wake patterns. The exception concerned staying out late. Adolescents with self-focused values were allowed by parents to stay out later in the evening, both on weekdays and on Saturdays. Moreover, parents reported normbreaking behavior (and sexual intercourse and smoking) correlated significantly with the self-focused value orientation. Overall, however, parents' reports of adolescents with self- and other-focused values did not differ much in these three domains. As we explain below, we believe that this is because these adolescents succeed in hiding their activities from their parents.

The situation was different for other domains—hiding or disclosing everyday life activities and inner life from adults, and long-term commitments versus short-term pleasures. One of the most salient findings in these domains was that the adolescents with self-focused values were more likely than those with other-focused values to hide from their parents information about what they did in the evening and with which friends. They also disclosed little about their thoughts and inner feelings. They reported that their parents knew little, that the parents were worried, and that the parents showed a lack of trust in them.

Parents agreed. The self-focused value orientation correlated significantly with parents' reports that the child seldom disclosed information about his or her whereabouts, that the parents knew little about what happened outside home, that they were more worried, and that they did not trust the child.

In our view, the likely reason why parents of adolescents with self-focused values know little about their sons and daughters normbreaking behaviors is that these children seldom spontaneously disclose information about what they are doing and with whom during leisure time, nor disclose how they think and feel about different matters. The major factor behind parents' knowledge about the child's whereabouts (or "monitoring," as parental knowledge measures have often been called in the literature) seems to be the child's voluntary disclosure of information, rather than parents' own control and regulation or parents' solicitation of information (Stattin & Kerr 2000; Kerr & Stattin 2000; Trost, Stattin & Kerr 1999). The findings in this study support this interpretation.

One domain in which parents can get independent information about the child's adjustment and behavior concerns school. In this domain, we also find differences between adolescents with self- and other-focused values both with regard to children's reports and parents' reports. According to the adolescents themselves, the subjects with self-focused values expressed poorer school adjustment (in addition to less school satisfaction and more truancy) and more task-irrelevant behavior (engagement in other more pleasurable activities when faced with demands on achievement and behavior). The parents of the adolescents with self-focused values also reported more school adjustment problems for their sons and daughters and more task-irrelevant behavior.

As we predicted, we found that adolescents with self-focused values had more problematic relations with their parents and teachers. All the different measures in this domain showed the same picture. The higher the adolescents' self-focused values, the more conflicts with mothers, the poorer the affective relations with mothers and fathers, the fewer the common family activities, the more negativistic parents were, and the poorer relationships were with teachers. For almost all the measures of adult relations, the adolescents with self-focused values differed significantly from the adolescents with other-focused values.

We have few analogous measures that assess how parents regard their relationships with their sons and daughters. For the two broader measures investigated here—parental conflicts with the child about everyday matters and common family activities—no significant differences existed between the parents of adolescents with self- and with other-focused values. However, self-focused values did correspond to more conflicts with the child about forgetting to do homework, and fewer common family activities.

In this study, we have argued that the way individuals function in one domain is lawfully linked to how they function in others and that values serve as an organizing principle for how adolescents think, feel, behave, and relate to others. Self-focused and other-focused value orientations should relate differently to various everyday life activities and personality, and the overall picture should be coherent. In the different domains covered—the social context of everyday activities, risky behavior, sleep-wake patterns, long-term commitments, hiding or disclosing information, and affective relations to adults—we see this coherent picture. Of course, we can not assume unidirectional causal effects between values and behavior in diverse domains, but rather a reciprocal interplay of factors. Values are as much developed from everyday experiences as they are guides or motivators of interests, activities, and behavior.

We also proposed that value orientations would be logically related to personality. Adolescents with self-focused values were presumed to have relatively more adventurous, unconventional personalities, whereas adolescents with other-focused values would have more conventional personalities. Our findings confirm this. A high self-focused value orientation was associated with being assertive, but also being more affected by feelings and more happy-go-lucky, tough-minded, self-assured, and willing to break rules. By contrast, a high other-focused value orientation was associated with being tender-minded and obedient rather than assertive.

Future life
Implications for future life

So far, we have been concerned with middle adolescence. It is now time to look at the possible long-term impact of adolescent values. What impact do self- and other-focused adolescent value orientations have on the life courses of individuals? We have argued that self-focused and other-focused values are reflected in interpersonal relationships. To the extent that adolescents' values have consequences for the future, we should see this in adult capacities for warm and caring relations and in attached versus detached relations to others.

Peer relations are vitally important as people navigate through adolescence. Adolescents need an interpersonal environment outside the family with which to identify and in which to mature. Peer relationships help adolescents build social skills and learn that others think and feel differently than they do. They allow adolescents to establish lasting relationships with agemates. Friendships are based on openness, affection, empathy, loyalty, and reciprocity, and friendships make adolescents sensitive to others' perspectives, roles, and feelings (Berndt 1992; Sullivan 1953). Adolescent friendships should also equip people with the ability to form lasting friendships and intimate relationships in the future.

To some extent, it could be argued that this should be true for adolescents with self-focused values. They certainly have ample opportunities for peer group interactions. Our findings showed that adolescents with self-focused values were highly involved with their peers, had large friendship networks, and spent much of their time with peers. They valued activities that involved others of their own age. This suggests that adolescents with self-focused values should be extraverted and interested in other people. If the adolescent experiences of being well integrated with peers prepares people to form new relationships in adulthood, then we should expect the adolescents with self-focused values to become the most socially competent adults.

On the other hand, these adolescents' peer-group activities seemed to exist at the expense of good relationships with adults. The adolescents with self-focused values had more strained relations with their parents and teachers. They were often away from home in the evening and seldom helped their parents with household tasks. They felt controlled by their parents, and they disclosed little of what they did in the evening and little of what they were feeling to their parents. They believed that their parents did not trust them and, according to their parents' reports, they were right. So, although adolescents with self-focused values were interested in others, the others were only peers with similar interests. They preferred the company of peers even though this meant that their relationships with their parents suffered.

For adolescents with other-focused values, peer involvement and time spent with peers was lower than for adolescents with self-focused values. However, they did not have bad relationships with peers; they were just less peer-dependent. They also had good relationships with adults. Generally, satisfying relationships with agemates, strong family ties and open communication with parents, as well as good, warm relationships with other adults, seemed to characterize the adolescents with other-focused values. It is this general capacity of adolescents with other-focused values to have close, caring, and satisfying peer and adult relations that suggests that they will develop and maintain deep, affectionate, caring, and lasting relationships in their future lives.

We expect to see continuity from adolescence to adulthood in people's ways of relating to others. The concern that adolescents with other-focused values have for others, both agemates and adults, suggests that they will have broader perspective-taking abilities than will adolescents with self-focused values (who interact mainly with peers) and should have a more pragmatic, instrumental interaction style.

To the extent that values are part of an individual's long-term goals, self-focused and other-focused value orientations should influence people's capacities for developing warm, caring relations to others in later life. Adolescents with other-focused values should be especially predisposed to attached relationships. Specifically, we predict that adolescents with other-focused values, relative to adolescents with self-focused values, should in adulthood: (a) be more sociable—interested in others and eager to affiliate with others, (b) have an attached, rather than detached, interpersonal style, and (c) have more warm, caring relationships with their partners and better family climates. We examine these propositions by looking at partner relationships, sociability, and detachment of thirty-seven-year-olds who had stated their value preferences more than twenty years earlier, when they were adolescents.

Attainment versus non-attainment of goals

As we have reported elsewhere (Stattin & Kerr, in press), we also wanted to examine the situation when future goals are not attained. If goals are important in the life trajectories of individuals, then it should matter whether or not they are able to fulfill value-relevant goals. If having satisfying personal relationships is a goal of adolescents with other-focused values, then having them or not should affect this group of adolescents more than the adolescents with self-focused values. We hypothesized that for the adolescents with other-focused values, value relevant goals would be forming close, fulfilling relationships, the most important of which would be the primary relationship with the partner. Failure to have formed satisfying partner relationships should compromise these people's well-being. Such a difference in well-being between those with satisfying and less satisfying partner relations should be less characteristic of adolescents with self-focused values.

Friendships, social support, and good partner relations have been linked to well-being in many studies (Apt, Hurlbert, Pierce, & White 1996; Argyle 1987; Brown 1994; Chiasson, et al. 1996; Ferroni & Taffe 1997; Kirchler & Wagner 1987; Thompson & Peebles 1992; Veenhoven 1984), and marital satisfaction has been identified as one of the most important predictors of well-being (Diener 1984), perhaps eclipsing all other predictors of happiness (Russell & Wells 1994). In the present case we specifically predicted that the future well-being of adolescents with other-focused values, but not adolescents with self-focused values, would depend upon whether they ended up having good or bad relationships with their partners.

Method
Sample

To answer our questions about the future implications of adolescent values, we used data from a Swedish birth-to-maturity study, which is led by the first author. This is a longitudinal sample of 212 subjects, 122 males and 90 females, born from 1955 to 1958 in Solna, a town near Stockholm. The subjects have been studied prospectively from birth into adulthood by researchers from the Clinic for the Study of Children's Development and Health at the Karolinska Hospital, Stockholm. They were assessed yearly from birth to age 18, with subsequent data collections made when they were 21, 25, and 37 years of age. In the present case, we use the data from age 37. Thus our predictions span more than twenty years.

Investigations of socioeconomic status, parents' age, mother's marital status, sibling order, gestational age and weight, and registered criminality have shown that the sample is representative of children in Swedish urban districts (Karlberg et al. 1968; Stattin & Klackenberg-Larsson 1990). Of the full sample, 163 subjects were interviewed and tested at age 15, 166 at age 16, 163 at age 17, and 161 at age 18. At these ages, all subjects were tested within four weeks of their birthdays. At the average age of 37, 185 subjects (91 percent of those who were still alive) were interviewed.

To determine whether the late-adolescent data were biased because of dropouts, those who participated in the data collection at age sixteen were compared with those who did not on relevant childhood measures (Terman-Merrill intelligence and social background at age five, and broad measures of internalizing and externalizing problems aggregated over ages four and five). The people who participated at age sixteen did not differ significantly on any of these measures from those who did not participate.

Material
Self- and other-focused adolescent values

A similar, but not identical measure of life values for the cross-sectional sample was obtained for the subjects in this longitudinal cohort. A life value instrument (Moore & Hindle 1968) was administered at age sixteen. The subjects were presented with sixteen different types of life values and were asked to rank order them on the basis of how important they were for them. The three other-focused values were "People," "Helping others," and "A peaceful world" and the four self-focused values were "Having enough money," "Having the freedom to do what I want," "Looking good," and "The opposite sex." The mean ranking (from

1 to 16; with higher scores meaning more important values) of the other-focused items was 10.4; for the self-focused items it was 8.9. The correlation between the two value scales was -.58 (p < .001).

Mid-life measures

Sociability was measured with the Extraversion-Sociability scale in the Eysenck Personality Questionniare (Eysenck & Eysenck 1975), and the Sociability scale in the EAS questionnaire (Buss & Plomin 1984).

Detachment was part of a personality questionnaire—the Karolinska Scales of Personality (KSP)—which was administered at the age of thirty-seven. The scales of this questionnaire are derived from theories of biologically-based temperament dimensions underlying psychiatric disorders (Schalling & Edman 1987; Schalling et al 1987). Detachment is assumed to be related to a syndrome of psychopathy including the schizoid or withdrawn type (Schalling 1978). The detachment scale consists of ten items: "It is easy for me to get close to people (rev.)", "I want to confide in someone when I am worried and unhappy (rev.)", "I avoid people who are interested in my personal life", "I feel uncomfortable when people take me into their confidence", "I am deeply moved by other people's misfortunes (rev.)", "I feel best when I keep people at a certain distance", "I prefer to avoid involving myself in other people's personality problems", "People generally think that I hide my feelings so that they have difficulties in understanding me", "I consider myself reserved and a little cold rather than kind and warm", and "People often come to me with their troubles (rev.)." Alpha reliability was 0.70 for the scale.

After the interview at the age of thirty-seven, the interviewers rated the subjects' expressed warmth on a five-point scale (with verbal descriptions of each scale point) ranging from (1) cold and unengaged, to (5) warm and hearty. The subjects themselves also reported on how closed or open they were in relations with others. On a three-point scale they were asked to indicate whether they considered themselves as (1) closed, (2) ordinary, or (3) open and sociable.

A composite measure of mid-life partner satisfaction was formed from interview questions and questionnaires. The individual items making up the broad partner-satisfaction measure were based on six open-interview questions: "How would you characterize your spouse (1 = only negative characteristics mentioned, 5 = only positive characteristics mentioned)?", "Do you and your spouse have any particular interests that hold you together (1 = no common leisure-time interests, no recreation together, 5 = share each other's interests, same amusements)?", "To give an overall impression of your relationship, how would you describe the home atmosphere (1 = very disharmonious, almost divorce atmosphere, 6 = unusually cordial relations, attitudes in harmony, open and warm home atmosphere)?", "How often does it happen that you spontaneously cuddle or caress each other (1 = seldom, 5 = daily)?", "Are you sexually well adjusted to each other (1= have no sexual life together, or very seldom, 6 = very well adjusted to each other)?", and "Do you receive encouragement and support from your partner when you have problems at work (1 = partner is more of an obstacle than a source of support, 5 = receive all the help I need)?"

A brief questionnaire about partner relations contained four main questions: "Does your partner talk to you about his/her problems (1 = never, 4 = always)?", "How warm are your feelings for your partner (1 = no warm feelings at all, 5 = very warm feelings)?", "How do you and your partner get along together (1 = badly, 5 = very well)?", and "How often does it happen that you get really angry with your partner (1 = very often, to 5 = very seldom)?" Alpha reliability was 0.82 for the full scale of ten items.

Family climate was measured with the Swedish Family Climate scale (Hanson 1989). It contains eighty-five adjectives which the subject is to mark as either appropriate or inappropriate. Four different scales are measured. For our purposes we used the Closeness scale, which consists of eighteen adjectives (e.g., happy, warm, soft, stable, easy) and the Distance scale which consists of eleven adjectives (e.g., intolerant, bad, cold). Satisfying psychometric properties, reliability and validity, have been presented by Hanson (1989).

Two well-being measures were used, one being a general life satisfaction measure and the other a measure of positive affect.

Life satisfaction was measured by a shortened version of Neugarten et al.'s Life Satisfaction Index A (Neugarten, Havighurst, & Tobin 1961). All items in the scale that referred directly or indirectly to past life were deleted before computing a scale index. Alpha reliability was 0.81 for the scale.

Positive effect was measured with the scale "General positive effect" in the Mental Health Inventory (MHI) of Veit and Ware (1983). Questions concerned subjects' feelings of being happy, satisfied, forward looking, relaxed, calm and peaceful, cheerful, lighthearted, etc., during the past month. Alpha reliability was 0.92 for the scale.

Results
Mid-life social relations

To avoid unnecessary drop-out of cases, we have calculated the correlations between each of the two value orientations in adolescence and the various sociability and family measures at the age of thirty-seven, but have refrained from using the dichotomized self- versus other-focused measure because it would have resulted in the loss of 40 percent of the cases. Table 3 presents correlations between the two adolescent value orientations and the sociability and family measures in midlife.

We made use of two different measures of sociability at the age of thirty-seven. One was the Extraversion-Sociability subscale in the Eysenck Personality Questionnaire (Eysenck & Eysenck 1975) and the other was the Sociability sub-scale in Buss and Plomin's EAS Scale (Emotionality, Activity, and Sociability: Buss & Plomin 1984). The findings are similar for both scales. There was a neg-ative correlation between adolescent self-focused values and the two sociability measures and a positive correlation between adolescent other-focused values and the sociability measures. This, despite the fact that adolescents with self-focused values were extensively involved in socializing with their peers and had rated having fun with their friends as one of their most important life values.

To make sure that these were really differences in sociability rather than

Table 3: Correlations between midlife interpersonal relations and adolescent self-focused and other-focuesed value orientations.[1]

	Other-focused values		Self-focused values	
	r	p	r	p
Sociability and attached relations to others				
Extraversion-Sociability (EPI)	.15	.05	-.17	.05
Sociability (EAS)	.26	.001	-.21	.01
Warmth (interviewer rating)	.08	n.s.	-.16	.05
Close vs. open (self-rating)	-.18	.05	.18	.05
Detachment (KSP)	-.24	.01	.19	.05
Partner and family relations				
Good partner relations (self-rating)	-.03	n.s.	-.18	.05
Family relations: Closeness (Family Climate scale)	.03	n.s.	-.10	n.s.
Family relations: Distance (Family Climate scale)	-.19	.05	.18	.05

[1] Because of the smaller sample size, limited number of comparisons, more than 20-year interval between measurements, and directional hypotheses, one-tailed tests are reported here.

social inhibition, we also compared the two adolescent groups on adult shyness. We found a correlation of -.36 (p < .001) between sociability and shyness, which is similar to what Cheek and Buss (1981) reported. Both the correlations between shyness, on the one hand, and self-focused and other-focused values, on the other, were nonsignificant (r = .04 and -.12, respectively). A partial correla-tion analysis showed that the correlations between the two sociability scales and adolescent values were only marginally reduced when controlling for shyness. Hence, the link between adolescent values and adult sociability could not be attributed to individual differences in shyness. As reported earlier in the section on personality differences in adolescence, neither value orientation was related to shyness in adolescence.

The interviewers rated the subjects after the test administrations and interviews had been done (this lasted about five hours for each person). As reported in Table 3, the interviewers considered the subjects who had been high in adolescent self-focused values less warm than subjects who had been low in self-focused values. No significant associations were obtained between the interview ratings and other-focused values.

Also, the subjects themselves were asked at the interview to indicate whether they perceived themselves as open or closed in their relationships with others. In agreement with the findings for the sociability measures, there was a significant negative correlation between adolescent self-focused values and this self-report of interpersonal openness, and a positive correlation for adolescent other-focused values.

Finally, to examine whether the adolescent value orientations were related to attached versus detached relationships, we made use of the "Detachment" scale from the Karolinska Scales of Personality. Adolescent self-focused values were positively related to detachment, and other-focused values were negatively related to detachment.

These results confirm our predictions that adolescents with other-focused values, later in life, will be relatively high in sociability and have an attached interpersonal style. Conventional sociability measures, observer ratings, and self-reports all converge to show this. At the same time it should be said that even though the correlations were significant and in the predicted direction, their magnitudes were not high. What is impressive is the robustness across methods, informants, and over twenty years.

As for family relations, in agreement with our predictions, subjects with high adolescent self-focused values reported poorer partner relations than subjects with low self-focused values. However, there was no link between adolescent other-focused values and midlife partner relations. Closeness in the family climate was not associated with self-focused or other-focused values. However, consistent with our propositions, self-focused values were positively linked and other-focused values were negatively linked to distance in the family climate.

Attaining versus not attaining important goals

Thus far, a correlational strategy has been adopted. In this section, however, we examine the hypothesis that relationship quality will moderate relations between value orientations and subjective well-being (Stattin & Kerr, in press). To do this we look at mean level differences. We argue that adolescents with other-focused values who have unsatisfying adult partner relationships should have lower life satisfaction and less positive affect than adolescents with other-focused values who end up having satisfying partnerships. Among adolescents with self-focused

Table 4: Levels of life satisfaction and positive affect for
participants with primarily self-focused and other-focused
value orientations with good and bad partner relations in mid-life[1]

	Partner Relations			
	Good	Bad	t	p
High other-focued values				
Life satisfaction	0.75	-0.14	2.87	.001
Positive affect	0.62	-0.30	3.20	.01
High self-focused values				
Life satisfaction	0.00	-0.37	1.34	n.s.
Positive affect	0.23	-0.69	4.21	.001

[1] T-test refer to differences between good and bad partner relations for the participants
with self-focused and other-focused value orientaions, spearately. These data are
shown graphically in Stattin & Kerr, in press.

values, we do not necessarily expect such differences.

To test these propositions, we divided adolescents with other-focused values
into two groups: those who had good adult relationships with their partners and
those who had bad relationships (dichotomized at the mean). We compared these
two groups on age-37 life satisfaction and positive affect. We performed the
same tests for the adolescents with self-focused values. The results are presented in Table 4.

Before examining these moderating effects, it should be noted that adolescents with other-focused values rated themselves as having more satisfying adult
lives than did adolescents with self-focused values (t = 3.33, p = .001; z-scores
were 0.18 and -0.13, respectively). Those with other-focused values also had significantly higher positive affect than did those with self-focused adolescent values (t = 2.16, p = .03; z-scores were 0.12 and -0.16, respectively). However,
these two groups did not differ on mid-life partner satisfaction (t = 0.45, n.s.; z-
scores were 0.14 and 0.03, respectively).

The results revealed that moderating conditions were important when the
outcome measure was life satisfaction. As expected, adolescents with other-
focused values who ended up with good partner relations had significantly higher life satisfaction than did those who ended up with bad partner relations. No
such differences appear for adolescents with self-focused values.

The results for positive affect showed no moderating effect of current conditions. Among both subjects with other- and self-focused adolescent values,
those with good partner relations reported significantly higher positive affect
than those with bad partner relations, Ms = .44 and -.26, p = .006 and Ms = .22
and -.51, p = .001 for other-focused and self-focused values and good and bad

partner relations, respectively.

In short, adult life satisfaction and positive affect are generally higher for people who, as adolescents, had other-focused values than for people who had self-focused values. Life satisfaction in mid-life is moderated by conditions that are relevant to adolescent life values. Among individuals with other-focused adolescent values, those with good partner relationships have higher life satisfaction than those with bad partner relations. Among individuals with self-focused adolescent values, life satisfaction does not depend upon good partner relationships. Good partner relations increase positive affect (experiences of positive emotions over the past month) for everyone.

General Discussion

Despite the fact that the topic of values has come up often in the history of psychology (Allport, Vernon, & Lindzey 1951; Rokeach 1971 1973), the systematic study of life values and their role for well-being and adjustment has not been a hot topic in adolescent research. Much of an individual's purposive, goal-directed activity is shaped by underlying values and preferences (cf., Coleman1990; Maslow 1950; Nurmi 1991, 1993; Schwartz 1994; Rokeach 1968). These values and preferences about what an individual desires are part and parcel of this individual's socialization history and unique experiences. Therefore, for developmental research, values and their role in socialization should be a central issue (Magnusson & Stattin 1998).

In this study, we have differentiated between values that parents and society try to neutralize—concern for only personal satisfaction and enjoyment—and values that parents and society try to inculcate—concern for others' well-being and the common good. We label these self-focused and other-focused values. Across the domains studied in adolescence we find a coherent and predictable pattern of relationships linked to these value orientations. Adolescents with these value orientations differ predictably in their everyday activities and personalities.

First of all, the adolescents with self-focused values were often away from home and spent much of their time out with their friends in the evening. They were more often engaged in unstructured leisure time activities, such as being out on the streets, and were less engaged in structured activities such as sports, music, theater, hobbies, church, scouts, and politics than were adolescents with other-focused values. In the evening, the adolescents with self-focused values were less often at home playing an instrument, reading a book, or painting, but more often out with their friends. They had fewer home responsibilities than did adolescents with other-focused values, and they were allowed to be out later in the evening.

Adolescents with self-focused values engaged more in risky behavior. The stronger these values, the higher the normbreaking, sexual intercourse, smoking, and drinking, and the more adolescents associated with delinquent friends. Adolescents with self-focused values also had their period of greatest alertness later in the day than adolescents with other-focused values. They preferred to stay up late in the evening and were tired and grouchy in the morning. They tended to perceive themselves as night-owls rather than as larks. Compared with the adolescents with other-focused values, they were less interested in academic pursuits, they had poorer relations with their teachers, and, when confronted with achievement demands, they easily shifted their attention to more desirable activities.

Perhaps most noteworthy, the adolescents with self-focused values seemed to guard their peer-oriented activities from parental insight. They hid their thoughts, feelings, and activities from their parents. Consequently, their parents knew little about their whereabouts and expressed less trust in them than did the parents of adolescents with other-focused values. Generally, the adolescents with self-focused values had poorer relationships with parents and teachers. There were more conflicts about daily routines at home, less affectionate relationships with mothers and fathers, and fewer common family activities. The adolescents with self-focused values also perceived their parents as having more negative attitudes and behaviors toward them than did adolescents with other-focused values (their parents used what they disclosed against them, made fun of things they said, and punished them for something they had said spontaneously at home). Moreover, even though they had more freedom to stay out late in the evening, those adolescents with self-focused values still thought that their parents controlled their behavior too much.

Values cannot be considered as separate from personality. In a previous study of our longitudinal sample, the adolescents with self-focused values were characterized as assertive, first and foremost, as well as less emotionally stable, more happy-go-lucky, tough-minded, self-assured, and willing to violate rules (Stattin & Kerr, in press). The adolescents with other-focused values were more tender-minded and obedient rather than assertive. These differences suggest that value orientations are, indeed, important aspects of adolescents' identities. The personality differences in these adolescents indicate that they have very different ways of relating to people. Self-focused adolescents, in particular, appear as we would expect them to—less conventional and concerned about others and more self-involved.

There are few models of adolescent development that try to integrate a number of domains. A notable exception is the work of Richard Jessor and co-workers (Jessor & Jessor 1977). Another elaborate model for how personal and social values affect behavioral intentions and actions through attitudes and subjective norms, is presented in Ajzen and Fishbein's theory of reasoned action (Ajzen & Fishbein 1980). In the present chapter, we have argued that self- and other-focused values might serve to organize individual functioning across domains in adolescence. As predicted, values do seem to have a coordinating role, underlying functioning and development in diverse domains in adolescence. It does not mean that they have a unidirectional effect on behavior. Values, as well as cognition, emotions, norms, and attitudes are part of one process—the individual acting as a whole (Magnusson 1988; Magnusson & Stattin 1998). Values are hypothetical constructs that describe part of the mental system. They are an effect of experiences and socialization, but they also influence what information we attend to in the environment and how we interpret it, our conduct, and the way we relate to other people. Thus, values are as much being shaped through home, school, and leisure experiences as they are responsible for people's behavior in these contexts.

Values could underlie and determine the short-term goals that direct an individual's thoughts and actions in current situations (Feather 1980; Pervin 1983), but they could also have implications for future life. We argue that the maintenance and establishment of warm, caring relationships is central to the life situation in adolescence and the future life situation. Self-focused and other-focused values should be reflected in interpersonal relationships and should have consequences for future life and well-being.

Our results show that having opportunities for, and experiences with peer interactions—belonging to a peer network that shares common activities and interests, and being outgoing in adolescence—does not, by itself, guarantee or promote sociability or the development of warm, friendly relations to others (c.f., Hartup & Stevens 1997). The adolescents with self-focused values were highly involved with their peers, and they had, in fact, rated "having fun with my friends" as one of the most important things in life. However, these intense peer relations seemed to exist at the cost of poor adult relations, and we expected that they would be less sociable and warm as adults. By contrast, adolescents with other-focused values had satisfying relations with agemates and strong family ties and open communication with parents. This more general capacity to have close, caring, and satisfying peer and adult relations was the ground for expecting future high sociability, attached relations to others, warm and caring partner relations, and a warm family climate among these adolescents.

The age-37 data confirmed these expectations. Subjects who had high adolescent self-focused values scored lower on commonly used sociability scales, had more detached interpersonal styles, were rated as less warm by an external observer, and considered themselves as more closed than subjects who were low on adolescent self-focused values. They also considered their partner relations to be poorer and their family climates as more distanced. By contrast, subjects who were high on other-focused values in adolescence scored higher on sociability, had more attached relations to others, and rated themselves as more open than did subjects who had been low on adolescent other-focused values. They also rated their family climates as less distanced. Overall, the findings confirm that adolescents with other-focused values have more warm relations to others later in their lives (both inside and outside of the family). It should also be noted that adolescent values were related to mid-life subjective well-being, defined as positive affect and life satisfaction. People with adolescent self-focused values reported less positive affect and lower life satisfaction in adulthood, whereas those with adolescent other-focused values reported higher life satisfaction in mid-life.

Besides providing a link between adolescent life values and future well-being, our findings offer some clues about the nature of these long-term associations. Each of these value orientations was associated with later life satisfaction in a different way. The satisfaction of subjects with other-focused vales in adolescence depended on the quality of their primary relationship. They were more satisfied with life if they lived in warm, caring relationships than if they did not. No such differences were found for subjects with adolescent self-focused values. These findings imply that certain life conditions in mid-life moderate the relations between values and life satisfaction. Individuals with other-focused values are more satisfied if they have better relationships. However, this difference in moderating conditions did not appear for positive affect, the other measure of subjective well-being. Moreover, we should not lose sight of the fact that in general the subjects with other-focused values had more positive emotion and were more satisfied with life at the age thirty-seven than subjects with self-focused adolescent values.

Overall, what can we conclude about the adolescent factors that determine future subjective well-being? Our results suggest, first, that adolescent self- and other focused values, which are highly abstract concepts (c.f., Glenn 1980), are associated with interpersonal relationships and the perception that one is living a good life more than twenty years later. In such a formative period as late adolescence, where considerable changes in identity, attitudes, and interests are taking place (Ryder 1965), the abstract ideas of humanistic and hedonistic values seem to have long-term implications for future well-being.

In the existing literature, the relations that are often found between values and behavior are not particularly strong. Values explain small proportions of the variance in individuals' behaviors in specific situations (Cohen & Cohen 1996). Because of this, one might conclude that values are unimportant. We agree that values explain small proportions of the variance in individual behaviors, but we do not conclude that they are unimportant. Values serve to organize individual functioning across domains and across time. What we have presented here is a coherent picture. We began with carefully selected values that we believed should be linked to basic socialization processes. Then, continuing with this theory-driven approach, we made predictions about the organization of behavior across domains and across time. We do not find huge effects on individual behaviors. What we do find, however, is that values are related in predicted ways to a broad range of theoretically relevant behavior and lifestyle factors. This, we believe, is evidence of their organizing function. So, do values matter? Yes, both in the short-term and in the long-term. Our findings suggest that we need to be more aware of adolescents' basic abstract ideas about the world in order to understand their future relations and happiness, and we need to be aware of whether or not they attain the goals related to these ideas.

References

Ajzen, I. & Fishbein, M. (1980). *Understanding attitudes and predicting social behavior*. Englewood Cliffs, NJ: Prentice-Hall.

Allport, G. W., Vernon, P. E., & Lindzey, G. (1951). *Study of values* (Rev. Ed.). New York: Houghton Mifflin.

Apt, C., Hurlbert, D. F., Pierce, A. P., & White, L. C. (1996). Relationship satisfaction, sexual characteristics and the psychosocial well-being of women. *Canadian Journal of Human Sexuality, 5*, 195–210.

Argyle, M. (1987). *The psychology of happiness*. New York: Methuen.

Bandura, A. (1972). The stormy decade: Fact or fiction? In D. Rogers (Ed.), *Issues in adolescent psychology*. (pp. 91–97). New York: Appleton-Century-Crofts.

Bear, G. G. & Rys, G. S. (1994). Moral reasoning, classroom behavior, and sociometric status among elementary school children. *Developmental Psychology, 30*, 633–638.

Berndt, T. J. (1992). Friendship and friends' influence in adolescence. *Current Directions in Psychological Science, 1*, 156–159.

Braithwaite, V. A. & Law, H. G. (1985). Structure of human values: Testing the adequacy of the Rokeach value survey. *Journal of Personality and Social Psychology, 49*, 250–263.

Brown, M. A. (1994). Marital discord during pregnancy: A family systems approach. *Family Systems Medicine, 12*, 221–234.

Buss, A. H. & Plomin, R. (1984). *Temperament: Early developing personality traits*. Hillsdale, NJ: Erlbaum.

Cairns, R.B. (1979). *Toward guidelines for interactional research*. Hillsdale, NJ: Erlbaum.

Cantor, N. & Kihlstrom, J. F. (1987). *Personality and social intelligence*. Englewood Cliffs, NJ: Prentice Hall.

Carlo, G., Koller, S. H., Eisenberg, N., Da-Silva, M. S., & Frochlich, C. B. (1996). A cross-national study on the relations among prosocial moral reasoning, gender role orientations, and prosocial behaviors. *Developmental Psychology, 32*, 231–240.

Cattell, R. B. (1962). *High School Personality Questionnaire*. Form A, 1962–63 edition.

Cheek, J. M. & Buss, A. H. (1981). Shyness and sociability. *Journal of Personality and Social Psychology, 41*, 330–339.

Chiasson, N., Dubé, L., & Blondin, J-E. (1996). Happiness. A look into the folk psychology of four cultural groups. *Journal of Cross-Cultural Psychology, 27*, 673–691.

Cohen, P. & Cohen, J. (1996). *Life values and adolescent mental health*. Mahwah, New Jersey: Lawrence Erlbaum.

Coleman, J.S. (1990). *Foundations of social theory*. Cambridge, MA: The Belknap Press of Harvard University Press.

Crosby, L. A., Bitner, M. J., & Gill, J. D. (1990). Organizational structure of values. *Journal of Business Research, 20*, 123–134.

Damon, W. & Hart, D. (1988). *Self understanding in childhood and adolescence*. New York: Cambridge University Press.

Diener, E. (1984). Subjective well-being. *Psychological Bulletin, 95*, 542–575.

Durgee, J. F., O'Connor, G. C., & Veryzer, R. W. (1996). Observations: Translating values into product wants. *Journal of Advertising Research, 36*, 90–99.

Eisenberg, N. (1986). *Altruistic emotion, cognition and behavior*. Hillsdale, NJ: Erlbaum.

Eisenberg, N., Carlo, G., Murphy, B., & Van Court, P. (1995). Prosocial development in late adolescence: A longitudinal study. *Child Development, 66*, 1179–1197.

Eisenberg, N., Lennon, R., & Roth, K. (1983). Prosocial development: A longitudinal study. *Developmental Psychology, 19*, 846–855.

Eysenck, H. J. & Eysenck, S. B. G. (1975). *Manual of the Eysenck Personality Questionniare*. London: Hodder & Stoughton.

Feather, N.T. (1980). Values in adolescence. In J.Adelson (Ed.), *Handbook of adolescent psychology*. New York: Wiley (p.247–294).

Ferroni, P. & Taffe, J. (1997). Women's emotional well-being: The importance of communicating sexual needs. *Sexual and Marital Therapy, 12*, 127–138.

Glenn, N. D. (1980).Values, attitudes, and beliefs. In O. G. Brim, Jr., and J. Kagan (Eds.), *Constancy and change in human development* (pp. 596–640). Cambridge, Ms: Harvard University Press.

Gärling, T., Lindberg, E., Montgomery, H., & Waara, R. (1985). Beliefs about the attainment of life values. *Umea Psychological Reports*, 181.

Hanson, K. (1989). *Family Climate. An adjective checklist for family diagnostis* [Familjeklimat. En adjektivlista for familjediagnostik]. Report nr 1 from the Department of Applied Psychology, Lund University.

Hartup, W. W. & Stevens, N. (1997). *Friendships and adaptation in the life course*. *Psychological Bulletin, 121*, 355–370.

Jessor, R. & Jessor, S.L. (1977). *Problem behavior and psychosocialdevelopment: A longitudinal study of youth*. New York: Academic Press.

Kandel, D.B. (1978). Similartity in real-life adolescent friendship pairs. *Journal of Personality and Social Psychology, 36*, 306–312.

Karlberg, P., Klackenberg, G., Engström, I., Klackenberg-Larsson, I., Lichtenstein, H., Stensson, J., & Svennberg, I. (1968). The development of children in a Swedish urban community: A prospective, longitudinal study: Parts I-VI. *Acta Pædiatrica Scandinavica Supplement, Whole No. 187*.

Kerr, M. & Stattin, H. (2000). What parents know, how they know it, and several forms of adolescent adjustment: Further evidence for a reinterpretation of monitoring. *Developemntal Psychology, 36*, 366–380..

Kerr, M. Stattin, H., & Trost, K. (1999). To know is to trust you: Parents' trust is rooted in child disclosure of information. *Journal of Adolescence, 22*, 737–752.

Kirchler, E. & Wagner, W. (1987). Marital satisfaction and conflict in purchasing decisions. *Social Behaviour, 2*, 99–103.

Lindberg, E., Gärling, T., & Montgomery, H. (1989). Subjective belief-value structures as determinants of preferences for and choices among housing alternatives. *Journal of Consumer Policy, 12*, 119–137.

Little, B. R. (1983). Personal projects: A rationale and method for investigation. *Environment and Behavior, 15*, 273–309.

Magnusson, D. (1988). Individual development from an interactionalperspective. In D. Magnusson (Ed.), *Paths through life* (Vol. 1).Hillsdale, NJ: Erlbaum.

Magnusson, D. & Stattin, H. (1998). Person-context interaction theories. In W. Damon & R. M. Lerner (Eds.), Handbook of child psychology. Volume 1: *Theoretical models of human development* (pp. 685–759). New York: Wiley.

Maslow, A. H. (1950). Self-actualizing people: A study of psychological health. *Personality symposia: Symposium 1 on values*, (pp. 11–34). New York: Grune and Stratton.

Miller, P. A. & Eisenberg, N. (1988). The relation of empathy to aggressive and externalizing/antisocial behavior. *Psychological Bulletin, 103*, 324–344.

Montemayor, R. & Eison, M. (1977). The development of self-conceptions from childhood to adolescence. *Developmental Psychology, 13*, 314–319.

Moore, T. & Hindley, C. B. (1968). "What Matters." Measure of adolescent values developed for du Centre International de l'Enfance. Manuscript.

Neugarten, B. L., Havighurst, R. J., & Tobin, S. S. (1961). The measurement of life satisfaction. *Journal of Gerontology, 16*, 141.

Nurmi, J.-E. (1991). How do adolescents see their future? A review of the development of future orientation and planning. *Developmental Review, 11*, 1–59.

Nurmi, J.-E. (1993a). Adolescent development in an age-graded context: The role of personal beliefs, goals, and strategies in the tackling of developmental tasks and standards. *International Journal of Behavioral Development, 16*, 169–189.

Nurmi, J.-E. (1993b). Self-handicapping and a failure-trap strategy: A cognitive approach to problem behaviour and delinquency. *Psychiatria Fennica, 24*, 75–85.

Nurmi, J.-E. (1997). Self-definition and mental health during adolescence and young adulthood. In J. Schulenberg, J. L. Maggs, & K. Hurrelmann, (Eds.), *Health risks and developmental transitions during adolescence* (pp. 395–417). New York: Cambridge University Press.

Offer, D. (1969). T*he psychological world of teenager: A study of normal adolescent boys*. New York: Basic Books.

Offer, D. & Offer, J. (1975). *From teenage to young manhood: A psychological study*. New York: Basic Books.

Pervin, L.A. (1983). The stasis and flow of behavior: Toward a theory of goals. In M. M. Page (Ed.), Nebraska Symposium on Motivation (pp.1–53). Lincoln: *Nebraska University Press*.

Rokeach, M. (1968). *Beliefs, attitudes and values*. San Francisco, CA: Jossey-Bass.

Rokeach, M. (1971). The measurement of values and value systems. In G. Abcarian & J. W. Soule (Eds.), *Social psychology and political behavior.* Columbus, OH: Charles Merrill.

Rokeach, M. (1973). *The nature of human values.* New York: Free Press.

Russell, R. J. & Wells, P. A. (1994). Predictors of happiness in married couples. *Personality and Individual Differences, 17*, 313–321.

Ryder, N. B. (1965). The cohort as a concept in the study of social change. *American Sociological Review, 30*, 843–861.

Schalling, D. (1978). Psychopathy-related personality variables and the psychophysiology of socialization. In R. D. Hare & D. Schalling (Eds.), *Psychopathic behavior. Approaches to research.* (pp.85–106). Chichester: Wiley.

Schalling, D. & Edman, G. (1989). Personality and vulnerability to psychopathology: the development of the Karolinska Scales of Personality (KSP). Karolinska Institute, Stockholm.

Schalling, D., Åsberg, M., Edman, G., & Oreland, L. (1987). Markers for vulnerability to psychopathology: Temperament traits associated with platelet MAO activity. *Acta Psychiatrica Scandinavica, 76*, 172–182.

Schwartz, S. H. (1992). Universals in the content and structure of values: Theoretical advances and empirical tests in 20 countries. In M. Zanna (Ed.), *Advances in experimental social psychology* (Vol. 25, pp. 1–65). Orlando, FL; Academic.

Schwartz, S. H. (1994). Are there universal aspects in the structure and contents of human values? *Journal of Social Issues, 50*, 19–45.

Stattin, H. & Kerr, M. (2000). Parental monitoring: A reinterpretation. *Child Development, 71*, 1070–1083.

Stattin, H. & Kerr, M. (in press). People who need people. . . . Adult life satisfaction is rooted in humanistic adolescent life values. *British Journal of Developmental Psychology.*

Stattin, H. & Klackenberg-Larsson, I. (1990). The relationship between maternal attributes in the early life of the child and the child's future criminal behavior. *Development and Psychopathology, 2*, 99–111.

Sullivan, H. S. (1953). *The interpersonal theory of psychiatry.* New York: Norton.

Thompson, M. S. & Peebles, W. W. (1992). The impact of formal, informal, and societal support networks on the psychological well-being of Black adolescent mothers. *Social Work, 37*, 322–328.

Veit, C. T. & Ware J. E. Jr. (1983). The structure of psychological distress and well-being in general populations. *Journal of Consulting and Clinical Psychology, 51*, 730–742.

Veenhoven, R. (1984). *Conditions of happiness.* Dordrecht: Reidel Publishing Company.

Whitbeck, L. B., Simons, R. L., Conger, R. D., & Lorenz, F. O. (1989). Value socialization and peer group affiliation among early adolescents. *Journal of Early Adolesce*, 436–453.

CHAPTER 3

Personal Goals During the Transition to Young Adulthood

KATARIINA SALMELA-ARO

Introduction

At no other stage of life is the struggle of purpose and meaning of life perceived to be greater than during adolescence and young adulthood, when the individual's mind is occupied with questions like: "What am I interested in?", "What is worth doing?", "What do I want from life?" It is only gradually, when young people make their decisions about adult roles, such as occupation and family, and commit themselves to behavior leading to these roles, that they are able to answer these questions. This thinking about the future plays an important role during adolescence and young adulthood, because young people's decisions have important consequences for their later adult lives. In fact, it has been suggested that individuals overall, and adolescents in particular, create their own future life in terms of their choices, decisions, and investments (Nurmi 1993). Accordingly, personal goals people construct have a key importance in this self-direction. At the same time, during this process of directing their lives into adulthood, adolescents and young adults end up at various self-definitions and form related identities and self-concepts. Moreover, all of this happens in their developmental environment, in the age-graded societal and cultural context, which also leads young adults to certain tracks and careers.

In this chapter, I will make an effort to investigate the role of young adults' motivation when they navigate through their life transition from adolescence to adulthood. To do this, I will first discuss personal goals in personality psychology as a way to analyze motivation. Next, I will review earlier research on young adults' personal goals and related appraisals in the context of various developmental transitions, and how these are associated with well-being. Finally, I will investigate, using a person-oriented approach, what kind of goal patterns young people have when they are faced with a transition from school to work, and how these are related to their well-being.

Developmental Tasks During Transition from Adolescence to Adulthood

Individual development takes place in the context of various age-graded developmental tasks (Havighurst 1948), role transitions (Elder 1985; Caspi 1987), challenges (Erikson 1959), institutional careers (Mayer 1986), age constraints (Neugarten, Moore, & Lowe 1985), and life-events (Baltes, Reese, & Lipsitt 1980). One period of human life-span during which people are faced with a variety of developmental tasks, normative demands, and institutional transitions is adolescence and young adulthood. The normative demands, challenges, and developmental transitions that young adults face are related to finishing one's education, getting started in an occupation, selecting a partner, and starting a family and rearing children (Havighurst 1948; Oerter 1986; Newman & Newman 1975).

In industrialized societies marriage, the completion of formal schooling, entry into full-time employment, moving out of the parental household, and becoming financially independent serve usually as markers of entry into adulthood (Marcia 1980). Culturally based, age-related expectations shape developmental transitions by providing a normative social timetable for various role transitions (e.g., parenthood, employment). The timing of these developmental milestones is also determined by institutional arrangements. The transition from school to work, for example, is shaped by the educational system and the labor market (Hurrelmann 1994). Despite the age-graded nature of these transitions, they seem to represent two key life themes, those to career- and work-related topics and those related to family and interpersonal relationships (see also Fleeson & Cantor 1995).

One major transition of young adulthood is that from school to work (Schulenberg, Maggs, & Hurrelmann 1997). This transition is influenced by several institutional, cultural, and societal factors typical of this life domain, such as the timing of educational transitions and related sequences, the amount of unemployment, and the gender role expectations (Hurrelman 1994). These factors also define the possible outcomes of this transition, such as the opportunities to enter a career that is suited to one's education or the likelihood of becoming unemployed. In this chapter I will focus on this transition.

It has been suggested that people do not only react to the age-graded transitions, developmental tasks, and action opportunities, but that they also make deliberate efforts to direct their own development across such transitions (Brandtstädter 1989; Lerner 1983). One process that has been assumed to play an important role in this self-direction process is individuals' motivation and goal construction (Nurmi 1991, 1993). In turn, young adults' success in dealing with their major age-graded transitions might be assumed the influence the ways in which they reconstruct and reappraise their goals later on (Nurmi & Salmela-Aro in press).

Personal goals

Individual motivation has been described by various concepts, such as future goals, personal strivings, possible selves, life tasks, and personal projects (Little

1983; Emmons 1986; Cantor, et al. 1987; Markus & Nurius 1986). Little (1996), as well as McAdams (1996), suggested that these middle-level constructs form the second floor of the house of personality (see Figure 1) between the traits or motives in the basement and self-identity in the attic.

Figure 1: The House of Personality and Motivation

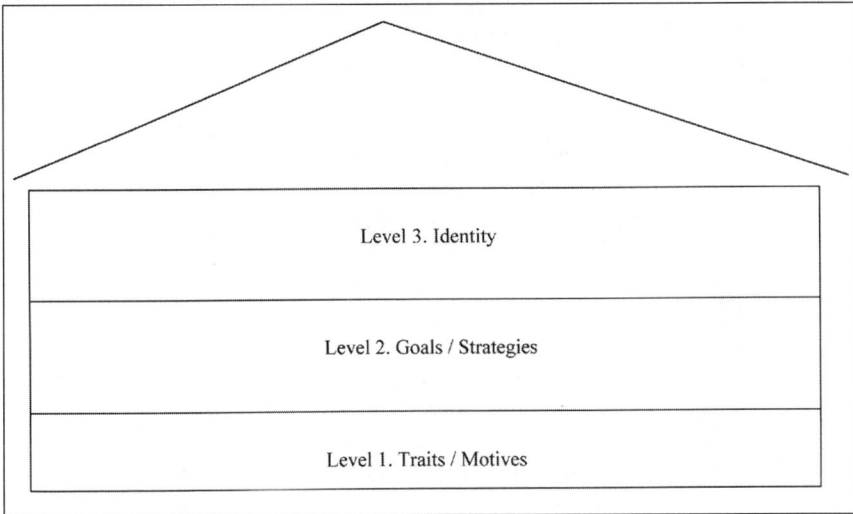

Level 3. Identity

Level 2. Goals / Strategies

Level 1. Traits / Motives

Referring to the first floor in "the House of Personality," McClelland (1985) defined a motive as a relatively enduring preference for a broadly defined class of emotionally charged incentives, such as having impact on others (power motive), doing things better (achievement motive), doing things with others (affiliation motive), and being engaged in an affectionate relationship (intimacy motive). It has also been suggested that individuals differ greatly in the strength of the aforementioned motives (McClelland 1985). The major personality traits characterize some of these differences. For example, Emmons (1989) has demonstrated links between both motive (e.g., intimacy and power mapping on to strivings) and trait (e.g., narcissism) domains. Although these motives and traits energize and loosely organize human behavior over extended periods of time, motives do not determine the specific ways in which a person satisfies her or his motives. Neither do motives directly relate to the development and use of strategies and plans necessary to achieve desired outcomes in the face of adversities.

Referring to the second floor of the house of personality, conative psychology and its goal theorists have suggested that individuals actively construe personally meaningful goals, such as future goals, personal strivings, possible selves, life tasks, and personal projects (Little 1983; Emmons 1986; Cantor

1990; Cantor et al.,1987; Markus & Nurius 1986), and then plan and engage in activities directed toward goal attainment. In contrast to broadly defined motives (for example achievement motive), personal goals constitute individualized and cognitively elaborated representations of what a person wants to achieve in his or her current life situation (for example, to get good grades in the next exam). These are called personal action constructs and they are typically examined by asking individuals to list their self-articulated goals (Nurmi 1993). It has been suggested that the goal construction is based on the comparison between the individual's motives, and the opportunities available in his or her developmental environments (Nuttin 1989). Several meta-theoretical perspectives offer a framework within which to interpret goal-directed action, such as control theory (Carver & Scheier 1990), living systems framework (Ford & Ford 1987), action theory (Brandtstädter 1989), and self-definition process model (Nurmi 1997).

Moreover, in the process of construal and actualization of their personal goals, people end up with various self-definitions (Nurmi 1997) on which basis they produce their identity. As has been suggested by McAdams (1996), this identity and related narratives and identity stories form the third level, the attic, of the house of personality. McAdams (1996) claims that the level of narrative storytelling provides the capacity for coherence in a way not afforded by other levels of his framework and related analogue of the house of personality.

Little (1983) was among the first who developed a methodology for assessing personal goals that combines open-ended idiosyncronic information about projects with standardized and quantifiable ratings. In this framework, personal goals are typically analyzed in three ways. First, the assessment begins with having respondents freely generate a list of their personal goals. These are then classified according to the domains of life they concern—the kinds of future events, transitions and challenges to which they refer to—such as education, occupation, family, children, property, and self-related topics (Little 1983; Nurmi 1992). It is possible also to analyze their content according to, for example, the motive to which they refer (Emmons 1997), whether goals are approach or avoidance type (Elliott & Church 1997), and the level of goal abstractness (Emmons 1992).

Second, to investigate further how people cognitively, emotionally, and behaviorally work on these personal goals, they have been investigated according to several appraisal dimensions, such as importance, progress, stress, support, and control beliefs (Cantor et al., 1987; Little 1983). These are typically summarized as three to five factors (Little 1989; Emmons 1989; Salmela-Aro 1992). Although the labels and weighting coefficients vary somewhat from study to study, the most robust dimensions appear to embody: (1) the degree of commitment or investment in the goal, (2) the degree to which the goal is perceived as stressful or challenging, and (3) the anticipated outcome or reward of the goal (see also Chambers 1997).

Young Adults Personal Goals, Life Situation and Well-being

Studies on personal goals suggest that the normative role sequence and age-graded developmental tasks and transitions, provide a basis for individuals' goals (Nurmi 1993). According to the self-direction model (Nurmi 1997), construction of such personal goals that optimize a person's possibilities to successfully deal with the forthcoming life-span transition (Baltes & Baltes 1990) requires a comparison of her or his individual motivation and the opportunities, challenges, and constraints typical of this particular transition. Consequently, individuals' personal goals have also been found to typically reflect the developmental tasks of their own age (Cross & Markus 1991; Nurmi 1992). Young adults goals are usually related to future occupation, education, family, and proper duty.

It has been assumed that personal goals also play an important role in the ways in which people direct their lives. It has been shown, for example, that the kinds of personal goals people have predict the life events they later face. Salmela-Aro and Nurmi (1997b) found in the context of transition to university that family-related goals predicted subsequent transitions in this same life domain. Similarly, Emmons (1991) showed that affiliation and intimacy strivings were correlated with the amount of interpersonal life events.

In turn, facing and going through a transition have important consequences for individuals' motivation and related goal construction. Every life-span transition consists of various changes in normative demands, tasks, challenges, and role expectations related to it. In order to deal with these new demands and role transitions successfully, individuals have to adapt their personal goals to fit them properly. For example, Salmela-Aro, Nurmi, Saisto, and Halmesmäki (2000) found that in the transition to parenthood, woman became less interested in achievement-related goals, whereas their interest in transition-specific goals, such as those related to birth and motherhood, increased. Moreover, life situation and related commitments have been found to predict young adults' subsequent goals. For example, Salmela-Aro and Nurmi (1997b) found students' life situations of being married and having children to predict subsequent family-related goals.

Moreover, several gender differences in personal goals have been found. For example, research on adolescents has shown that girls produce more family- (Greene & Wheatley 1992) and also more education-related goals (Nurmi 1989) than boys, who emphasize more material values (Solantaus 1987; Cross & Markus 1991; Strough, Berg, & Sansone 1996). Similarly, in the transition to parenthood, women were interested in social issues while men were interested in achievement and property (Salmela-Aro, et al. 2000).

Personal Goals and Well-being

Personal goals have also been found to have consequences for individuals' well-being. Although the majority of earlier studies have focused on goal appraisals (for reviews see Austin & Vancouver 1996; Karniol & Ross 1996), the content of young adults' personal goals have also been found to predict well-being. For example, Salmela-Aro and Nurmi (1997b) found among university students that personal goals that concerned major age-graded developmental tasks, such as future family and achievement-related topics, predicted high subjective well-being. In turn, high subjective well-being also predicted interest in these types of personal goals. Those who felt high well-being in the beginning of their studies later turned to family-related goals (Salmela-Aro & Nurmi 1997b). Intimacy strivings have also been found to be positively related with young adults well-being (Emmons 1991).

One possible explanation for these results is that the goals which reflect the age-graded developmental tasks help individuals to successfully deal with the key challenges of their developmental environment, and consequently benefit their overall life adaptation and subsequent well-being (Heckhausen 1999; Nurmi 1997). By way of contrast, personal goals that do not focus on age-graded demands lead to low well-being, because they do not help the individuals to focus on the major demands of their current life situation. For example, low self-esteem predicted interest in self-related goals which later were associated with low well-being (Salmela-Aro & Nurmi 1997a).

A Study on Personal Goals in the Transition from School to Work

Although a lot of research has been carried out on personal goals, this research has several limitations. First, the majority of studies have focused on goal appraisals (reviews: Austin & Vancouver 1996; Heckhausen 1999). Second, although many researchers have emphasized the impact of personal goals on life-span development, only a few longitudinal studies have been carried out in the context of life-span transitions. Third, although some studies have focused on different groups of individuals who appraise their goals differently, the majority of research has applied a variable-oriented approach, and only few studies have tried to explore the patterns of goals individuals typically have. In other words, to try to investigate the naturally occurring groups of individuals who differ according to their goals (see e.g., Cairns, Bergman, & Kagan 1998).

Consequently, using data from A Transition from School to Work study (Nurmi & Salmela-Aro in press), the following research problems were investigated:

(1) What kind of personal goals young adults have when they are faced with a transition from school to work and do these goals differ according to gender?

(2) What kind of goal patterns do young adults typically report, i.e., what kind of "naturally occurring" homogenous groups of the participants could be identified on the basis of their goal contents?

(3) How stable are these goal patterns across this particular transition?

(4) And finally, how are young adults' goal patterns associated with their well-being during the transition from school to work?

Methods

Subjects

The study is a part of the Transition from School to Work study. In this study, 250 young adults (129 males, 121 females, for age M = 24.27, SD = 4.07) who were facing a transition from school to work were investigated. 117 participants attended a business-oriented vocational school and 133 attended an institute of technology.

The participants were investigated three times:

(1) Two hundred and fifty young adults were investigated at the beginning of the last spring of their curriculum. They were asked to complete: the Personal Project Analysis (PPA; Little 1983), the revised Beck's Depression Inventory (BDI; Beck, Ward, Mendelsohn, Mosck, & Erlaugh 1961), the revised Mood Scale (Diener & Emmons 1984), the Perceived Stress Scale (Cohen, Kamerck, & Mermelstein 1983), the Brief Symptom Inventory (Emmons 1991), alcohol consumption CAGE-scale (Mayfield, McLeod, & Hall 1974) and a background questionnaire.

(2) About eight months after the first measurement, and about four months after the participants had graduated, they were asked to fill in the PPA, and a Work Status Questionnaire (WSQ; Nurmi & Salmela-Aro 1995). Two hundred and twenty participants (106 men, 114 women) from the original sample (response rate 88 percent) returned them.

(3) About eighteen months after the first measurement, the same young adults were again asked to fill in the PPA, and the WSQ sixteen months after completing their studies. Two hundred young adults (95 men, 105 women) from the original sample (response rate 80%) returned the questionnaires.

Measurements

The Personal Project Analysis inventory (PPA). The participants were asked to fill in a revised version of Little's (1983) Personal Project Analysis inventory. They were asked to describe six of their current personal projects. In this study we were only interested about the contents of personal goals.

Content analysis of the PPA. Each project mentioned by the participants was classified independently by two assessors in nine categories on the basis of their contents. The categories were similar to those used most often in earlier studies

(Little 1983; Nurmi 1991; education, work, family, social relations, self, health, property, hobbies, and daily hassles). Content analysis reliabilities for these three measurements measured by the percentage agreement between two independent raters, were 0.97, 0.90, 0.95, respectively.

Depression. Lack of personal well-being was assessed using a revised version of Beck's (Beck   et al., 1961) Depression inventory. The participants were not asked to choose one of the four alternatives of twenty-one sets of items but rather to rate thirteen items on a five point scale ranging from not at all true of me (1) to very true of me (5). The Cronbach alpha reliabilities were 0.88, 0.88, 0.89, respectively.

Mood. Mood was assessed by five bipolar mood adjectives such as happy-sad on a five point scale (according to Diener & Emmons 1984). The Cronbach alpha reliabilities were 0.80, 0.83, 0.85, respectively.

Stress. Stress was assessed by the use of a short version of Cohen, Kamarck, and Mermelstein (1983) perceived stress scale. It included seven questions on a five point scale ranging from not at all true of me (1) to very true of me (5). The questions covered the stress felt during the last month. The Cronbach alpha reliabilities of the scale were 0.80, 0.79, 0.65, respectively.

Physical symptoms. The amount of physical symptoms during the last half year was assessed by the use of the brief symptom inventory (Emmons 1991) which included twelve symptoms, such as headache, to be answered on a scale from 5 ("daily") to 1 ("not at all"). The Cronbach alpha reliabilities for this scale were 0.81, 0.69, 0.72, respectively.

Use of alcohol. The use of alcohol was assessed by an alcoholism screening test, the CAGE (Mayfield, Mcleod & Hall 1974), which included four questions to be answered on 1 ("not at all") to 5 ("very often") scale. The Cronbach Alpha reliabilities for this scale were 0.80, 0.78, 0.76, respectively.

Work Status. To obtain information about the participants' previous and current work status, they were asked to fill in the Work Status Questionnaire (WSQ, Nurmi & Salmela-Aro 1995) in the measurements 2 and 3. In this questionnaire, they were first asked about their current life situation by means of six questions ("Yes" = 1, "No" = 0): (1) "Are you at work?", (2) "Are you working in your own business?", (3) "Are you a student?", (4)"Are you unemployed at the present?", (5) "Are you staying at home with the children?", and (6) "Are you now in the army or in the civil service?"

Amount and type of jobs. Next, the participants were asked to write down all the jobs they had had since finishing school. Four numbered lines were provided to list these. For each job, they were further asked to evaluate the extent to which it was appropriate to their previous education ("Yes" = 2, "To some extent" = 1,

"No" = 0). The answers to this question were re-coded as a dichotomous variable: 1 = work that was appropriate to previous education (categories 2 and 1 in the original question) and 0 = was not appropriate to the participant's education.

Based on the six questions concerning their life situation, the participants were first grouped into three groups: (1) The *unemployed* group included those who were currently unemployed; (2) The *not in work* group included those who were neither at work nor unemployed (those who were studying, who were at home with children, or who were in the army); and (3 and 4) those who were working on a full-time basis. This group which consisted of participants who had full-time work, was divided further into two groups based on the information its members gave about if their work was appropriate to their previous education or not. (3) The 'professional work' group included those who were working in a profession for which their education had fitted them. (4) The 'other work' group included those who were working in a profession that was not appropriate to their education.

The numbers of participants in the *professional work, other work, not in work and unemployed groups* in measurement 2 were 106, 40, 36, and 34, respectively. Men and women were equally distributed in these categories ($\chi2 = 1.17$, ns.). Based on this variable, dummy-coded variables were created for each work status group. The numbers of participants in measurement 3 were in the professional work, other work, not at work and unemployed groups were 73, 80, 27 and 20, respectively. Men and women were again equally distributed in these categories ($\chi2 = 1.48$, ns.).

Background. In the background questionnaire, their grades in high-school and their marital status was asked.

Results

Goals at Time 1

In order to investigate what kinds of "naturally occurring homogenous groups" of young adults could be identified in the sample according to their personal goals, I carried out a clustering by cases analysis. In this analysis, the eight different goal content variables (standardized) related to education, work, family, social relations, self, health, property, hobbies, and daily hassles at each measurement point, were used as criteria variables. A hierarchical cluster procedure was used. In each case, we finished clustering when the seventh group solution emerged.

The results for the measurement of time 1 showed the following types of young adults with different goal patterns (see Figure 2 and Table 1). First, a cluster with high interest in daily hassles emerged (n=20, 8 percent) from the total sample. Second, the emerging cluster was the one including those who had high interest in property (n = 39, 16 percent). Third was a cluster with high interest in social relations (n = 40, 16 percent). Fourth was a cluster with a high interest in work and family-related issues (n = 33, 13 percent). Fifth was a cluster with high interest in self and hobbies as well (n = 26, 10 percent). Sixth was a cluster with a high interest in health (n = 55, 22 percent), and finally, seventh was a cluster with high interest in education (n = 36, 15 percent). The largest group was that with interest in health and the smallest was that with interest in daily issues.

Figure 2: Personal Goals

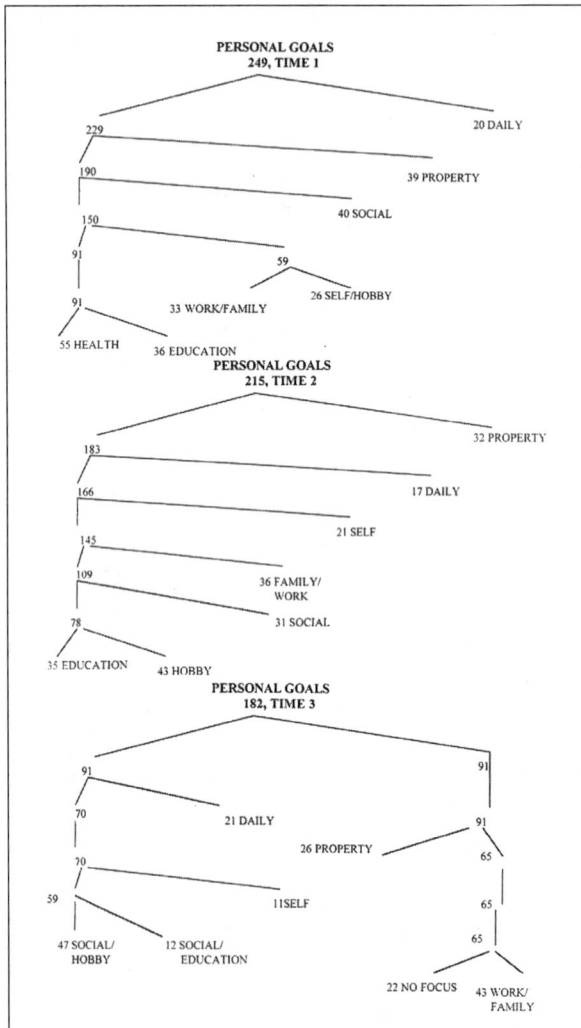

Table 1: Means and Standard Deviations for Clusters at Time 1

	Clusters							
N	**33**	**26**	**40**	**39**	**55**	**20**	**36**	
Goals	**Family and Work**	**Self and Hobby**	**Social Relations**	**Property**	**Health**	**Daily**	**Education**	**F**
Education								
M	1.39^{ab}	1.27^{b}	1.52^{ab}	1.15^{b}	1.62^{ab}	1.50^{ab}	1.89^{a}	3.61^{**}
SD	0.05	0.67	0.64	0.74	0.65	0.69	1.24	
Work								
M	1.58	0.96^{bc}	0.98^{b}	0.82^{bc}	0.95^{b}	0.75^{bc}	0.64^{c}	12.30^{***}
SD	0.70	0.45	0.48	0.45	0.30	0.44	0.59	
Family								
M	1.21^{a}	0.11^{c}	0.40^{bc}	0.59^{b}	0.64^{b}	0.35^{bc}	0.11^{c}	15.77^{***}
SD	0.78	0.33	0.55	0.55	0.56	0.59	0.32	
Friends								
M	0.00^{c}	0.19^{c}	1.10^{a}	0.26^{b}	0.00^{c}	0.20^{b}	0.03^{c}	76.08^{***}
SD	0.00	0.40	0.30	0.44	0.00	0.41	0.17	
Hobby								
M	0.61^{b}	1.54^{a}	0.68^{b}	0.54^{bc}	0.44^{bc}	0.65^{b}	0.14^{c}	12.21^{***}
SD	0.56	0.99	0.73	0.64	0.57	0.88	0.35	
Health								
M	0.00^{c}	0.27^{c}	0.65^{b}	0.46^{b}	1.09^{a}	0.75^{b}	0.17^{c}	29.75^{***}
SD	0.00	0.45	0.58	0.51	0.35	0.64	0.38	
Self								
M	0.21^{b}	1.12^{a}	0.15^{b}	0.33^{b}	0.25^{b}	0.05^{b}	0.11^{b}	14.00^{***}
SD	0.42	0.91	0.36	0.62	0.44	0.22	0.32	
Property								
M	0.00^{c}	0.04^{c}	0.00^{c}	1.05^{a}	0.02^{c}	0.30^{b}	0.00^{c}	141.87^{***}
SD	0.00	0.20	0.00	0.22	0.13	0.57	0.00	
Daily Hassles								
M	0.03^{b}	0.00^{b}	0.00^{b}	0.00^{b}	0.00^{b}	1.00^{a}	0.00^{b}	579.50^{***}
SD	0.17	0.00	0.00	0.00	0.00	0.00	0.00	

Note: ***P<.001 **P<.01

Analyses of the amount of women and men in different goal types showed that the amount of women and men was different in property and social relations clusters: men were over-represented in the property cluster and women, in turn, in the social relations cluster ($\chi2(6) = 17.68$, p<.001; Table 2). Moreover, the cluster numbers differed according to their marital status, $\chi2(6) = 16.29$, p<.01. Those who were interested in work and family, health, or daily goals were more often married. In turn, those interested in social, property, or education goals were more often single.

Table 2: The Amount of Women and Men in Clusters at Time 1

| | | | Clusters at Time 1 | | | | |
Goals	Family/ Work	Self/ Hobby	Social relations	Property	Health	Daily	Education
N	33	26	40	39	55	20	36
Male	22	13	12	26	25	8	22
Stand. Resid.	1.8	-0.2	-3.0	2.0	-1.1	-0.9	1.4
Female	11	13	28	13	30	11	11
Stand. Resid.	-1.8	0.2	3.0	-2.0	1.1	0.9	-1.4

Note: $\chi^2(6) = 17.68$, $p<.001$

Goals at Time 2

The following types of young adults with different goal patterns were found at time 2 (see Figure 2 and Table 3). First, a cluster with high interest in property (n = 32, 14 percent) emerged from the whole sample. Second was a cluster with high interest in daily issues (n = 17, 8 percent). Third was a cluster with high interest in self (n = 21, 10 percent). Fourth was a cluster with high interest in both work and family (n = 36, 16 percent). Fifth was a cluster with high interest in social relations (n = 31, 14 percent). Sixth was a cluster with high interest in education and health (n = 35, 16 percent), and finally, seventh was a cluster with high interest in education (n = 43, 21 percent). The largest group was those with interest in hobbies and the smallest was that related to daily issues. This time no differences in gender distribution were found between the clusters, $\chi^2(6) = 4.32$, ns.

Goals at Time 3

The following types of young adults with different types of goal orientations were found at time 3 (Figure 2 and Table 4): First emerged a cluster with high interest in daily issues (n = 21, 10 percent). Second was a cluster with high interest in property and health-related issues (n = 26, 13 percent). Third was a cluster with high interest in self (n = 11, 6 percent). Fourth was a cluster with high interest in social relations and hobbies (n = 47, 23 percent). Fifth was a cluster with high interest in education and also to social relations (n = 12, 6 percent). Sixth was a cluster with high interest in work and family (n = 43, 22 percent), and finally, seventh was a cluster with no specific interest (n = 22, 11 percent). The largest group was that related to social relations and hobbies and smallest was that related to self. Again, no differences in gender distribution were found between the clusters, $\chi2(6) = 8.19$, ns.

Table 3: Means and Standard Deviations for Clusters at Time 2

				Clusters				
N	35	36	43	21	17	32	31	
Goal	Educ./ Health	Work and Family	Hobby	Self	Daily	Property	Social Relations	F
Educ.								
M	1.15^a	0.53^b	0.65^b	0.81^b	0.35^b	0.47^b	0.77^{ab}	3.68***
SD	1.08	0.56	0.69	0.81	0.61	0.57	0.50	
Work								
M	0.89^b	1.50^a	0.86^b	0.81^b	1.24^{ab}	0.84^b	1.19^{ab}	7.96***
SD	0.47	0.74	0.52	0.40	0.56	0.47	0.54	
Family								
M	0.49^b	1.25^a	0.05^c	0.67^b	0.53^b	0.6^b	0.19^c	21.98***
SD	0.51	0.55	0.21	0.48	0.51	0.75	0.40	
Friends								
M	0.11^c	0.53^b	0.30^c	0.33^c	0.24^c	0.34^c	1.25^a	19.97***
SD	0.32	0.51	0.46	0.58	0.44	0.55	0.44	
Hobby								
M	0.20^b	0.78^a	0.84^a	0.62^{ab}	0.65^{ab}	0.53^{ab}	.55^{ab}	2.59*
SD	0.41	0.68	1.15	0.92	0.79	0.62	0.57	
Health								
M	1.14^a	0.22^c	0.12^c	0.29^c	0.29^c	0.72^b	1.03^a	27.22***
SD	0.55	0.42	0.32	0.46	0.59	0.63	0.55	
Self								
M	0.20^c	0.06^c	0.23^c	1.81^a	0.18C	0.44B	0.23C	37.78***
SD	0.41	0.23	0.43	0.60	0.53	0.67	0.43	
Property								
M	0.00^c	0.00^c	0.00^c	0.00^a	0.12^b	1.09^a	0.00^c	248.57***
SD	0.00	0.00	0.00	0.00	0.33	0.30	0.00	
Daily Hassles								
M	0.00^c	0.08^c	0.00^c	0.10^c	1.53^a	0.06^c	0.29^b	57.19***
SD	0.00	0.28	0.00	0.30	0.62	0.25	0.53	

Note: ***p<.001, *p<.05

Table 4: Means and Standard Deviations for Clusters at Time 3

			Clusters					
N	47	43	11	26	22	21	12	
Goals	Social/ Relats. Hobby	Work and Family	Self	Property Health	No Focus	Daily	Educat.	*F*
Educ.								
M	0.51^b	0.49^b	0.45^b	0.38^b	0.59^b	0.86^b	2.33^a	17.37***
SD	0.55	0.55	0.52	0.70	0.67	0.65	0.78	
Work								
M	0.89^b	1.49^a	1.00^b	1.00^b	0.86^b	0.71^b	0.50^b	10.29***
SD	0.52	0.59	0.45	0.40	0.35	0.56	0.52	
Family								
M	0.45^b	1.12^a	0.55^b	0.58^b	0.00^c	0.00^c	0.75^b	17.87***
SD	0.54	0.59	0.69	0.58	0.00	0.00	0.62	
Friends								
M	0.89^a	0.09^b	0.00^b	0.23^b	0.00^b	0.19^b	0.83^a	27.84***
SD	0.52	0.29	0.00	0.43	0.00	0.40	0.39	
Hobby								
M	1.00^a	0.37^b	0.64^{ab}	0.58^{ab}	0.23^b	0.48^b	0.25^b	4.76*
SD	1.02	0.54	0.50	0.58	0.43	0.75	0.45	
Health								
M	0.66^b	0.35^b	0.55^{ab}	1.12^a	0.59^b	0.38^b	0.33^b	5.25***
SD	0.66	0.48	0.52	0.77	0.67	0.50	0.49	
Self								
M	0.57^b	0.09^c	2.45^a	0.11^c	0.14^c	0.14^c	0.25^{bc}	37.92***
SD	0.71	0.37	0.69	0.33	0.35	0.36	0.45	
Property								
M	0.13^c	0.07^c	0.00^c	1.19^a	0.00^c	0.48^b	0.00^c	33.39***
SD	0.34	0.26	0.00	0.57	0.00	0.68	0.00	
Daily hassles								
M	0.17^b	0.21^b	0.18^b	0.04^b	0.00^b	1.37^a	0.33^b	33.81***
SD	0.38	0.41	0.40	0.20	0.00	0.48	0.49	

Note: ***$p<.001$, *$p<.05$

Stability of Goal Pattern

Next, in order to analyze the stability of goal patterns during the transition from school to work, cluster types in measurement 1 and 2 were cross-tabulated and analyzed by use of log-linear models. The results concerning stability of interests between times 1 and 2 revealed that there was stability ($\chi(2(36) = 71.74$, p<.001) concerning interest related to work and family (St. Res. = 3.3, p<.05), self (St. Res. = 1.9, p<.05), property (St. Res. = 2.8, p<.05), daily issues (St. Res. = 4.0, p<.05), and social relations (St. Res. = 2.8, p<.05). Moreover, the results showed that it was not typical for young adults to turn their interest from self and hobbies to social relations (St. Res. = -2.1, p<.05), from social relations to property (St.Res. = -2.3, p<.05), or from property to education (St. Res. = -2.2, p<.05). In turn, it was likely for young adults in the transition to work life from school to turn interest from education to hobbies (St. Res. = 2.8, p<.05).

Analogous analyses across the measurement of 2 and 3 showed stability ($\chi2(36) = 63.99$, p<.001) concerning social relations (St. Res. = 2.6, p<.05), work and family (St. Res. = 2.3, p<.05) and daily-related (St. Res. = 4.5, p<.05) goals. Moreover, it was typical for young adults to turn interest from hobbies to no focus (St. Res. = 4.1, p<.05) of goals in later years.

Goals and Life-situation

Next, I was interested in investigating how individuals who showed different goal patterns at time 1 while still at school would differ in their life-situation at time 1, time 2, and time 3. The results showed first that those who had interest in social or daily-related goals at time 1 had had higher grades in their high school ($\chi2(6, 242) = 2.41$, p<.02, Table 7). Moreover, those young adults who were interested in work and family related goals at time 1 were more likely to work later on in a profession after graduation that was in accordance with their education ($\chi2(6) = 13.29$, p<.03; Table 5). Also, those young adults who were interested in education-related goals at time 1 were unlikely to be in a work that was in accordance with their education at time 2 (seeTable 5). Next, those young adults who were interested in social relations-related goals at time 1 were also more likely to be in other life situations than full-time work at time 2 after graduation ($\chi2(6) = 13.20$, p<.03; Table 5). In turn, it was not likely to be in life situations other than full-time work if being previously interested in either property or education-related goals at time 1.

Next, I investigated how individuals who showed a certain goal pattern at last measurement time, would differ in their life situation at the same time, time 3. First, these results showed that those young adults who were interested in work and family-related goals at time 3 were less likely to be unemployed at the same time, at time 3 ($\chi2(6) = 15.17$, p<.02; Table 6). In turn, those who were interested in education or social relations-related goals at time 3 were more likely to be at a life situation other than full-time work, such as taking care of children at home at the same time ($\chi 2(6) = 17.29$, p<.04; Table 6).

Goals and Well-being

Finally, in order to analyze the relations between well-being at time 1 and goal clusters at time 1, the differences were analyzed in clusters according to their well-being using *ANOVA's*. First, the results for mood showed that those interested in social goals at time 1 were to some extent happier at the same measurement time, time 1, than those interested in self- or property-related goals (F(6, 242) = 1.90, p = .08, Table 7). The results showed further that those interested in property-related goals at time 1 scored highest at the same measurement time on depressive symptoms and stress, and, on the contrary, those interested in work and family-related goals at measurement time 1, scored lowest on depressive symptoms (F(6,242) = 1.80, p = .10, Table 7) and on stress (F(6,242) = 1.79, p = .10, Table 7).

Finally, in order to analyze the relations between interests at time 1 and physical well-being at time 1 in terms of symptoms and the use of alcohol, we first compared the clusters at time 1 according to their amount of physical symptoms. The results showed that those who were interested in property at time 1 had more symptoms at the same measurement time than those who were inter-

Table 5: Relations Between Clusters at Time 1 and Life Situation at Time 2

Life Situation	Family/ Work	Self/ Hobby	Social Relations	Property	Health	Daily	Education	N
Other than working full-time								
No	21	20	27	31	47	14	18	178
Standard Resid	0.6	0.5	-2.2	1.9	1.6	-0.6	-2.0	
Yes	3	3	11	2	5	4	8	96
Standard Resid	-0.6	-0.5	2.2	-1.9	-1.6	0.6	2.0	

Note: $\chi 2(6) = 13.20$, p<.03

Life Situation	Family/ Work	Self/ Hobby	Social Relations	Property	Health	Daily	Education	N
Work in accordance with one's own education								
No	7	12	20	18	21	11	19	108
Standard Resid	-2.2	0.2	0.3	0.5	-1.7	0.9	2.5	
Yes	17	11	18	15	31	7	7	106
Standard Resid	2.2	-.2	-.3	-.5	1.7	-.9	-2.5	

Note: $\chi 2(6) = 13.29$, p<.03

ested in education-related goals $(F(6, 242) = 2.25, p = .03$, see Table 7). Furthermore, the results showed that those who were interested in property-related goals at time 1 used more alcohol at the same time than others $(F(6, 242) = 2.68, p<.01$, table 7). Again, no cross-lagged prospective relations were found and thus they are not presented.

Finally, the results showed only cross-sectional associations, neither goals nor well-being predicted prospectively each other.

Conclusions

This study was an attempt to explore the ways in which young adults differ along their personal goal patterns and what consequences these have on their success while at the important crossroad in their life—the transition from school to work. Instead of a variable-oriented approach, a person-oriented approach was chosen in order to analyze the goal patterns young adults showed during the transition period from school to work life. The advantage of the use of a person-oriented approach is that the results refer to certain individuals rather than to variables,

Table 6: Relations Between Clusters at Time 3 and Life Situation at Time 3

Life Situation	Family/ Work	Social Relations	Self	Property/ Health	No Focus	Daily	Education
Work in not accordance with one's own education							
No	42	39	9	20	20	18	7
Standard Resid	0.7	1.4	0.4	1.5	1.3	0.1	2.9
Yes	5	3	2	6	1	3	5
Standard Resid	0.7	1.4	0.4	1.5	1.3	0.1	2.9

Note: $\chi2(6) = 17.29, p<.04$

Life Situation	Family/ Work	Social Relations	Self	Property/ Health	No Focus	Daily	Education
Unemployed							
No	46	35	11	25	17	18	9
Standard Resid	2.3	-1.8	1.2	1.3	-1.2	-0.5	-1.6
Yes	1	8	0	1	4	3	3
Standard Resid	-2.3	1.8	-1.2	-1.3	1.2	0.5	1.6

Note: $\chi2(6) = 15.17, p<.02$

and it is possible to estimate how a big proportion of the sample showed a particular goal pattern. In this study, I focused using this person-oriented approach to investigate motivational constructs on the second floor of the house of personality, personal action constructs.

My first aim was to examine the kinds of goal patterns young adults typically showed in the transition from school to work. The results showed, first, that a group of young adults who were interested in work and family was found at each measurement time during transition period from school to work life. Thus, these two types of goals, work and family, seem to "go together", i.e., to form a combined interest type, indicating a strong and equally engaged emphasis on both life areas. These two goals might be assumed to be markers of normative developmental tasks for these young adults (Havighurst 1948; Nurmi 1993). Based on the results, it seems that there is a group of young adults for whom the normative focus in life is the most important one. This family and work oriented young adults group might be called a normatively-oriented group or traditionalists in the way they planned and thought of their future life. Furthermore, the amount in this group increased during the transition to work life. So, it seems that young adults become more traditional as they grow up.

Second, the results showed that some of the goal patterns resembled those described previously as motive types (McClelland 1985), such as those related to achievement (education-related group), nurturing (social), and power (property). This result suggests that some of the goal patterns identified here reflect

Table 7: Relations Between Clusters at Time 1 and Well-being at Time 1

Well-being	Daily		Property		Social Relations		Family/ Work		Self/ Hobby		Health		Education	
Time 1	M	SD	M	SD	M	SD	M	SD	M	SD	M	SD	M	SD
Grads at High School	8.10[a]	.72	7.79[b]	.75	8.18[ab]	.67	7.73[b]	.69	7.71[b]	.70	7.82[b]	.72	7.73[b]	.65
Health	1.86[ab]	.55	1.94[a]	.68	1.75[ab]	.46	1.70[ab]	.31	1.80[ab]	.47	1.78[ab]	.42	1.50[b]	.38
Alcohol	1.55[b]	.55	2.16[b]	.68	1.27[ab]	.69	1.82[ab]	.59	1.71[ab]	.74	1.75[ab]	.63	1.65[b]	.59
Mood	4.29[ab]	.75	4.74	1.05	5.29[a]	.79	5.16[ab]	.93	4.70[b]	.82	5.03[ab]	1.03	4.96[ab]	.77
Depression	2.17	.74	2.21	.91	1.84	.59	1.80	.57	2.09	.71	2.12	.76	1.99	.69
Stress	2.81	.53	2.93	.75	2.64	.58	2.57	.50	2.88	.53	2.81	.63	2.69	.58

Note: The means in the same row that do not share subscipts differed at p<.05 in *Tukey's test*.

more general motive types described to be involved on the "first floor of the house of personality."

Moreover, the results also showed that at each time during this transition there seems to be a small group of individuals who were interested in daily hassles. It might be that these young adults are not ready to orient themselves into future adult roles and rather focus more on the present and daily issues. It is possible that these young adults later do not find other interests for their life. Future study in which we follow these young adults might give an answer to this hypothesis.

My next aim was to examine whether the young adults' goal patterns were similar across the three measurements during transition from school to work life.

The results showed some stability on personal goals, such as those goals related to normative developmental tasks, interest in work and family. Moreover, stability was found also among social, self, daily, and property-related interests during a transition period from school to work. Based on these results, it seems that young adults navigate their transition period from school to working life by forming their life structure around interests that they already had formed while still at school. It might be that during transition periods people direct their lives by personal goals which they set for themselves and are resistant to change them (see Heckhausen 1999). However, the results also revealed change in interests. The results showed, for example, that those young adults who still were interested in education at the end of their vocational school typically moved to their interests to hobbies and later on to no focus. These results showed also that young adults reconstructed their personal goals particularly in those life-domains which were closely related to the transition they were going through, such as those related to their education. This is in line with some of our earlier results according to which people seem to re-direct their focus according to the demands and challenges of a specific transition period (Salmela-Aro et al., in press).

The results of the present study showed only a few gender differences in young adults' personal goals: young women were interested in goals related to social issues and young men in property related issues before their graduation at vocational schools. This finding, which supports the earlier findings (see for example Strough et al., 1996), is a very typical gender-prototype finding and it was found only before graduation.

According to the results of the present study young adults' goal patterns were related to their life situation. As would be expected, the results showed first that normatively-oriented young adults, i.e., who have work and family-related goals, were more often in a life situation as married. In turn, those interested in material aspects of life or friends were less often married. These results are also in line with the suggestions according to which people direct their own lives (Lerner 1983) by personal goals (Nurmi 1991). The young adults of this study seemed to produce their life by setting personal goals which were based on their current life situation. It might be that goals and life-situation form accumulative cycles, according to which goals lead to certain life situations which again strengthen interests in the same life arena (see also Salmela-Aro & Nurmi 1997b).

The next aim was to analyze the relations between goal patterns young adults have and their consequences for their professional work life situation. I was also interested in examining what kind of consequences and antecedents these different goal patterns have for young adults' lives in terms of their work life situation. The results showed that young adults' goal patterns seemed to have some consequences for their life situation and so the results showed that young adults' interest types were related to some extent to their life situation. Interestingly, it seems, for example, that those normatively-oriented young adults who had interest in work and family seem to be sheltered from unemployment and lead to employment in a profession related to their own education. This result is in line with earlier findings in which it is assumed that personal goals play a role in the ways in which people direct their lives (Salmela-Aro & Nurmi 1997a, 1997b; Emmons 1991). In turn, interest in education seems to be related to a life-situation in which one is not working in a profession related to one's own profession. Moreover, those young adults interested and oriented toward friends while at school were less likely to be able to find work. Furthermore, they seem to be later also doing something else other than working, such as taking care of children. It might be that these young adults find the meaning of life in social aspects rather than working life. This is in line with the findings of Emmons (1991) according to which affiliation and intimacy strivings were associated with interpersonal life events. Moreover, those interested in material aspects were able to find work. This result shows also that goals orient one's life situation. Those young adults who value material aspects of life direct to working life as a way to earn money. These results show that interest patterns orient young adults according to their similar life situation.

Finally, in this study, the aim was to analyze the relations between goal patterns young adults have and their related well-being. In this study, however, only results based on correlations between goal patterns and well-being were found. The results showed that those young adults who were interested in social goals were, to some extent happier, than others who did not focus on social goals. This result is in line with earlier results. For example, according to Emmons (1991) intimacy goals lead to high well-being. Moreover, those interested in normative aspects, such as work and family, experienced less depressive aspects. The basis for this result might be, as has been suggested by Nurmi (1993), according to which personal goals related to developmental tasks, such as this normative orientation is related to high well-being. Previously Salmela-Aro and Nurmi (1997b) also found that goals which concern major age-graded developmental tasks, such as future family, predict high subjective well-being. Relations between ill-being and goal interests revealed also small associations between material aspects and intrapersonal orientation in terms of self-related project pattern and low well-being. So, these results based on young adults showed that interpersonal and normative orientations seemed to be related to positive emotions and intrapersonal or material orientation to negative emotions. These results are in line with the suggestions according to which normative, external orientation (e.g., Havighurst 1948) or social orientation (Emmons 1991, 1996) is related to high well-being. In turn, self-related (Little 1993; Salmela-Aro & Nurmi 1997a; Salmela-Aro, Pennanen, & Nurmi in press) or material orientation

(Emmons 1996; Kasser & Ryan 1993, 1996; Ryan et al., 1999) is related to low well-being. Kasser and Ryan (1996), for example, found that individuals who strongly value extrinsic goals, such as wealth, relative to intrinsic goals, such as relatedness, experience less well-being. Moreover, focusing on self-goals does not promote dealing with developmental tasks, and maybe therefore lead to depression (Salmela-Aro, Pennanen, & Nurmi in press). It has been suggested that over-excessive thinking about oneself and focusing inward may have negative affective and cognitive consequences (Ingram 1990; Nolen-Hoeksema, Parker, & Larsen 1994) and those who focus on internal aspects are more likely to become depressed and suffer from low self-esteem.

No prospective predictions were found, however, between goal patterns and well-being. It might be that the relations between well-being and goal patterns are such fast processes that they do not predict each other in a longer time period. Furthermore, in this study the results are based on groups of young adults with similar goal patterns. It might be that the results using variable orientation are more powerful. In addition, the results are based on goal contents, and not how people appraise their goals. However, the main conclusion of this chapter is that the person-oriented approach advocated here with the personal action construct at the second level of the house of personality brings the developmental and personality psychology back into understanding how one really is.

Consequences for Clinical Applications

This study focused on young adults who were at an important crossroad in their lives: moving from school to work. Important contributions in terms of adolescents' personal goals and their relations to their positive well-being, life-situation, and adaptation are possible to raise. One way how young adults seem to direct their lives is by producing personal goals. Based on the results of this study, these goals are related to young adults' life situation and also to some extent to their well-being. The results showed that it would be important for young adults during transition to working life to focus on those personal goals forming the key developmental tasks during this time, such as future professional career and family. In turn, those who focus on other life themes in this period of life such as education, friends, or self-related issues might be in danger of not being able to achieve the tasks which are expected from them and which are markers at entry into adulthood. The use of personal goals as units of personality research affords the opportunity for therapeutic activities to be centered directly on the units that have been assessed. Personal goals can serve as the direct focus for clinical, counseling, or development activities. This practical accessibility and mutability of personal goal units make them particularly attractive to applied fields, such as occupational therapy and counseling (see also Christiansen, Little, & Backman 1998; Christiansen, Backman, Little, & Nguyen 1999). One possibility would be to create a goal program for adolescents, the aim of which would be to enhance their well-being. This process would involve themes, such as how to set personal goals, which goals are better and which are worse in terms of adaptation, how to achieve these goals in the immediate future, and how to believe in a valuable future. During the program young adults would be able to learn how to identify positive life goals in terms of normative expectations, and focus on goal attainment.

References

Austin, J. & Vancouver, J. (1996). Goal constructs in psychology: Structure, process and content. *Psychological Bulletin*, 120, 338–375.

Baltes, P. B. & Baltes, M. M. (1990). Psychological perspectives on successful aging: The model of selective optimization with compensation. In P. B. Baltes & M. M. Baltes (Eds.), *Successful aging. Perspectives from behavioral sciences* (pp. 1–34). Cambridge: Cambridge University Press.

Baltes, P., Reese, H., & Lipsitt, L. (1980). Life span developmental psychology. *Annual Review of Psychology*, 31, 65–110.

Beck, A. T., Ward, C. H., Mendelsohn, M., Mosck, L., & Erlaugh, J. (1961). An inventory of measuring depression. *Archives of General Psychiatry*, 4, 561–571.

Brandtstädter, J. (1989). Personal self-regulation of development: Cross-sequential analyses of development-related control beliefs and emotion. *Developmental Psychology*, 25, 96–108.

Cairns, L., Bergman, L., & Kagan, J. (Eds, 1988), *Methods and models for studying the individual*. Thousand Oaks, CA: SAGE.

Cantor, N. (1990). From thought to behavior. "Having" and "doing" in the study of personality and cognition. *American Psychologist*, 45, 735–750.

Cantor, N., Norem, J. K., Niedenthal, P. M., Langston, C., & Brower, A. M. (1987). Life tasks, self concept ideals, and cognitive strategies in a life transition. *Journal of Personality and Social Psychology*, 53, 1178–1191.

Carver, C. & Scheier, F. (1990). Origins and functions of positive and negative affect: A control-process view. *Psychological Review*, 97, 19–35.

Caspi, A. (1987). Personality in the life course. *Journal of Personality and Social Psychology*, 53, 1203–1213.

Chambers, N. (1997). *Personal project analysis: The maturation of a multi-dimensional methodology*. Carleton University, Canada.

Christiansen, C., Little, B., & Backman, C. (1998). Personal projects: A useful concept for occupational therapy. *American Journal of Occupational Therapy*, 52, 439–446.

Christiansen, C., Backman, C., Little, B., & Nguyen, A. (1999). Occupational therapy and well-being: A study of personal projects. *American Journal of Occupational Therapy*, 53, 91–100.

Cohen, J., Kamarck, T., & Mermelstein, R. (1983). A global measure of perceived stress. *Journal of Health and Social Behavior*, 24, 385–396.

Cross, S. E. & Markus H. R. (1991). Possible selves across the lifespan. *Human Development*, 34, 230–255.

Diener, E. & Emmons, R. A. (1984). The independence of positive and negative affect. *Journal of Personality and Social Psychology*, 47, 1105–1117.

Elder, G. H. Jr. (1985). Perspectives on the life course. In G. H. Elder, Jr. (Ed.), *Life course dynamics* (pp. 23–49). Ithaca, NY: Cornell University Press.

Elliot, A. J. & Church, M. A. (1997). A hierarchical model of approach and avoidance motivation. *Journal of Personality and Social Psychology*, 72, 218–232.

Emmons, R. A. (1986). Personal strivings: An approach to personality and subjective well-being. *Journal of Personality and Social Psychology*, 51, 1058–1068.

Emmons, R. A. (1989). Exploring the relations between motives and traits: The case of narcissism. In D. M. Buss & N. Cantor (Eds.), *Personality psychology: Recent trends and emerging directions*. New York: Springler-Verlag.

Emmons, R. A. (1991). Personal strivings, daily life events, and psychological and physical well-being. *Journal of Personality*, 59, 455–472.

Emmons, R. A. (1992). Abstract versus concrete goals: Personal striving level, physical illness, and psychological well-being. *Journal of Personality and Social Psychology*, 62, 3–9.

Emmons, R. A. (1996). Striving and feeling. Personal goals and subjective well-being. In P. M. Gollwitzer & J. A. Bargh (Eds.), *The psychology of action-linking cognition and motivation to behavior* (pp. 313–337). New York: Guildford Press.

Emmons, R. A. (1997). Motives and life goals. In R. Hogan, J. Johnson & S. Briggs (Eds.), *Handbook of personality psychology*. San Diego: Academic Press.

Erikson, E. H. (1959). *Identity and the life cycle*. New York: International Universities Press.

Fleeson, W. & Cantor, N. (1995). Goal relevance and the affective experience of daily life. Ruling out situational explanations. *Motivation and Emotion*, 19, 25–57.

Ford, D. & Ford, M. (1987). Humans as self-constructing living systems: An overview. In M. Ford & D. Ford (Eds.), *Humans as self-constructing living systems: Putting the framework to work*. (pp. 1–46). Hillsdale, NJ: Erlbaum.

Greene, A. L. & Wheatley, S. M. (1992). "I've got a lot to do and I don't think I'll have the time": Gender differences in late adolescent's narratives fo the future. *Journal of Youth and Adolescence*, 21, 667–686.

Havighurst, R. J. (1948). *Developmental tasks and education*. (3rd ed.). New York: Mc Kay.

Heckhausen, J. (1999). *Developmental regulation in adulthood: Age-normative and sociostructural constraints as adaptive challenges*. Cambridge: Cambridge University Press.

Hurrelman, K. (1994). Introduction: Interdisciplinary and international approaches to research on adolescence. In K. Hurrelmann (Ed.), *International handbook of adolescence* (pp. 1–15). Westport, CT: Greenwood Press.

Ingram, R. (1990). Self-focused attention in clinical disorders: Review and a conceptual model. *Psychological Bulletin*, 107, 156–176.

Karniol, R. & Ross, M. (1996). The motivational impact of temporal focus: thinking about the future and the past. *Annual Review of Psychology*, 47, 593–620.

Kasser, T. & Ryan, R. (1993). A dark side of the American dream: Correlates of financial success as central life aspiration. *Journal of Personality and Social Psychology*, 65, 410–422.

Kasser, T. & Ryan, R. (1996). Further examining the American dream: Different correlates in intrinsic and extrinsic goals. *Personality and Social Psychology Bulletin,
22*, 80–87.

Lerner, R. M. (1983). A "goodness of fit" model of person-context interaction. In D.
Magnusson, & V. L. Allen (Eds), *Human development: An interactional perspective (pp. 279–294)*. New York: Academic Press.

Little, B. R. (1983). Personal projects: A rationale and method for investigation.
Environment and Behavior, 15, 273–309.

Little, B. R. (1989). Personal project analysis: Trivial pursuits, magnificent obsessions,
and the search for coherence. In D. M. Buss & N. Cantor (Eds.), *Personality psychology: Recent trends and emerging directions.* New York: Springler-Verlag.

Little, B. (1993). Personal projects and the distributed self. In J. Suls (Eds.),
Psychological perspectives on the self. (Vol4). Hillsdale, NJ: Lawrence Erlbaum.

Little, B. (1996). Free traits, personal projects and idio-tapes: Three tiers for personality
psychology. *Psychological Inquiry, 7*, 340–344.

Marcia, J. E. (1980). Identity in adolescence. In J. Adelson (Ed), *Handbook of adolescent psychology.* New York: Wiley.

Markus, H. & Nurius, P. (1986). Possible selves. *American Psychologist, 41*, 954–969.

Mayer, K. (1986). Structured constraints of the life course. *Human Development, 29*,
163–170.

Mayfield, D., McLeod, G., & Hall, P. (1974). The CAGE questionnaire: Validation of a
new alcoholism screening instrument. *American Journal of Psychiatry, 131*,
1121–1123.

McAdams, D. (1996). Personality, modernity and the storied self: A contemporary
framework for studying persons. *Psychological Inquiry, 7*, 295–321.

McClelland, D. C. (1985). *Human motivation.* Glenview, IL: Scott, Foresman.

Neugarten, B. L., Moore, J. W., & Lowe, J.C. (1985). Age norms, age constraints, and
adult socialization. *American Journal of Sociology, 70*, 710–717.

Newman, B. M. & Newman, P. R. (1975). *Development through life. A psychosocial
approach.* Homewood: The Dorsey Press.

Nolen-Hoeksma, S., Parker, L. E., & Larsen, J. (1994). Ruminative coping with
depressed mood following loss. *Journal of Personality and Social Psychology, 67*,
92–104.

Nurmi, J.-E., (1989). Planning, motivation and evaluation in orientation to the future: A
latent structure analysis. *Scandinavian Journal of Psychology, 30*, 64–71.

Nurmi, J. -E. (1991). How do adolescents see their future? A review of the development
of future orientation and planning. *Developmental Review, 11*, 1–59.

Nurmi, J. -E. (1992). Age differences in adult life goals, concerns, and their temporal
extension: A life course approach to future-oriented motivation. *International
Journal of Behavioral Develpoment, 15*, 487–508.

Nurmi, J. -E. (1993). Adolescent development in an age-graded context: The role of
personal beliefs, goals, and strategies in the tackling of develpomental tasks and

standards. *International Journal of Behavioral Development, 16*, 169–189.

Nurmi, J.-E. (1997). Self-definition and mental health during asolescence and young adulthood. In J. Schulenberg, J. Maggs & K. Hurrelmann (Eds.), *Health risks and developmental transitions during adolescence.* (pp. 395–419). Cambridge: Cambridge University Press.

Nurmi, J.-E. & Salmela- Aro, K. (1995). *Work status questionnaire.* University of Helsinki.

Nurmi, J.-E. & Salmela- Aro, K. (in press). Goal construction, reconstruction and well-being in a life-span context: A transition from school to work. *Journal of Personality.*

Nuttin, J. (1984). *Motivation, planning and action. Relational theory of behavioral dynamics.* Lawrence Erlbaum: Leuven University Press.

Oerter, R. (1986). Developmental tasks through the life span: a new approach to an old concept. In P. B. Baltes, D. L. Featherman, & R. M. Lerner (Eds.), *Life-span development and behavior. Vol. 7* (pp. 233–269). Hillsdale, NJ: Lawrence Erlbaum.

Ryan, R., Chirkov, V., Little, T., Sheldon, K., Timoshina, E., & Deci, E. (1999). The American deream in Russia: Extrinsic aspirations and well-being in two cultures. *Journal of Personality and Social Psychology Bulletin, 25*, 1509–1524.

Salmela-Aro, K. (1992). Struggling with self: The personal projects of students seeking psychological counselling. *Scandinavian Journal of Psychology, 33*, 330–338.

Salmela-Aro, K. & Nurmi, J.-E. (1997a), Positive and negative self-related goals and subjective well-being. Journal of Adult Development, 4, 179-188.

Salmela-Aro, K. & Nurmi, J.-E. (1997b), Goal contents, well-being and life context during transition to university: A longitudinal study. *International Journal of Behavioral Development, 20 (3)*, 471–491

Salmela-Aro, K., Nurmi, J.-E., Saisto, T. & Halmesmäki, E. (2000). Changes in women's and men's personal goals during transition to parenthood. *Journal of Family Psychology,* 14, 171–186.

Salmela-Aro, K., Pennanen, R. & Nurmi, J.-E. (in press). Self-focused goals: What they are, how they function and how they relate to well-being. In P. Schmuck & K. Sheldon (Eds.), *Life-goals and well-being.* Berlin: Pabst Science Publishers.

Schulenberg, J., Maggs, J. & Hurrelmann, K. (1997). Negotiating developmental transitions during adolescence and young adulthood: Health risks and opportunities. In J. Schulenberg, J. Maggs & K. Hurrelmann (Eds.), *Health risks and developmental transitions during adolescence* (pp. 1–19). Cambridge: Cambridge University Press.

Solantaus, T. (1987). Hopes and worries of young people in three European countries. *Health Promotion, 2*, 19–27.

Strough, J., Berg, C. A., & Sansone C. (1996). Goals for solving everyday problems across the life span: Age and gender differences in the salience of interpersonal concerns. *Developmental Psychology, 32*, 1106–1115.

CHAPTER 4

The Role of Achievement and Social Strategies in the Transition into Young Adulthood

SANNA ERONEN

Times of transition may offer a window on personality in many respects. Transition situations have been found to arise from social and biological changes that require persons to organize their activities around new tasks (Caspi & Moffit 1993; see also Ruble & Seidman 1996). It has been suggested that personality differences are best revealed during transitions into unpredictable new situations (Caspi & Moffit 1993). Therefore, assessing behavior during these novel, ambiguous, and uncertain life-points can give crucial information to researchers.

People do not just face ordinary transitions during young adulthood: this time phase has been considered especially important for later lifespan development. First of all, the age period from the early teens to the middle twenties makes a unique contribution to the development of lifespan memory: events that occur during this phase are better remembered than events that occur during other phases of people's lives (Belli, Schuman, & Jackson 1997; Fitzgerald 1988). This may be due to the fact that this time period has been considered to be the most important with respect to the formation of identity (Erikson 1959; Fizgerald 1988; Havighurst 1959; Rubin, Wetzler, & Nebes 1986). Conceptualizations about and attitudes toward the self are formed, which means that environmental feedback in terms of successes and failures may have an especially strong influence on an individual's self-concept (Nurmi 1997). It has been shown that the majority of young adults are exploring their identity even when they are twenty years or older (Meeus 1996). This may reflect the fact that the end of adolescence is individually defined in Western culture, and it is more dependent on the extent to which a person has achieved independence and self-reliance in various aspects of development than any single role transition (Arnett & Taber 1994). However, there are some developmental tasks which are not only topical during young adulthood, such as finding a congenial social group and getting started in education or an occupation, but which may also be determining factors for later well-being (Havighurst 1948). Therefore, it is essential to study the extent to which an individual's personality can facilitate or hinder the achievement of these tasks. According to the dynamic interactionist paradigm, personality differences, such as individual ways of dealing with situations, can be assumed to affect personal adaptation during the transition process, whereas the achievement of developmental tasks during transition may again shape the individual's personality (Asendorpf & Wilpers 1998; Magnusson 1990).

This chapter focuses on the transition phase from secondary school to new educational environments. During this period young adults have to face at least two challenges: first, they have to fulfill the new academic demands of the environment, and second, they have to adapt to new social circles by making friends and acquaintances. This process is conceptualized from the social-cognitive viewpoint in terms of cognitive-motivational strategies. Because it has been suggested that people translate their personal skills and goals into action via strategies (e.g., Cantor 1990; Nurmi 1997), it is to be expected that such strategies have a major role in the adaptation process. Moreover, the feedback from the environment might also be expected to influence such strategies in particular, because they have been suggested to be more situation-specific (e.g., Cantor, 1990) than stable personality traits, being immune to changes in the environment (Asendorpf & Wilpers 1998). Therefore, this theoretical framework may be useful when reciprocal processes of interaction with the environment are studied. After all, individual personality is characterized by enormous flexibility alongside its stability (Epstein 1990).

Achievement Strategies and Success in Studies

There has been increasing interest in the cognitive and motivational strategies people apply in achievement contexts (e.g., Dweck & Legget 1988; Jones & Berglas 1978; Norem & Cantor 1986; Onatsu-Arvilommi & Nurmi in press; Pintrich, Marx, & Boyle 1993; Winne 1997). These strategies have been suggested to consist of various psychological processes, such as anticipation of behavioral outcomes, affects, planning of and investing effort in the task at hand, monitoring behavior, and evaluating goal attainment in terms of causal attributions (Dweck & Leggett 1988; Norem 1989). The use of these types of strategy has also been shown to be associated with how successful people are in various achievement or study situations (Dweck & Legget 1988; Jones & Berglas 1978; Norem & Cantor, 1986; Onatsu & Nurmi in press). If people expect to do well, they typically set task-related goals, construct plans for their realization, and invest a high level of effort in carrying them out (Norem 1989; Nurmi 1993). This enhances the probability of success in the task at hand, and strengthens images of competence in future situations. In turn, it has been suggested that a person who is anxious or anticipates failure often tries to avoid the situation (Peterson & Seligman, 1984), or behaves in a way that will provide an excuse for potential failure (Jones & Berglas, 1978). These types of behavior typically decrease the likelihood of success in the task at hand, and consequently may lead to low well-being.

Several types of achievement strategy have been described earlier. For example, Cantor with her colleagues (Cantor 1990; Norem & Cantor 1986) described two types of strategy among young people who were successful in a university environment. An optimistic strategy was characterised by straightforward striving for success based on high outcome expectations and positive past experiences, and on the desire to enhance an already strong image of competence (Cantor 1990; Norem 1989). In contrast, typical of students using a defensive-pessimistic strategy was having defensively low expectations and feeling very anxious and out of control before performance. However, these negative expectations did not become self-fulfilling prophesies, but rather served as a protective attributional cover and motivator before performance, thus leading to a successful outcome (Cantor 1990; Norem & Cantor 1986).

In turn, other types of strategy have been found to be associated with poor performance and problem behavior. For example, Berglas and Jones (1978) described a self-handicapping strategy in the context of academic underachievement. Because self-handicappers are concerned about potential failure, they concentrate on task-irrelevant behavior in order to create an excuse for it, instead of formulating task-related plans. Although this strategy provides them with attributional benefits, it also decreases the likelihood of success. Another prototypical example of a maladaptive behavioral pattern is learned helplessness (Abramson et al., 1978; Seligman 1975), which can also be conceptualized as a strategy (Cantor 1990). Helpless individuals have been shown to lack belief in personal control, and therefore to be passive in achievement-related situations rather than formulating task-oriented plans (Diener & Dweck 1978).

Social Strategies and Interpersonal Relationships

Cognitive and motivational patterns also play an important role also in initiating and maintaining interpersonal relationships (Crick & Dodge 1994; Eronen & Nurmi in press; Eronen, Nurmi, & Salmela-Aro 1997; Langston & Cantor 1989). They have been conceptualized in various different terms: Langston and Cantor (1989) described these patterns as *social strategies*, Crick & Dodge (1994) as *social problem-solving strategies*, Goffman (1959) as *self-presentation strategies*, and Eronen et al. (1997) as *social reaction styles*. Even though these conceptualizations overlap, there are also some important differences. Strategic self-presentation has been defined as an attempt to regulate one's own behavior to create a particular impression on others (Jones & Pittman 1982). Social strategy, in turn, has been used to refer to the intricate organization of the feelings, thoughts, effort-arousal, and actions by which people accomplish their personally meaningful goals (Cantor 1990; Langston & Canto 1989). Social problem-solving strategies consist of interpreting contextual information, selecting a behavioral goal and mentally producing and evaluating the alternative behavioral responses evoked by a specific situation (Crick & Dodge 1994). Social reaction styles refer to the ways in which people typically feel and react in challenging social situations by anticipating behavioral outcomes and related affects, and planning of and investing effort in the situation at hand (Eronen et al., 1997). It is apparent that the psychological processes behind these concepts are rather similar. Even though the term social strategy is used in this chapter to refer individuals' interpersonal thoughts and affects, the reader is encouraged to compare the results and theoretical ideas with those that have been presented in the context of kindred concepts.

Adaptive social strategies have been suggested to be typified by optimism, positive affects and approach-orientation toward others, providing a basis for success in initiating social relationships (Eronen et al., 1997; Langston & Cantor 1989). On the other hand, pessimism and avoidance are typical of various types of maladaptive patterns (Arkin, Lake, & Baumgardner 1986; Eronen et al., 1997; Leary & Kowalski 1990; Langston & Cantor, 1989). Although individuals often use these strategies to minimize the likelihood of being evaluated unfavorably, the resulting tendency is to diminish positive feedback from others (Arkin et al., 1986; Cantor 1990; Leary & Kowalski 1990). Therefore, applying maladaptive strategies at the beginning of their studies may have detrimental long-term consequences for individuals' well-being, such as predisposing them to feelings of loneliness (Jones & Carver 1991).

It might be assumed that social strategies also have short-term consequences which are reflected in the online person perception and interpersonal behavior. For example, socially anxious and shy people have been shown to display more reticence and withdrawal, and to be less responsive in interpersonal situations, than non-shy individuals (Cheek & Buss 1981; Jones & Carpenter, 1986; Lord & Zimbardo 1985). Moreover, a protective self-presentational style is often typified by withdrawal from social interaction, and by self-handicapping behaviors (Arkin, Appleman, & Burger 1980; Arkin et al., 1986).

Individuals' social strategies might also be assumed to be reflected in the ways in which they perceive other people. For example, it has been shown that individuals subjectively interpret other people's behavior in the light of their own personality (e.g., Gara et al., 1993; Markus & Smith 1981). They have been shown to use the same categories in describing others as they do in describing themselves (Hirschberg & Jennings 1980; Lewicki 1983; Schrauger & Patterson 1974), suggesting that an individual self-schema provides an interpretive framework for organizing other people's schema-relevant behaviors (Markus et al., 1985). It has also been proposed that people may project their undesirable traits onto other individuals on a defensive level (for a review, see Holmes, 1978), or as a cognitive result of supression (Newman, Duff, & Baumeister 1997). Another possibility is that they project the cause of their feelings onto others. For example, a socially anxious person may perceive others as threatening and intrusively active (Daleiden & Vasey 1997).

Achievement, Social Strategies, and Life Events

Although age-graded, normative developmental tasks are faced by most young adults, there are substantial differences in the sequencing and timing (Hagestad & Neugarten 1985), as well as in the number and severity of the non-normative life events people face (Baltes, Reese, & Lipsitt 1980). If certain types of life event happen to, or even accumulate for, some people but not for others, an interesting question concerns the psychological processes that might be responsible for this individual variation. However, only a few studies have concerned the extent to which people's typical ways of responding in various situations predispose them to positive and negative life events (Headey & Wearing 1989; Magnus et al., 1993; Swearingen & Cohen 1985). Achievement and social strategies are two possible predisposing factors that may influence what life events people experience.

It is also possible that life events predict subsequent well-being. Although some researchers have concluded that they have no impact on it (Brickman et al., 1978; Costa, McCrae, & Zonderman 1987; Diener 1984; Swearingen & Cohen 1985), some others have pointed to an influence over and above the effects of personality (Headey & Wearing 1989; Suh et al., 1996). Therefore, it is possible that people who use functional strategies face positive life events which enhance their well-being, whereas self-protective strategies may increase negative events and subsequent depression and low self-esteem.

Three Studies about Cognitive-motivational Strategies

This chapter seeks to answer four questions: (1) What kind of strategies do students deploy in study and social contexts? (2) Do achievement and social strategies predict academic achievement, well-being, life events and satisfaction with peer relationships? (3) Do social strategies predict interpersonal behavior and person perception, and finally, (4) Does feedback from the new environment (e.g., academic achievement, life events and satisfaction with peer relationships) predict change in the strategies young adults deploy?

Study 1: Achievement and Social Strategies and Transition to University

The first aim of study 1 was to examine what types of achievement and social strategies people apply in the context of transition to university, and how such strategies are related to subsequent academic success and satisfaction and personal well-being on the one hand, and to social adjustment on the other hand. Secondly, I wanted to investigate the extent to which the tendency to use a certain strategy is an individual characteristic that shows some stability across time.

I was also interested in examining whether academic success and satisfaction might predict the achievement strategies people later apply. Entrance to university or college provides a real testing ground for the achievement strategies used at secondary school. Therefore, individuals may undergo substantial change in their preferred strategies over the course of life transition (Cantor, Brower, & Korn 1985), and first academic successes or failures may have far-reaching consequences. Similarly, I was interested in the extent to which the social life situation, such as peer relationships and feelings of loneliness, predicted change in the social strategies people deploy.

Because the aims of this study were explorative, the clustering-by-cases procedure was used to identify "naturally-occurring" subgroups of participants who differed in the types of achievement and social strategies they applied. This person-oriented approach (Caspi & Silva 1995; Magnusson 1990) seemed to fit well with research on cognitive-motivational strategies, which have often been described in terms of a typology of people who apply different strategic patterns in challenging situations.

In Study 1, a group of students was examined twice according to their achievement and social strategies and several well-being measures, first at the beginning of their university studies and then two years later. Their academic satisfaction, feelings of loneliness and satisfaction with peer-relationships were also studied twice, first in their second year of university studies and again two years later. Academic success during the first three years of their studies was coded from university archives.

Participants

The first study is part of the Helsinki Longitudinal Study (HELS-study). The participants were eighteen to thirty-three-year-old undergraduates at the University of Helsinki who were taking introductory courses in various subjects (Biology, Geography, Economics, English, Finnish, French, History, Psychology, and Sociology). Women were over-represented in the study, since females form the majority of students in humanities and social sciences.

Procedure

First, 306 students (224 women, 82 men) were examined at the beginning of their first autumn term at the university. They were asked to fill in the Cartoon Attribution Strategy Test (CAST; Nurmi, Salmela-Aro, & Haavisto 1997), the Strategy Attribution Questionnaire (SAQ; Nurmi, Haavisto, & Salmela-Aro 1995), a revised version of Beck's (Beck et al., 1979) Depression Inventory and a Rosenberg's Self-Esteem Scale.

One year after the first measurement, 272 participants (70 men, 202 women) from the original sample rated their satisfaction with their grades during the first year of their study, and filled in the revised UCLA Loneliness Scale (Russel, Peplau, & Cutrona 1980), and a short peer-relationships measure (retention rate 82 percent). The total number of courses the participants had passed was also coded from university archives.

Two years after measurement 1, 254 participants (65 men, 189 women) from the original sample filled in a questionnaire involving the CAST (retention rate 82 percent). The total number of courses they had passed during their second year of study was coded from university archives.

Three years after measurement 1, 256 participants (66 men, 190 women) forming an original sample filled in a questionnaire involving a revised version of the BDI, Rosenberg's Self-Esteem scale, the Revised UCLA Loneliness scale and the Peer relationship measure and rated their satisfaction with their studies (retention rate 84 percent). Again, the total number of courses they had passed during their third year of study was coded from university archives.

Measurements

Only a brief overview of the measures is given. For more detailed information see Eronen et al., 1997 or Eronen et al., 1998.

Measurement 1

Social and Achievement Strategies. Social and achievement strategies were assessed using the Cartoon Attribution Strategy Test (CAST; Nurmi, Haavisto, & Salmela-Aro 1997).

The Cartoon Attribution Strategy Test was used to measure the participants' thoughts, feelings and plans in achievement and social situations. The participants were first given the following instruction: "On the following pages, you are presented with cartoons showing some situations related to one person's life. Let us call him/ her person A. Your task is to write down what Person A is thinking in different situations and what he or she is going to do. Let us imagine that Person A is quite similar to you."

The participants were then presented with the two social and two study situations in the form of two-picture cartoons. Before the first picture of each cartoon pair was shown, a written description of the four situations was given (e.g., "Fellow students are telling Person A that there will be a party in the evening," or "Person A has a big exam the day after tomorrow". The participants were then asked to write down answers to the following questions: "What does Person A think?", and "What does Person A do?" Then the second picture was shown together with a description of Person A receiving information that the situation had ended in either success or failure. The subjects were then asked to write down their answer to the following question: "What might have been the reasons for this outcome?"

The participants' answers to questions concerning (a) the thoughts and actions and (b) the reasons for the outcome were classified independently by two raters. The following six categories for thoughts and actions were used separately in study and social situations: planning, task-irrelevant behavior/ avoidance, positive affects, negative affects, secondary benefit seeking, and initiation of the task (the inter-rater reliability was 0.80 for the scale). The reasons that the participants gave for the outcome were not used in this study.

Subjective well-being. Depression was assessed using the revised Beck's Depression Inventory (BDI; Beck et al., 1979; Nurmi, Salmela-Aro, & Haavisto 1995). The participants were asked to rate thirteen items on a five-point Likert scale that ranged from "Not at all true of me" (1) to "Very true of me" (5). These thirteen items were drawn from the original set of twenty-one second-mildest statements, because they were expected to measure best a depression tendency among the normal population. The Cronbach alpha reliability was 0.87 for the scale.

Self-esteem was assessed on Rosenberg's self-esteem scale (Rosenberg 1979) consisting of ten statements concerning the self. The participants rated the items on a four-point scale that ranged from "Not at all true of me" (1) to "Very true of me" (4). The Cronbach alpha reliability was 0.85 for the scale.

Measurement 2

Subjective satisfaction with interpersonal relationships. Loneliness was assessed using the revised UCLA Loneliness scale (Russell et al., 1980), which consists of 20 statements that are concerned with the extent to which people think they are lonely. The participants rated the items on a five-point scale that ranged from "Not at all true" (1) to "Very true" (5). The Cronbach alpha reliability was 0.92 for the scale.

Peer relations were assessed using the Peer-Relationship Questionnaire developed for the needs of this study. The participants were asked in three questions the extent to which they had contacts with their friends and peers. They were given five alternatives (1 = "Daily", 5 = "Less" than once every six months").

Academic success and satisfaction. Academic success was measured in the following way: The number of courses the participants had passed during their first two academic years were coded from university archives. In the Finnish university system, there is no term fee and each student is free to decide how many courses he/ she takes each term. In this type of system, the number of courses students pass during the term varies substantially, and this discriminates clearly successful students from unsuccesful ones. *Academic satisfaction* was assessed using four questions, in which the participants rated their satissfaction with their grades on a four-point scale ranging from "not at all" (1) to "very satisfied" (4). The Cronbach alpha reliability was 0.85 for the scale.

Measurement 3

Achievement and social strategies were again measured using the CAST. The testing and scoring procedures were identical to those used in Measurement 1. The inter-rater reliability for the content analysis was 0.90.

Measurement 4

The participants filled in the Revised UCLA Loneliness scale, the Peer-relationships measure, the BDI, and Rosenberg's self-esteem scale. The Cronbach alpha reliabilities were 0.90, 0.82, 0.89 and 0.68, respectively.

Participants' academic achievement was again coded from university archives.

Results

Types of Achievement and Social Strategies used in University Environments

Achievement Strategies. To examine what types of achievement strategies young people apply in the context of transition to university, a cluster analysis by cases (detailed procedure is described in Eronen et al., 1998) were carried out to classify the participants according to the extent to which they showed planning, task-irrelevant behavior, positive affects, negative affects, and initiation of the task in the achievement situations described in the CAST.

Four groups of people were identified in both measurements 1 and 3: those who used (1) optimistic, (2) defensive pessimistic, (3) impulsive, and (4) self-handicapping strategies. A description of these strategy groups is presented in Figure 1. This shows that those who deployed an optimistic strategy were typified by a high level of positive feelings in both measurements. On the other hand, those who used a defensive-pessimistic strategy showed a high level of planning in measurements 1 and 3. Impulsive strategy users were characterized by high task-initiation throughout the study, and those who belonged to the self-handicapping strategy group showed high levels of negative affect and task-irrelevant behavior in both measurements.

Social Strategies. Similarly, to examine what types of social strategies young people apply in interpersonal situations, a cluster analysis by cases was carried out (the detailed procedure is described in Eronen et al., 1997) to classify the participants according to the extent to which they showed planning, positive affects, negative affects, avoidance, secondary benefit-seeking, and initiation of the task in the social situations described in the CAST.

Three groups of people were identified in both measurements 1 and 3: those who used (1) planning-oriented, (2) avoidant and (3) impulsive strategies. A description of these strategy groups is presented in Figure 2. Members of the

Figure 1: The Four Achievement-Strategy Groups at Measurements 1 and 3

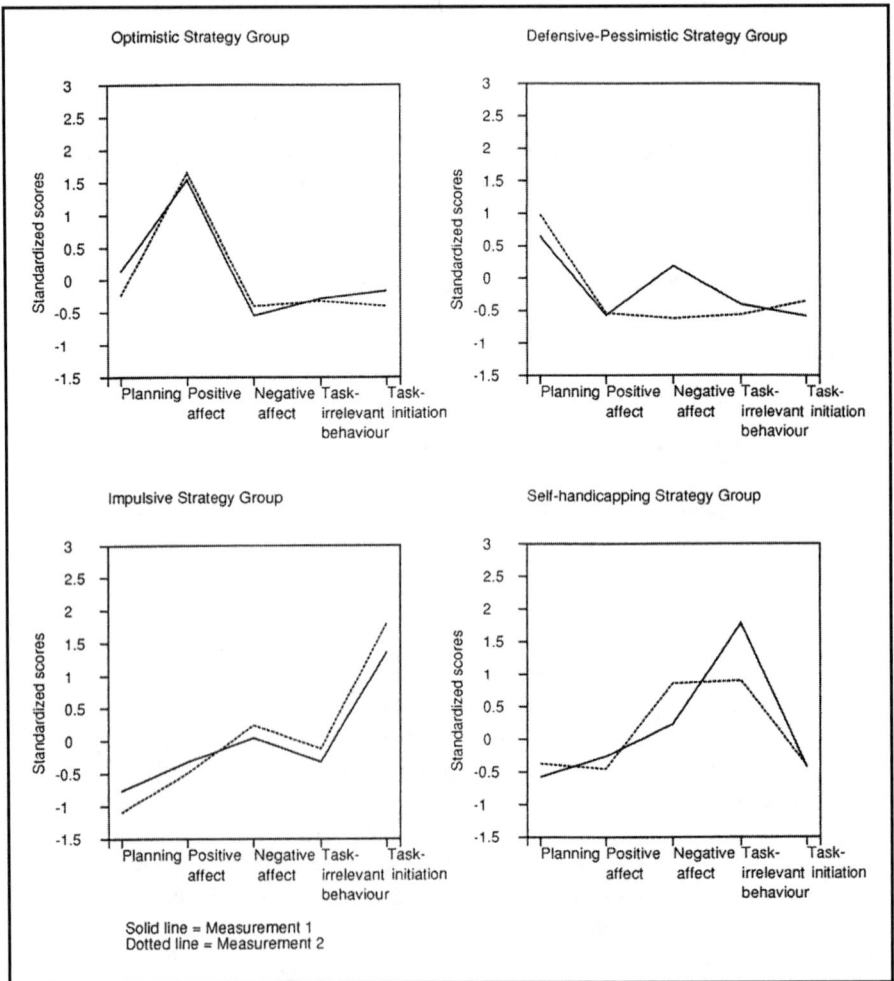

planning-oriented strategy group were above-average in planning from measurement 1 to measurement 3. Avoidant strategy users were typified by high levels of negative affect and avoidance throughout the study, whereas impulsive students showed high levels of task initiation in both measurements, and an extremely high level of secondary benefit-seeking in measurement 3.

Figure 2: The Three Social-Strategy Groups at Measurements 1 and 3

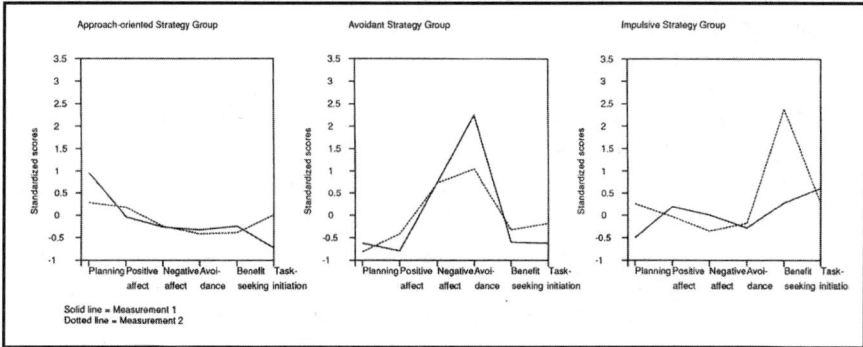

Achievement and Social Strategies in University Environments: Associations and Consequences

Well-being. Univariate ANOVAs were used to examine the extent to which achievement and social strategies were associated with depression and self-esteem at measurement 1. The results showed that social strategies had a statistically significant main effect for depression (F = 3.66, p<.03), whereas achievement strategies had not (F = 2.28, p<.08). There were no interactions between achievement and social strategies (F = .79, p<.58). Those who used an avoidant social strategy showed a higher level of depression at Time 1 (M = 2.3, SD = .90) than those who deployed planning-oriented (M = 1.95, SD = .64) or impulsive (M = 1.99, SD = .62) strategies when tested using Duncan's Multiple Range Test.

Both social (F = 3.28, p<.04) and achievement strategies (F = 3.77, p<.02) had statistically significant main effects for self-esteem at Time 1, but there were no interactions between the two (F = 1.39, p<.22). Avoidant social-strategy users showed a lower level of self-esteem (M = 2.94, SD = .67) than planning-oriented (M = 3.21, SD = .48) or impulsive (M = 3.15, SD = .47) strategy users. Those who deployed a defensive-pessimistic achievement strategy reported the lowest level of self-esteem (M = 3.06, SD = .51), whereas those in the optimistic strategy group reported the highest level (M = 3.21, SD = .49).

Academic Achievement. Next, the users of different achievement and social strategies were compared according to both the number of courses they had passed during the first two years and their satisfaction with their studies. The first univariate ANOVA showed that only achievement strategies had a statistically significant main effect on the number of courses the participants had passed (F = 3.95, p<.01). Those who deployed optimistic (M = 42.2, SD = 20.6) or self-handicapping (M = 43.5, SD = 21.9) strategies at Time 1 had passed fewer courses than the impulsive (M = 53.4, SD = 24.9) or defensive-pessimistic (M = 50.7, SD = 25.4) strategy users during the following two years. The results showed further that neither achievement (F = .47, p<.70) nor social strategies (F = 1.16, p<.33) used at Time 1 had a statistically significant main effect on satisfaction with studies at Time 2.

Interpersonal satisfaction. The results of the first univariate ANOVA showed that social strategies at Time 1 had a statistically significant main effect on feelings of loneliness (F = 8.31, p<.001) at Time 2. The participants who deployed an avoidant strategy during their first year at university reported a higher level of loneliness in their second year (M = 2.05, SE = .08) than those who used planning-oriented (M = 1.73, SE = .04) or impulsive (M = 1.78, SE = .05) strategies. Achievement strategies did not contribute to the prediction of loneliness (F = .83, p<.48).

The results showed further that social strategies used at Time 1 had a marginally significant main effect on the number of students the participants had come to know well at Time 2 (F = 2.78, p<.06). Planning-oriented strategy users knew more students well (M = 3.33, SE = .08) than avoidant strategy users (M = 2.88, SE = .17). Achievement strategies did not contribute to the prediction (F = .84, p<.47).

Stability and Change in the Achievement and Social Strategy Groups. The extent to which people show stability in the use of a special achievement or social strategy across a three-year period was examined next. It was decided to investigate the extent to which the number of courses passed and satisfaction with studies measured at Time 2 predicted change in achievement strategy from Time 1 to Time 3. Similarly, the question whether loneliness and the number of new friends predicted change in social strategy use from Time 1 to Time 3 was addressed. Separate logistic regression analyses were carried out for the dummy variables related to the use of a specific strategy (see for details Eronen et al., 1997; Eronen et al., 1998).

When achievement strategies were studied, logistic regression analysis revealed substantial stability in the use of optimistic ($\Delta\chi2 = 3.70$, p<.05, Wald = 3.85, R = .08) strategies from Time 1 to Time 3, but entering the number of courses passed and satisfaction with studies did not add to the prediction. There was no stability in the deployment of defensive pessimistic strategies, but adding the number of courses passed and satisfaction with studies increased the prediction ($\Delta\chi2$ = 12.16, p<.005). Passing many courses (Wald = 3.91, R = .08, p<.05) and satisfaction with studies (Wald = 4.11, R = .08, p<.05) increased the likelihood of defensive-pessimistic strategy use. It was also shown that a self-handicapping strategy used at Time 1 marginally predicted the same strategy use at Time 3 ($\Delta\chi2$ = 3.40, p<.07). Moreover, passing many courses and satisfaction with studies added to the prediction ($\Delta\chi2$ = 13.95, p<.001): the more satisfied the students were with their studies at Time 2, the less likely they were to use self-handicapping strategies at Time 3 (Wald = 9.86, R = -.16, p<.005). Deployment of an impulsive strategy showed no stability, and neither the number of courses passed nor the satisfaction with studies contributed to the prediction.

When social strategies were studied, logistic regression analyses revealed substantial stability in the use of planning-oriented strategies (χ^2 = 3.94, p<.05, Wald = 3.84, R = .08, p<.05) from Time 1 to Time 3. Moreover, loneliness and the number of new friends added to the prediction ($\Delta\chi^2$ = 6.49, p<.05): having many friends at Time 2 increased the deployment of a planning-oriented strategy (Wald = 3.87, R = .08, p<.05), whereas loneliness made no unique contribution. The deployment of an avoidant social strategy showed only marginal stability ($\Delta\chi^2$ = 2.81, p<.10), and entering loneliness and the number of new friends also increased the prediction ($\Delta\chi^2$ = 9.09, p<.05). Having many friends at Time 2 decreased the use of an avoidant strategy from Time 1 to Time 3 (Wald = 6.07, R = -.12, p<.05), whereas loneliness had no unique impact. The results showed futher that the use of an impulsive strategy at Time 1 only marginally predicted the same strategy use at Time 3 ($\Delta\chi^2 2$ = 2.74, p<.10), and neither loneliness nor the number of new friends added to the prediction.

Summary of the Findings

In Study 1, four achievement strategies (optimism, defensive pessimism, impulsiveness, and self-handicapping), and three social strategies (planning-orientation, avoidance, and impulsiveness) were revealed at the two measurement points. Closer study of achievement strategies revealed higher academic achievement among defensive-pessimistic and impulsive strategy users than those who used optimistic or self-handicapping strategies. High academic achievement and satisfaction with studies also increased the deployment of defensive-pessimistic strategies, whereas the use of self-handicapping decreased among those who were satisfied with their studies. The optimists showed the highest level of self-esteem at the beginning of their studies, and the defensive pessimists showed the lowest level, despite their high academic achievement.

As far as social strategies were concerned, those who deployed an avoidant strategy at the beginning of their studies showed a higher level of subsequent loneliness and got to know a smaller number of their fellow students well than among the planning-oriented and impulsive strategy users. They also showed the highest level of depression at the beginning of their studies. Moreover, having new friends increased the deployment of planning-oriented strategies, and decreased the use of avoidance.

Study 2: Social Strategies, Interpersonal Behavior and Person Perception

The aim of Study 2 was to examine the extent to which individuals' social strategies are associated with their subsequent social behavior and perceptions of other people. It was predicted that planning-oriented and impulsive strategies would be associated with adequate interpersonal behavior, whereas avoidance would be associated with behavioral deficits. It was also hypothesised that planning-oriented and impulsive strategy users would perceive others more positively than those who deployed avoidant strategies.

Participants and Procedure

The participants were eighteen-to forty-year-old students (M = 24.3, SD = 5.4) at an institute of health care (30 men, 62 women) aiming at the professions of physiotherapist, X-ray nurse, foot therapist, optician, hospital technician and, dental technician. Their social strategies were studied at the beginning of their studies, and their interpersonal behavior and ways of perceiving other people six months later.

Measurements

Measurement 1

The Cartoon Attribution Strategy Test. The procedure of this test (CAST) was described in the context of Study 1, and the testing and scoring procedures were identical to those used in that study. The following six categories were applied to measure the participants' social strategies: planning, positive affects, negative affects, social avoidance, secondary benefit-seeking, and initiation of the task (the inter-rater reliability was 0.82).

Measurement 2

Interpersonal behavior. The participants' interpersonal behavior was measured on the Behavioral Strategy Rating Scale (BSR; Eronen & Nurmi1996), which consists of seventeen statements. The participants were asked to rate the typical behavior of their seven classmates on a five-point scale that ranged from "I agree" (5) to "I disagree" (1). The following four subscales were used to measure each participant's peer-rated social behavior: (1) Social responsiveness (three items, e.g., "He/she is an easy person to talk to"), (2) Openness (two items, e.g., "He/she often shares his/her private thoughts with someone"), (3) Social avoidance (three items, e.g., "He/she prefers to be alone or with only one other person"), (4) Incisiveness (four items, e.g., "He/she often seems to have disagreements with people"). The Cronbach alpha reliabilities for these subscales were 0.67, 0.83, 0.77, and 0.84, respectively.

Perceived Behavior of Others. Measurement of the participants' typical ways of perceiving other people was also based on the same BSR ratings as that of their interpersonal behavior. This time, however, the mean of the ways in which the participant evaluated his/her seven randomly-chosen classmates was used to form indices of social perception. The following four subscales were again applied: (1) Social responsiveness, (2) Openness, (3) Social avoidance, and (4) Incisiveness. The Cronbach alpha reliabilities were 0.61, 0.83, 0.51, and 0.72, respectively.

Results

Social Strategies, Interpersonal Behavior and Person Perception in a Peer Group

To investigate the extent to which self-reported social strategies were associated with interpersonal behaviors and person perception, homogenous subgroups of different strategy users were first formed by using cluster analysis by cases. The participants were classified according to the extent to which they showed planning, positive affects, negative affects, social avoidance, secondary benefit-seeking and initiation of the task in the CAST.

Three groups of people were identified: those who deployed planning-oriented, impulsive, and avoidant social strategies. A description of these strategy groups is presented in Figure 3. At the next step, univariate ANOVAs were used to compare the three strategy groups in terms of interpersonal behavior. The results revealed that those who deployed an avoidant strategy (F = 5.22, p<.01, M = 2.23, SD = .81) showed a lower level of openness than the planning-oriented (M = 2.99, SD = .67) or impulsive (M = 2.87, SD = .62) strategy users. Avoidant strategy users also behaved in a less responsive way (F = 2.4, p<.10, M = 2.61, SD = .73) than the planning-oriented (M = 3.05, SD = .76) and impulsive (M = 3.13, SD = .76) strategy users. However, this effect was only marginally significant. Avoidant strategy users also behaved in an avoidant way (F = 3.75, p<.05, M = 2.35, SD = .93) when compared to the planning-oriented students (M = 1.65, SD = .63). Avoidant behavior among the impulsive strategy users fell between these two extremes (M = 1.91, SD = .64). Finally, the planning-oriented strategy users showed a higher level of incisiveness (F = 5.32, p<.01, M =

Figure 3: The Three Social-Strategy Groups

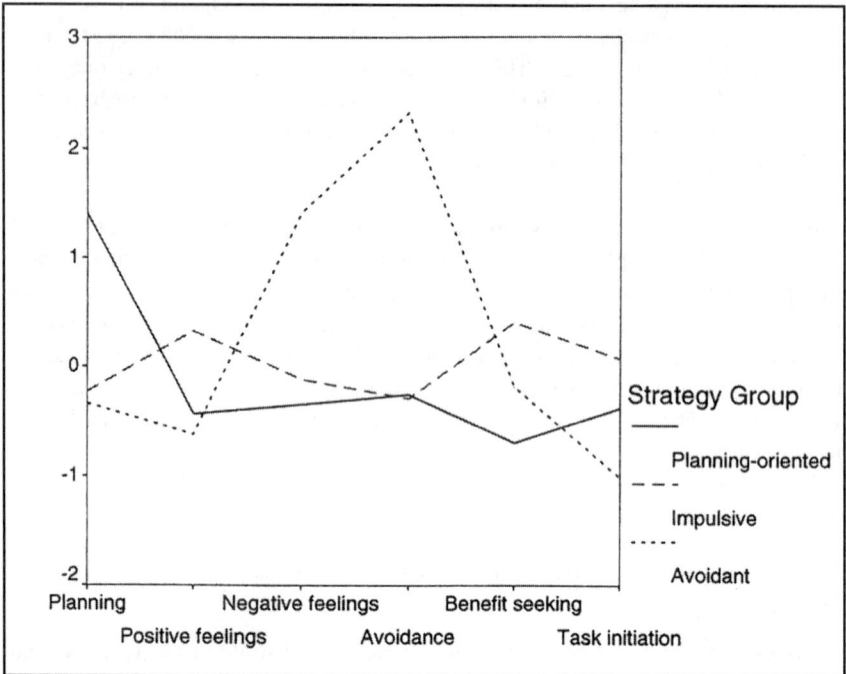

2.59, SD = .54) than the impulsive (M = 2.12, SD = .52) and avoidant (M = 2.22, SD = .61) strategy users.

Univariate ANOVAs were also used to study the person perception of the students in the three strategy groups. The results showed that those who deployed a planning-oriented strategy perceived their classmates to be more open (F = 3.24, p<.05, M = 3.15, SD = .59) than the impulsive strategy users (M = 2.71, SD = .63). Avoidant strategy users fell between these two groups (M = 2.80, SD = .43). The avoidant strategy users perceived their class-mates as showing a lower level of responsiveness (F = 3.44, p<.05, M = 2.59, SD = .59) than the planning-oriented (M = 3.23, SD = .63) and impulsive (M = 3.02, SD = .61) strategy users. Moreover, the avoidant strategy users perceived others as showing a higher level of incisiveness (F = 3.46, p<.05, M = 2.57, SD = .35) than the planning-oriented (M = 2.24, SD = .50) or the impulsive students (M = 2.20, SD = .40). There were no differences in the levels of avoidance the three strategy-group members perceived in the behavior of their class-mates (F = .07, p>.90).

Summary of the Findings

The results revealed that the behavior of the avoidant strategy users was rated as more avoidant and less open and responsive than the behavior of the planning-oriented and impulsive strategy users. Planning-oriented students showed the highest level of incisiveness according to their classmates.

Avoidant strategy users also perceived the behavior of their classmates negatively: they rated their peers as showing higher levels of incisiveness and lower levels of responsiveness than the other strategy users. Those who deployed a planning-oriented strategy perceived their classmates as most open.

Study 3: The Accumulation of Positive and Negative Life Events

This study investigated the achievement and social strategies as two possible predisposing factors that may influence what life events people experience. Another matter of interest was whether life events would predict subsequent well-being. Some researchers have concluded that they have no impact on subjective well-being (Brickman et al., 1978; Costa, McCrae, & Zonderman 1987; Diener 1984; Swearingen, & Cohen 1985), whereas others have pointed to an influence over and above the effects of personality (Headey & Wearing 1989; Suh et al., 1996). It was assumed here that positive life events would have a positive impact on well-being, whereas negative events would increase depressive feelings and lower self-esteem.

Participants and Data-Collection Procedure

This study is part of the Helsinki Longitudinal Study (HELS), and the participants were described in the context of Study 1.

The study consisted of five measurement points.

(1) Three-hundred and six students (224 women, 82 men) eighteen- to thirty-two-year-old ($M = 21.62$, $SD = 2.98$) were examined at the beginning of their first autumn term at the university. They were first informed about the study and their agreement to participate was sought. None of them refused. Next, they were asked to fill in the Cartoon Attribution Strategy Test (CAST; Nurmi, Haavisto, & Salmela-Aro 1997), the Strategy Attribution Questionnaire (SAQ; Nurmi, Salmela-Aro, & Haavisto 1995), a revised version of Beck's (Beck et al., 1979) Depression Inventory and Rosenberg's self-esteem scale (Rosenberg 1979). This was done during one classroom hour. All the students who were present in the class during the day of the study were included in the sample.

(2) One year after the first measurement, the participants in the original sample were asked to fill in a life-event questionnaire. The questionnaire was mailed

to the participants and it was also returned by mail. Two-hundred and seventy-two (70 men, 202 women) participants from the original sample returned it. The retention rate was 89 percent.

(3) Two years after measurement 1, the participants in the original sample were again asked to fill in a life-event questionnaire. The questionnaire was sent and returned by mail. This time, 252 participants (65 men, 187 women) from the original sample returned it (retention rate 82 percent.)

(4) Three years after measurement 1, the participants in the original sample were asked to fill in a life-event questionnaire, the BDI and Rosenberg's self-esteem scale. The questionnaires were sent and returned by mail. Two-hundred and fifty-six participants (66 men, 190 females) returned them (retention rate 84 percent.)

(5) Four years after measurement 1, the participants in the original sample were asked to fill in the BDI and Rosenberg's self-esteem scale. The question-naires were sent and returned by mail. Two-hundred and forty-two participants (63 men, 179 females) returned them (retention rate 80 percent.)

Only the students who returned the first four questionnaires were included in this study, leaving us with 229 participants (56 men, 173 women). Two-hundred and ten students (54 men, 156 females) returned all five questionnaires, and they are included in the analyses of measurement five.

Measurements

Measurement 1

The participants' achievement and social strategies were measured using the CAST and the SAQ.

The Cartoon Attribution Strategy Test. The procedure for this test (CAST) was described in the context of study 1. In this study, two sumscores concerning thoughts and actions were calculated for both social and study situations: *optimistic planning* and *pessimistic avoidance*. A sumscore for *self-serving attributional bias* concerning causal attributions was also calculated separately in social and study situations. The intention was to measure the extent to which people tend to take the credit for success, but to deny responsibility for failure (Zuckerman 1979).

Depression. Depression was assessed using a revised version of Beck's Depression Inventory (Beck & al., 1979; Nurmi, Salmela-Aro, & Haavisto 1995). The Cronbach alpha reliability was 0.87.

Self-esteem. Self-esteem was assessed using a Rosenberg's self-esteem scale

(Rosenberg 1979). The Cronbach alpha reliability was 0.85.

Measurement 2

Positive and negative life events. Positive and negative life events were assessed by asking the participants to rate whether twenty different types of positive (e.g., "Starting a new job," "Engagement"), or negative (e.g., "Losing a job," "Divorce") event had happened to them during the last year.

Given the theoretical notion that people construct their own future (Cantor 1990; Nurmi 1993), it was decided to take into account the controllability of the life events the subjects were facing.

In order to examine the controllability of life events, an independent sample of thirty participants was asked to rate whether they evaluated the events as positive or negative (2 = "Very positive," -2 = "Very negative"), and whether they saw them as being in their control or not (5 = "Very much," 1 = "Not at all"). These independent evaluations were used as basis for calculating the controllability scores for the positive and negative life-event sumscores for the study sample. First, each individual life-event score was multiplied by the mean of the controllability rating it received in the independent sample. All the life events that were evaluated as positive were then counted, and the same was done with those evaluated as negative.

Measurement 3

Positive and negative life events were assessed and scored using the identical procedure to that used in measurement 2.

Measurement 4

Positive and negative life events were again assessed and scored using the identical procedure to that used in measurements 2 and 3.

Similarly, the participants again filled the Revised Beck's Depression Inventory and Rosenberg's Self-esteem Scale. The Cronbach Alpha reliabilities were 0.89 and 0.86.

Measurement 5

The participants filled in the Revised Beck's Depression Inventory and Rosenberg's Self-esteem Scale. The Cronbach Alpha reliabilities were 0.89 and 0.87.

Results

Patterns of Positive and Negative Life Events.

Cluster analysis by case was used to identify homogenous subgroups of participants who differed according to the extent to which they faced positive and negative life events during their first three years at university (details of the procedure are given in Eronen and Nurmi 1999).

Four types of groups were identified: (i) those who had enjoyed many positive (M = 16.68, SD = 4.40) and few negative events (M = 5.59, SD = 3.88, n =
55), (ii) those who reported many negative (M = 22.48, SD = 6.55) and few positive events (M = 5.48, SD = 4.06, n = 21), (iii) those who had experienced many
positive (M = 16.66, SD = 4.65) and many negative events (M = 17.05, SD =
3.77, n = 26), and (iv) a group that reported few positive (M = 4.14, SD = 3.42)
and few negative events (M = 5.21, SD = 4.18, n = 123).

Achievement and Social Strategies, and Future Life Events.

The results of several univariate ANOVAs and pairwise comparisons, which
were made using Duncan's Multiple Range Test, showed that the students in the
different life-event groups deployed different types of achievement and social
strategies at the beginning of their studies. The participants who enjoyed many
positive life events during the first three years at university reported a lower level
of pessimistic avoidance in study situations at the beginning of their studies (F =
2.63, p<.05, M = 22.30, SD = 17.69) than those who experienced many negative
events (M = 35.16, SD = 22.61), more use of self-serving attributional bias in
study situations (F = 3.22, p<.02, M = 32.73, SD = 56.29) than those who experienced many negative events (M = -7.14, SD = 59.76) and a higher level of optimistic planning in social situations (F = 2.47, p<.06, M = 67.23, SD = 22.25)
than those who faced only a few life events (M = 57.32, SD = 27.78). The participants who faced many positive and many negative events, fell between the
more extreme groups according to their self-reported strategies at measurement
1, whereas those who faced only a few positive and negative events resembled
those who faced mostly negative events in some respects: they reported as low a
level of positive attributional bias in study situations, and the lowest level of
optimistic planning in social situations. According to the other variables, however, they were in between the other groups.

The results showed further that the four groups did not differ according to
pessimistic avoidance or self-serving attributional bias in social situations, or to
optimistic planning in study situations. Moreover, the results were similar for
men and women.

Self-esteem, Depression, and Future Life Events

Univariate ANOVAs and pairwise comparisons were carried out in order to compare the four life-event groups according to self-esteem and depression. The results showed that those who enjoyed many positive life events during their first year at university showed a tendency to report a higher level of self-esteem at the beginning of their studies (F = 2.56, p<.06, M = 3.26, SD = .44) than those who experienced many negative events (M = 2.91, SD = .65). However, the group which later reported many negative life events showed a higher level of depression at the beginning of their studies (F = 4.50, p<.01, M = 2.52, SD = .86) than those who experienced many positive (M = 1.90, SD = .56), many positive and many negative (M = 1.93, p<.01), or a few positive and a few negative events (M = 2.04, SD = .70).

Life Events as Predictors of Subsequent Well-being

In the last part of the study, several univariate analyses of variance were carried out to examine the extent to which the pattern of positive and negative life events the participants were facing predicted their subsequent self-esteem and depression, when the impact of the dependent variable at Time 1 was controlled as a covariate (for the details, see Eronen & Nurmi 1999). The results showed that the students who experienced many positive (F = 4.70, p<.01, M = 3.41, SD = .40) or many positive and negative events (M = 3.42, SD = .42), showed a higher level of self-esteem than those who faced many negative (M = 3.12, SD = .59) or a few positive and a few negative events (M = 3.25, SD = .49), even after controlling for self-esteem at Time 1. Moreover, those who enjoyed many positive life events showed the lowest level of depression in their fifth year at university (F = 2.90, p<.05, M = 1.90, SD = .53), whereas those reporting many negative events showed the highest level (M = 2.28, SD = 1.03), even after controlling for the original level. Those who experienced many (M = 2.11, SD = .73) or a few life events (M = 2.12, SD = .73) showed a level of depression that was between the two extremes.

Summary of the Findings

Four types of students were identified in this study: the first goup enjoyed mainly positive life events, whereas the second group experienced mostly negative events. The third group was typified by many positive and negative events, and the fourth group experienced a small number of both types. Moreover, achievement and social strategies and life-event patterns formed cumulative developmental cycles: the more active strategies and higher well-being the students showed at the beginning of their studies (i.e., high levels of self-esteem and optimistic planning in social situations, self-serving attributional bias in study situations, and low levels of depression and pessimistic avoidance in study situations), the more likely they were to experience many positive life events during their first three years at university. Students who faced many negative events showed the opposite pattern, and the groups who experienced many or few positive and negative events were in between these two extremes. Negative life events also increased subsequent depression and decreased levels of self-esteem, whereas positive life events had the opposite impact.

Discussion

This chapter focused on the transition phase from secondary school to new educational environments. Emerging adulthood was approached in the context of two topical developmental tasks, i.e. finding a congenial social group and getting started in an education (Havinghurst 1948). I was particularly interested in investigating the role of cognitive-motivational strategies during these transactions (Cantor 1990; Nurmi 1997). The results presented above showed that achievement strategies contributed to young adults' success in dealing with academic tasks, and social strategies influenced their success in dealing with interpersonal challenges. These strategies may therefore open up intervention in situations in which people have difficulties directing their lives.

Achievement Strategies and Success in Studies

Four types of achievement strategies were identified in the two measurements of Study 1. Optimistic strategy users were typified by a high level of positive and a low level of negative feelings. This strategy was related to high self-esteem and low academic achievement. Defensive pessimists showed a high level of planning at both measurements 1 and 3, and a high level of negative feelings at measurement 1. Their academic achievement was high during the first two years, but despite this their self-esteem was low. Self-handicapping strategy users dispalyed high levels of negative feelings and task-irrelevant behavior, and both their academic achievement and self-esteem were low. Impulsive students were characterized by a high level of spontaneous task-initiation, a high level of academic achievement, and an average level of self-esteem.

Social Strategies, Interpersonal Behavior and Satisfaction

Three types of social strategies were identified in Studies 1 and 2. A planning-oriented strategy, which was typified by interpersonal planning and positive affects, predicted frequent contacts with peers and a low level of loneliness. It was also associated with a low level of depression and a high level of self-esteem. The opposite pattern was true for users of the avoidant strategy, which was typified by a high level of avoidance and negative affects. Impulsiveness, which was characterized by spontaneous task initiation and secondary benefit-seeking in the context of social relationships, also predicted frequent peer contacts and a low level of loneliness.

The results of Study 2 revealed that three strategies were reflected in individuals' social behaviors in consistent ways. The behavior of planning-oriented students was rated as more responsive, open and incisive, and less avoidant than the behavior of other strategy users. The avoidant strategy users showed the opposite pattern, and the impulsive strategy users were in between these two extremes. It was further shown that the students in the three strategy groups also perceived other peoples' behavior differently. Planning-oriented strategy users saw their classmates as open, responsive and non-incisive, whereas those who used an avoidant strategy perceived others as unresponsive and incisive.

Life Events and Predisposing Strategies

The results of Study 3 showed first that different people seem to be faced with different patterns of positive and negative life events. One quarter of the students enjoyed mainly positive life events during their first years at university, whereas approximately 10 percent faced mostly negative events. A similar number experienced many negative and many positive events, whereas about half of the participants had largely uneventful lives: they faced only few positive and few negative events.

Moreover, the achievement and social strategies people apply, and their well-being, predisposed them to these life-event patterns. Typical of the young adults who faced many positive and few negative events was that they showed a high level of optimistic planning in social situations, and a low level of pessimistic avoidance and a high level of self-serving attributional bias in study situations. Their level of self-esteem was high and their depression was low. The opposite pattern was true for those who faced many negative and few positive events, whereas the strategies and well-being of those who faced many or few positive and negative events were in between these two extremes. The results also suggested that life events had consequences for well-being: facing mostly positive events enhanced self-esteem and lowered depressive feelings, whereas the opposite was true for those facing many negative events.

The Cumulation of Positive and Negative Development

The findings of these studies suggest that strategies seem to develop on the basis of the feedback people receive about their success in dealing with developmental challenges. When focus was on achievement strategies, the results showed that low academic satisfaction increased the subsequent deployment of self-handicapping, whereas passing many courses increased the use of defensive-pessimistic strategies. Social strategies seemed to form cumulative cycles with environmental feedback: using a planning-oriented strategy increased the number of new friends, which again increased the deployment of this strategy. Making new friends also decreased the use of an avoidant strategy.

The results of Study 2 may give some insight into the findings concerning social strategies. Both the behavior of avoidant-strategy users and their perceptions of other peoples' behavior showed a rather self-protective and restricted pattern. Withdrawn behavior may make it difficult to establish new friendships, and perceiving others in a negative light may enhance feelings of loneliness. On the other hand, the positive or negative tone of an individual's perceptions may be signaled to others through behavior, and approval or rejection from others may create self-fulfilling prophesies and therefore maintain and reinforce the type of strategy the individual deploys (e.g., Jones 1986). Since both achievement and social strategies also showed substantial stability across the two-year transition period to university, they may be described as important aspects of individual personality.

The results presented in this chapter support the dynamic-interactionist paradigm of personality development. Individuals' personalities, i.e., cognitive strategies and well-being, predisposed them to different feedback from the environment, such as social relationships, life events and academic achievement. This feedback, again, predicted their subsequent cognitive strategies and well-being. Conceptualizing personality through a social-cognitive framework may emphasize its flexibility more than if personality differences are described as stable personality traits (Mischel & Shoda 1995; Showers & Cantor 1985). This leads to the discussion of the practical implications which follows.

Practical Implications

The fact that achievement and social strategies seemed to play an important role in the contexts of topical developmental tasks and the accumulation of positive and negative life events provides a basis for the development of clinical applications. The stabilility of these patterns suggests that, at least partly, they are a dispositional part of individual personality. However, they also seemed to develop according to environmental feedback, which implies that there are situational factors that modify individuals' cognitive-motivational patterns.

In academic environments, students' desires to achieve good grades and avoid negative evaluation are often encouraged by the teachers because it has been thought to enhance their motivation to study. However, this may also reinforce their performance goals rather than their striving to learn (Dweck & Leggett 1988). This again has been shown to have detrimental side effects: if students are oriented toward achievement and evaluation instead of learning, they have been shown to deploy helplessness strategies if they assess their present abilities as low (Diener & Dweck 1978, 1980). This fear of negative evaluation may create the need to prove certain abilities instead of improving them, which does not facilitate learning. This striving may be especially strong at university, where the competition among students is high. People who come to university have often been at the top of their class, and it may be frustrating for them to notice that, in the new environment, hard work may lead only to average success. Since they have not been used to coping with negative feedback, it might be useful, paradoxically, to teach them how to fail instead of teaching them ways to succeed. It has been reported that people start to use immature strategies when they face unsolvable tasks (Diener & Dweck 1978, 1980). Therefore, it would seem to be essential to create a supportive atmosphere where failures are seen as a natural part of the learning process. This could be done by utilizing principles of reattribution therapy: helping people to make external and unstable attributions of failure (e.g., I did not try hard enough, the task was too difficult) and internal and stable attributions of success (Abramson, Seligman, & Teasdale 1978). Moreover, it might also be useful to give students individual guidance and feedback during the time they are studying for an exam or writing an essay instead of giving them a grade after the final work has been done. This could also diminish intermittent feedback (e.g., getting a good grade after a low level of effort or vice versa), which has been shown to increase the deployment of self-handicapping strategies (Berglas & Jones 1978). Finally, group learning has also been suggested to be an effective way to encourage students to participate in and commit themselves to rather than competing with each other's success (for a review, see Johnson, Maruyama, Johnson, Nelson, & Skon 1981). This type of behavior can be expected to facilitate the deployment of functional achievement strategies and enhance learning. It can also enhance students' peer contacts and therefore support their interpersonal well-being and the development of active social strategies as well.

There are several possibilities for clinical intervention in the cognitive and motivational patterns that regulate the interpersonal behavior of individuals. Prominent approaches have been described in the context of the information-processing perspective (e.g., Daleiden & Vasey 1997; Lochman & Lenhart 1993). The model assumes that there are four points of entry for effective change in individuals' cognitions: First, attempting to change the encoding-stage process so that attention is no longer excessively allocated to one type of stimulus, such as that which signals the possibility of threat. The second point of entry emphasizes correction at the biased and distorted interpretation stage, such as when ambigious information about other people is seen in a negative light, which was typical of the avoidant strategy users (see also Eronen & Nurmi 1999), and which has also been shown to be typical of anxious, aggressive, and depressive individuals (e.g., Daleiden & Vasey 1997; Hall & Davidson 1996; Quiggle, Garber, Panak, & Dodge 1992; Waldman 1996). Other common distortions during the interpretation stage include adopting a negative attributional style and expecting negative outcomes (Daleiden & Vasey 1997). More adaptive self-talk and attributional style instead of anxious or threatening interpretations could therefore be encouraged (Abramson et al., 1978; Kendall 1994). The third stage of the model involves interventions aimed at changing individuals' goals. It has been shown that anxious, avoidant and depressive people usually want to avoid anxiety-provoking situations (Daleiden & Vasey 1997; Quiggle et al., 1992), and that they appraise their interpersonal goals negatively (Salmela-Aro & Nurmi 1996). Consequently, interventions that encourage individuals to adopt a new goal, for example to confront the situation despite their anxious feelings, have been suggested to be useful (Daleiden & Vasey 1997; Kendall 1994). Finally, increasing individuals' ability to generate, select and enact effective responses and behaviors should result in improved performance (Daleiden & Vasey 1997; Kazdin 1987). It would be important to practice both the production and deployment of adequate social strategies and interpersonal problem-solving skills.

The results of strategy research could be especially useful when community-based interventions are planned. The major idea is that they are conducted within the community, and therefore schools and universities are ideal places for them. These approaches emphasise the need to intergrate and treat "problem individuals" and adaptively behaving peers together (Kazdin 1987). Various psycho-educational programs that focus on learning about personal development, strategies and skills may be useful and not too time-demanding (see Brown 1998). Supporting socialization into adulthood is a challenging task for teachers and other professionals involved in young adults' lives. If we are able to help them to accomplish their interpersonal and academic goals, we might expect such a help to have cumulative and long-lasting positive effects on their future life-span development, behavior and well-being.

References

Abramson, L. Y., Seligman, M. E. P., & Teasdale, J. D. (1978). Learned helplessness in humans: critique and reformulation. *Journal of Abnormal Psychology, 87*, 49–74.

Arkin, R. M., Appleman, A. J., & Burger, J. M. (1980). Social anxiety, self-presentation, and self-serving bias in causal attribution. *Journal of Personality and Social Psychology, 38*, 23–25.

Arkin, R. M., Lake, E. A., & Baumgardner, A. H. (1986). Shyness and self-presentation: In: W. H. Jones, J. M. Cheek, & S. R. Briggs (eds.), *Shyness: Perspectives on research and treatment* (pp. 189–204). New York: Plenum Press.

Arnett, J. J. & Taber, S. (1994). Adolescence terminable and interminable: When does adolescence end? *Journal of Youth and Adolescence, 23*, 517–537.

Baltes, P. B., Reese, H. W., & Lippsitt, L. P. (1980). Life-span developmental psychology. *Annual Review of Psychology, 31*, 65–100

Beck, A. T., Rush, A. J., Shaw, B. F., & Emery, G. (1979). *Cognitive therapy of depression*. Chichester, N Y: John Wiley.

Belli, R. F., Schuman, H., & Jackson, B. (1997). Autobiographical misremembering: John Dean is not alone. *Applied Cognitive Psychology, 11*, 187–209.

Berglas, S. & Jones, E. E. (1978). Drug choise as a self-handicapping strategy in response to noncontingent success. *Journal of Personality and Social Psychology, 36*, 405–417.

Boekaerts, M. (1996). Personality and the psychology of learning. *European Journal of Personality, 10*, 377–404.

Brickman, P., Coates, D., & Janoff-Bulman, R. (1978). Lottery winners and accident victims: Is happiness relative? *Journal of Personality and Social Psychology, 36*, 917–927.

Brown, N. W. (1998). *Psychoeducational groups*. United States: Taylor & Francis.

Cantor, N. (1990). From thought to behavior: "Having" and "Doing" in the study of personality and cognition. *American Psychologist, 45*, 735–750.

Cantor, N., Brower, A., & Korn, H. (1985). Cognitive bases of personality in a life transition. In: E. Roskam (Ed.), *Measurement and Personality Assessment* (pp. 323–331). Noth-Holland: Elsevier Science Publishers.

Cantor, N., Zirkel, S. & Norem, J. K. (1993). Human personality: Asocial and reflexive? *Psychological Inquiry, 4*, 273–277

Caspi, A. (1987). Personality in the life course. Journal of Personality and Social *Psychology, 53*, 1203–1213.

Caspi, A. & Moffit, T. (1993). When do individual differences matter? A paradoxical theory of personality coherence. *Psychological Inquiry, 4*, 247–271.

Cheek, J. M. & Buss, A. H. (1981). Shyness and sociability. Journal of Personality and *Social Psychology, 41*, 330–339.

Costa, P. T. Jr., McCrae, R. R., & Zonderman, A. B. (1987). Environmental and disposi-otional influences on well-being: Longitudinal follow-up of an American national sample. *British Journal of Psychology, 78*, 299–306.

Crick, N. R. & Dodge, K. A. (1994). A review and reformulation of social information.processing mechanisms in children's social adjustment. *Psychological Bulletin, 115*, 74–101.

Daleiden, E. L. & Vasey, M. W. (1997). An information-processing perspective on childhood anxiety. *Clinical Psychology Review, 17*, 407–429.

Diener, E. (1984). Subjective well-being. *Psychological Bulletin, 45*, 542–575.

Diener, C. I. & Dweck, C. S. (1980). An analysis of learned helplessness: II. The pro-cessing of success. *Journal of Personality and Social Psychology, 39*, 940–952.

Dweck, C. S. & Leggett, E. L. (1988). A social-cognitive approach to motivation and personality. *Psychological Review, 95*, 256–273.

Epstein, S. (1990). Cognitive-experiental self-theory. In L. Pervin (Ed.), Handbook of *Personality: Theory and Research* (pp. 165–192). New York: Guilford.

Erikson, E. H. (1959). *Identity and the life cycle.* New York: International University Press.

Eronen, S. & Nurmi, J.-E. (1996). *Behavioral Strategy Rating Scale.* University of Helsinki.

Eronen, S. & Nurmi, J.-E. (1999). Life events, predisposing cognitive strategies and well-being. *European Journal of Personality, 13*, 129–148.

Eronen, S. & Nurmi, J.-E. (1999). Social reaction styles, interpersonal behaviours and person perception: A multi-informant approach. *Journal of Social and Personal Relationships, 16*, 315–333.

Eronen, S. & Nurmi, J.-E. (in press). Sociometric status of young adults: Behavioural correlates and cognitive-motivational antecedents and consequences. *International Journal of Behavioural Development.*

Eronen, S., Nurmi, J.-E., & Salmela-Aro, K. (1997). Planning-oriented, avoidant, and impulsive social reaction styles: A person-oriented approach. *Journal of Research in Personality, 31*, 34–57.

Eronen, S., Nurmi, J.-E., & Salmela-Aro, K. (1998). Optimistic, defensive-pessimistic, impulsive and self-handicapping strategies in university environments. *Learning and Instruction, 8*, 159–177.

Fizgerald, J. M. (1988). Vivid memories and the reminiscent phenomenon: The role of a self narrative. *Human Development, 31*, 261–273.

Gara, M. A., Woolfork, R. L., Cohen, B. D., Goldston, R. B., Allen, L. A., & Novalany, J. (1993). Perception of self and other in major depression. *Journal of Personality and Social Psychology, 102*, 93–100.

Goffman, E. (1959). *The presentation of self in everyday life.* New York: Anchor.

Hagestad, G. O. & Neugarten, B. L. (1985). Age in the life course. In R. H. Binstock & E. Shanas (Eds.), *Handbook of aging and the social sciences.* New York: Van Nostrand Reinhold, pp. 35–61.

Hall, P. & Davidson, K. (1996). The misperception of anger in behaviorally hostile men. *Cognitive Therapy and Research, 20*, 377–389.

Havighurst, R. J. (1948). *Developmental tasks and education* (3rd ed.). New York: McKay. (Original work published 1948)

Headey, B. & Wearing, A. (1989). Personality, life events, and subjective well-being: Toward a dynamic equilibrium model. *Journal of Personality and Social Psychology, 57*, 731–739.

Hirschberg, N. & Jennings, S. J. (1980). Beliefs, personality, and person perception: A theory of individual differences. *Journal of Research in Personality, 14*, 235–249.

Hokoda, A. & Fincham, F. D. (1995). Origins of children's helplessness and mastery achievement patterns in the family. *Journal of Educational Psychology, 87*, 375–385.

Holmes, D. S. (1978). Projection as a defensive mechanism. *Psychological Bulletin, 85*, 677–688.

Johnson, D. W., Maruyama, G., Johnson, R., Nelson, D., & Skon, L. (1981). Effects of cooperative, competitive, and individualistic goal structures on achievement: A meta analysis. *Psychological Bulletin, 89*, 47–62.

Jones, E. E. (1986). Interpreting interpersonal behavior: The effects of expectancies. *Science, 234*, 41–46.

Jones, E. E. & Berglas, S. (1978). Control of attributions about the self through self-handicapping: The appeal of alcohol and the rate of underachievement. *Personality and Social Psychology Bulletin, 4*, 200–206.

Jones, E. E. & Pittman, T. S. (1982). Toward a general theory of strategic self-presentation. In J. Suls (Ed.), *Psychological perspectives on the self* (Vol 1, pp. 231–262). Hillsdale, NJ: Erlbaum.

Jones, W. H. & Carpenter, B. N. (1986). Shyness, social behavior and relationships. In W. H. Jones, J. M. Cheek, & S. R. Briggs (Eds.), *Shyness: Perspectices on research and treatment* (pp. 227–238). New York: Plenum Press.

Jones, W. H. & Carver, M. D. (1991). Adjustment and coping implications of loneliness. In C. R. Snyder & D. R. Forsyth (Eds.), *Handbook of social and clinical psychology*, 682–689.

Kendall, P. C. (1994). Treating anxiety disorders in children: Results of randomized clinical trial. *Journal of Consulting and Clinical Psychology, 62*, 100–110.

Langston, C. A. & Cantor, N. (1989). Social anxiety and social constraint: When making friends is hard. *Journal of Personality and Social Psychology, 56*, 649–661.

Leary, M. R. & Kowalski, R. M. (1990). Impression management: A literature review and two-component model. *Psychological Bulletin, 107*, 34–47.

Lewicki, P. (1983). Self-image bias in person perception. *Journal of Personality and Social Psychology, 45*, 384–393.

Lochman, J. E. & Lenhart, L. A. (1993). Anger coping intervention for aggressive children: Conceptual model and outcome effects. *Clinical Psychology Review, 13*, 785–805.

Lord, C. G. & Zimbardo, P. G. (1985). Actor-observed differences in the perceived stability of shyness. *Social Cognition, 3*, 250–265.

Magnus, K., Diener, E., Fujita, F., & Pavot, W. (1993). Extraversion and neuroticism as predictors of objective life events: A longitudinal analysis. *Journal of Personality and Social Psychology, 5*, 1046–1053.

Magnusson, D. (1990). Personality development from an interactional perspective. In L. E. Pervin (Ed.), *Handbook of Personality: Theory and Research*, pp. 193–222. New York: The Guilford Press.

Markus, H. & Smith, J. (1981). The influence of self-schema on the perception of others. In N. Cantor & J. F. Kihlström (Eds.), *Personality, cognition and social interaction*. Hillsdale, N J: Erlbaum.

Markus, H., Smith, J., & Moreland, R. L. (1985). Role of the self-concept in the perception of others. *Journal of Personality and Social Psychology, 49*, 1494–1512.

Meeus, W. (1996). Studies on identity development in adolescence: An overview of research and some new data. *Journal of Youth and Adolescence, 25*, 569–598.

Mischel, W. (1977). The interaction od person and situation. In D. Magnusson & N. S. Endler (Eds.), *Personality at the crossroads: Current issues in interactional psychology* (pp. 333–352). Hillsdale, NJ: Lawrence Erlbaum Associates, Inc.

Mischel, W., Shoda, Y. & Rodriguez, M. L. (1989). Delay of gratification in children. *Science, 244*, 933–938.

Mischel, W. & Shoda, Y. (1995). A cognitive-affective system theory: reconceptualizing situations, dispositions, dynamics, and invariance in personality structure. P*sychological Review, 102*, 246–268.

Newman, L. S., Duff, K. J., & Baumeister, R. F. (1997). A new look at defensive projection: Thought suppression, accessibility, and biased person perception. *Journal of Personality and Social Psychology, 72*, 980–1001.

Norem, J. (1989). Cognitive strategies as personality: Effectiveness, specifity, flexibility, and change. In D. M. Buss & N. Cantor (Eds.), *Personality Psychology: Recent Trends and emerging directions*. New York: Springer-Verlag.

Norem, J. & Cantor, N. (1986). Defensive pessimism: Harnessing anxiety as motivation. *Journal of Personality and Social Psychology, 51*, 1208–1217.

Norem, J. & Illingworth, K. S. S. (1993). Strategy-dependent effects of reflecting on self and tasks: Some implications of optimism and defensive pessimism. *Journal of Personality and Social Psychology, 65*, 822–835.

Nurmi, J. -E. (1993). Adolescent development in age-graded context: The role of personality beliefs, goals, and strategies in the tackling of developmental tasks and standards. *International Journal of Behavioural Development, 16*, 169–189.

Nurmi, J. -E. (1997). Self-definition and mental health during adolescence and young adulthood. In J. Schulenberg, J. L. Maggs & K. Hurrelmann (Eds.), *Health risks and developmental transitions during adolescence.*

Nurmi, J. -E., Haavisto, T., & Salmela-Aro, K. (1997). *CAST-käsikirja.* [A manual for CAST]. Helsinki: Psykologien kustannus.

Nurmi, J.-E., Onatsu, T., & Haavisto, T. (1995). Underachievers' cognitive and behavioral strategies - Self-handicapping at school. *Contemporary Educational Psychology, 20,* 188–200.

Nurmi, J. -E. & Salmela-Aro, K. (1995). Unpublished data. *University of Helsinki*

Nurmi, J. -E., Salmela-Aro, K., & Haavisto, T. (1995). The strategy and attribution questionnaire: Psychometric properties. European Journal of Psychological Assessment, 11, 108–121.

Onatsu-Arvilommi, T. & Nurmi, J. -E. (in press). The role of task-avoidant and task-focused behaviors in the development of reading and mathematical skills during the first school year: A cross-lagged longitudinal study. *Journal of Educational Research.*

Peterson, C. & Seligman, M. E. P. (1984). Causal explanation as a risk factor for depression: Theory and evidence. *Psychological Review, 91,* 347–374.

Quiggle, N. L., Garber, J., Panak, W. F., & Dodge, K. A. (1992). Social information processing in aggressive and depressive children. *Child Development, 63,* 1305–1320.

Renshaw, P. D. & Asher, S. R. (1983). Children's goals and strategies for social interaction. *Merrill-Palmer Quarterly, 29,* 353–374.

Rosenberg, M. (1979). *Conceiving the self.* Malabar, Florida: R. E. Krieger Publishing Company.

Rubin, D. C., Wetzler, S. E., & Nebes, R. D. (1986). Autobiographical memory across the lifespan. In D. C. Rubin (Ed.), *Autobiographical memory*, pp. 202–221. New York: Camridge University Press.

Russell, D., Peplau, L. A., & Cutrona, C. E. (1980). The revised UCLA loneliness scale: Concurrent and discriminant validity evidence. *Journal of Personality and Social Psychology, 39,* 472–480.

Salmela-Aro, K. & Nurmi, J.-E. (1996). Uncertainty and confidence in interpersonal projects: Consequences for social relationships and well-being. *Journal of Social and Personal Relationships, 13,* 109–122.

Schrauger, J. S. & Patterson, M. B. (1974). Self evaluation and selection of dimensions for evaluating others. *Journal of Personality, 42,* 569–585.

Seligman, M. E. P. (1975). *Helplessness: On depression, development and death.* San Francisco: Freeman.

Suh, E., Diener, E., & Fujita, F. (1996). Events and subjective well-being: Only recent events matter. *Journal of Personality and Social Psychology, 70,* 1091–1102.

Swearingen, E. M. & Cohen, L. H. (1985). Life events and psychological distress: A prospective study on young adolescents. *Developmental Psychology, 21,* 1045–1054.

Zirkel, S. & Cantor, N. (1990). Personal construal of life tasks: Those who struggle on independence. *Journal of Personality and Social Psychology, 58,* 172–185.

Zuckerman, M. (1979). Attribution of success and failure revised, or: The motivational bias is alive and well in attributional theory. *Journal of Personality, 47,* 245–287.

Waldman, I. D. (1996). Aggressive boys' hostile perceptual and response bias: The role of attention and impulsivity. *Child Development, 67,* 1015–1033.

Part Two

Future Planning and Identity Explorations
in Educational and Vocational Settings

CHAPTER 5

Future-orientation in Educational and Interpersonal Contexts

LARS-ERIK MALMBERG[1]

Introduction

"What do you want to be when you grow up?" is a question adolescents are often asked by their parents, relatives, family members, peers, teachers and others. The answers given to this question stem from young people's "maps" about the future, including the major routes, available areas, potential shortcuts, blind alleys, and pitfalls of the navigation to adulthood. Studies on adolescents' "maps" about the future, i.e., their future-orientation (for reviews see Nurmi 1991; Malmberg 1998), have investigated the goals adolescents set up, how they plan to reach them, and how goals and planning are related to their self-definitions. There are, however, two important areas that have not been studied so far. The first issue to be investigated is the extent to which adolescents' future-orientation is an individual or an interpersonal process. In other words, do young people plan their futures by themselves or through interaction with other people? Second, what is the role of adolescents' developmental environments, such as education, in their future-orientation? Education is assumed to be an important socialization agent in the navigation from adolescence to adulthood. Apart from acquiring academic skills and factual knowledge, one of the officially stated goals of the educational system is to support adolescents' self-images and their integration into the adult world, i.e., their future lives (National Board of Education 1994). Consequently, the aim of this chapter is to investigate how other people and educational environments influence adolescents' future-orientation.

Future-orientation

According to Nurmi (1989), future-orientation consists of setting a goal ("What do I want?"), planning the means to reach the goal ("How can I get it?"), and evaluating the outcomes of related behavior ("What are the consequences or results?"). After the pursuit of a goal ends in success or failure, people may also need to revise their earlier goals or plans. This may include withdrawing from earlier goals or setting new ones, finding new means for reaching the same goal, or changing the evaluation standards for success and failure.

[1] I am thankful to the following institutions for financial support: the Foundation of Åbo Akademi University, Waldemar von Frenckell's Foundation and Johann Jacobs Foundation. Study 1 was conducted in cooperation with Janusz Trempala, to whom I direct my gratitude.

Socioculturally constructed norms influence what goals, means for reaching goals, and ways of celebrating success or coping with failure are considered appropriate. That is, the action sequences are guided by collective representations (Buchmann 1989), developmental tasks (Havighurst 1953), or normative expectation about development (Heckhausen & Krueger 1993). This conceptualization of future-orientation is in line with action (Leontiev 1975; Eckensberger & Meacham 1984; Boesch 1991) and developmental theories (Brim 1981): On the one hand, people construct their own futures; on the other, their goals simultaneously reflect certain sociocultural contexts in a certain historical period (Brandtstädter 1998). For example, adolescents' hopes and interests have consistently been found to reflect the major developmental tasks of adulthood, i.e., their future education, occupation, partnership, and family life across a variety of cultures, while their worries typically have mirrored general societal hardships, e.g., threat of unemployment (e.g., Nurmi 1989; Malmberg & Norrgård 1999). Hence, future-orientation encompasses a person's goals, plans, and potential outcomes, which serve as a "map" for the self in a certain sociocultural context (Nurmi 1989, 1993).

In the literature on future-orientation, planning has been regarded as an intrapersonal cognitive process aimed at constructing the means to reach a goal (e.g., Scholnick & Friedman 1987). A variety of constructs such as degree of realism (Verstraeten 1980), clarity of plans (Pulkkinen 1990), complexity of planning (Nurmi 1989), amount of planning (Kosonen 1983; Jusi 1987), and exploration (Nurmi et al., 1995) have been employed to operationalize the planning construct. Future-oriented information gathering, exploration, and planning a sense of mature occupational choices (Kosonen 1983; Jusi 1987), commitment (Nurmi et al., 1995; Kalakoski & Nurmi 1998), and life orientation (Pulkkinen & Rönkä 1994) are important because they have been shown to lead to well-being and positive adjustment in the long run.

Contexts for Future-orientation

Macro level features of society shape the ways in which proximal developmental contexts are structured. Historical events and processes, such as economy, legislation, and even wars and catastrophes influence the labor market, the educational system, and socioeconomic stratification and regulate the availability of action opportunities in these contexts for the individual (e.g., Buchmann 1989; Hurrelmann 1993). Moreover, cultural features, such as gender-roles (e.g., Rauste-von Wright 1987; Gordon & Lahelma 1991), age-related expectations (Neugarten, & Datan 1973), lifestyles and value systems (e.g., Roos 1988), and the strictness of these normative expectations regulate the kind and amount of social control that is imposed on the individual (e.g., Buchmann 1989; Triandis 1989). Literature has pointed out several proximal contexts as salient for and supportive of adolescents' cognitive and social development. Among these are the home (Pulkkinen 1990; Nurmi & Pulliainen 1991), school (e.g., Entwistle 1990; Anderman & Maehr 1994), peer groups (e.g., Brown 1990), work (e.g., Fine et al. 1990), leisure activities (e.g., Silbereisen, et al. 1986; Evans & Poole 1991), mutual friendships (e.g., Little et al. 1999), and mass media (e.g., Arnett 1995). The present study will focus on four contexts: family, peers, schools, and mass media.

Family

The structure of the family has changed in Western society during the twentieth century. For example, the number of children per family has decreased, divorce rates have increased, and women participate more in the workforce, while fewer males are breadwinners (e.g., Buchmann 1989). Regardless of these structural changes in family life, its nucleus remains the melting pot of material, cognitive and autonomous support of the development of offspring.

The family's role for adolescents' future planning has been investigated in several studies. For example, Brown (1990) suggested that adolescents would rather turn to their parents than to their peers in matters regarding their long-term future plans, such as college or occupational choice. Pulkkinen (1990) found that several family interaction patterns, such as having time for one's child, a harmonious rhythm of life, explanation of norms and consideration of the children's opinions, predicted adolescents' future optimism. Interestingly, mother's illness predicted clarity of plans of girls, while several familial changes predicted clarity of plans in boys. Similarly, Nurmi, and Pulliainen (1991) found that family discussion influenced optimism of mid-adolescents. Moreover, Nurmi (1989) found that late adolescents who reported a negative home atmosphere planned their future more than those who reported a positive home atmosphere.

Studies including measures of the parents' socioeconomic status (SES) have shown that adolescents from higher SES families express more educational hopes and articulated plans that extended further into the future, than those of adolescents' from a lower SES (e.g., Trommsdorff, Lamm, & Schmidt 1979). These studies are in line with general sociological studies, which show that parents' SES is strongly related to the expected length and level of their children's education (e.g., Härnqvist 1999).

Peers, leisure, and mass media

Youth culture, leisure activities, same-sex and opposite-sex peers and friends have become increasingly important for Western adolescents during the last century (Chisholm & Hurrelmann 1995). The impact of peers and friends becomes increasingly important during the adolescent years, while the parents' role simultaneously diminishes (Eriksson 1968; Hurrelmann 1993; Rubin, Bukowski, & Parker 1997). Adolescents interact in cliques, crowds, peer groups, or close friendships. Together with peers, adolescents "hang out," engage in free time activities or sports, or watch television or videos (Fine et al. 1990; Arnett 1995). With their friends or best friends, they discuss topics that concern issues of intimacy, dating, sexuality, common perspectives, interests, and doubts, i.e., topics they discuss less with their parents (Rubin et al. 1997). Small groups can provide identity prototypes, values, or lifestyle ideologies that are different from those of parents (Brown 1990). It is likely that topics such as future partnership and family life are discussed in close friendships.

Schools

The structure and content of the educational system, i.e., its age-stratification, enrollment capacity, length and content of studies, and entrance and assessment criteria are regulated through legislation, financing, and curricula (Bourdieu 1977; Andres 1999). One important structural feature of education is the socioeconomic background of students. Pupils' achievements, educational aspirations, and selection of educational track have been found to be related to their socioeconomic background in several countries (e.g., Kuusinen 1992; Härnkvist, 1999). Educational track, in turn, influences the kinds of goals students have. For example, vocational school students have voiced more adulthood-oriented goals and fewer education related goals than those who pursue further studies (Trommsdorff, et al. 1979; Hurrelmann 1987; Klaczynski & Reese 1991).

Teaching content is transmitted through the teachers' pedagogical ideologies, classroom interaction styles, and attitudes (e.g., Ames 1992; Malmberg, Wanner, Sumra, & Little 2000). Several studies on students' perceptions of their school life show that schools, teachers, and their pedagogical ideologies affect students' well-being (e.g., Brunell et al. 1996), self-esteem (Korpinen 1990; Keltikangas-Järvinen 1992), and action-control beliefs (Little 1998). Consequently, it might be argued that schools also serve as sources for adolescents' future-orientation and future planning.

However, some authors have criticized the educational system for not fulfiling the role of preparing adolescents for the future (Hurrelmann 1987; Andersson 1990, 1994; Aittola, Jokinen & Laine 1994; Anderman & Maehr 1994). This criticism focuses mainly on subject content in schools, which is irrelevant to the challenges of adulthood (Hurrelmann 1987; Andersson 1990). Moreover, students have been shown to perceive activities at school as irrelevant because they do not prepare students for democracy nor do they stimulate students' independence, participation in society, or the ability to take responsibility for themselves (Andersson 1994). Aittola et al. (1994) pointed out that other contexts, such as work, media, and peers have become more important for adolescents and young adults as learning environments than school.

Educational transitions have also been shown to have an impact on students' motivation (Anderman & Maehr 1994), self-esteem (Zimmerman et al. 1997), and future exploration (Kalakoski & Nurmi 1998). For example, Kalakoski and Nurmi (1998) found that exploration of educational and occupational issues increased from the seventh grade to the shift to secondary education. Students' exploration of family related issues was not affected by the transition to secondary education. This educational transition is crucial for two reasons. The effects of parents' SES on students' choice of track is obvious (Rinne & Salmi 1998), and students' grade point averages dictate which track they can enter.

Self-evaluation and Future Planning

It has been suggested that the ways in which adolescents think about themselves provide a basis for their future-orientation (Nurmi 1989). For example, high-self esteem has been related to voicing more educational hopes (Nurmi 1989), realization of goals (Malmberg 1996b), positive probability estimations (Malmberg & Trempala 1997), optimism (Trommsdorff 1994), and internal attributions (Nurmi 1989). Moreover, Rauste-von Wright (1987) showed that high achieving, high self-esteem girls were socially oriented, while low achieving, low self-esteem girls were likely to withdraw from future planning.

Gender Differences

Boys' and girls' future-orientations have been shown to reflect sociocultural gender roles and age norms. For example, girls have been found to report more hopes and worries about family life than boys (Solantaus 1987). Girls have also been found to explore their future family (Kalakoski & Nurmi 1998) more than boys (Nurmi, et al. 1995). However, girls estimate the likelihood of their educational goals as occurring more probable than boys (Malmberg & Trempala 1997). Greene and Wheatley (1992) found that, compared to young men, young women anticipated and experienced their transition to adulthood as more stressful, more rapid, and as including more decisions (Greene & Wheatley 1992).

Research Questions

The following research questions are investigated in the present study:

(1) To what extent is adolescents' future planning an intrapersonal versus an interpersonal process? In other words, do young people plan their future alone or in the context of their parents, peers, school, or mass media?

(2) To what extent, and from what sources, do adolescents gather information

about their future education, occupation, and family life?

(3)   How are adolescents' intrapersonal characteristics, such as control beliefs and self-esteem, related to their future planning and information gathering?

(4)   How are the educational tracks and transitions related to adolescents' future planning and information gathering?

(5)   Are there gender or age differences in these processes?

Finland

Finland is a Scandinavian country with five million inhabitants. The dominant religion is Protestantism. Finland urbanized rapidly in the 1960s and 1970s, while simultaneously expanding its educational system (e.g., Roos 1988). The population is divided into Finnish speakers (92.9 percent) and Swedish speakers (5.8 percent). Even though the language forms an important part of one's identity, both Swedish and Finnish speakers regard themselves as Finns (e.g., Nyman-Kurkiala 1997).

The Finnish educational system consists of a nine-year comprehensive school, after which students, aged fifteen to sixteen choose either three-year vocational studies or general secondary school (also known as "academic track," or "Gymnasium"). About half of this age group, more boys than girls, select vocational school studies, while more girls than boys select general secondary school. Vocational school students can head into the workforce or continue in higher vocational training in several fields. General secondary school students can choose higher vocational studies or university studies, after which they can join the workforce as well.

Students' future planning in schools is supported by guidance counseling lessons and individual tutoring. In the upper part of comprehensive school (grades seven to nine) guidance counseling is part of the regular curricula and normally includes one to three weeks of workforce experience. It is to a lesser extent included and available in secondary and vocational schools. The aims of guidance counseling are acquisition of self-related knowledge and exploration of different occupational options (Eskelinen 1993). Because Finnish schools are encouraged to develop school-wise curricula, some variation between schools can be found as far as content, timing and duration is concerned.

Study 1

Sample

Study 1 included a total of 194 students of about seventeen years of age. The sub-samples included 103 general secondary school students (39 boys and 52 girls; age: M = 17.15, SD = .36) and 91 students from vocational schools (69 boys and 34 girls age: M = 17.37, SD = .59). Data were collected in 1995 by questionnaires according to standardized procedures by a network of guidance counselors and teachers. All students were enrolled in schools for Swedish speakers. The socioeconomic backgrounds of the students in the two educational tracks represented educational stratification in Finland quite well (see Malmberg 1998). This sample has also been compared with Polish adolescents (see Malmberg & Trempała 1997, 1998; Trempała & Malmberg 1998).

Measures

Future Planning was investigated by asking the participants: "How much time do you spend planning your future in the following situations?" Then, they were asked to estimate how much time they spent in seventeen situations by using a seven-point scale (0 = not at all, 6 = very much). Based on these ratings, the following scores were calculated. Planning alone was measured with two items ("on your own," "only when you are alone"; α = .69), planning with peers, with three items (with "friends at school," "friends outside school," and "best friend; α = .73), planning at home with four items ("at home," "with "mother," "father," and "sister/brother"; α = .81), planning at school with four items ("with teachers," "in lessons," "at school," and "with guidance counselor"; α = .75), and using mass media for planning purposes was measured with four items ("when watching TV-programs," "watching news," "reading magazines" and "newspapers"; α = .85).

Self-esteem was measured by six items (Rosenberg 1965) on four point scales (α= .82) and control beliefs with three items, e.g., "Do you think you are able to influence the way your future educational / career / family plans will work out?" (0 = very uncertain, 4 = very certain; α = .63).

Choice of further studies was measured with one item including four response options (0 = go to work, 1 = continue studies at the institute level, 2 = continue studies at the university level, or 3 = military service).

Results

Intrapersonal or interpersonal future planning?

In order to investigate to what extent adolescents plan their future alone or together with others, a 2 (Gender) x 2 (Schooltype) MANOVA was performed on the five future planning variables. The MANOVA revealed a main gender effect (F[5,186] = 4.46; p<.01) and a main educational track effect (F[5,186] = 2.65; p<.05) but no interaction effect (F[5,186] = 0.83; p = ns.). The results presented in Figure 1 show that adolescents reported most planning alone (M =

4.48; SD = 1.32), next most together with peers (M = 4.08; SD = 1.06), then at home (M = 3.48; SD = 1.31), then when using mass media (M = 2.47; SD = 1.28) and least at school (M = 2.14; SD = 1.08). In Figure 1, non-overlaps of the standard error bars between groups indicate significant mean-level differences.

Gender and educational track differences

Figure 1: Adolescents' Intrapersonal and Interpersonal Future Planning

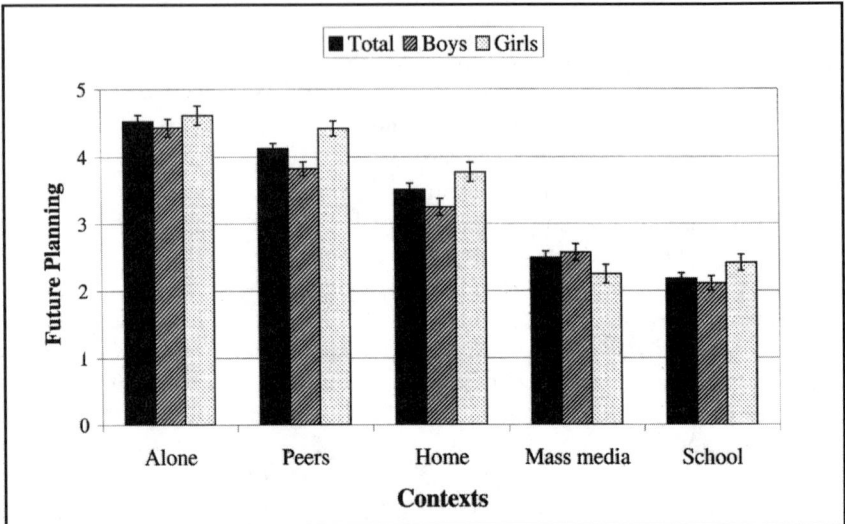

Note: Non-overlap of the standard error bars indicates statistically significant differences between groups.

The subsequent univariate tests showed that girls reported more future planning together with peers (F[1,193] = 15.54; p<.001) and at home (F[1,193] = 7.38; p<.01) compared with boys. General secondary school students reported more planning alone (F[1,193] = 7.02; p<.01) and when using mass media (F[1,193] = 7.64; p<.01) than the vocational school students reported.

Planning and self-definitions

In order to investigate the relationship between intrapersonal and interpersonal future planning, and how both kinds of planning were related to self-evaluation, Pearson product moment correlations were calculated. As shown in Table 1, planning alone was correlated with planning in all the other contexts (r from 0.20 to 0.42). Likewise, all planning variables were moderately intercorrelated (0.29 to 0.46). The more the adolescents planned with friends (0.24) and at home

(0.15), the higher was their control over the future.

Table 1: Correlations between adolescents'
future planning and self-evaluations

	Alone	**Peers**	**Home**	**Mass**	**School**	**Control**
Alone						
Peers	.30***					
Home	.42***	.46***				
Mass Media	.26***	.28***	.33***			
School	.20**	.29***	.41***	.42***		
Control	.00	.24**	.15*	.14	.10	
Self-esteem	.13	.10	.13	.16*	.19**	.18**

* p<.05, ** p<.01, *** p<.001 (two-tailed)

Transitions and future planning

In order to explore how future planning would vary according to adolescents' choices for future education, a series of x 2 (Gender) ANOVA (Educational choice) for each planning variable was performed. Significant gender effects were found in both student groups who were heading for vocational institutes. Vocational school girls reported more planning with peers (F[1,74] = 11.87; p<.01) and at home (F[1,74] = 4.47; p<.05) than boys. General secondary school girls reported more planning at home (F[1,33] = 5.40; p<.05) and at school (F[1,33] = 8.38; p<.01) than boys.

Study 2

Sample

Study 2 comprised a total of 460 Finnish students from three school types: 218 students from comprehensive school (grade 9; 108 boys and 110 girls; age: M = 15.36; SD = .48), 130 students attending the last year of general secondary school (third year, grade 12; 51 boys and 79 girls; age: M = 18.14; SD = .37) and 112 students attending the last year of vocational school (third year, grade 12; 75 boys and 37 girls; age: M = 18.72; SD = .69; see Malmberg 1996a, 1996b, 1998). Data were collected in 1993, from all three school types in three cities and an additional group of vocational school students from a fourth city. As in Study 1, educational track reflected the socioeconomic background of the students in Finland quite well.

Measures

Information gathering. The respondents were asked about to which degree they had gathered information about their future ("With whom have you discussed / thought of your future studies / occupation / family life?"), on five-point scales (0 = I haven't discussed / thought of it at all, 4 = I have discussed / thought of it a lot.") For each of the three life domains, they responded to eight items: "with friends at school," "with friends outside school," "with teachers," "in lessons," "at home (mother / father / siblings)," "with guidance counselor," "when I have read magazines / books," and "when I have watched TV-programs."

In order to investigate differences in adolescents' information gathering in the three content areas, domain-specific variables were computed, i.e., information gathering about future education (α = .75), occupation (α = .65), and family life (α = .70).

To examine with whom adolescents plan their future, the items were combined context-wise into five variables. Information gathering when using *mass media* (magazines / books / TV) consisted of six items (α = .87). Information gathering at *school* focused on formal education (with teachers, in lessons, and with guidance counselors) and consisted of nine items (α = .84). Information gathering with *peers* (peer-relations outside school), consisted of three items (α = .85). Information gathering with *school friends* (peer-relations at school) consisted of three items (α = .81). Information gathering at *home* focused on discussions with parents and siblings, and consisted of three items (α = .72).

Self-evaluation. Self-esteem was measured with the ten-item Rosenberg (1965) four-point scale (α = .79) and control beliefs again with three items (α = .66).

Choice of future studies. Choice of further educational track was probed with two questions: (1) "What will you do after comprehensive / general secondary / vocational school?" Participants responded to this question by choosing one out of several structured options or an open-ended alternative response. (2) "Which alternatives do you have for your future studies?" The participants responded to this question by writing all schools they had considered. If the responses to the first two questions verified each other, the students were categorized straightforwardly into four groups: comprehensive school students heading for vocational school (N = 90), comprehensive school students heading for general secondary school (N = 124), general secondary school students heading for vocational institutes (N = 43), and general secondary school students heading for universities (N = 76). If either of the responses was left blank the response to the other question was used. Students who indicated some alternative future plan (e.g., "take a year off," "military service") or did not indicate any plan at all were categorized as "others". Vocational school students responded to an open-ended question: "Which occupational plans do you have?" They were then categorized into three groups: Those clearly heading for further studies (N = 57), those clearly heading for working life (N = 33) and those who had other or unclear options (N = 22; e.g., "wait and see," "military service").

Figure 2: Adolescents' Information Gathering in Different Contexts, According to School Type

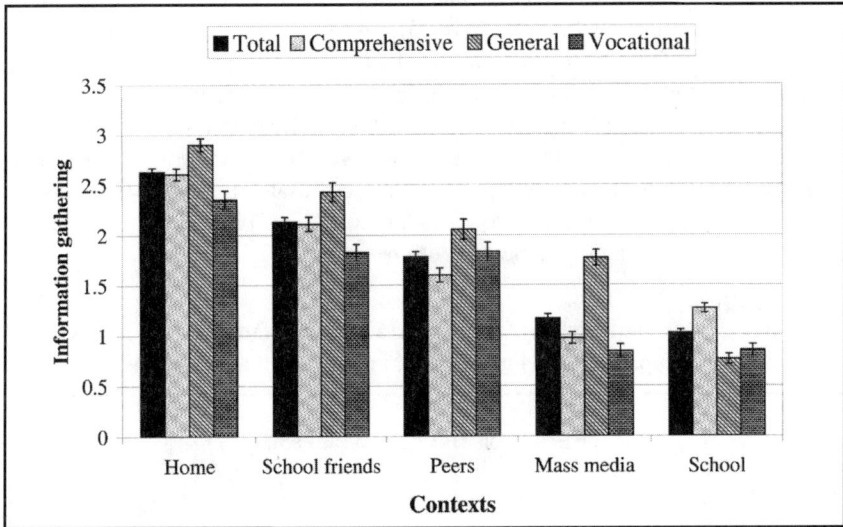

Results

Information gathering in several contexts. In order to investigate with whom adolescents report having gathered information about the future, a 2 (Gender) x 3 (School type) MANCOVA was performed. Age was inserted as a covariate since the design included one group of fifteen-year-olds and two groups of eighteen-year-olds. The MANCOVA revealed main effects of gender (F[6,447] = 23.72; p<.001), and school type (F[6,447] = 14.74, p<.001), as well as an interaction effect (F[6,447] = 2.09; p<.05). As shown in Figure 2, students gathered the most information at home (M = 2.54; SD = 0.91), then with school friends (M = 2.13; SD = 1.02), then with peers (M = 1.79; SD = 1.07), and least when using mass media (M = 1.17; SD = 0.92) and at school (M = 1.02; SD = 0.67).

Information gathering and gender. The univariate tests showed that girls reported gathering information more at home (F[1,456] = 12.09; p<.001), together with school friends (F[1,456] = 97.46; p<.001), with peers (F[1,456] = 36.66; p<.001) and when using mass media (F[1,456] = 10.07; p<.01) than boys. Boys and girls reported the same amount of information gathering at school.

Information gathering and educational track. Univariate tests by school type showed effects on information gathering at home ($F[2,456] = 10.12$; $p<.001$), with school friends ($F[2,456] = 5.98$; $p<.001$), when using mass media ($F[2,456] = 36.75$; $p<.001$) and at school ($F[2,456] = 8.05$; $p<.001$). As shown in Figure 3, general secondary school students gathered more information at home and with school friends than comprehensive school students, while vocational school students gathered the least (Scheffé, $ps<.05$). General secondary school students gathered more information from mass media than did comprehensive and vocational school students (Scheffé, $ps<.05$). In contrast, comprehensive school students gathered more information at school than did general secondary school students, who in turn gathered more than vocational school students did (Scheffé, $ps<.05$). When age was included as a covariate, the school type effects decreased for peers from ($F[2,455] = 6.60$; $p<.001$) to ($F[2,455] = .87$; $p = $ n.s.), indicating that information gathering with peers increased with age.

Figure 3: Boys' and Girls' Information Gathering about Future Education, Occupation, and Family Life, in Three School Types

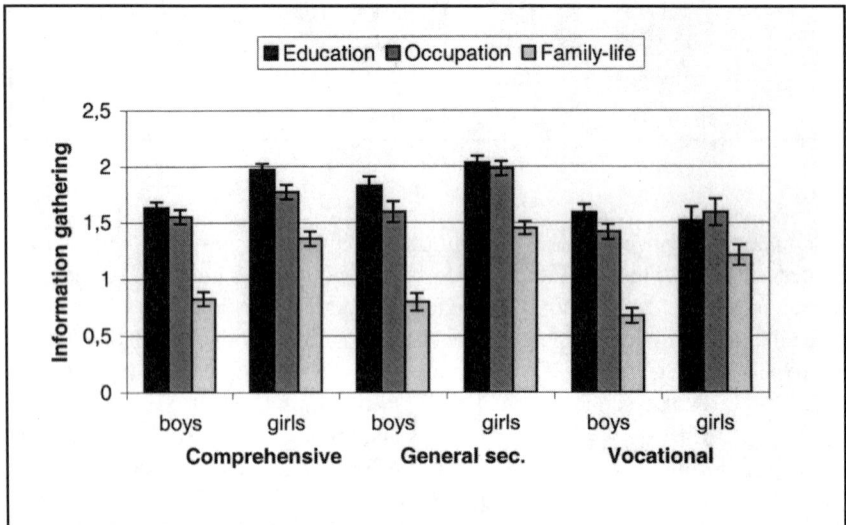

Information gathering and choice of future studies. In order to investigate information gathering according to the students' choices of further education, 2 (Gender) x 2 (Choice) MANOVAs were performed among the comprehensive school students, and a 2 (Gender) x 3 (Choice) MANOVA among the vocational school students. Among the comprehensive school students, the main effects of gender (F[5,203] = 17.89; p<.001) and track (F[5,203] = 3.62; p<.01) were significant, while no interaction effect was found. As in the analysis of the total sample, girls gathered more information than boys did at home, with friends at school, with peers, and when using mass media. Comprehensive school students heading for vocational school gathered more information with peers (F[1,207] = 4.72; p<.05) and in school (F[1,207] = 6.63; p<.05) than those heading for general secondary school. Main effects for gender also were found among the general secondary school students (F[5,111] = 9.05; p<.001) and the vocational school students (F[5,102] = 2.58; p<.001). General secondary school girls gathered more information than boys did at home (F[1,118] = 19.65; p<.001), with school friends (F[1,118] = 30.52; p<.001), and with peers (F[1,118] = 20.70; p<.001). Vocational school girls gathered more information with school friends (F[1,106] = 11.22; p<.001) and with peers (F[1,106] = 5.18; p<.001) than boys did.

Information gathering about future education, occupation, and family life. In order to investigate to what extent adolescents gathered information about their future education, occupation, and family life respectively, 2 (Gender) x 3 (Educational Track) MANOVA was performed. The results revealed statistically significant effects for gender (F[1,447] = 30.79; p<.001), educational track (F[1,447] = 4.03; p<.001), and their interaction (F[1,447] = 3.07; p<.01). When the total mean levels for information gathering in the three life domains were inspected in Figure 3, students reported gathering more information about their future education (M = 1.79; SD = .61) and occupation (1.70; SD = .68) and less about their future family life (M = 1.06; SD = .67). Univariate tests showed that girls gathered more information than boys did across all three domains (education: F[1,456] = 7.31; p<.01; occupation: F[1,456] = 9.94; p<.01; and family life F[1,456] = 86.92; p<.001). Likewise, educational track had a significant effect on all three content domains (education: F[2,455] = 10.94; p<.01; occupation: F[2,455] = 9.94; p<.01; and family life F[2,455] = 3.44; p<.001). General secondary school students gathered more information about all three content areas than either vocational school students or comprehensive school students (Scheffé; ps<.05). Comprehensive school boys and vocational school students reported the least information gathering about future education and occupation and general secondary school girls reported the most.

Information gathering and self-definitions In order to investigate the relationships between information gathering, and self-esteem and control beliefs, a correlation matrix was produced. As shown in Table 2, all information gathering variables were intercorrelated from α = 0.17 to 0.45. Moreover, the higher the

control beliefs participants reported, the more information they gathered at home
($\alpha = 0.14$) and with peers ($\alpha = 0.18$).

Table 2: Correlations between Finnish students'
information gathering and self-evaluations

	Alone	Peers	Home	Mass	School	Control
Alone						
Peers	.36***					
Home	.22***	.45***				
Mass Media	.22***	.33***	.25***			
School	.30**	.31***	.19***	.17***		
Control	.14**	.09	.18***	-.11*	.10*	
Self-esteem	.02	-.13**	.04	-.02	-.09*	.20***

* $p<.05$, ** $p<.01$, *** $p<.001$ (two-tailed)

Discussion

The present study investigated adolescents' future planning and related information gathering in intrapersonal, interpersonal, and institutional settings. The discussion is organized according to the research questions.

Intrapersonal or Interpersonal Planning?

The first aim was to investigate to what extent future planning is an intrapersonal or an interpersonal process, i.e., to what extent do adolescents plan their future
alone or with others. Planning has mainly been conceptualized as an intrapersonal process in previous research (e.g., Scholnick & Friedman 1987; Nurmi
1989), while investigations of the interactive features of this planning have been
less frequent (Goodnow 1987). The findings from Study 1 showed that seven-
teen-year-olds planned most when they were alone, next most with peers, then at
home, then when using mass media, and least at school. The correlations
between planning alone and planning with others suggest that intrapersonal and
interpersonal planning are related: the more the adolescent plans with others, the
more he or she plans alone. Because the present study was cross-sectional, it
does not provide information about to what extent planning in one context could
support, undermine, or compensate for planning in another. Such questions need
to be answered in future studies on adolescents' future planning.

These findings were replicated in Study 2, in which fifteen and eighteen-
years-old adolescents were found to gather future-related information most often
at home, with school friends, and with peers, but less frequently when using
mass media and in school. The intercorrelations between gathering information
in different contexts indicate that the more information the adolescent gathers in
one context, the more he or she reports searching for information in other con-

texts as well. Taken together, these findings show that apart from the importance of the family on adolescents' future planning (Pulkkinen 1990; Nurmi & Pulliainen 1991), peers and school friends also play an important role. However, mass media and school are regarded as less important contexts for future planning and information gathering. The minor role that school plays in adolescents' future thinking is in line with criticism raised recently toward the educational system (Andersson 1990, 1994; Aittola et al. 1994): schools have lost their function as learning or socialization environments during recent decades. However, the low importance of schools is counterbalanced by the importance of school friends in information gathering. Thus, placing young people in a school context provides them with ample opportunities to plan and gather information about their future from their friends and peers.

Overall, the result reflects adolescents' individuation and autonomy vis-a-vis their parents (Eriksson 1968; Hurrelmann 1993), while at the same time (in Study 2) home still exceeds the importance of peers (Brown 1990).

About what do adolescents gather information?

The second aim of this chapter was to investigate to what extent adolescents gather information about their central developmental tasks, i.e., education, occupation, and family life (Havighurst 1953; Buchmann 1989; Nurmi 1989; Hurrelmann 1993). The findings from Study 2 showed that adolescents gathered more information about their future education and occupation than about their future family life. This finding is similar to the findings of Nurmi, Seginer and Poole (1995), who found that Finnish adolescents reported less exploration in the family domain than in education and working life. One explanation for why young people plan their future education and occupation more than their family life is that the transitions to further studies or occupations are closer compared to the transition to family life (Kalakoski & Nurmi 1998). Several studies indicate that adolescents anticipate the transition from school to working life earlier than they anticipate the transition to family life (Nurmi 1989; Malmberg, 1996b). Another possible explanation is that family-related topics are regarded as more intimate, private, and shared with fewer people (e.g., Brown 1990), and there-fore, adolescents report gathering less information about this topic than about educational and occupational issues. There is an evident need for future studies discriminating between how important a particular future topic is, how much it is discussed with others, and how the emotional or supportive tone of this infor-mation gathering is evaluated.

Future planning and educational tracks and transitions

The third aim of the chapter was to investigate how adolescents planning and information gathering vary according to chosen or anticipated educational tracks. The findings from Study 1 showed that general secondary school students planned more on their own than vocational school students. Both Study 1 and 2 showed that general secondary school students planned or gathered more information when using mass media than vocational school students. A likely explanation for this finding is that the educational tracks reflect the parents' SES: the more educated parents are, the more likely it is that their children use written information as a source of information (Brunell 1993). In a future study, it would be worthwhile to investigate which specific sources adolescents use for this information gathering, for example, which particular magazines or television programs. Another interesting topic is the role of rapidly growing data technology: To what extent do adolescents use modern information technology, such as "surfing" on the Internet or "virtual libraries," as a means for exploring the future.

In Study 1, school was evaluated by adolescents as the least used context for gathering information about the future. However, when the educational track differences were observed, comprehensive school students gathered more information at school than did general secondary school students, who in turn gathered more than vocational school students did in this context. Moreover, among the comprehensive school students, those bound for vocational schools gathered more information at school and with peers than those bound for general secondary school. These results may reflect the fact that guidance counseling is more established in comprehensive schools than in the secondary stage of education (Eskelinen 1993). This finding is also in line with that of Kalakoski and Nurmi (1998), who found that educational exploration increases as students approach the transition from comprehensive school to secondary school.

When transitions on the secondary stage were observed, findings in both Study 1 and 2 showed that vocational and comprehensive school girls heading to studies at occupational institutes planned more than boys did at home, with peers and at school. No differences were found between general secondary school boys and girls heading for university studies.

Future planning and gender

The final aim was to investigate gender differences in future planning and information gathering. Several consistent gender patterns were found. In Study 1, girls planned their future at home and with their peers more than boys. In Study 2, girls gathered more information than boys did at home, with school friends, with peers, and when using mass media. Also, girls who pursued studies at the institute level planned more than boys. These results are in line with gender differences found in studies on adolescents' occupational planning (Kosonen 1983; Jusi 1987) and exploration (Nurmi, et al. 1995).

Conclusion

This study examined the ways in which adolescents' construct their future "maps" through interaction with others in several contexts, such as at home, with peers, at school, and when using mass media. Four central findings emerged. First, intrapersonal planning, i.e., planning alone, is associated with planning in other contexts: at home, with peers and friends, when using mass media, and at school. Second, adolescents co-plan their future most often when they are at home or with peers, and less often when using mass media. When at school, they gather information primarily from their peers rather than from formal education. Third, students' information gathering at school reflects the organization of guidance counseling for students at different stages of the educational system. Finally, girls plan more and gather more information about their future than boys do across all stages of education, reflecting specific gender role socialization.

References

Aittola, T., Jokinen, K., & Laine, K. (1994). Nuoret, koulu ja uudet oppimisympäristöt [The young, school and new learning environments]. *Kasvatus, 25,* 472–482.

Ames, C. (1992). Classroom structures: goals, structures, and student motivation. *Journal of Educational Psychology, 84,* 261–271

Anderman, E. M. & Maehr, M. L. (1994). Motivation and schooling in the middle grades. *Review of Educational Research, 64,* 287–309.

Andersson, B.-E. (1990). Are adolescents given a relevant preparation for the adult role? A Swedish perspective. *European Journal of Psychology of Education, 5,* 45–57.

Andersson, B.-E. (1994, June). Does school stimulate young people's development. Paper presented at the Fourth Nordic Youth Research Conference: Young in Europe, conditions, changes and alterations, June, 2–4, in Stockholm, Sweden.

Andres, L. (1999). Rational choice or cultural reproduction? Tracing transitions of young Canadians to higher education. *Nordisk Pedagogik, 18,* 197–206.

Arnett, J. J. (1995). Adolescents' use of media for self-socialization. *Journal of Youth and Adolescence, 24,* 519–533.

Boesch, E. E. (1991). *Symbolic action theory and cultural psychology.* Berlin: Springer.

Bourdieu, P. (1977). Cultural reproduction and social reproduction. In J. Karabel & A. H. Halsey (Eds.), *Power and ideology in education* (pp. 473–486). New York: Oxford University Press.

Brandtstädter, J. (1998). Action perspectives on human development. In R. M. Lerner (Ed.), *Theoretical models of human development* (5th ed., pp. 807 – 863). New York: Wiley.

Brim, O. G. (1981). Foreword. In R. M. Lerner & N. A. Busch-Rossnagel (Eds.), *Individuals as producers of their development. A life-time perspective* (pp. xv–xvii). New York: Academic Press.

Brown, B. B. (1990). Peer groups and peer cultures. In S. S. Feldman & G. R. Elliot (Eds.), *At the threshold. The developing adolescent* (pp. 171–196) Cambridge, MA: Harvard University Press.

Brunell, V. (1993). Hur står det till med läskunnigheten i den Finlandssvenska skolan? [How do students comprehend what they read in the Finland-Swedish schools?] In P. Linnakylä & H. Saari (Eds.), *Oppiiko oppilas peruskoulussa? Peruskoulun arviointi 90-tutkimuksen tuloksia* (pp. 5–26). Jyväskylä: Institute for Educational Research.

Brunell, V., Kannas, L., Levälahti, E., Tynjälä, J., & Välimaa, R. (1996). *Livskvaliteten i skolan. Elevuppfattningar i Finland och utomlands om grundskolan som psykoso-cial miljö.* Jyväskylä: University of Jyväskylä.

Buchmann, M. (1989). *The script of life in modern society. Entry into adulthood in a changing world.* Chicago: The University of Chicago Press.

Chisholm, L. & Hurrelmann, K. (1995). Adolescence in modern Europe. Pluralized transition patterns and their implications for personal and social risks. *Journal of*

Adolescence, 18, 129–158.

Eckensberger, L. H. & Meacham, J. A. (1984). The essentials of action theory: A framework for discussion. *Human Development, 27,* 166–172.

Entwistle, D. R. (1990). Schools and the adolescent. In S. S. Feldman & G. R. Elliot (Eds.), *At the threshold. The developing adolescent* (pp. 197–224). Cambridge, MA: Harvard University Press..

Eriksson, E. H. (1968). *Identity. Youth and crisis.* New York: W.W. Norton

Eskelinen, T. (1993). *Opotunnit. Opetusintentiot, mielekkyys ja vastavuoroisuuden kokemukset peruskoulun oppilaanohjaustunnilla.* [Career counselling lessons—teaching intensions, meaningfulness and experiences of reciprocality during counselling lessons in the comprehensive school]. (University of Joensuu Publications in Education, No. 15). Joensuu: University of Joensuu.

Evans, G. & Poole, M. E. (1991). *Young adults: Self-perceptions and life contexts.* London: The Falmer Press.

Fine, G.A., Mortimer, J.T., & Roberts, D.F. (1990). Leisure, work and mass media. In S.S. Feldman & G.R. Elliot (Eds.) *At the threshold. The developing adolescent* (pp. 225–252). Cambridge, MA: Harvard University Press.

Goodnow, J. J. (1987). Social aspects of planning. In S. L. Friedman, E. K. Scholnick, & R. R. Cocking (Eds.), *Blueprints for thinking. The role of planning in cognitive development* (pp. 321–355). Cambridge: Cambridge University Press.

Gordon, T. & Lahelma, E. (1991). Koulutus ja sukupuoli. [Education and gender]. In T. Takala (Ed.) *Kasvatus sosiologia* (pp. 119–161) Porvoo: WSOY.

Greene, A. L. & Wheatley, S. M. (1992). "I've got a lot to do and I don't think I'll have the time": Gender differences in late adolescent's narratives of the future. Journal of *Youth and Adolescence, 21,* 667–686.

Havighurst, R. J. (1953). *Human development and education.* New York: Longmans, Green and Co.

Heckhausen, J. & Krueger, J. (1993). Developmental expectations for the self and most other people: Age grading in three functions of social comparisons. *Developmental Psychology, 29,* 539–548.

Hurrelmann, K. (1987). The importance of school in the life course: Results from the Bielefeld study on school-related problems in adolescence. *Journal of Adolescent Research, 2,* 111–125.

Hurrelmann, K. (1993). Introduction: Interdisciplinary and international approaches to research on adolescence. In K. Hurrelmann (Ed.), *International handbook of adolescence* (pp. 1–15). Westport, CT.: Greenwood Press.

Härnkvist, K. (1999). Explaining the recruitment to post-secondary education: The case of Sweden. *Nordisk Pedagogik, 18,* 207–216.

Jusi, K. (1987). *Abiturienttien uranvalinta ja uranvalintavarmuuden kehittyminen* [Upper secondary school students' career choice and the development of career commitment] (Työvoimapoliittisia tutkimuksia, Nro 71). Helsinki: Ministry of labor.

Kalakoski, V. & Nurmi, J-E. (1998). Identity and educational transitions: Age differences in adolescent exploration and commitment related to education, occupation and family. *Journal of Research on Adolescence, 8,* 29–47.

Keltikangas-Järvinen, L. (1992). Self-esteem as a predictor of future school achievement. *European Journal of Psychology of Education, 7,* 123–130.

Klaczynski, P. A. & Reese, H. W. (1991). Educational trajectory and "action orientation": Grade and track differences. *Journal of Youth and Adolescence, 20,* 441–462.

Korpinen, E. (1990). *Peruskoululaisen minäkäsitys* [Comprehensive school students' self-concept] (Research reports A:34). Jyväskylä: Institute for Educational Research.

Kosonen, P. (1983). *Uranvalinnan valmiuksia peruskoulun päättoluokalla* [Career choice readiness at the end of comprehensive school] (Työvoimapoliittisia tutkimuksia Nro 39). Helsinki: Ministry of labor.

Kuusinen, J. (1992). Hyvät, huonot ja keskinkertaiset. [The good, bad and average]. *Kasvatus, 23,* 47–56.

Leontiev, A. N. (1975). *Toiminta, tietoisuus, personallisuus.* [Action, awareness and personality; Orig. Dejatel'nost, coznanie, litπnost] (Trans. P. Hakkarainen). Helsinki: Kansankulttuuri.

Little, T. D. (1998). Sociocultural influences on the development of children's action-control beliefs. In J. Heckhausen & C. Dweck (Eds.), *Motivation and self-regulation across the life span* (pp. 281–315). New York: Cambridge University Press.

Little, T. D., Brendgen, M., Wanner, B., & Krappmann, L. (1999). Children's reciprocal perceptions of friendship quality in the sociocultural contexts of East and West Berlin. *International Journal of Behavioral Development, 23,* 63–89.

Malmberg, L.-E. (1996a). How do Finnish students prepare for their future in three school types? The relation between content of plans, information gathering and self-evaluations. *British Journal of Educational Psychology, 66,* 457 –469.

Malmberg, L.-E. (1996b). Finnish adolescents' future interests, worries and time extension: Effects of educational track, gender and self-evaluation. *Nordisk Pedagogik, 16,* 213 – 224.

Malmberg, L.-E. (1998). *Education and students' future-orientation: Adolescents' future preparation, future goals and self-evaluation in educational contexts in Finland and Poland* (Dissertation). Vasa: Åbo Akademi University.

Malmberg, L.-E. & Norrgård, S. (1999). Adolescents' ideas of normative life-span development and personal future goals. *Journal of Adolescence, 22,* 33–47.

Malmberg, L.-E. & Trempała, J. (1997). Anticipated transition to adulthood: The effect of educational track, gender and self-evaluation on Finnish and Polish adolescents' future orientation. *Journal of Youth and Adolescence, 26,* 517 – 537.

Malmberg, L.-E. & Trempała, J. (1998). Future planning both at school and in other contexts: the case of Finnish and Polish general-secondary and vocational-school students. *Scandinavian Journal of Educational Research, 42,* 207–226.

Malmberg, L.-E., Wanner, B., Sumra, S. & Little, T. (2000). Agency-beliefs about school achievement: Tanzanian primary school students in two city schools. *Zimbabwe Journal of Educational Research, 12,* 126–150.

National Board of Education (1994). *Grunderna för grundskolans läroplan 1994* [The basis of the curriculum for comprehensive school, 1994]. Helsingfors.

Neugarten, B. L. & Datan, N. (1973). Sociological perspectives on the life cycle. In P. B. Baltes & K. W. Schaie (Eds.), *Life-span developmental psychology. Personality and socialization* (pp. 53–69). New York: Academic Press.

Nurmi, J.-E. (1989). *Adolescents' orientation to the future. Development of interests and plans, and related attributions and affects in the life-span context* (Commentationes Scientarium Socialium, 39). Helsinki: Societas Scientiarum Fennica.

Nurmi, J.-E. (1991). How do adolescents see their future ? A review of the development of future-orientation and planning. *Developmental Review, 11,* 1–59.

Nurmi, J.-E. (1993). Adolescent development in an age-graded context: The role of personal beliefs, goals, and strategies in the tackling of developmental tasks and standards. *International Journal of Behavioral Development, 16,* 169–189.

Nurmi, J.-E. (1998). *How do adolescents see and create their future.* Key-note paper presented at the 6th Biennial Conference of the EARA (European Association for Research on Adolescence), 03.06.–07.06.1998, in Budapest, Hungary. OR: reference to chapter in the forthcoming book?

Nurmi, J.-E., Poole, M. E., & Seginer, R. (1995). Tracks and transition—A comparison of adolescent future-oriented goals, explorations and commitments in Australia, Israel and Finland. *International Journal of Psychology, 30,* 355–375.

Nurmi, J.-E. & Pulliainen, H. (1991). The changing parent-child relationship, self-esteem, and intelligence as determinants of orientation to the future during early adolescence. *Journal of Adolescence, 14,* 35–51.

Nurmi, J.-E., Seginer, R. & Poole, M. E. (1995). Searching for the future in different environments: A comparison of Australian, Finnish and Israeli adolescents' future orientations, explorations and commitments. In P. Noack, M. Hofer & J. Youniss (Eds.), *Psychological responses to social change. Human development in changing environments* (pp. 219–237). Berlin: Walter de Gruyter.

Nyman-Kurkiala, P. (1997). *Ung och finlandssvensk* [Young and Finland-Swedish]. (Rapporter från institutet för finlandssvensk samhällsforskning vid Åbo Akademi, nr. 32). Vasa: Åbo Akademi University.

Pulkkinen, L. (1990). Home atmosphere and adolescent future orientation. *European Journal of Psychology of Education, 5,* 33–43.

Pulkkinen, L. & Rönkä, A. (1994). Personal control over development, identity formation, and future orientation as components of life orientation: A developmental approach. *Developmental Psychology, 30,* 260–271.

Rauste-von Wright, M-L. (1987). *On the life process among Finnish adolescents. Summary of a longitudinal report* (Commentationes Scientarium Socialium, 35).

Helsinki: Societas Scientiarum Fennica.

Rinne, R. & Salmi, E. (1998). *Oppimisen uusi järjestys* [New order of learning].
Tampere: Vastapaino.

Roos, J. P. (1988). *Elämäntavasta elämänkertaan—Elämäntapaa etsimässä* [From lifestyle to life-stories—in search of life-style]. Jyväskylä: Gummerus.

Rosenberg, M. (1965). *Society and the adolescent self-image.* Princeton, NJ: Princeton
University Press.

Rubin, K. H., Bukowski, W., & Parker, J. G. (1997). Peer interactions, relationships,
and groups. In W. Damon (Eds.), *Handbook of Psychology, Vol. 3: Social, emotional, and personality development* (ed. By N. Eisenberg)(pp. 619–700). New York:
Wiley.

Scholnick, E. K. & Friedman, S. L. (1987). The planning construct in the psychological
literature. In S. Friedman, E. Scholnick, & R. Cocking (Eds.), *Blueprints for thinking. The role of planning in cognitive development* (pp. 3–38). Cambridge:
Cambridge University Press.University Press.

Silbereisen, R. K., Noack, P. & Eyferth, K. (1986). Place for development: Adolescents,
leisure settings, and developmental tasks. In R. K. Silbereisen, K. Eyferth, & G.
Rudinger (Eds.), *Development as action in context. Problem behavior and normal
youth development* (pp. 87–107). Berlin: Springer.

Solantaus, T. (1987). Hopes and worries of young people in three European countries.
Health Promotion, 2, 19–27.

Triandis, H. C. (1989). The self and social behavior in differing cultural contexts.
Psychological Review, 96, 506 –520.

Trempała, J. & Malmberg, L-E. (1998). The anticipated transition to adulthood: effects
of culture and individual experience on Polish and Finnish Adolescents' future orientation. *Journal of Psychology, 132*, 255–266.

Trommsdorff, G., Lamm, H., & Schmidt, R. W. (1979). A longitudinal study of adolescents' future orientation (time perspective). *Journal of Youth and Adolescence, 8*,
131–147.

Trommsdorff, G. (1994). Future time perspective and control orientation: Social conditions and consequences. In Z. Zaleski (Ed.), *Psychology of future orientation.* (pp.
39–62; Publication of the Faculty of Social Sciences, No 32). Lublin: Catholic
University of Lublin.

Verstraeten, D. (1980). Level of realism in adolescent future time perspective. *Human
Development, 23*, 177–191.

Zimmermann, M. A., Copeland, L. A., Shope, J. T., Dielman, T. E. (1997). A longitudinal study of self-esteem: implications for adolescent development. *Journal of
Youth and Adolescence, 26*, 117–141.

CHAPTER 6

Adolescents' Career Exploration in the Context of Educational and Occupational Transitions

BAERBEL KRACKE AND EVA SCHMITT-RODERMUND

Introduction

In industrialized societies work is central to adults' definitions of themselves and the ways in which they live (Vondracek 1998). Consequently, becoming aware about a future occupation and preparing for the transition from school to work is regarded as a central developmental task in the transitional period of adolescence (Havighurst 1948; Erikson 1968). Indeed, the more adolescents approach the period of transition from school to work, the more important the developmental task of preparing for a future place in work life becomes (Dreher & Dreher 1985) and the greater effort adolescents put into exploring educational and occupational issues (Kalakoski & Nurmi 1998). In fact, in late adolescence, educational and occupational issues are more important identity issues than other youth-typic developmental tasks like intimate relationships, thinking about a future family, or becoming independent from parents (Dreher & Dreher 1985; Kalakoski & Nurmi 1998). The importance of work for adolescents' lives also becomes evident when the consequences of the lack of work are considered. Being unemployed has disastrous consequences for adolescents' psychological well-being (e.g., Meeus, Dekovic, & Iedema 1997).

While work is central to people's lives in today's world, the access to the world of work becomes increasingly complicated for adolescents because of the permanently changing labor market due to technological development and a changing economy (Raab & Rademacker 1996). This results in increasing demands for individual qualifications, on the one hand, and a shortage of available training positions and jobs, on the other. According to a recent youth survey in Germany, 88 percent of the 12-to-24-year-olds interviewed regard the increasing unemployment rates as the most urgent problem overshadowing their future lives (Münchmeier 1997). This seems a very realistic perception of the employment situation. In January 1996, the unemployment rates of adolescents and young adults under 25 years old varied regionally from 8 percent to 18 percent. Among the 20- to 25-year-olds, however, the rates were higher on average because they often stay in educational programs financed by the state so that their unemployment is more "hidden" (Bauereiss, Bayer, & Bien 1997).

Because adolescence is a transitional stage, many activities like learning in school can be seen as preparation for the adult world. The significance of these preparational activities is partly dependent on the perceived accessibility of the adult world. Concerning the world of work, accessibility is reflected, for instance, by the level and type of expected qualifications and the availability of training positions. The more difficult access to the adult world becomes, the more important become preparational activities (like learning in school to meet qualification demands in general) and information seeking behaviors concerning future occupations in particular. According to sociologists and educationalists, further demands for a successful development of today´s youth are individual flexibility, readiness for life-long learning, and the ability to self-direct their lives (Brater 1997; Raab 1996).

The purpose of this chapter is to examine the activities that serve information gathering in preparation for the school to work transition, i.e., occupational exploration. Exploration in general can be regarded as a fundamental adaptational behavior which is functional for the orientation of the individual in his or her social and material world (Keller, Schneider, & Henderson 1994). Thus, the study of antecedents and consequences of exploration is a potentially important research issue in every phase of life. Although exploration is an important adaptational behavior throughout the life-span, adolescence is traditionally seen as a period where exploration, particularly in the course of identity formation, becomes important (Erikson 1968; Marcia 1980; Grotevant 1987). Furthermore, because in times of rapid social change adolescents are confronted with an adult world that increasingly provides less orientation for their personal future, exploration becomes more and more a core issue in the study of adolescent development. Therefore, in order to understand how adolescents navigate through their lives in today's world, we need to learn more about the phenomenology of adolescents' explorational behaviors, as well as about antecedents and consequences of adolescent exploration. Greater insight could help the establishment of intervention programs which aim at facilitating successful coping with the demands of an increasingly complex context.

In the following, we will first address theoretical considerations about the character and functionality of exploration. We will then discuss factors which account for individual variation in exploration and look at the consequences of exploration. In each section, we will first give a short review of the existing research literature and then present some examples of our own empirical research. Before reporting our findings, details of the samples and measures will be presented. In the final section, we will discuss theoretical and practical implications of our findings.

Character and Function of Exploration: Background and Earlier Studies

The process of exploration is central to career choice and career development theory (Stumpf, Colarelli, & Hartmann 1983; Super, Savickas, & Super 1996). In the field of adolescent identity formation (Erikson 1968; Marcia 1980), exploration is crucial for a satisfactory commitment to a choice. Grotevant (1987) defined identity exploration "as problem-solving behavior aimed at eliciting information about oneself or one's environment in order to make a decision about an important life choice" (p. 204). This rather general notion can be applied to every life domain. For the specific domain of occupation, career exploration as a problem-solving behavior is aimed at eliciting internal or external information in order to choose, prepare for, enter, adjust to, or progress in an occupation (Jordaan 1963). In adolescence, occupational exploration means that individuals must identify their interests and abilities, balance them with labor market opportunities, and gradually develop an occupational preference (Super, Savickas, & Super 1996).

Problem-solving behavior includes not only the gathering of relevant information but also how systematic and goal-oriented the information-seeking behavior is. That is why researchers usually address three different aspects of exploration, i.e., internal exploration (exploring, reflecting one's interests, abilities, experiences), external exploration (exploring by talking to people, reading information brochures, visiting job fairs) and planful exploration (Stumpf, Colarelli & Hartmann 1983; Blustein & Phillips 1988; Kracke 1997; Kalakoski & Nurmi 1998). Exploration is operationalized either by one scale, which contains the aspects internal, external, and planful exploration (Kracke 1997; Kalakoski & Nurmi 1998) or by three correlated scales assessing the three aspects independently (Stumpf, Colarelli, & Hartmann 1983). Sometimes, occupational exploration, is just assessed by a list of information seeking activities (e.g., Vocational Exploration Behavior Checklist (VEBC) by Krumboltz 1964, cf. Stumpf, Colarelli & Hartmann 1983; Career Development Inventory [CDI] by Super, Thompson, Lindeman, Jordaan, & Myers 1979). Thus, although occupational exploration is a major construct in career development theory, there is no unique conception of its content or dimensionality. The same holds for general exploration. Schmitt-Rodermund and Vondracek (1999), for instance, were interested in adolescents' general explorational behavior. They conceptualized exploration as engagement in different activities in five areas, namely leisure, school, technology, movies, and music. A composite score indicated the breadth of the adolescents' activities.

Besides the content of exploration, the individual variability of explorational behavior is another important issue. Several studies have shown that there is considerable variation in the extent to which individuals explore at one given point in time (Jordaan 1963; Stumpf, Colarelli, & Hartmann 1983, Grotevant 1987) and over their life-courses (Waterman, Geary, & Waterman 1974; Bosma 1985; Grotevant 1987). While interindividual variations in exploration can be partly explained by differences in personality and social factors (Grotevant 1987), intra-individual variations in the intensity of exploration across the life-course can be expected to occur because explorational activities become particularly functional before transitions occur (Super 1990). In adolescence, seen as a life-period in which transitions in various life domains take place, explorational activities are very intense compared to other life phases. However, empirical findings concerning the existence of intra-individual variation in explorational activity are ambiguous, as Kalakoski and Nurmi (1998) report in their review of the relevant literature. While some studies show that there is an age-related increase in exploration and commitment (Bosma 1985) or that individuals progress from less advanced identity statuses to more advanced during adolescence, other studies show that there is no change in identity exploration and commitment during the adolescent years (e.g., Grotevant & Thorbecke 1982).

Kalakoski and Nurmi (1998) present two hypotheses why intra-individual change in exploration should occur. The maturation hypothesis states that changes in exploration are caused by maturational processes like physiological changes or cognitive development. The transition hypothesis states that changes in exploration reflect changes in the sociocultural environment such as institutional transitions, e.g., the transition from school to apprenticeship or university which provokes intensified preparational activities. Their own empirical findings support the transition hypothesis. In their Finnish sample, the students showing the highest intensity of exploration were those who were close to the transition from secondary school to vocational or senior high school. Students who had already undergone this transition were less actively involved in exploration of educational and occupational issues. While Kalakoski and Nurmi's findings are based on cross-sectional analyses of students from different grades, in the following study of Kracke (Kracke, in prep.) we were able to examine the development of exploration longitudinally.

Study I: Situational Preconditions for Career Exploration Among German Students

Sample and measurement

The longitudinal study of Kracke followed 240 students of middle track schools[1] from the beginning of ninth grade to the end of tenth grade, at three measurement points across the period of one and a half years before their transition from secondary school either to apprenticeship or to higher track schools. The adolescents were about fifteen years old at the first measurement point (M = 15.27; SD = .66), and 40.4 percent (n = 97) were female.

Career exploration was assessed by a six-item scale that addressed exploration of the self and of the environment as well as the planfulness of exploration (e.g., "I try to get information about occupations I am interested by various means (e.g., reading, talking, work experience)." "I try to find out which occupations best fit my strengths and weaknesses." The ratings for each item ranged from 1 = "does not apply" to 4 = "fully applies"; Cronbach's alpha in ninth grade was .70 and in tenth grade .77, respectively (Kracke 1997).

Change in exploration was studied across six months between the first assessment at the beginning of ninth grade and the second assessment at the end of ninth grade. In this time period, German middle-track schools offer a special curriculum for occupational preparation. The first assessment took place before the school organized occupational preparation had started, while the second assessment occurred directly after the school intervention had ended.

Results

The first set of analyses which examined the effect of time and gender on occupational exploration revealed that, first, girls (T1: M = 3.27, SD = .42; T2: M = 3.25, SD = .46) explored more intensively than boys (T1: M = 2.98, SD = .56; T2: M = 2.95, SD = .59) (effect of gender: F = 24.03, p < .000) at the two measurement points and, secondly, that the intensity of exploration over time did not change (effect of time: F = .30, p = ns). Overall, the adolescents showed rather intensive explorational activities at both assessments. Correlational analyses, however, showed that the stable group mean did not reflect the intra-individual changes in explorational activity. For all adolescents, explorational activity at both measurement points correlated with r = .42 (p < .000) indicating only a moderately high stability. Girls (r = .40, p > .000) and boys (r = .37, p > .000) did not differ substantially.

Our next aim was to look for factors which could explain the intra-individual variation in development of exploration across the time-period studied. At this point in the analyses, we were looking for factors which reflected the specific situation of the adolescents studied and not for fundamental influencing factors, such as personality or parent-child relationships, which will be studied in more detail in the following section of this chapter.

Jordaan (1963) and Ertelt (1992) pointed out situative circumstances which could cause differential trajectories of exploration. We will focus on three possible factors: (1) It could be that students change their explorative behavior according to their *educational plans* for the time after tenth grade. Some students might intend to start an apprenticeship, which would need ongoing intensive exploration until a contract with a future employer is fixed. Other students, however, might intend to change school track in order to enter university after twelfth/thirteenth grade. These students would have more time to make their decisions and could reduce their level of exploration. (2) A further reason for the differential intensification of exploration could be the different level of information about vocational issues at the beginning of the school intervention. It could be that students who lack more information intensify exploration, while those who are already well informed reduce or do not change their exploratory activity. (3) Research about coping with developmental tasks in adolescence (Dreher & Dreher 1985; Silbereisen 1986) and results from curiosity research about the conditions which promote the approach of a new object (e.g., Lugt-Tappeser & Schneider 1987) point to the fact that to understand explorative behavior one has to consider *how difficult* and, thus, how threatening, adolescents *perceive a developmental task* to be. Adolescents who think it is difficult to get an idea about their occupational future might avoid exploration while adolescents who see no difficulty might intensify their explorational activities.

In order to examine the effect of educational plans, MANOVAs with repeated measurement were conducted. The between-subject-factor was educational plans at the first measurement point. Four educational goals were differentiated[2]: (1) higher track school, (2) apprenticeship, (3) apprenticeship and higher track school, and (4) not decided (neither higher track school nor apprenticeship). Because previous analyses had not revealed significant interactions between gender and educational plans the following results leave out gender to reduce

Table 1: Means, Standard Deviations, F-Values and Effect-Sizes
for Exploration at MP1 and MP2 by Educational Plans

	M (SD)				F			Eta^2		
	HT N=63	AP N=71	APHT N=60	ND N=12	Plan	MP	Plan x MP	Plan	MP	Plan x MP
Exploration	3.13	3.12	3.12	2.89	1.56	0.05	2.31+	.02	.00	.03
T1	(.51)	(.54)	(.54)	(.63)						
Exploration	2.98	3.19	3.14	2.85						
T2	(.61)	(.54)	(.47)	(.64)						

Note: HT = high track, AP = apprenticeship, APHT = apprenticeship and high track,
ND = not decided

complexity.

Table 1 reveals a marginal effect of the interaction between educational plans and measurement point. The means show that students who plan to change to a higher track school after having finished middle-track school reduce their exploration slightly, while the other students' level of activity remains rather stable. This effect becomes even clearer if one examines those students who were asked about their explorational activities at three measurement points. This group of adolescents is a selective group of youths who did not have a contract for an apprenticeship at the end of tenth grade and therefore were asked again about the intensity of their occupational exploration. Table 2 shows (more pronounced than in the previous analysis) that students who want to continue school

Table 2: Means, Standard Deviations, F-Values and Effect-Sizes
for Exploration at MP1, MP3, and MP3 by Education al Plans

	M (SD)				F			Eta^2		
	HT N=47	AP N=17	APHT N=33	ND N=5	Plan	MP	Plan x MP	Plan	MP	Plan x MP
Exploration	3.17	3.12	3.08	3.27	.90	.66	3.26**	.03	.01	.09
T1	(.50)	(.70)	(.46)	(.65)						
Exploration	3.03	3.20	3.24	2.90						
T2	(.58)	(.67)	(.46)	(.48)						
Exploration	2.79	2.97	3.18	3.37						
T3	(.64)	(.81)	(.60)	(.30)						

Note: HT = high track, AP = apprenticeship, APHT = apprenticeship and high track,
ND = not decided

education reduce their explorational activity across the time studied.

Multiple regression analyses were run in order to examine the effect of the level of occupational information at the first measurement point[3], and the perceived difficulty of the developmental task occupational preparation[4] on the development of career exploration across the six months time period. In each analysis, exploration at measurement point one and gender were controlled. Table 3 shows the results.

Over and above the already reported findings concerning the moderate stability of exploration and the clear gender difference, which together account for nearly 20 percent of the explained variance, the level of information and the perceived difficulty of the occupational orientation task have effects on the change of exploration. These effects are small but give interesting hints for situational effects on explorational activities. As expected, adolescents who perceive occupational orientation as a difficult task reduce their explorational activity over

Table 3: Impact of Level of Occupational Information
and Perceived Difficulty of the Occupational Orientation Task on
Occupational Exploration at Time 2

Variable	r	Beta	R^2	R^2 Change	F
1. Step					
Exploration T1	.42***	.42***	.17	.17	***
2. Step			.19	.02	*
Exploration T1	.25***	.38***			
Gender		.15*			
3. Step			.21	.02	*
Exploration T1		.35***			
Gender		.16*			
Information Level	-.20**	-.14*			
4. Step			.22	.01	+
Exploration T1		.36***			
Gender		.17*			
Information Level		-.11+			
Perceived Difficulty	-.10+	-.11+			

Note: n = 209

time. Contrary to our expectations, however, is the effect of the level of occupational information on exploration. It was not the adolescents who were well informed that reduced exploration, but those who had reported at time one that they lacked information. For better understanding of this result one has to note that the level of lacking information and the perceived difficulty of the occupational orientation task are positively correlated ($r = .23$, $p < .000$). This means that a lack of occupational information does not necessarily lead to information seeking behavior, but that it can also have the effect of supressing a threatening activity.

In sum, we found that factors such as educational plans, level of occupational information, and perceived difficulty of the occupational orientation task partly contribute to explain why adolescents change their explorational activities in different ways during ninth grade. This has various practical implications. First, it underlines the request of Super (1990) and Ertelt (1992) to orient work-related school intervention programs more toward individual interests and individual preconditions. Furthermore, there is an important hint for educational programs in that information deficit does not necessarily lead to more information seeking. Consequently, students with comparably higher information deficits should not only receive more information but also an intensive treatment on how to handle such information.

Individual and Social Factors Promoting Career Exploration: Theoretical Background and Previous Research

The extent of exploration not only varies due to contextual or situational factors, but also in relationship with the topic. Factors which may account for the variation of exploration in the domain of occupation, as well as in other areas of exploration, were not yet systematically studied. Research in the realm of identity development, however, showed internal and external sources of influence. Concerning internal sources, certain personality characteristics have turned out to be positively related with exploration. Concerning external sources, parental behaviors have proved to be of particular importance in explaining variation in exploration. These two major sources of influence will be discussed in greater detail in the following review. In addition, some of our own results will be presented.

Grotevant (1987) names self-esteem, ego-resiliency, openness to experience, and self-monitoring as important personality characteristics which account for variation in general exploration. In that vein, Blustein and Phillips (1988) reported that decision-making style relates to occupational exploration. Their findings suggest that a more thinking-oriented and systematic style in decision making increases the likelihood of serious exploration. Moreover, Blustein (1989) showed that internal control beliefs facilitate exploration. Common to these personality characteristics is their reflection of what Savickas (1993, 1997) calls a "syndrome of adaptability", i.e., the ability to respond suitably and constructively to developmental demands.

The second important source of influence on exploration is context (Blustein 1997; Schmitt-Rodermund & Silbereisen 1998). In this chapter we will focus on the family as one important context (Blustein, Walbridge, Friedlander, & Palladino 1991; Grotevant & Cooper 1987; Vondracek 1993). Safe and secure family relationships early in life have been shown to promote curiosity and exploratory activity, an idea which was first put forward by the authors of attachment theory (Bowlby 1982; Ainsworth 1989). Furthermore, Baumrind (1989) identified two independent factors of parental behaviors as especially important for the development in childhood and adolescence. The first is child-centeredness and includes parental love, responsiveness to the child's needs, and parental involvement. The second addresses parental expectations that their children act in a mature and responsible manner. Parenting that shows both awareness of needs and high expectations is called authoritative parenting. These parents provide a warm family climate, set standards, and promote independence.

Adolescents from authoritative families tend to be responsible, self-reliant, adaptable, creative, curious, and socially competent (Baumrind 1989; Steinberg, Mounts, Lamborn, & Dornbusch 1991).

While the work of Baumrind and others on parents' educational style focus mainly on the behavior of the parents, individuation theory provides an additional theoretical view on the family with adolescent children. Youniss and Smollar (1985), as well as Grotevant and Cooper (1987), focus on the changing relationship between parents and their maturing children. Due to physical and cognitive maturation, adolescents increasingly strive for autonomy, try to distance themselves emotionally from their parents, and demand an input into family decision making (Steinberg & Silverberg 1986) while remaining emotionally connected to their parents. Parents on the other hand have to adapt their control demands to their maturing offspring. Thus, a new pattern of parent-child relationships has to be negotiated in adolescence.

Addressing the promotion of exploration in particular, Grotevant and Cooper (1987), as well as Vondracek (1993), point to a specific family interaction process beyond warmth and support. They hold that, if parents are willing to discuss issues openly, if they are open for new information and developments from their children, or if they promote independent thinking and action, adolescents would be more active in exploration.

In one of our earlier studies, the three aspects of parenting, authoritativeness, individuation, and openness for adolescents' issues were found to be positively correlated with adolescents' occupational exploration (Kracke 1997). Another study showed that richness of the home environment in terms of books and other cultural goods, and joint activities with parents also facilitated adolescents' exploratory activities (Schmitt-Rodermund & Vondracek 1999).

In sum, exploration-enhancing parental behaviors can be characterized as oriented toward the adolescents' developmental needs for independence and emotional support in an intellectually open and stimulating atmosphere.

As Schmitt-Rodermund and Vondracek (1999) have pointed out, such parental behaviors not only directly effect exploration but also indirectly facilitate an active approach to the world by stimulating the development of the above described personality characteristics, which in turn enhance exploration[5]. They found that parenting strongly affected childhood exploration, which in turn related to exploration during adolescence. There was no direct path of parenting behaviors to exploratory activities in adolescence when breadth of childhood exploration was included in the analysis. One aspect of goal directedness was also relevant for adolescent exploration. Adolescents who were achievement oriented, reported a broader range of interests and more activities than those who were not very ambitious.

These findings show, firstly, that parental behaviors and personality characteristics are influential for exploration, and secondly, that exploration in adolescence has a strong continuity from childhood onward. Thus, roots for an adaptive approach to the world in later life are already developed through early life experiences.

While the findings of Schmitt-Rodermund and Vondracek were based on retrospective data about childhood experiences and parenting, the following study on individual and parental impacts on exploration has the advantage of a longitudinal design.

Study II: Individual and Social Factors Promoting Career Exploration

Figure 1:

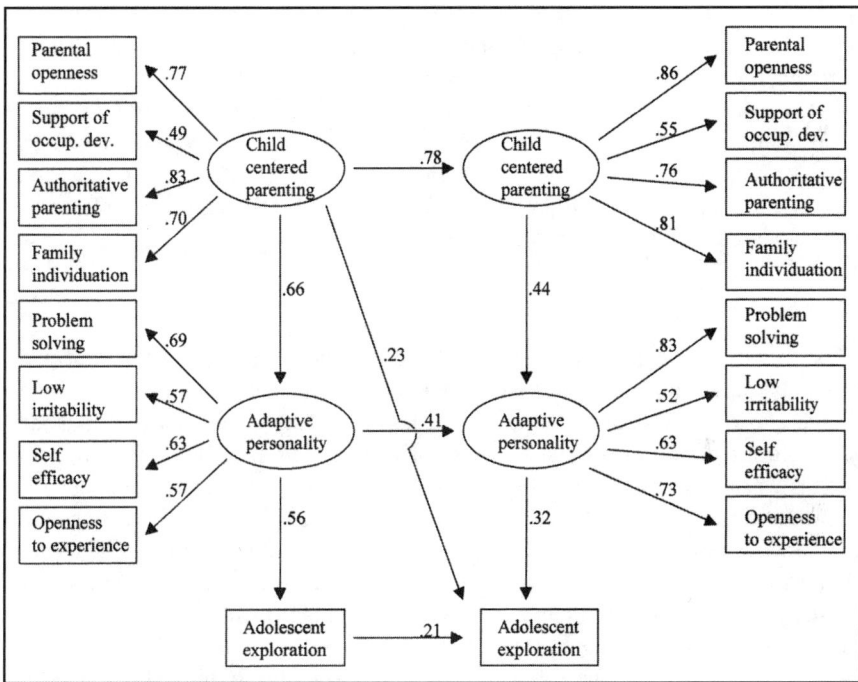

Sample and measurement

We examined the influence of personality characteristics and parental behaviors on occupational exploration in the sample of West German middle track students that was described earlier in Study I.

The following analyses were carried out with data from the first two measurement points, which took place in the first and the second half of ninth grade with an interval of six months in between. One hundred ninety-seven students with complete data sets were included. Parental behaviors were assessed by four scales which were partly self-developed, partly adapted from other research. They are intended to reflect parental behaviors which are oriented to the adolescents' needs and, at the same time, tap relational issues according to individuation theory. The two self-constructed scales were *parental openness to adolescents' issues* consisting of five items (e.g., "When I criticize my parents, they listen and think about it." Cronbach Alpha at T1 .75), and *parental support in occupational preparation* comprising six items (e.g., "My parents encourage me to seek information about as many occupations as possible." Cronbach Alpha at T1 .83); the adapted scales were *individuation* from Youniss and Smollar (1985) (four items, e.g., "Even if my parents don't like my opinion I openly express what I think." Cronbach Alpha at T1 .62), and *authoritative parenting* from Lamborn et al. (Lamborn, Mounts, Steinberg, & Dornbusch 1991) (eight items, e.g., "I can count on my parents to help me out if I have some kind of problem." Cronbach Alpha at T1 .78).

The personality characteristics studied were those identified by Grotevant (1987) as exploration-enhancing, namely, *problem solving competence* (Hofer, Noack, Wild, and Kracke 1996), *self-efficacy* (Schwarzer 1986), *low irritability*, and *openness to experiences* (Windle & Lerner 1986). Occupational exploration was assessed by the six-item scale described in Study I.

Results

First, bivariate correlations were calculated in order to check for the expected relations between parental behaviors and personality characteristics, on the one hand, and occupational exploration, on the other. The results showed that the correlations between parental behaviors and exploration at both measurement points were on average $r = .33$ (ps < .001), indicating a moderate but meaningful relation between parenting and occupational exploration. Parenting and exploration also correlated at this level across the six-month period. The correlations between an active and open personality and exploration were cross-sectionally, as well as longitudinally, between .17 and .45 (ps from < .05 to < .001), also indicating a moderate but substantial relationship. Problem solving competency and openness for new experiences were more closely related with exploration than self-efficacy and low irritability.

In the second step, a model was tested utilizing structural equation analysis (AMOS; Arbuckle 1997) with maximum likelihood estimation based on covariance analyses. The model postulated that child-centered parental behaviors had a direct as well as an indirect effect on occupational exploration. The indirect influence should be effective because parental behaviors of this kind should promote an active, self-conscious, and planful personality which itself should be positively related to occupational exploration. In order to test whether parental behaviors and personality characteristics could predict change in exploration across the six-month period, exploration at measurement points one and two were included in the model. Furthermore, to check for the stability of parenting and personality, as well as for possible effects of exploration on change in these variables, parenting behaviors and personality characteristics measured at time two were also included.

Figure 1 shows the model which best fit the data. Only significant path coefficients (ps < .05) are depicted. According to the fit indicators chi-square/degree of freedom-ratio (Chi2/df = 224.31/121, p < .01), Goodness of Fit Index (GFI = .89) and RMSEA (RMSEA = .07), the model represents the empirical data quite well. The depicted results show a high stability of parental behaviors as perceived by the adolescents and a moderate stability of the assessed personality characteristics. Occupational exploration is not very stable over the observed period of six months. As already seen in the bivariate correlations, the personality characteristics which express a general positive adaptive behavior have strong effects on occupational exploration at each measurement point. In contrast to the cross-sectional correlational analyses we find no direct cross-sectional effect of parental behaviors on exploration. The former existing positive correlation seems to be mediated entirely through the strong relation between adolescent-centered parental behaviors and adaptive personality characteristics. Furthermore, we can observe a significant cross-lagged effect of parenting at T1 on exploration at T2 over and beyond the stability of exploration. Personality characteristics do not predict change in exploration over time. This might be due to the rather high cross-sectional correlations between personality and exploration.

In line with previous research in the realm of identity development, the

Figure 2:

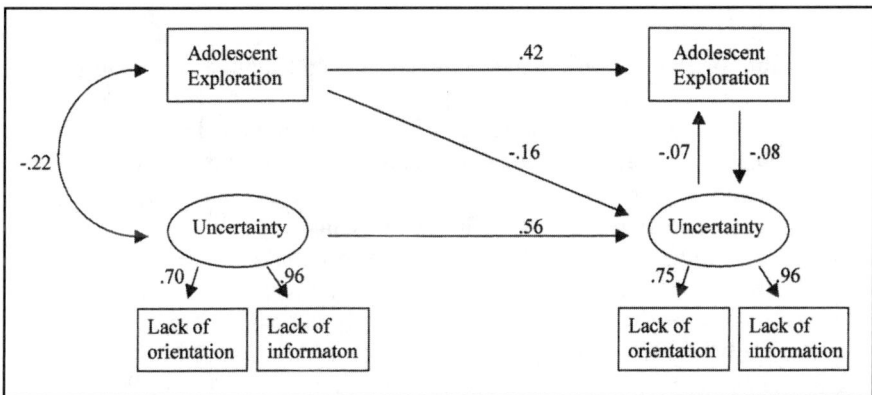

results revealed that child-centered parental behaviors are important for the development of occupational exploration. Such a family life seems to facilitate a successful approach of the developmental tasks by encouraging adolescents actively to discover the adult world. Furthermore, we find that adolescent-centered parenting stimulates the development of personality characteristics, which, in turn, fits with more intensive occupational exploration.

Consequences of Exploration

Engagement in the identity exploration process produces both affective and cognitive consequences (Grotevant 1987; Jordaan 1963). Affective reactions accompany exploration and are important to consider because they evaluate explorational experiences and outcomes, thus, shaping future explorational activities and expectations about the consequences of exploration. Affective reactions in the course of the explorational activity could be anxiety or happiness; affective reactions in response to the outcomes of exploration could be disappointment or satisfaction. Cognitive reactions are based on the amount and content of information that is gathered in the process of exploration. While some individuals think they know enough about the occupation in question, others may judge the same information as insufficient. The information gained can contribute to the developing sense of identity (Grotevant 1987).

In the following, we will address the cognitive and affective outcomes of exploration, as well as the relationship between exploration and identity status. Cognitive outcomes of occupational exploration will be exemplified by uncertainty concerning future occupational plans: Satisfaction with their apprenticeship will serve as an example for affective outcomes of occupational exploration.

Study III: Exploration and the Reduction of Uncertainty

Sample and measurement

The impact of explorational activities on changes in cognitive uncertainty concerning future occupational plans was examined in the previously described sample of West German middle track students (see Study I and II); 207 students with complete data on measurement points one and two were included (Kracke 1998). Uncertainty was assessed by two indicators. The two scales assessing *lack of specific occupational information* (seven items, e.g., "I do not feel well informed about the vocational possibilities which I could pursue when my time at school has finished." Cronbach's Alpha .81) and *general uncertainty about occupational plans* (nine items, e.g., "I still do not know which occupation would fit my strengths and weaknesses." Cronbach's Alpha .84) were adapted from the Questionnaire of Occupation and Apprenticeship Choice [Fragebogen zur Berufs- und Ausbildungswahl (LPS-HS) by Seifert & Bergmann (1992)].

Results

We tested a model which postulated that more intense exploration at the first measurement point would lead to the reduction of cognitive uncertainty across the observed period of six months between measurement points one and two. Furthermore, we assumed cross-sectional correlations between exploration and uncertainty at each measurement point. The model was tested employing structural equation analysis (AMOS, Arbuckle 1997) with maximum likelihood estimation based on covariances.

Figure 2 shows the model which best fit the data. All depicted path coefficients are significant (ps < .05). Modification indices suggested a path from uncertainty T2 to exploration at T2 instead of the postulated reciprocal relationship. The model fit indicates that the resulting model represents the empirical data quite well (Chi2 = 12.74, df = 7, p = .08, GFI = .98, RMSEA = .06). The results show a high stability of cognitive uncertainty and a moderate stability of exploration. As expected, more intense exploration at T1 accompanies less uncertainty at T1. The significant cross-lagged effect indicates that more intense exploration at T1 leads to a decrease of uncertainty between T1 and T2. This finding is in line with our expectations and underscores the positive consequences of exploration. Adolescents who explored more intensely reduced their uncertainty more than the general trend to reduce uncertainty, as depicted by decreasing means (Lack of Information T1: M = 2.07; SD = .59; T2: M = 1.90, SD = .56; General Uncertainty T1: M = 2.40, SD = .64; T2: M = 2.21, SD = .71; F(2;192) = 56.09, p < .000). The general trend to reduce uncertainty might be due to the effects of the school curriculum of occupational counseling between the two measurement points. It is very important to note, however, that beyond such planned interventions, which aim at cognitive effects, individual variation in explorational activity contribute to additional change.

At T2, the direction of the cross-sectional effect goes from uncertainty to exploration, suggesting that higher uncertainty predicts lower levels of exploration and vice versa. With respect to one part of the uncertainty construct, namely, lack of information, this was even found as a cross-lagged effect in Study I, which examined situational effects on exploration. It seems as if those students most in need of intensive exploration are the ones who pursue exploratory behaviors comparatively little and who do not take any opportunities offered which could improve their situation. In other words, this finding suggests that exploration requires at least some level of cognitive certainty as a "secure" base.

Our analyses might have tapped a process that could be described as a vicious cycle.

Study IV: Exploration and Satisfaction with Apprenticeship

One affective response to exploration could be the satisfaction with an attained goal. In the following, we will present a study on the longer term consequences of occupational exploration in school. We were interested in whether occupational exploration in the school years were related to later satisfaction with the apprenticeships the adolescents had started (Kracke 1999). More specifically, we wanted to examine Super's assumption that more intensive exploration leads to the choice of an occupation that fits well to one's interests and abilities, and which, in turn, results in higher satisfaction with one's occupation.

Sample and measurement

Data of thirty-six adolescents in their second year of apprenticeship were available from the longitudinal study on West German middle-track students (Kracke in prep.; details on the original sample and design of the study see previous). Exploration was assessed by the already introduced six-item scale (Kracke 1997). The fit between occupational demands and individual abilities was measured by five items (e.g., "In my apprenticeship I can develop my abilities." Cronbach Alpha .77). Satisfaction with the current apprenticeship was assessed by four items (e.g., "I am satisfied with my apprenticeship." and "I would always choose this apprenticeship again." Cronbach Alpha .77).

Correlational analyses showed that occupational exploration at the end of ninth grade was indeed positively correlated with satisfaction with the current apprenticeship ($r = .40$, $p < .05$), but was not correlated with the fit between apprenticeship and individual abilities ($r = .10$, $p = $ ns). Having an apprenticeship which fits to one's abilities and interests was positively correlated with the satisfaction with apprenticeship ($r = .66$, $p < .001$).

Exploration and identity status

Schmitt-Rodermund and Vondracek (1999) examined the relationship between adolescent exploration and identity status. Exploration was assessed by the breadth of activities and identity status by one of four alternative statements concerning the adolescents' current life situation. The statements addressed identity diffusion, identity foreclosure, moratorium, and identity achievement (see Schmitt-Rodermund & Vondracek 1999). Using analyses of variance, the adolescents' exploratory activity was compared with the four identity status groups.

The results showed that identity achievers reported a broad range of interests and exploratory activities. Adolescents in identity diffusion had only few interests and did not engage in extensive exploratory activities. Adolescents in moratorium, and those with a foreclosed identity, fell between these extremes. Furthermore, the level of exploration was related to occupational choice. Independently of age, adolescents who had already made up their minds about what future occupation they wanted to pursue had explored more than those who currently had no idea of what they might do. These differences are consistent with Marcia's view of identity development as well as with empirical findings on commitment and exploration in adolescence (Marcia 1980; Waterman 1989; Bosma 1992).

Summarizing the results of our studies on the consequences of exploration in general, and on occupational exploration in particular, we can state that, over a shorter period of time, exploration contributes to an increased knowledge about educational and occupational options and that it reduces cognitive uncertainty about one's own abilities and aims. This is perfectly in line with the finding that adolescents who express a sense of achieved identity tend to explore most intensively. Over longer time-periods, such as two or three years, between occupational preparation in school and being involved in an apprenticeship, we still find relationships between exploration and satisfaction with the current work. However, we do not find a relationship between exploration and the fit of work, and own interests, which we had expected to be the link between exploration and satisfaction with apprenticeship. This latter relationship may rather be due to a third variable which we have not yet measured. One could speculate that satisfaction with the chosen apprenticeship is not only a reflection of the given work conditions, but is also partly a result of the individual's ability to be active in shaping his or her work environment. Thus, an underlying third variable that contributes to the relationship between exploration and satisfaction with apprenticeship could be an individual's general high level of adaptability. The fit between the individual's abilities and interests and the job characteristics, however, might be more due to objective circumstances and be less changeable by the individual. These questions should be addressed more deeply in future research.

Discussion

Conclusions

The purpose of our chapter was to investigate one component of adolescents' navigation through their lives, namely exploration. Guided by our current research interests, we concentrated mainly on one central area of adolescents' lives, i.e., preparation for a future career. We examined our own data, which

spanned one and a half years, to see how career exploration developed in adolescents who were about two years before the transition from school to work.
Furthermore, we were interested in antecedents and consequences of change in
the individual intensity of the explorational activities with regard to a future
occupation. We also addressed precursors and correlates of general exploration
assessed by the number of activities in different areas in which the adolescents
were engaged.

Our results showed that exploration, seen as information seeking behavior
directed to the self and the environment in order to prepare for decisions in the
important life domain of occupational future, was more intense in adolescent
girls than in boys. Moreover, exploration in West German ninth graders of middle-track schools turned out to be only moderately stable across a period of six
months. We found that situational factors, such as educational plans, the level of
information about possible careers, and the perceived difficulty of the developmental task "career orientation" systematically contributed to the intra-individual trajectories of career exploration.

When examining factors which should be effective longterm, we found that
various facets of adolescent-centered parenting also predicted change in career
exploration. Personality characteristics reflecting a high level of adaptability to
developmental issues, however, turned out to be significantly correlated with
concurrent exploration but had no impact on change in career exploration. A
positive short-term consequence of career exploration was a decrease in cognitive uncertainty about the future career and, as a positive longterm consequence,
a higher satisfaction with the apprenticeship could be observed.

One major conclusion that can be drawn from our results of a prospective
longitudinal study on career exploration (Kracke in prep.), as well as of a retrospective study on general exploration (Schmitt-Rodermund & Vondracek 1999)
is that similar factors, which were shown to be relevant in previous research on
exploration in identity development, are also influential for exploration in the
domain of career development. Taking an even more general perspective on our
results, one can state that, when exploration is seen as one of various possible
adaptive behaviors, those parental behaviors and personality characteristics
which also promote other forms of adaptive activity in adolescents are particularly influential. Thus, our findings again underscore that parenting which is oriented toward the adolescents' needs, e.g., for behavioral and ideological autonomy, as well as provides emotional support promotes the development of adolescents who are able to navigate through their lives.

Furthermore, our findings concerning the situational conditions influencing
career exploration should stimulate thinking about career counseling. In particular, our observation that adolescents who lack more information about career
planning (or about their own interests and abilities) tend to reduce their explorational efforts, has practical importance for teachers of career-orientation class-

es. Our findings concerning the consequences of exploration are instructive in the light of Blustein's (1997) summary of empirical findings on the effects of exploration being far from unequivocal regarding generally positive consequences. He speculates that this is due to the consequences of exploration often being assessed in too narrow a sense, e.g., when one expects exploration to lead directly to the desired career, or assumes that the self-concept can be fully realized. Therefore, he suggests taking a broader perspective when looking for possible consequences. The lack of an association of exploration and fit between abilities and job opportunities in our data might be due to further aspects beyond exploration that we were not yet able to tap in our research.

By providing some empirical support for the often assumed positive function of exploration in general, and career exploration in particular, as well as by pointing out factors promoting exploration, our research presented here seems to have been rather fruitful so far. The limitations of our research are that findings are not generalizable to all German adolescents facing the transition from school to work. Thus, further research should also address adolescents in other school tracks, and should explore differences possibly stemming from living under different socio-economic conditions. Furthermore, studies on career development should follow individuals over much longer time periods than we were able to do in our studies. In the light of the findings of Schmitt-Rodermund and Vondracek's (1999) retrospective analyses regarding the continuity of explorational activities from childhood to adolescence, investigations should start early in childhood and follow the individuals as far as possible into their working lives.

Practical Implications

Our final considerations address the question of practical implications. Our findings, first, point to the importance of exploration for information gathering as a specific task in occupational preparation and for identity formation as a more general task in the development of a healthy self. Consequently, stimulating exploration can be seen an important goal in itself. Efforts to this end should not only start in adolescence but—as the findings of Schmitt-Rodermund and Vondracek (1999) demonstrate—should already be considered in early childhood. As parents seem to play a central role in providing a context facilitating exploration, they should be the first to address the issue.

The second important social context to be mentioned is school. From preschool or kindergarten onward, teachers should stimulate information seeking in a planful, reflective manner. School curricula in Germany traditionally schedule occupational preparation for the last two or three years of school. However, there is considerable variation between individuals due to earlier influences or personality differences. Thus, teachers should monitor their students carefully to avoid those who are less used to exploring because of contextual or temperamental factors, lagging behind, or losing motivation. If teachers, when approaching occupational preparation in school, considered individual needs to a greater extent, the usefulness of this regular intervention—mostly regarded as low in quality and effect by adolescents—is very likely to improve.

The content of school interventions aimed at occupational preparation in Germany is mostly guided by matching theories in the tradition of Holland (1985). One aim of the school curriculum is to foster a good fit between adolescents' interests and abilities, on the one hand, and job characteristics, on the other. Holland's empirical work showed the fit between personality characteristics and job characteristics to be a good predictor for later satisfaction with the job. Unfortunately, due to the limited time for the occupational preparation process available in school, in many cases no match between abilities and occupational choice can be found, so that the consequence of the counseling process is often disappointment for the adolescent. Therefore, parents and schools should do more to stimulate the explorational process, making the students aware of their abilities and interests as early as possible. A wide range of possible occupations should be introduced in a second step, before a matching procedure is finally initiated, so that students are helped to come up with satisfactory commitments for their professional futures. Ideally, such a procedure would be accompanied by optional individual career consultations. This, of course, needs much more time for occupational preparation courses than is currently provided.

References

Ainsworth, M.D.S. (1989). Attachments beyond infancy. *American Psychologist, 44*, 709–716.

Arbuckle, J.L. (1997). *AMOS user's guide*. Version 3.6. Chicago, IL: Small Waters Corporation.

Bauereiss, R., Bayer, H., & Bien, W. (1997). *Familienatlas II. Lebenslagen und Regionen in Deutschland—Karten und Zahlen* [Family-Atlas II. Lifesituations and regions in Germany. Cards and numbers]. Opladen: Leske+Budrich.

Baumrind, D. (1989). Rearing competent children. In W. Damon (Ed.), *Child development today and tomorrow* (pp. 349–378). San Francisco: Jossey-Bass.

Blustein, D.L. (1989). The role of goal instability and career self-efficacy in the career exploration process. *Journal of Vocational Behavior, 35*, 194–203.

Blustein, D. L. (1997). A context-rich perspective of career exploration across the life-roles. *Career Development Quarterly, 45*, 260–274.

Blustein, D. L. & Phillips, S. D. (1988). Individual and contextual factors in career exploration. *Journal of Vocational Behavior, 33*, 203–216. .

Blustein, D. L., Walbridge, M. M., Friedlander, M. L., & Palladino, D. E. (1991). Contributions of psychological separation and parental attachment to the career development process. *Journal of Counseling Psychology, 38*, 39–50.

Bosma, H.A. (1985). *Identity development in adolescence. Coping with commitments.* Groningen, NL: Rijkuniversiteit Te Groningen.

Bowlby, J. (1982). *Attachment and loss*. Vol. 1: Attachment. New York: Basic Books.

Brater, M. (1997). Schule und Ausbildung im Zeichen der Individualisierung [School and apprenticeship in time of increasing individualization]. In U. Beck (Hrsg.), *Kinder der Freiheit* [Children of freedom]. Frankfurt: Suhrkamp.

Bynner, J. (1998). Education and family components of identity in the transition from school to work. *International Journal of Behavioral Development, 22*, 29–53.

Dreher, E. & Dreher, M. (1985). Entwicklungsaufgaben im Jugendalter. Bedeutsamkeit und Bewaeltigungskonzepte [Developmental tasks in adolescence. Significance and coping]. In D. Liepmann & A. Stiksrud (Eds.), *Entwicklungsaufgaben und Bewältigungsprobleme in der Adoleszenz* (pp. 56–70). Goettingen: Hogrefe.

Erikson, E.H. (1968). *Identity, youth, and crisis*. London: Faber & Faber.

Ertelt, B.-J. (1992). Entscheidungsverhalten und Berufswahl [Decision making and occupational choice]. In Bundesanstalt für Arbeit (Hrsg.), *Handbuch zur Berufswahlvorbereitung* [Handbook for occupational preparation]. (S. 90–105). Nürnberg: Bundesanstalt für Arbeit.

Grotevant, H.D. (1987). Toward a process model of identity formation. *Journal of Adolescent Research, 2*, 203–222.

Grotevant, H.D. & Cooper, C.R. (1986). Exploration as a predictor of congruence in adolescents´ career choices. *Journal of Vocational Behavior, 29*, 201–215.

Grotevant, H.D. & Cooper, C.R. (1987). The role of family experience in career exploration: A life-span perspective. In P.B. Baltes, D.L. Featherman & R.M. Lerner (Eds.), *Life-span development and behavior* (pp. 231–258). Hillsdale, NJ: Erlbaum.

Grotevant, H. D. & Thorbecke, W. L. (1982). Sex differences in styles of occupational identity formation in late adolescence. *Developmental Psychology, 18*, 396–405.

Havighurst, R. J. (1948). *Developmental tasks and education.* New York: McKay.

Heinz, W. R., Kelle, U., Witzel, A., & Zinn, J. (1998). Vocational training and career development in Germany: Results from a longitudinal study. *International Journal of Behavioral Development, 22*, 77–101.

Hofer, M., Noack, P., Wild, E. & Kracke, B. (1996). *Individuation und sozialer Wandel.* 2. Fortsetzungsantrag an die Deutsche Forschungsgemeinschaft [Proposal for a grant of the German Research Council for measurement points five and six of the Mannheim-Leipzig Youth Longitudinal Study on Individuation and Social Change]. Mannheim: University of Mannheim.

Holland, J. L. (1985). *Making vocational choices. A theory on vocational personalities and work environments.* Englewood Cliffs, NJ: Prentice-Hall.

Jordaan, J. P. (1963). Exploratory behavior: The formation of self and occupational concepts. In D. E. Super, R. Starishevsky & N. Matlin (Eds.), *Career development: Self-concept theory* (pp. 42–78). New York: College Entrance Examination Board.

Jugendwerk des Deutschen Snell (Eds.) (1992). Jugen '92 [Youth '92]. Opladen: Leske & Bodrich.

Kalakoski, V. & Nurmi, J. E. (1998). Identity and educational transitions: Age differences in adolescent exploration and commitment related to education, occupation, and family. *Journal of Research on Adolescence, 8*, 29–47.

Keller, H., Schneider, K. & Henderson, B. (1994). Preface: The Study of exploration. In H. Keller, K. Schneider & B. Henderson (Eds.), *Curiosity and exploration* (pp. 1–14). Berlin, Heidelberg: Springer.

Kracke, B. (1997). Parental behaviors and adolescents' career exploration. *Career Development Quarterly, 45*, 341–350.

Kracke, B. (1998). *Reduzierung von Unsicherheit durch aktive Exploration bei Jugendlichen im Berufsorientierungsprozeß* [Reducing uncertainty about future careers by occupational exploration in adolescents]. Paper presented at the 41th Meeting of the Deutsche Gesellschaft fuer Psychologie, 27.9.–1.10., Dresden.

Kracke, B. (1999). *Career exploration and the transition to apprenticeship.* Paper presented at the Meetings of EARLI, August 1999, Goeteborg.

Kracke, B. (in prep.). *Adolescents' occupational preparation.* Habilitation thesis. University of Mannheim.

Lamborn, S. D., Mounts, N. S., Steinberg, L. & Dornbusch, S. (1991). Patterns of competence and adjustment among adolescents from authoritativem authoritarian, indulgent, and neglectful families. *Child Development, 62*, 1049–1065.

Lugt-Tappeser, H. & Schneider, K. (1987). Ängstlichkeit und das Erkunden eines neuen Objektes bei Vorschulkindern [Anxiety and exploration of a novel object in preschool children]. *Zeitschrift für Entwicklungs- und Pädagogische Psychologie, 19*, 300–313.

Marcia, J. E. (1980). Identity in adolescence. In J. Adelson (Ed.), *Handbook of adolescent psychology* (pp. 159–187). New York: Wiley.

Meeus, W., Dekovic, M., & Iedema, J. (1997). Unemployment and identity in adolescence: A social comparison perspective. *Career Development Quarterly, 45*, 369–387.

Münchmeier, R. (1997). Die Lebenslage junger Menschen [Young people's life situation]. In Jugendwerk der Deutschen Shell (Eds.), *Jugend '97* (pp. 277–301) [Youth '97]. Opladen: Leske + Budrich.

Raab, E. (1996). (Kein) Leben ohne Arbeit—Einzelbefunde zu den Arbeitsorientierungen von Jugendlichen. In. E. Raab, E. (Hrsg.). *Jugend sucht Arbeit. Eine Längsschnittuntersuchung zum Berufseinstieg Jugendlicher* [Youth searches work. A longitudinal study on the transition from school to work] (S. 185–192). München: DJI-Verlag.

Raab, E. & Rademacker, H. (1996). Strukturen der Berufseinmündung [The transition to work]. In E. Raab (Hrsg.), *Jugend sucht Arbeit* [Youth searches work] (S. 19–32). München: DJI-Verlag.

Raskin, P. M. (1985). Identity and vocational development. In A. S. Waterman (Ed.), *Identity in adolescence: Process and concepts* (pp. 25–42). San Francisco: Jossey-Bass.

Savickas, M. L. (1985). Identity in vocational development. *Journal of Vocational Behavior, 27*, 329–337.

Savickas, M.L. (1993). Predictive validity criteria for career development measures. *Journal of Career Assessment, 1*, 93–104.

Savickas, M. L. (1997). Career adaptability: An integrative construct for life-span, life-space theory. *Career Development Quaterly, 45*, 247–259.

Schmitt-Rodermund, E. & Silbereisen, R. K. (1998). Career maturity determinants: Individual development, social context, and historical time. *The Career Development Quarterly, 47*, 16–31.

Schmitt-Rodermund, E. & Vondracek, F. W. (1999). Breadth of interests, exploration, and identity development in adolescence. *Journal of Vocational Behavior, 55*, 298–317.

Schulenberg, J. E., Vondracek, F. W., Crouter, A. C. (1984). The influence of the family on vocational development. *Journal of Marriage and the Family, 46*, 129–142.

Schwarzer, R. (Ed.)(1986). *Skalen zur Befindlichkeit und Persönlichkeit* [Scales for Psychological Health and Personality] . Research Report 5, Institute for Psychology, Free University Berlin.

Seifert & Bergmann (1992). *Fragebogen zur Berufs- und Ausbildungswahl für Schüler* (LPS–HS) [Questionnaire of Occupation and Apprenticeship Choice]. Universität Linz.

Silbereisen, R. K. (1986). Entwicklung als Handlung im Kontext. Entwicklungsprobleme und Problemverhalten im Jugendalter [Development as action context. Developmental problems and problem behavior in adolescence]. *Zeitschrift fuer Sozialisationsforschung und Erziehungssoziologie, 6*, 29–46.

Silbereisen, R. K., Vondracek, F. W. & Berg, L. A. (1997). Differential timing of initial vocational choice: The influence of early childhood family relocation and parental support behaviors in two cultures. *Journal of Vocational Behavior, 50*, 41–59.

Steinberg, L. D., Mounts, N., Lamborn, S. D. & Dornbusch, S. M. (1991). Authoritative parenting and adolescent adjustment across varied ecological niches. *Journal of Research on Adolescence, 1*, 19–36.

Steinberg, L.D. & Silverberg, S.B. (1986). The vicissitudes of autonomy in early adolescence. *Child Development, 57*, 841–851.

Stumpf, S. A., Colarelli, S. M., & Hartman, K. (1983). Development of the Career Exploration Survey (CES). *Journal of Vocational Behavior, 22*, 191–226.

Super, D. E. (1990). A life-span, life-space approach to career development. In D. Brown & L. Brooks (Eds.), *Career choice and development* (pp. 197–261). Jossey-Bass Publishers.

Super, D. E., Savickas, M.L., & Super, C. M. (1996). The life-span, life-space approach to careers. In D. Brown & L. Brooks (Eds.), *Career choice and development* (3rd ed., pp. 121–178). San Francisco: Jossey-Bass.

Super, D. E., Thompson, A. S., Lindeman, R. H., Jordaan, J. P., & Myers, R. A. (1979). *Career Development Inventory*. Palo Alto, Ca.: Consulting Psychologists Press.

Vondracek, F. W. (1993). Promoting vocational development in adolescence. In R. M. Lerner (Ed.), *Early adolescence—perspectives on research, policy, and intervention* (pp. 277–292). New York, Hillsdale: Erlbaum.

Vondracek, F. W. (1994). Vocational identity development in adolescence. In R. K. Silbereisen & E. Todt (Eds.), *Adolescence in context* (pp. 284–303). New York: Springer.

Vondracek, F. W. (1998). Career development: A lifespan perspective (Introduction to the special section). *International Journal of Behavioral Development, 22*, 1–6.

Wallace-Broscius, A., Serafica, F.C. & Osipow, S.H. (1994). Adolescent career development: Relationships to self-concept and identity status. *Journal of Research on Adolescence, 4*, 127–149.

Waterman, A. S. (1989). Curricula interventions for identity change: Substantive and ethical considerations. *Journal of Adolescence, 12*, 389–400.

Waterman, A. S., Geary, P. S., & Waterman, C. K. (1974). A longitudinal study of changes in ego identity status from the freshman to the senior year at college. *Developmental Psychology, 10*, 387–392.

Windle, M. & Lerner, R. M. (1986). Reassessing the dimensions of temperamental individuality across the life span. The revised Dimension of Temperament Survey (DOTS-R). *Journal of Adolescent Research, 1*, 213–230.

Youniss, J. & Smollar, J. (1985). *Adolescents' relations with mothers, fathers, and friends*. Chicago: University of Chicago Press.

Notes

1. In West Germany, after four years in primary school students move to one of three tracks of secondary school, which they then attend for six years. The lower track (Hauptschule) usually leads to blue collar apprenticeships or unskilled labor. The middle track (Realschule) usually leads to white collar apprenticeships or special schools for intermediate qualified social work or administration. After 10th grade, about one third of the middle track students move to the higher track. The higher track (Gymnasium) continues to 13th grade and leads to a university bound qualification. In East Germany, secondary education was not divided into three tracks. After 10th grade, dependent on their prior achievement, students applied for apprenticeships or moved to the Gymnasium, which ended after 12th grade.

2. The educational plans variable results from the combination of two items which could be rated with "does not apply" (1), "rarely applies" (2), "somehow applies" (3), "fully applies" (4). Both items were introduced with the following sentence: "If you think about the time after middle track school, what plans do you have at the moment?" The first item was: "I want to start an apprenticeship." The second item was: "I want to change to a higher track school." Students who ticked the first item "3" or "4" and at the second item "1" or "2" were grouped as "Apprenticeship". Those who ticked the first Item "1" or "2" and at the second item "3" or "4" were grouped as "School". Those who had ticked high values at both items were grouped as "Apprenticeship and school". Low values at both items indicated being "not decided".

3. Information level was assessed with a seven item scale. The items were selected from the questionnaire "Fragebogen zur Berufs- und Ausbildungswahl (LPS-HS)[Questionnaire of Occupation and Apprenticeship Choice]" by Seifert and Bergmann (1992). The scale grasps a lack of knowledge about opportunities and demands regarding apprenticeships and occupations and sources of information. Cronbach's Alpha ranges from .81 to .83 across the three points of measurement.

4. The perceived difficulty of the occupational orientation task was assessed with one item. "How difficult do you think is to know which occupation you will have some day and how to reach this goal?"

5. Schmitt-Rodermund and Vondracek (1999) examined the influence of personality characteristics and parental behaviors on adolescents´ general exploration in a national survey of 325 East and 608 West German youth between 13 and 19 years of age (Jugendwerk der Deutschen Shell, 1992) who attended low, middle or high track schools in the 10th grade or below (for details about the scales see Schmitt-Rodermund & Vondracek, 1999).

Part Three

The Role of Family in
Adolescents' Future-orientation and Decision-making

CHAPTER 7

Adolescents' Future: A Comparison of Young People's and their Parents' Views

MARGHERITA LANZ, ROSA ROSNATI, ELENA MARTA, AND EUGENIA SCABINI

Introduction

Defining future life plans is considered to be an important developmental task during adolescence. Young people are assumed to make choices that involve imagining themselves as future adults: the attainment of educational goals, the acquisition of a professional identity, and the formation of a family are the most important markers of achieving adult status. In other words, future orientation is a developmental task whose pursuit facilitates the transition to adulthood (Seginer 1995). This task has recently become complex, especially due to the fact that today the transition to adulthood takes place as a double transition, the first lasting from adolescence to the phase of young-adulthood and the second, from this to full adulthood. This transition as it occurs in complex Western societies has become fragmented into a variety of pathways from which to choose that retain a minimum of ritual and are characterized by ample space for choice and decision-making concerning the particular mode and timing of the transition (Scabini 1995; Cigoli 1995).

In the recent past young people had to finish school, get a job, marry and have children. Today these "rites of passage" no longer constitute moments in a precise sequence of events because life-paths increasingly allow for changing one's mind regarding personal and professional choices. Nowadays, young people may choose to study and work at the same time, to enter the job market and then leave it in order to attend specialization courses or to live with their girl or boy friend while finishing their education, and so on. Each adolescent must find his/her own path to adult status and define his/her own strategy. This fragmentation of the transition to adulthood, connected as it is to the spread of growth strategies based on "trial and error," on taking "small steps" at a time, or on simply waiting (Heinz 1996)—in other words, the spread of the so-called "paradigm of reversibility" (Ricolfi 1984)—makes it difficult for present-day adolescents to plan for their futures. The paradigm of reversibility—with its corollary, the "experimentation model"—is based on adolescents' belief of being able to make choices that are never definitive but always subject to change—in all areas of life. For example, one can begin a specific course of study but change it after a year or two; one can commit oneself in a romantic relationship or to marriage with the assumption that one's choice of partner can be questioned at any time.

The adoption of this paradigm results in the loss of the framework provided by a unitary and stable value system to which one can refer for guidance in life and in the affirmation of a fragmented and self-referential value system.

Life has been transformed into a complex succession of situations that adolescents perceive as being transitory and that need to be selected and organized. Young people, therefore, have many more opportunities but, at the same time, may be confused and plagued by doubts. The task they must face is not at all simple: they are required to conceive of themselves as being "a planning agency for life's decisions" (Heinz 1996) and to direct their own present and future lives. As Beck (1992) has underlined, the situation of transition demands flexibility and a sense of self-direction but, at the same time, requires long-term aspirations and a certain persistency, as well. In order to successfully bring about the transition, therefore, adolescents must be able to quickly and capably select from among immediate options while simultaneously keeping their sights fixed on goals which, given the present organization of society, can only be realized in what seems like a very distant future.

Future Orientation: A Theoretical and Empirical Framework

Psychosocial theory about future planning is not recent. Lewin (1946) had already pointed out that while the child lives only in a present dimension, as he grows older his temporal dimension comes to include most of his past and future, as well. During adolescence, the maturation of cognitive functions enables the subject to make predictions about reality and to prefigure different alternatives regarding the future. According to Piaget and Inhelder' s theory (1955) at this age the individual develops hypothetical-deductive thought by means of which he can take into account not only directly perceivable situations but also possible events. Thus, during adolescence an expansion of the temporal dimension takes place that allows the subject to coherently organize sequences of actions leading to the attainment of a specific goal, even if it is deferred in time. The "total temporal perspective" is considered by Lewin to be one of the basic dimensions of the *space of life*.

The particular importance of the temporal perspective in adolescence lies in an expanded "future" dimension, which assumes particular prominence during this age. In adolescence, the future is initially conceived of as a sphere of possibility. A clearly defined need arises to project oneself forward in time and a person begins to differentiate between fantasy and reality by setting goals and prefiguring the most suitable means of reaching them (Leccardi 1996).

Through socialization, people learn which goals are realistic in a certain socio-cultural context in accordance with its structural constraints (labor market and educational tracks) and cultural constraints (e.g., role-transitions and gender roles) (Buchmann 1989; Hurrelmann 1993). Moreover, people also learn what are appropriate and non-appropriate ways to realize goals, at which age their goals can be reached and how to deal with success and failure after an action has been completed. Ultimately, we learn what sort of person one becomes according to a society's socio-culturally defined developmental tasks, collective representations, social times, or normative expectations about development. Adolescents find that they must make choices (those related to school and work, in the first place) that force them to devise plans concerning themselves as future adults and therefore not only to take into consideration their own aspirations, but also to think about how best to actualize their plans and the probability of success—considerations that are connected to knowledge about the external conditions of the context in which the plans are to be realized.

There are two research traditions associated with adolescent thinking and preparation for the future. The first has investigated how young people see their personal futures in terms of hopes, goals, expectations, and concerns (Lewin 1948; Trommsdorff, Burger, and Fuchusle 1982; Nuttin 1984; Seginer 1988a; Nurmi 1991): it has been suggested that young people set future-oriented goals by comparing their individual motives to their view of the future and their personal perception of future possibilities (Nurmi, Poole, and Seginer 1995). These goals and hopes are then realized by constructing different plans and strategies (Nurmi 1991, 1993). Results are consistent and show that adolescents are mostly concerned with future jobs and education, secondly, with leisure time and material possessions and, finally with marriage and building their own family (Gillies, Elmwood, and Hawtin 1985; Nurmi 1987, 1989; Seginer 1988a 1988b; Malmberg and Norgard 1997).

The results of numerous studies demonstrate that young people, irrespective of their age and cultural milieu, tend to visualize their futures up until the end of the second and the beginning of the third decade of life. Nurmi's research showed that young people on average expect their goals to be realized by the time they are around twenty years old, according to a sequence that appears to reflect a "cultural prototype" of development during the life cycle: finishing one's education, first of all, then finding work, and finally, building a family and the material foundations of one's own existence.

The other research tradition that is closely related to thinking about and preparing for the future, concerns identity formation (Nurmi 1991): planning the future is part of identity construction. It is by planning the future that one begins the process of defining a personal system of co-ordinates around which one's identity takes shape. Self-concept is modified and rebuilt by future expectations and life plans. In other words, the question "Who I am?" can elicit a proper answer only if the subject is able to find a solution to the question, "Who do I want to become and who can I become?"

Through interaction with their parents, peers, and the wider social context adolescents internalize the normative aspects of development during the individual life cycle (that is, the age at which it is expected that an individual will become independent from his parents, find work, marry and have children). In fact, according to Ricci Bitti (1993), to talk about temporal perspective means to make reference to the process of formulating plans and goals which take shape partly in response to individual needs and in part are dictated by the objectives put forward by the social structure into which an individual's life plans come to be channeled. Thus, the adolescent's temporal perspective takes the form of a sort of "personal agenda" into which social time and individual time are integrated. The first refers to time that is regulated by society and is governed by a number of precepts and norms which establish when, in which order, and for how long various activities should be carried out (Rampazzi 1985). The second, an expression of the adolescent's personal identity, originates in all the processes activated in order to define and construct the self and to actualize an individual's choices within his own relational network.

Perhaps it is the topic of expectations more than any other that highlights the reciprocal relationship existing between the individual and society. In effect, the adolescent's individual plans are influenced by a set of economic, social, and cultural factors: in short, they are determined by what we might define as the *social structure*, identified by Lewin (1946) as the fundamental element in a "total temporal perspective." This concept gathers together such aspects as values, and norms, a sense of social timing that identifies the most advantageous age at which to undertake various transitions (e.g., finishing one's studies, beginning one's working life, marriage and the birth of a first child), the laws governing the labor market that regulate young people's entry into the work place and assign more or less prestige to particular salary levels and professions, etc.

Much research has highlighted social influence on adolescents' future plans. From the 1970s onward a consistent body of research has investigated adolescents' educational and occupational expectations. These studies have revealed that gender differences exist in adolescents' aspirations: females have lower educational and occupational expectations for their careers than males, reproducing the same differences existing in the labor market (Mooney Marini and Greenberg 1987; Aneshensel and Rosen 1980; Mooney Marini and Brinton 1984). This discrepancy is based on a commonplace assumption that females attempt to mesh their future roles in the family and the labor market, giving highest priority to the former (Aneshensel and Rosen 1980). This process sheds light on the existence of factors which lead to sex-segregation and which exist prior to the entrance of women into the labor market and are related to the process of sex-role socialization.

If the studies carried out in the 70s and early 80s showed that adolescents' conception of the future mirrored traditional roles (Lamm, Schmitdt, and

Trommsdorf 1976), more recent research reveals that these differences have diminished substantially and all but disappeared in the areas of school and work. Nurmi (1987,1989) points out, in fact, that girls express aspirations related to educational and occupational fields just as frequently as boys. The same results have been obtained in the Italian context during the 1990s: a recent study (Rosnati 1995) demonstrated that female adolescents have educational and occupational expectations for their careers which are as high as or even higher than those of males.

The influence of social factors acts directly on adolescents by means of the representations of the social environment they build over the years, but this is also modified by individual factors (interests, self-esteem levels, values, etc.) and family factors (parents' child-rearing styles, levels of expectations, family history, and quality of relationships). Within a family, in effect, norms, values and models are transmitted from one generation to the next which influence adolescents in terms of what form their future planning will take. Families transmit their legacies to future generations, therefore, and at the same time, mediate the influence exerted by the social environment (Reiss and Olivieri 1991). It is not only necessary to bear in mind that people who live in the same socio-cultural context share a certain number of myths (Buchmann 1989; Boesch 1991) about "positive spirals" and "negative spirals" but to remember that they also share family myths.

The Role of Family in Adolescents' Future-Orientation

Many studies on adolescence have highlighted the importance of the family background within which development takes place (Grotevant and Cooper 1983; Youniss and Smollar 1985; Scabini and Galimberti 1995). The family is the major context for individual development: it helps to shape personality, behavioral repertoire, and relationship style. Thus, the family affects all the individual's interpersonal behavior (Bell, Cornwell, and Bell 1988). In recent years, these assumptions have led to an increasing awareness of the importance of the family in the study of adolescence (Dornbuch, Petersen, and Hetherington 1991; Sherrod, Haggerty, and Featherman 1993). This means that we should examine adolescents in terms of family context rather than simply from an individual point of view. Whatever it is that the child experiences and that also shapes development is constructed conjointly with parents and emerges from the environment created by the family process (Youniss and Smollar 1985; Sroufe 1991). Thus, adolescence is an event which involves the whole family system (Cigoli 1985; Scabini 1995).

From this brief description of adolescent development, we can infer that the elaboration of a personal identity, as well, should not be considered a uniquely individual task, but rather one that involves the whole family. The family affects adolescents' future planning in different ways: by mediating the influence of the social context, but also by directly proposing models and values and making explicit its expectations for the young person's future. A less direct type of influence exists, moreover, which acts through the quality of family relationships. But we have to emphasize that while there is a consistent body of research pointing to social influence on adolescents' expectations, only a few studies have focused on the influence exercised by family context on the younger generation's future planning.

Nurmi (1987) found that parents may motivate their children to become interested in different domains relevant for their futures. Family climate and the parents' relationship as a model for family life may motivate adolescents either to plan their own future families or, conversely, not to. Moreover, family context may also provide a basis for adolescents' internality and optimism concerning the future. In previous studies, parental support was found to increase adolescents' internality and optimism (Pulkkinen 1984) in thinking about the future. Trommsdorff (1983) found that adolescents who perceived themselves as being more supported by parents were more optimistic and believed they would be able to influence their own futures. Finally, adolescents also learn the basic planning skills and coping strategies through interaction with parents. Nurmi (1987) showed that mothers' levels of life planning correlated positively with the level of adolescents' educational plans, suggesting that the basis for future planning is learned within the family context.

Nurmi and Pulliainen (1991) showed that active family interaction supplied a positive model for family life and seemed to encourage adolescents to think actively about their own future marriages and families. Also, educational and occupational expectations are affected not only by economic, social, and cultural factors—as we have already seen—but also by values and patterns transmitted by the family from one generation to the next. Several studies carried out in the United States by Aneshensel and Rosen (1980) found that there was a significant influence exercised by parents, and especially by mothers, on adolescents' life plans. It is clear that the family plays an important role in the transition to adulthood by supporting offspring and guiding their choices.

Adolescents' Future Orientation in the Italian Context

In Italy, we find that the quality of family relationships is generally high, that there is an almost complete absence of intergenerational conflict coexisting with an arduous process of integration into society for young people (due to the difficulty of finding work or a place to live); young people also want to have the option of trying various alternatives in both the affective as well as occupational spheres of life. All these factors increasingly defer adolescents' transition to adulthood and heighten the risk that young-adulthood no longer represents a preparatory phase, but rather a breakdown in the generational transition.

Various Italian studies have shown that the temporal extension of adolescents' future perspectives has been reduced in length (Ricci Bitti 1993): today young people's goals and plans mostly address the immediate future and, to a lesser extent, have to do with the distant future, in contrast to the "future-centric" conception of one's existence typical of former generations. According to Cavalli and De Lillo (1996), this is a consequence of the younger generation's adaptation to a world that is uncertain, changeable, and not easily predictable.

The good quality of family relationships proves to be both an optimum context for children's self-fulfillment and a hindrance to the generational transition (Scabini and Cigoli 1997). The phenomenon of young people remaining within the family for an extended period, widespread in Mediterranean countries (Cordon 1997), and their adherence to a paradigm of "reversibility" are made possible in part by the fact that present-day families, unlike their predecessors, are willing to tolerate, both affectively and economically, a long transition to adulthood in the younger generations. In the culture of Italian families, parents and offspring are united in sharing the same ideal: self-fulfillment in the adolescent/young adult. This self-fulfillment mostly concerns the sphere of work and leisure time while the prospect of making the generational leap by forming one's own family and assuming parental responsibilities is relegated to a remote future.

Parents and children share the same representation of the transition to adulthood, as demonstrated by a recent study (Scabini and Cigoli 1997): they prefer to postpone this transition—marked as it is by uncertainty—as much as possible in order to achieve self-fulfillment in the spheres of affection and work.

The influence of the family relational context on adolescents' future orientation has also been found in Italy, with some features unique to this country, however. A recent study carried out on an Italian sample of families with late adolescents has revealed that the quality of parent-child communication and support, and above all, the quality of the mother-child relationship, influences the levels of adolescents' aspirations, particularly in academics (Rosnati 1996a). This means that adolescents who can rely on a supportive family are able to set their sights high and undertake a demanding course of study in order to achieve a prestigious position in the working world.

Other studies on Italian families with adolescents have demonstrated that the most important variable influencing an adolescents' educational and occupational expectations is their parents', and especially their mother's, aspirations for their offspring. The family's socio-economic status, adolescent's self-esteem, and academic achievement are only of secondary importance (Manganelli Rattazi and Capozza 1993; Maganelli and Canova 1995; Rosnati 1996b). The findings of this research reveal that the mother has a predominant role in the elaboration process of adolescents' aspirations, in particular those of her daughter. The mother exercises an important influence, not only because she directly affects her children's aspirations, but also because she conveys her husband's expectations to them. In other words, she plays the role of mediator within the family context. Thus, the mother plays a significant role in the elaboration process of her child's personal identity. The pivotal role played by mothers in the family relational network has been highlighted by other international studies: adolescents communicate more openly with their mothers (Youniss and Ketterlinus 1987; Noller and Callan 1990), usually seek their advice and help (Greene and Grimsley 1990), and perceive a greater emotional closeness with them.

The Italian situation is unique in that the mother plays a central role in the family with adolescents, not only from the expressive point of view, but from the instrumental one as well (Carrà and Marta 1995; Manganelli Rattazzi and Capozza 1993; Rosnati 1995). In other words, not only does the mother have the task of child-rearing but also the function of socialization and transmission of norms and values, tasks that have traditionally been part of the father's role. We can infer from this data a kind of "relational loss of balance" in families with adolescents: the mother is the relational fulcrum of the family while the father maintains a more distant position. Nevertheless, recent studies carried out by Carrà and Marta (1995) show that Italian fathers, due to their more peripheral position in the family, are more accurate than mothers in their perceptions regarding the quality of their relationships with offspring. The quality of the father-child relationship constitutes, therefore, an important protective factor in the adolescent's psycho-social development.

Aims of the Study

All these results taken together reveal that the elaboration of future plans cannot be considered as an individual task but rather occurs in the relational family network, corroborating the assumption that the family relational network influences adolescents' preparation for the transition to adulthood and shapes their future expectations.

The key purpose of the present study is to analyze the influence of the family on adolescents' future planning and therefore on their preparation for the transition to adulthood. All the above mentioned studies have taken into account only adolescents' points of view and their own perceptions of parental expectations, while few exceptions have compared both generations. Our aim, following the family perspective, is to consider how the adolescent's future plans develop within the family relational network, with a comparison of the two generations. In order to conduct a true "family research" as defined by Feetham (1988) and Larsen and Olson (1990), we assume that the family is the unit of analysis both from a theoretical and a methodological point of view. This implies that we have to consider both children's and parent's standpoints and to combine the perspectives of different family members (Larsen and Olson 1990).

The specific aim of the present study is, first, to compare parents' and adolescents' perspective regarding adolescent's future orientation and, secondly, to analyze the relationship between parent-child communication and adolescents' future orientation. In our opinion, this contribution represents the first step in understanding the mutual involvement of parents and children in the adolescents' construction of the future. In order to reach our objectives, we made use of multiple temporal dimensions and we carried out data analysis on two levels. On the first analytical level, we analyzed separately parent's and children's data and then compared the respective generations of adults/parents and children/adolescents in order to highlight generational differences and similarities with respect to the content of the temporal perspective. On the second level, the analytical unit is constituted by the dyad parent (father or mother)-child (male or female). We then proceeded to compare parents and offspring from the same family in order to analyze more closely the degree of similarity in parents' and children's perceptions of the temporal perspective. In this second analytical level, the influence exerted by parents' and children's gender will be taken into consideration.

In this study, the concept of temporal perspective includes, besides such topics as hopes and fears for the future, the age of goal realization, the levels of control (control belief) that adolescents attribute to themselves, and the probabilities of actualizing those goals (optimism/pessimism).

Method

Participants

The sample was composed of 482 adolescents, 361 fathers and 394 mothers. The mean age of adolescents was 14.9 years old ($SD = 2.16$; range 12/20). Females comprised 53.2 percent and males 46.8 percent.

The mean age of the fathers was 46.6 years old (range 30/65; $SD = 5.76$) and 43.29 for mothers (range 30/61; $SD = 5.37$). All the couples had been married, on average, for 19.8 years (range 3/37; SD 4.94). Of mothers, 39.8 percent were housewives or pensioners, 7.9 percent of fathers were pensioners. The socio-economic status of the families was medium to high.

Only the families that had not experienced divorce and that had all three members responding to the questionnaire were used for this project, for a total of 325 triads.

The sample was formed with the cooperation of the secondary schools of Milan and was representative of intact families living in Milan and its periphery, with a child/student of twelve to twenty years of age.

After the headmasters and the teachers of the schools had given their consent, students were asked to fill in a questionnaire. Questionnaires were group administered in an ordinary classroom situation during the last semester of the 1997 school year in the presence of two researchers. The subjects were further asked to bring home a copy of the questionnaire to both parents and to return it within ten to fourteen days.

Measurements

Adolescents questionnaire

Future hopes and fears. Adolescents were requested to write down their hopes and fears for their own futures. There were nine numbered lines allowed for the hopes and nine for the fears and each respondent was free to write down up to nine hopes and nine fears.

The subjects were further asked to assess (1) the age when these hopes and fears could come true (temporal extension); (2) the extent to which the occurrence of each hope and fear depended on external or internal factors through a four-point bipolar rating scale (1-totally outer factors / 4-totally up to me; control belief); and finally (3) the probability that each hope or fear could be actualized on a five-point bipolar rating scale (1-it will surely happen / 5-it won't happen; level of realization).

Content analysis and scoring. Each hope and fear reported by adolescents was then coded independently by two assessors and placed in one of the eleven life domain categories worked out during the pre-analysis and based on those used most frequently in the literature (Seginer 1992; Nurmi 1994; Nurmi et al. 1995): work/career, schooling/education, marriage/family, leisure activities (traveling, sport, and music), property (becoming a rich [wo]man, owning a house, etc.), friends, health/life/death, love/dating/sex, self in general (becoming famous, being happy, etc.), self as an adolescent (becoming a good boy-girl, scared to put on weight, etc.), and global/political issues (peace and war). Content analysis reliability, measured by the percentage rates of agreement between the two rates of agreement between the two raters was 95 percent for adolescents' hopes and 93 percent for adolescents' fears.

The following scores were calculated both for adolescent data:

(1) the total number of hopes and fears;
(2) the thematic differentiation index, which is the total number of future life domains contemplated;

(3) the salience index, which is the total number of hopes or fears concerning a specific life domain category;

(4) the relative score, that is, the salience index divided by the number of total hopes or fears expressed by all the subjects which can range from 0 to 1; and

(5) the number of domains shared by parents and children.

Parent-adolescent communication. The respondents were requested to answer twenty items on a five-point scale ranging from "strongly agree" to "strongly disagree" from the Parent-Adolescent Communication Scale by Barnes and Olson (1985). This scale measures the quality of parent-offspring communication and is composed of two sub-scales.

The Openness scale focuses on the free flowing exchange of information, both factual and emotional, as well as on the perception of the lack of constraint and degree of understanding and satisfaction experienced in the interaction. Examples of items regarding Openness in communication are: "My father/mother is always a good listener," "When I ask questions, I get honest answers from my father/mother."

The Problems scale focuses on the negative aspects of communication: hesitancy to share, negative styles of interaction, and selectivity and caution in what is shared. Examples of items measuring the existence of Problems in communication are: "There are topics I avoid discussing with my father/mother," "I don't think I can tell my father/mother how I really feel about some things." The consistency of the scale was measured on an Italian sample composed of 1120 adolescents and parents with the Cronbach's Alpha equal to .82 (Lanz 1997). The adolescents were requested to appraise communication with their mothers and separately with their fathers.

Parents' Questionnaire. Questionnaires analogous to those filled out by adolescents were administered to parents: they were asked to assess their hopes and fears for their child's future . For the content analysis and scoring of hopes and fears, we used the same categories and indices used for adolescents. Content analysis reliability, measured by the percentage rates of agreement between the two rates of agreement between the two raters was, 92 percent for parents' hopes and 90 percent for fathers' fears. They also filled out the parent's version of the Parent-Adolescent Communication Scale by Barnes and Olson.

Results

The adolescents' point of view

The analysis of the mean scores of the numbers of hopes and fears showed that the adolescents have an optimistic vision of the future: the mean number of

Table 1: Means and Standard Deviation of Number of Future
Orientation Statements and Thematic Differentiation Index

	Adolescents		Parents		
	Mean	SD	Mean	SD	t
Number of hopes	4.49	2.03	2.49	1.52	12.80**
Number of fears	2.73	1.64	1.64	1.41	9.33**
Thematic differentiation index for hopes	3.47	1.46	2.18	1.22	15.27**
Thematic differentiation index for fears	2.29	1.30	1.43	1.14	9.67**

** $p<.01$

hopes quoted is greater than that of fears.

The means for the salience indeces for each of the eleven domains of adolescents' hopes are given in Figure 1.

The results showed the adolescents most often mentioned expectations related to future occupation, future family, education, and leisure activity. These results confirm the findings of numerous studies carried out on adolescents' future orientation (Nurmi 1993; Seginer 1995). The analysis of the "relative

Figure 1: Means of Salience of Hopes for Each Life Domain

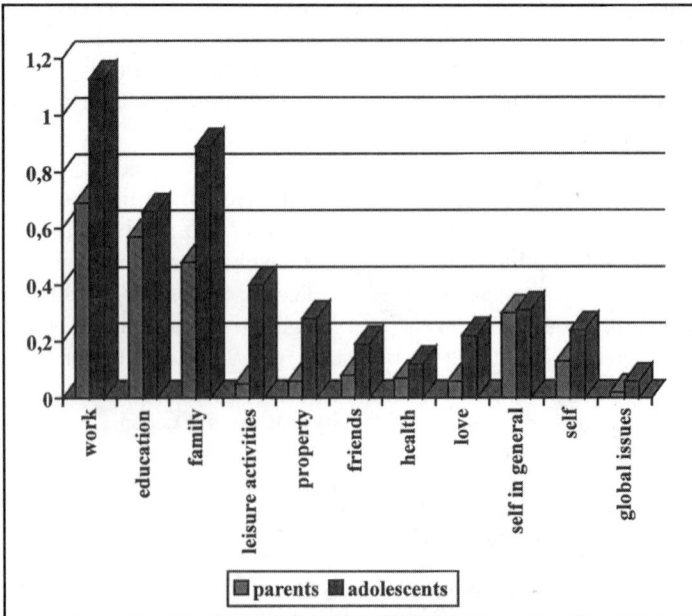

Table 2: Relative[a] Frequency of Hopes and Fears of Different Domains

Domains	Hopes				Fears			
	Adolescents		Parents		Adolescents		Parents	
	Mean	SD	Mean	SD	Mean	SD	Mean	SD
Works	0.35	(0.23)	0.35	(0.22)	0.35	(0.19)	0.37	(0.28)
Education	0.28	(0.16)	0.36	(0.23)	0.41	(0.22)	0.34	(0.24)
Family	0.31	(0.14)	0.26	(0.12)	0.37	(0.20)	0.18	(0.10)
Leisure activities	0.27	(0.15)	0.18	(0.10)	0.27	(0.11)	0.19	(0.08)
Property	0.23	(0.10)	0.21	(0.19)	0.32	(0.28)	0.13	(0.05)
Friends	0.22	(0.08)	0.13	(0.08)	0.36	(0.20)	0.31	(0.24)
Health	0.19	(0.09)	0.17	(0.09)	0.49	(0.27)	0.44	(0.25)
Love	0.21	(0.08)	0.14	(0.06)	0.37	(0.22)	0.21	(0.14)
Self in general	0.29	(0.20)	0.31	(0.23)	0.48	(0.29)	0.33	(0.21)
Self	0.24	(0.14)	0.22	(0.14)	0.36	(0.19)	0.28	(0.21)
Global issues	0.24	(0.09)	0.21	(0.14)	0.38	(0.20)	0.24	(0.14)

[a] Number of hopes/fears related to each domain divided by the total number of subject's hopes/fears

scores" (Table 2) revealed similar pattern of results.

The mean salience scores for fears are presented in Figure 2. First of all, comparing Figure 1 and Figure 2, we can point out that, in general the mean

Figure 2: Means of Salience of Fears for Each Life Domain

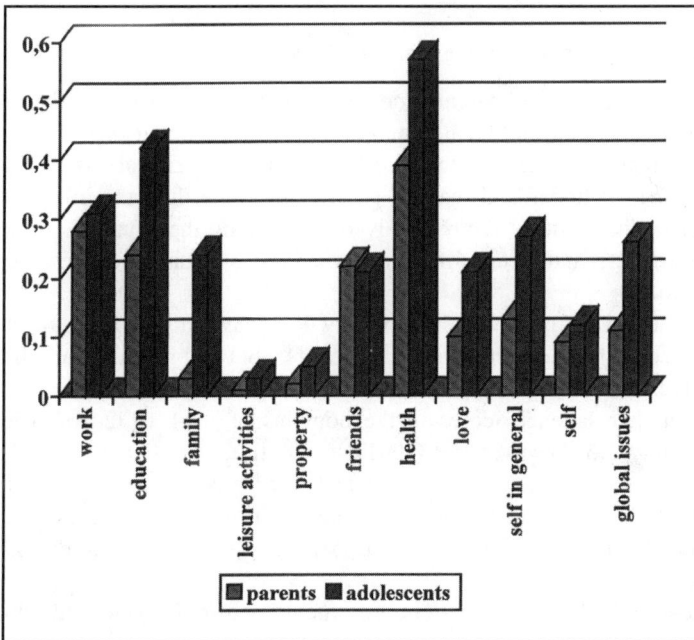

salience scores regarding fears are lower than those regarding hopes. In other words, fears are spread in more domains than hopes. As matter of fact, regarding fears, no relevant domains emerged except for health and education, while the hopes are gathered into four domains. The results for the "relative scores" concerning fears (Table 2) showed a similar pattern of results.

Parents' point of view

The analysis of the mean scores of parents' hopes and fears showed that the parents also have an optimistic vision of the future for their children: the mean number of hopes quoted is greater than that of fears.

The salience indices for each of the eleven domains of hopes and fears are presented in Figure 1. The results showed that parents most often mentioned expectations related to future occupation, future family, and education. Parents thus turn out to be most interested in goals having to do with the transition to adult life (normative). The analysis of the "relative scores" (Table 2) revealed a similar pattern of results.

The mean salience scores for fears are presented in Figure 2. First of all, comparing Figure 1 and Figure 2, we can point out that, in general the mean salience scores regarding fears are lower than those regarding hopes. The domains most frequently mentioned were work, education, friends and health. The results for the relative scores were similar to those of salience scores.

The comparison between the two generations

The comparison between parents and their offspring indicates, firstly, that the adolescents have more articulated and complex views about their own futures and are increasingly attentive to more life areas than their parents: in fact, the mean number of hopes and fears is greater, as is the thematic differentiation index. The adolescents, directly involved in planning their futures, are able to embrace a greater number of life domains and thus to have a more articulated perspective.

Our data reveal, however, that not only do adolescents express expectations more related to the perspective of the life course, but that parents share the same perspective. The comparison[2] of the two generations showed that adolescents obtained higher salience scores in the domains of work ($t(324) = 6.30$, $p < 0.001$), family ($t(324) = 6.25$, $p < 0.001$), leisure time ($t(324) = 9.58$, $p < 0.001$), wealth ($t(324) = 6.11$, $p < 0.001$), and affectivity ($t(324) = 5.07$, $p < 0.001$) than their parents. In the domains of school, health, self in general, self as an adolescent, and global political issues the two generations obtain similar salience scores.

Likewise, both parents and children mentioned those typical life domains that are socially shared as far as growing up and becoming an adult are concerned, such as future occupation, future family, and future education. The t-test analyzes showed significant differences between parents and adolescents for the domains of school ($t(324) = 3.25$, $p < 0.001$), family ($t(324) = 6.51$, $p < 0.001$), and world ($t(324) = 3.19$, $p < 0.002$). Here, also, adolescents obtained higher salience scores than did their parents.

If these data lead us to believe that parents' plans regarding their children's future differ substantially from those of adolescents themselves, at least in terms of the domains mentioned, the t-tests carried out on the relative scores show significant differences only with respect to hopes concerning school, to which parents assign greater importance than offspring ($t(100) = 3.49$, $p < 0.001$).

Parents and offspring differ the most in terms of the domains regarding hopes, as opposed to fears, in which differences in only four domains were found. Taken together, these preliminary results show that the adolescents took into account those domains associated both with the transition to adulthood and existential matters (such as love, sex, friends, etc.); on the contrary, parents focused on life areas essentially related to adult life, underestimating aspects more closely related to the existential worlds of actual adolescents.

The parent-child agreemen. The comparison of the dyads

In the second part of our study, the analytical unit is constituted by the dyads father/child and mother/child. In this case, fathers and offspring and mothers and offspring from the same family were compared. Since the variability due to gender turns out to be particularly important in family relationships, subsequent calculations took into account this factor.

First of all, we calculated for each dyad the number of domains held in common, that is, quoted both by children and fathers or by children and mothers. The range for shared domains regarding hopes is between 0 and 4; for fears it is between 0 and 3.

Table 3: Number of Shared Domains: Percentage

Number of Shared Domains Works	Hopes				Fears			
	Father/ Adolescent		Mother/ Adolescent		Father/ Adolescent		Mother/ Adolescent	
	Male	Female	Male	Female	Male	Female	Male	Female
0	27.1	31.1	22.9	22.6	65.0	63.3	63.6	61.6
1	38.6	32.8	37.9	35.0	27.9	28.8	25.7	26.0
2	24.3	26.6	26.4	31.6	7.1	5.6	8.6	9.6
3	9.3	9.6	11.4	10.7	0.0	2.3	2.1	2.8
4	0.7	0	1.4	0.0	–	–	–	–

As these percentages demonstrate (Table 3), about a third of the dyads do not share even a single hope, while the percentage doubles in the case of fears. No differences linked to adolescent gender emerged, no significant results being given by the chi squared.

In order to understand which expectations and fears parents and children share, we calculated the percentage of dyads in agreement for each domain. We took into consideration the content categories that were mentioned by at least 15 percent of the subjects (Nurmi 1993).

This procedure demonstrated that, in the realm of hopes, parents and off-spring, irrespective of gender, share above all the domains related to work (male/father 50.7 percent; female/father 43.5 percent , male/mother 53.6 percent; female/mother 49.7 percent), school (male/father 23.6 percent; female/father 23.6 percent; male/mother 32.1 percent; female/mother 29.4 percent) and family (male/father 23.6 percent; female/father 29.4 percent; male/mother 27.1 percent; female/mother 32.8 percent), that is, the domains connected to a normative transition. Furthermore, in the case of fears only, males share with their parents worries about health (male/father 17.1 percent; male/mother 20.0 percent). Fears related to wealth and leisure time were not chosen by either the father/offspring or the mother/offspring dyads.

In order to further analyze the hopes in the three domains (profession, education, future family) that were chosen most frequently either by mothers and children or by fathers and children, we also calculated the age of realization, control belief, and probability of actualization. For the purpose of parents' and children's expectations, we applied the paired t-test. As regards the age of realization (Table 4) results showed that both parents and children conceived of the three major life areas (school, work, future family) in terms of an equal "temporal stepping", confirming the idea of a "cultural prototype" proposed by Nurmi (1991): finishing one's education (first) getting a job, (second) and getting married (third). The temporal perspective for achieving goals in these domains is by the age of thirty, both for parents and offspring, irrespective of the child's gender. Differences were found in both dyads regarding the domain of school: males and females think they will be able to finish their studies sooner than their parents think likely.

With respect to the category of work, it was found that males agreed with both mothers and fathers on a realization age while females hoped to realize their goals in this domain sooner than their parents thought likely. In other words, mothers and fathers who expressed agreement with their daughters' occupational aspirations expected them to be realized at a later age than their daughters did. As for the domain of family, the only significant difference found was between fathers and sons: sons expect to form a family at an earlier age than their fathers

Table 4: Temporal Extension of Hopes by Adolescent's and Parents' Gender

	Son	Father		Daughter	Father		Son	Mother		Daughter	Mother	
Extension as Age	Mean (SD)	Mean (SD)	t (df)	Mean (SD)	Mean (SD)	t (df)	Mean (SD)	Mean (SD)	t (df)	Mean (SD)	Mean (SD)	t (df)
Work	25.58 (6.67)	23.82 (3.78)	ns	22.98 (3.29)	24.20 (3.69)	2.08 (48)	24.24 (7.01)	24.88 (4.64)	ns	22.69 (3.76)	24.27 (3.30)	2.63* (55)
School	21.04 (4.56)	22.68 (3.47)	2.30* (24)	19.78 (4.61)	22.71 (3.58)	3.41 (38)	20.59 (4.53)	22.45 (3.30)	3.34* (30)	20.15 (4.13)	22.52 (3.70)	3.61* (40)
Family	28.37 (3.85)	30.26 (3.23)	2.60* (25)	26.53 (3.76)	27.26 (2.08)	ns	29.00 (3.74)	29.57 (2.33)	ns	27.12 (3.34)	28.04 (2.67)	ns

*$p < 0.05$

think possible.

Turning now to the levels of control (Table 5), it was found that in both dyads, male and female adolescents expressed a more internally located control than their parents did regarding the domains of work and school. The adolescents believe themselves to be more capable of determining the course of events concerning school and work than their parents think possible. The only exception was found in the father/daughter dyad, who agree with respect to control belief concerning school. On the one hand, these results may indicate that parents underestimate their children's capacities but, on the other hand, may express the adult generation's greater awareness of the difficulties that a young person may encounter in the course of finishing his/her education and entering the work

Table 5: Control Belief of Hopes by Adolescent's and Parents' Gender

	Son	Father		Daughter	Father		Son	Mother		Daughter	Mother	
Extension as Age	Mean (SD)	Mean (SD)	t (df)	Mean (SD)	Mean (SD)	t (df)	Mean (SD)	Mean (SD)	t (df)	Mean (SD)	Mean (SD)	t (df)
Work	3.08 (6.67)	2.64 (3.78)	3.14* (54)	3.17 (0.52)	2.71 (0.78)	3.56* (55)	3.01 (0.81)	2.67 (0.72)	2.38* (58)	3.11 (0.64)	2.84 (0.57)	2.97* (63)
School	3.58 (4.56)	3.16 (3.47)	3.03* (28)	3.53 (0.50)	3.36 (0.68)	ns	3.58 (0.73)	3.22 (0.40)	2.68* (35)	3.71 (0.45)	3.43 (0.62)	2.92* (45)
Family	2.87 (3.85)	3.07 (3.23)	ns	2.96 (0.48)	3.14 (0.48)	ns	2.92 (0.56)	3.08 (0.58)	ns	2.89 (0.55)	3.07 (0.46)	ns

*$p < 0.05$

place. With respect to the family domain no significant differences were found.

The same life areas (school and work) also differentiated the two generations in terms of the probability estimation of goal realization (Table 6). In this case, however, both sons and daughters were found to be more pessimistic than their parents, giving evidence of not believing that their expectations are realisable. In particular, males and females differ from fathers with respect to the work and school domains. Differences between mothers and children were found regarding the work domain in the case of daughters only and regarding the school domain in the case of sons only. In the family domain, daughters were found to differ from both parents in their perceptions of the possibilities of realizing this expectation. The probability of realization is linked to knowledge of the external conditions existing in the social context in which the plan is to be realized. It is not by chance that the areas the adolescents believe to be the least realisable are those to do with work and school, areas which, in the Italian con-

Table 6: Level of Realization of Hopes by Adolescent's and Parents' Gender

	Son	Father		Daughter	Father		Son	Mother		Daughter	Mother	
Extension as Age	Mean (SD)	Mean (SD)	t (df)	Mean (SD)	Mean (SD)	t (df)	Mean (SD)	Mean (SD)	t (df)	Mean (SD)	Mean (SD)	t (df)
Work	2.79 (0.92)	2.23 (0.77)	3.14* (55)	2.64 (0.70)	2.27 (0.82)	2.42* (54)	2.81 (0.97)	2.50 (0.74)	ns	2.68 (0.76)	2.33 (0.78)	2.82* (64)
School	2.55 (0.83)	2.11 (0.54)	3.44* (28)	2.33 (0.81)	1.95 (0.72)	2.17* (42)	2.38 (0.86)	2.10 (0.70)	2.28* (34)	2.21 (0.77)	1.99 (0.56)	ns
Family	2.20 (0.69)	2.19 (0.75)	ns	2.39 (0.78)	2.0 (0.66)	2.63* (40)	2.28 (0.80)	2.07 (0.67)	ns	2.28 (0.73)	1.97 (0.66)	2.65* (46)

* $p < 0.05$

text, are especially problematic.

As for fears regarding the health domain, fathers and sons who chose this domain did not differ with respect to the age of realization, control belief, and the probability of realization.

Quality of Communication, Control Belief and Level of Realization

In order to test the relationship between the quality of communication and the number of domains shared by parents and offspring, we calculated the correlation index in the various dyads (mother/child; father/child). This analysis didn't give significant results. Thus, the number of shared domains does not turn out to be connected to relationship quality.

For each of the three domains most frequently chosen, we probed the relationship between the quality of communication and levels of control and optimism expressed by the adolescents. For each domain a series of ANOVAs were carried out with two factors between (communication quality [high/low] X gender).

The interaction between the two factors turned out to be significant for the level of realization in the work domain ($F(1) = 5.07$, $p < 0.05$). The analysis of the interaction revealed that daughters who report better communication with their fathers have a higher level of optimism with respect to their professional aspirations (M = 2.53, SD = 0.70) as compared to male (M = 2.91, SD = 0.92) and as compared to girls who perceive worse communication (M = 2.82, SD = 0.84).

Perceptions regarding communication with mothers is a significant factor for control levels ($F(1)$ = 5.88, p < 0.005) in the domain of school. In particular, adolescents who report above average communication with their mothers were found to have more internally located control (M = 3.44, SD = 0.63) as compared to adolescents who perceive worse communication (M = 3.66, SD = 0.47).

It is worth emphasizing that communication quality influences the variables of control and optimism with respect to the realization of hopes. In general we can hypothesize that being able to count on good relationships makes it possible for the adolescent to plan his/her future, to feel responsible, and to be able to imagine the future in an autonomous way, that is, in a different way from how his/her own parents imagine it.

Discussion and Conclusion

The aims of the present study were, first, to compare parents' and adolescents' perspectives regarding adolescents' future orientation and, secondly, to analyze the relationship between parent-child communication and adolescents' future orientation.

The data showed that parents and adolescent offspring from Italian families share a positive vision of the future, characterized more by hopefulness than by fear. When imagining their children's future, however, parents "anchor" it to a limited number of domains while the younger generation evidences a more composite and complex vision of the domains constituting their future lives. In addition, while parents list hopes and fears regarding only the life domains connected to a normative transition to the adult world (school, work, family, success), their children, in accordance with other research (Nurmi 1987, 1989; Seginer 1988a, 1988b), consider other areas less clearly linked to a stereotypical transition, such as leisure time, wealth and affectivity/sexuality to be integral parts of their future lives. The presence of long-term goals in children's and parents' representations can be seen as a necessary precondition for the setting of personal goals, exploring future options, obtaining information useful for planning, and committing oneself to making the transition (Seginer 1992).

The presence, in the offspring's data, of goals having less to do with the stereotypical aspects of assuming roles and more to do with areas that the adolescent, for the first time in his/her life, is able to manage independently, can be understood as an indicator of the younger generation's capacities and needs. These capacities are those necessary for facing the transition to adulthood, taking into account the multiplicity of life's aspects and joining social aspects and social time with personal aspects and personal time—inseparable elements for the construction of one's own agenda (Ricci Bitti 1993). The needs are of two kinds: on the one hand, those connected to the difficult transition the adolescent is living and to his/her condition as a human being in formation who "stands on the threshold" of life with different and more complex needs and aims than in childhood, but which are also greater and more diversified than those of parents, who have already completed the transition; on the other hand, those connected to the necessity of engaging him/her self in realizing long-term aspirations, but also aspirations that can be actualized in the immediate future.

Nowadays short term aspirations assume a crucial role because they allow adolescents to articulate their cognitive, emotional, and social skills while waiting to carry out the transition to adulthood. We can hypothesize that this protects the youngster from possible feelings of frustration and dissatisfaction that might arise from pursuing goals that appear to be reachable only in the distant—or too distant—future. This confirms Beck's hypothesis (1992) that young people need to set goals that they can easily govern and reach in the short-term, such as the management of their leisure time, as well as pursuing long-term goals which require greater dedication and even tenacity. In order to direct their own life, it is necessary for them to have both long- as well short-term aspirations. Moreover, we use the term "capacities" because the adolescents in the study, who are perhaps less naïve than their parents, truly see themselves as being a "planning agency for all of life's decisions" (Heinz 1996). We can further hypothesize that they believe themselves to be able to combine all the domains that interest them and reach the highest levels in their pursuits.

As the results showed, for both generations, the domains that are the most important, in terms of both hopes and fears, are those most connected to the normative areas, but to these we must add the domain of the self in general. In our opinion, this result could be understood as an indicator of the fact that parents and offspring conceive of the other domains not as self-referential areas, but as elements that, in a different manner, contribute to the definition and structuring of the self.

The comparison between the generations allowed us to highlight the differing degrees of involvement on the part of parents and children in planning the latter's future. In fact, while it was very clear that the generations shared a hopeful vision of adult life, it should be noted that adolescents expressed their hopes with greater incisiveness. This discrepancy between parents and children was more evident when parents' and adolescents' future hopes and fears were compared within family. There are only a few areas of hopes and fears, i.e., those related to work, school, family, and health that were chosen to be common. These areas once again essentially involve adult life and demonstrate the importance the transition to adult status assumes for both generations. The results concerning communication and hopes and fears enable us to underline that the agreement on hopes and fears was not related to the quality of communication. We can suppose that open communication allows for both sharing and expressing diversity among family members' points of view. Moreover, the data showed that parents and adolescents chose most frequently work domain as common topics of their future orientation, evidencing the centrality of this domain for both generations' future perspectives.

If, on the one hand, parents and children confirm the hypothesis that a "cultural prototype" exists regarding future orientation (Nurmi 1991) in that they agree on the order of the various normative steps involved in future planning (finishing one's education, entering the work force, building a family) and locate the actualization of these goals between the second and third decade of life, on the other hand, they differ as to temporal extension, control belief, and the possibility that their children's goals can be realized.

Adolescents and parents seem to have two different approaches. The young people believe themselves to be able to reach their goals and to be able to do so sooner than their parents think possible and yet, at the same time, they believe they are less likely to realize their aims. This result suggests two interpretations: this relative "pessimism" of adolescents may reflect a certain realism in the youngsters who, although seeing themselves as being competent, do not deny the objective difficulties of finding work today or finishing a course of study. Conversely, it could attest to a certain "fragility" in the adolescent, attributable to either the fear of "failing" or to the need to better understand how to manage his/her abilities and competencies in a world that inspires fear. Parents, for their part, have less faith in their children's opportunities but express greater optimism in their assessment of the probability of realizing goals.

The results also showed gender differences. Girls anticipated that they will finish their studies and enter the work force sooner than their parents think is likely, both being future events that they believe themselves able to control to a greater extent than in their parents' opinion. However, they shared perceptions with their parents as to the age at which they will realize the goal of starting a family and the possibility of controling this event, but are decidedly more pessimistic as far as the realization of all these goals is concerned.

The boys, in turn, anticipated that they will finish their studies sooner than their parents expect; they differ however only from their fathers' expectations about when they will start a family. While they agree with both parents on when they will enter the work force, they show a more internally situated locus of control and greater pessimism than their parents do as to the possibility of realizing school and work goals. They shared with parents the type of control they feel able to exert and the possibility of realization in the family domain.

The overall analysis of these data paint a surprising picture that differs from the results reached by earlier studies (Manganelli Rattazzi and Capozza 1993;

Rosnati 1996a): we find that there is greater agreement in perceptions of future expectations, not between mothers and daughters as previous studies have pointed out, but between mothers and sons, especially with respect to the two domains most closely connected to the transition to adulthood: family and work. This indicates that future plans are more fully shared by sons and mothers than by daughters and mothers. This may be due to the social and cultural transformations underway in our country which affect to a greater extent the development of female identity in the younger generations and result in less sharing between females of different generations (mother/daughter).

Other gender differences turned up regarding temporal extension, control belief, and the possibility of realizing set goals: parents and daughters showed a perceptual agreement concerning the family and school domains—while differences were found with respect to the work domain; parents and sons, however, showed perceptual sharing with respect to the domains of work and family, while differences were found in the area of school. This result implies that starting a family is a domain shared by the two generations both as an objective to be reached and in terms of means and age, which was found both among boys and girls. However, in the case of school and work, we find several differences linked to gender.

As regards the possibility of realizing their future plans, it seems that daughters experience within the family a situation of greater perceptive divergence from their mothers as compared to boys, and yet mothers are traditionally described as being their preferred confidantes. Bearing in mind that in Italy the entry of women into the work force in great numbers and the equal treatment of sons and daughters in terms of professional prospects are recent phenomena, we believe that the perceptual divergence found between girls and their mothers regarding the work domain is a clear indicator of the social changes underway in our country. Although mothers and daughters prioritize the choice of work in the daughters' future plans, they show substantial differences regarding the means to adopt in order to actualize this goal. The generation of mothers seems to counterbalance that of their daughters. The daughters predict an earlier entry into the work force, they see themselves as bearing more responsibility in realizing this event, and imagine it in essentially pessimistic terms. The mothers, perhaps being less naïve, are more realistic and aware of social ties and economic contingencies, and consequently perceive that their daughters will commence work at a later age, are more likely to take into consideration the possible influence situational factors can have on realizing this goal, and show greater optimism.

These results cause us to reflect upon possible future scenarios: In coming years, will the perceptual divergences between mothers and daughters regarding future occupational aspirations decrease or increase? What might the effects be of one or the other scenario? And, will daughters' aspirations find adequate fulfillment?

In order to complete the picture, we should add that communication with fathers also exerts a positive influence on daughters' expectations about realizing professional goals. We can underline that the girls are sensitive, as far as our object of analysis is concerned, to the relationship with both parents.

In closing, we can assert that the family seems to carry out a real function of mediation, orientation, and personalized adjustment within the social context (Scabini 1995). In this study, the family was found to be composed of two generations (adults and adolescents) that appear to find commonality and the possibility of encounter, especially with respect to patterns having to do with being adults and social stereotypes and role models. The lack of substantial differences found in the agreement between adolescents with mothers, and also with fathers, regarding domains mentioned in their children's future planning, once again confirms the cohesiveness of the adult generation.

These preliminary results suggest that hopes and fears for the future are only partially shared by the two generations. The parents appear to focus primarily on the transition to adult status but at the same time defer its actualization. In this, they reveal their role in "lengthening," or temporally extending, the family transition (Scabini and Cigoli 1997), thus making it possible for offspring to take time to evaluate which choices to make and possibly to experiment with "trial" choices.

This study has made it possible to shed light on the complex intergenerational relational interaction underlying Italian adolescents' future orientation. It is only on the basis of an intergenerational approach that future research will be able to study and verify the effect of family relationships on future orientation.

The present study demonstrates that navigating through adolescence is not a solitary voyage for young people, but profoundly involves their parents, as well. From this derives the importance of investigating the adolescent universe not only from a purely individual point of view but also from the relational perspective by taking into consideration the primary context of socialization for adolescents—their families—and, in particular, their relationships with their fathers and mothers.

Recent Italian and international surveys show a clear increase in the importance families have in the lives of modern day adolescents as compared to past generations. In recent years the family has assumed a crucial role in young people's transition to adulthood and not only in Mediterranean countries, like Italy, where the phenomenon of the young adult is widespread, but also in other contexts in which this role has traditionally been less pronounced. As our results showed, the family carries out an important function of mediation with the social realm and of providing personalized guidance for its younger generation who thus feel supported in the difficult passage to adult status.

There are several practical implications of the present research's results for psycho-social workers. First of all, they provide useful information for those who organize and run courses aimed at helping parents to carry out parental functions and roles during the children's adolescence. Secondly, they offer precise information on gender differences in future orientation to those who run services aimed at providing academic or professional guidance to adolescents. Finally, the present study's results can be profitably used in the context of the family clinic in order to shed light on the complex interactions usually present in families in these joint phases of the life cycle of parents and their adolescent children.

References

Aneshensel, C.A. & Rosen, B.C. (1980). Domestic roles and sex differences in occupational expectations. *Journal of Marriage and the Family, 2*, 121–131.

Barnes, H. & Olson, D. (1985). Parent adolescent communication and the circumplex model. *Child Development, 56*, 438–447.

Bell, L., Cornwell, E. & Bell , D., (1988). Peer relationships of adolescent daughters: A reflection of family relationships patterns. *Family Relations, 37*, 171–174.

Beck, U. (1992). Risk society: Towards a new modernity. London: Sage.

Boesch, E.E. (1991). Symbolic action theory and cultural psychology. Berlin: Springer.

Buchmann, M. (1989).*The script of life in modern society. Entry into adulthood in a changing world*. Chicago: The University of Chicago Press.

Capozza, D. & Manganelli Rattazzi, A.M. (1995). Aspettative giovanili d'istruzione e occupazione all'inizio degli anni '90 [Young peolple education and occupational expectations at the beginning of the Ninties]. In F. Bimbi (ed.), *Le radici del cambiamento. Uno sguardo di genere sulla società veneta* [The roots of change. A gender look at the Venetian society]. Milano: Franco Angeli, pp.88–119.

Carrà, E. & Marta, E. (Eds.) (1995). *Relazioni familiari e adolescenza* [Family relationships and adolescence]. Milano: Angeli.

Cavalli, A. & De Lillo, A. (Eds.) (1993). *Giovani anni '90: terzo rapporto IARD sulla condizione giovanile in Italia* [Young people of the Nineties: third report IARD about the juvenile conditions in Italy], Bologna: Il Mulino.

Cavalli, A. & De Lillo, A. (1996)(Eds.). *Quarto rapporto IARD sulla condizione giovanile in Italia* [Fourth report IARD about the juvenile conditions in Italy]. Supplemento a Laboratorio IARD, 4.

Cigoli, V. (1985). Adolescenza. In E. Scabini (Ed.) *L'organizzazione famiglia tra crisi e sviluppo* [Family organisation between crisis and development] (pp. 202–239). Milano: Franco Angeli.

Cigoli, V. (1995). Transizioni familiari [Family transition]. In E. Scabini & P. Donati (Eds.), *Nuovo lessico familiare* [New family lexicon] (pp.107–116). Milano: Vita e Pensiero.

Cordon, J.A.F. (1997). A comparative study. *Journal of Family Issues, 18*, 576–607.

Cospes (1995). L'età incompiuta [The unfinished age]. Torino: Elle Di Ci.

Dornbusch, S.M., Petersen, A.C., & Hetherington E.M. (1991). Projecting the future research on adolescence. *Journal of Research on Adolescence, 1*,57–82.

Feetham, S.L. (1988). *Developing programs of research of families*. Paper presented at University of Pennsylvania School of Nursing, March,1,Philadelpia, PA.

Gillies, P., Elmwood, J. M., & Hawtin, P. (1985). Anxieties in adolescents about employment and war. *British Medical Journal, 291*, 383.

Greene, A. & Grimsley, M. D. (1990). Age and gender differences in adolescents' preferences for parental advice: Mum's the word. *Journal of Adolescence Research, 5*, 396–413.

Grotevant, H. D. & Cooper, C. R. (1983). *Adolescent development in the family.* London: Jossey-Bass.

Heinz, W.R. , (1996). L'ingresso nella vita attiva in Germania e Gran Bretagna. In A. Cavalli & O. Galland (Eds.), *Senza fretta di crescere* [The prolonged adolescence] (pp. 83–102)-Napoli:Liguori.

Hurrelman, K. (1993). Introduction: Interdisciplinary and international approaches to research on adolescence. In K. Hurrelmann (Ed.) *International handbook of adolescence* (pp. 37–71). Westport, CN: Greenwood Press.

Lamm, H., Schmidt, R.W., & Trommsdorff, G. (1976). Sex and social class as determinants of future orientation in adolescent. *Journal of Personality and Social Psychology, 34,* 317–326.

Lanz, M. (1997). Parent-offspring communication scale: applicazione ad un campione italiano [Parent-offspring communication scale: validity on an Italian sample]. *Bollettino di Psicologia Applicata,224,* 33–38.

Larsen, A. &. Olson, D. (1990). Capturing the complexity of family systems: integrating family theory, family scores and family analysis. In T. Draper & A. Marcos. *Family variables. Conceptualization, measurement and use* (pp. 19–47). London : Sage Publication.

Leccardi, C. (1996). *Futuro breve: le giovani donne e il futuro* [Brief future: young women and future]. Torino: Rosenberg & Sellier.

Lewin, K. (1946). Behavior and development as a function of total situation. In L.Carmichael, *Manual of child psychlogy.* (pp.) New York: Harper.

Lewin, K. (1948). Resolving social conflicts. New York: Harper.

Malmberg, L-E & Norrgard, S. (1997). Adolescents' ideas of normative life-span development and personal future goals. *Journal of Adolescence* (in press).

Manganelli, A.M. & Canova, I. (1995). *Progetti di istruzione, aspettative giovanili e influenze familiari* [Educational plans, juvenile expectations and family influences]. Quaderni di Psicologia, 17, Bologna: Patron Editore.

Mangannelli Rattazzi, A.M. & Capozza, D. (1993). Famiglia, ruoli sessuali e aspettative giovanili [Family, sex roles and juvenile expectations]. In M. Cusinato (Ed.) *Ruoli e vissuti familiari. Nuovi approcci* [Roles and family life experiences. New approaches] (pp. 84–103) Firenze: Giunti.

Mooney Marini, M. (1987). Measuring the process of role change during the transition to adulthood. *Social Science Research, 16,* 1–38.

Mooney Marini, M. & Brinton, M.C., (1984). Sex-typing in occupational socialization. In B.Reskin (Ed.) *Sex segregation in the workplace* (pp. 192–232). Washington: National Academic Press.

Mooney Marini, M. & Greenberg, E. (1978). Sex differences in occupational aspirations and expectations. *Sociology of Work and Occupations, 5,* 147–178.

Noller, P. & Callan, V. (1990). Adolescents' perceptions of the nature of their communication with parents. *Journal of Youth and Adolescence 19,* 349–362.

Nurmi, J.-E. (1987). Age, sex, social class, and quality of family interaction as determinants of adolescents' future orientation: A developmental task interpretation. *Adolescence, 22,* 977–991.

Nurmi, J.-E. (1989). Adolescents' orientation to the future: development of interest and plans, and related attributions and affects, in the life-span context. *Commentationes Scientiarum Socialium, 39.* Helsinki: The Finnish Society for Sciences and Letters.

Nurmi, J.-E. (1991). How do adolescents see their future? A review of the development of future orientation and planning. *Development Review, 11,* 1–59.

Nurmi, J.-E. (1993). Adolescent development in an age-graded context. The role of personal beliefs, goals and strategies in the tackling of development tasks and standards. *International Journal of Behavioral Development, 16,* 169–189.

Nurmi, J.-E. (1994). The development of future-orientation in a life-span context. In Z. Zaleski, (Ed.). *Psychology of Future Orientation* (pp. 63–74) Lublin: Catholic University of Lublin Press, Faculty of Social Sciences.

Nurmi, J.-E. & Pulliainen, H. (1991). The changing parent-child relationship, self-esteem, and intelligence as determinants of orientation to the future during early adolescence. *Journal of Adolescence, 14,* 35–51.

Nurmi, J.-E. Poole, M. E., & Seginer R. (1995). Tracks and transition—A comparison of adolescent future-oriented goals, explorations, and commitments in Australia, Israel, and Finland. *International Journal of Psychology, 30,* 355–375.

Nuttin, J. R. (1984). *Motivation, planning, and action. A relational theory of behavior dynamics.* Louvain: Lawrence Erlbaum Associates.

Piaget, J. & Inhelder, B., (1955). *De la logique de l'enfant à la logique de l'adolescent* [From the child logic to the adolescent logic]. Paris: PUF,

Pulkkinen, L. (1984). A longitudinal perspective on future-orientation in late adolescence. Paper presented at the XXIII International Congress of Psychology, September, Acapulco.

Pulkkinen, L. (1990). Home atmosphere and adolescent future orientation. European *Journal of Psychology of Education, 1,* 33–43.

Rampazzi, M. (1985). Il tempo biografico. In A. Cavalli (Ed.) *Il tempo dei giovani* [The time of the young people] (pp.149–283). Bologna: Il Mulino.

Reiss, D. & Oliveri, M. (1991). The family's conceptions of accountability and competence: a new approach to the conceptualization and assessment of family stress. *Family Process, 30* 193–214.

Ricci Bitti, P. (1993). Organizzare la vita quotidiana e progettare il futuro: l'esperienza temporale degli adolescenti [To organise daily life and to plan the future: adolescents' temporal experience]. In A. Palmonari (Ed.), *Psicologia dell'adolescenza* [Psychology of adolescence] (pp. 147–157). Bologna: Il Mulino.

Ricolfi, L. (1984). Il paradigma della reversibilità [The paradigm of reversibility]. In A. Tarozzi & G. Bongiovanni (Eds.), *Le imperfette utopie* [The imperfect utopias] (pp.31–57). Milano: Franco Angeli.

Rosnati, R. (1995). Adolescenti e aspettative per il futuro: una prospettiva familiare [Adolescents and future expectations: a family perspective]. In Carrà, E., &. Marta, E. (Eds.) *Relazioni familiari e adolescenza* [Family relationship and adolescence] (pp. 78–98). Milano: Franco Angeli.

Rosnati, R. (1996a). Gender Differences and Adolescent Life Plans: a Family Point of View. In M. Cusinato (Ed.), *Research on family resources and needs across the world* (pp. 375–394). Padova: LED,

Rosnati, R. (1996b). La famiglia di fronte al futuro scolastico e professionale degli adolescenti [Family and adolescents' educational and occupational future plans]. In C. Castelli & L. Venini (Eds.), *Psicologia dell'orientamento scolastico e professionale* [Psychology of educational and professional orientation] (pp. 122–141). Milano: Franco Angeli.

Scabini, E. (1995). *Psicologia sociale della famiglia* [The social psychology of the family]. Torino: Bollati Boringhieri.

Scabini, E. & Galimberti, C. (1995). Adolescents and young adults: A transition in the family. *Journal of Adolescence, 18*, 593–606.

Scabini, E., & Marta, E.(1996). Families with late adolescents: social and family topics. In Cusinato M. (Ed.), *Research on family resources and needs across the world.* (pp. 177–197). Padova: LED.

Scabini, E. & Cigoli, V. (1997). An evolutionary slowdown or a breakdown in the generational transition? *Journal of Family Issues, 18*, 608–626.

Seginer, R. (1988a). Adolescent facing the future: Cultural and sociopolitical perspective. *Youth and Society 19*, 314–333.

Seginer, R. (1988b). Social milieu and future orientation: The case of kibbutz vs. urban adolescents. *International Journal of Behavioral Development, 11*, 247–273.

Seginer, R. (1992). Future orientation: Age-related differences among adolescent females. *Journal of Youth and Adolescence, 21*, 421–437.

Seginer, R. (1995). Hopes and fears of anticipated adulthood. In G.Trommsdorff (Ed.), *Kindheit und jugend in verschienden kulturen* [Childhood and adolescence in different cultures]. Juventa Verlag Weheim und Muchen, pp.225–247.

Sherrod, L., Haggerty, R., & Featherman., D., (1993). Introduction: Late adolescence and the transition to adulthood. *Journal of Reserach on Adolescence, 3*, 217–226.

Sroufe, L. W. (1991). Assessment of parent-adolescent relationships: Implications for adolescent development. *Journal of Family Psychology, 5*,21–45.

Trommsdorff, G. (1983). Future orientation and socialization. *International Journal of Psychology, 18*, 381–406.

Trommsdorff, G., Burger, C., & Fuschule, T. (1982). Social and psychological aspects of future orientation. In M. Irle (Ed.), Studies in decision making (pp. 167–194). Berlin: De Grutyer.

Youniss, J. & Ketterlinus, R. (1987). Communication and connectedness in mother- and father-adolescent relationship. *Journal of Youth and Adolescence,16*, 265–280.

Youniss, J. & Smollar, J. (1985). Adolescent relations with mothers, fathers and friends. Chicago: University of Chicago Press.

Notes

1. The parents' scores is the mean of scores obtained by both mother and father.
2. Since the salience scores showed a distribution that was concentrated between the values of 0 and 1, a square root transformation was carried out before the t-test adjusted Bonferroni analysis.

CHAPTER 8

Family Context and the Development of Adolescent Decision-making

BRUNA ZANI, HARKE A. BOSMA, DJURRE H. ZIJSLING,
AND TERRY M. HONESS

Introduction

It has been suggested that the adolescence is a socially constructed object and a "joint developmental enterprise" between parents and adolescents (Youniss 1983; Scabini 1995). This means that the way in which adolescence is construed by parents and adolescents is likely to have important implications for the mutual accommodations which take place in the family, and the development of adolescents' self-direction. Recent perspectives in the psychological literature of teenagers and families emphasize changes occurring with age in the patterns of these relationships, from an asymmetrical to a more mutual and symmetrical pattern (Goodnow and Collins 1990; Grotevant and Cooper 1983; Noller and Callan 1991; Youniss and Smollar 1985).

This process of mutual accommodation is probably based on a conception of adolescent behaviors that are seen as appropriate to this period of development. This affects features of family life, such as the pace at which autonomy is given, the way rules are applied and the authority that is exerted by parents, as well as adolescent responses to the actions of parents. It is likely that the degree of concordance between adolescent and parental constructions will influence the quality of family relationships, leading to conflict when considerable divergence exists. Adolescence is, therefore, considered as a phase of transformation of the pre-existing bonds. This implies the need to focus attention on the major developmental tasks for both adolescents and parents, such as the dynamics between autonomy and control, the development of adequate ways of communication, and the management of conflict and disagreements.

In addition, the role of the social/cultural context in which adolescent development takes place is currently being increasingly acknowledged in the literature (Gecas and Seff 1990). Indeed, much of the research work is primarily concerned with North-American adolescents. This raised questions about the generalizability of findings to adolescents living in other cultural settings.

This position has implications on the methodological level. Whereas most studies on parent-adolescent relationships are based on reports from adolescents only and on cross-sectional data, we assume it is desirable, if not necessary, to (a) consider the different perspectives of parents and adolescents on the family functioning and on their relationships, (b) pursue longitudinal research, and (c) analyze the possibility of cultural/national variation in the time table and in the content of normative expectations concerning adolescent development.

Major Changes in Parent-adolescent Relationships

According to what might be described as this social-relational perspective, changes in parent-adolescent relationships are gradual and continuous, rather than simply dictated by age or maturation (Laursen and Collins 1994). In particular, as Smetana and Asquit (1994) have underlined, parents' views and behaviors change slowly, and parents are slow to relinquish control over day-to-day matters they consider important to their children's well-being. In contrast, adolescents expect to have more behavioral autonomy and earlier control over normative activities than parents expect to grant. These discrepancies regarding the timing of self-governance are likely to lead to conflict (Holmbeck and O'Donnell 1991).

In respect of *autonomy*, for example, Smetana (1988) reported that parents and their children show changes in conceptions of parental authority versus adolescent autonomy between eleven and sixteen years of age. Adolescents conceive parental authority as appropriate on "moral" (e.g., lying to parents) and "conventional" issues, but not on such issues as choice of friends or style of dress, which tend to lead to conflicts (Smetana and Asquit 1994). These results are consistent with recent perspectives on adolescent development in an age-graded context (Nurmi 1993): young persons' and parents' conceptions of adolescence probably reflect age-graded normative expectations about appropriate adolescent behavior in the particular social-cultural context. This implies the possibility of cultural variation in the time table of normative expectations, as well as in their content.

In this regard, Kagitcibasi (1990) argues that parents' beliefs about child development and socialization are powerful contextual meaning systems that influence child-rearing behaviors. Cultural differences become particularly clear during adolescence, generating broad differences as regards freedom of action allowed in the various domains of everyday life. According to Kagitcibasi, the degree of separation and individual autonomy induced in child socialization is a crucial factor that shows cultural variability.

Communication is generally considered to be one of the basic dimensions of parent-adolescent relationships (Olson et al. 1983): supportive communication in the family stimulates the development of more positive identities and higher levels of social and coping skills in adolescents (Noller and Callan 1991). Research findings showed that there are differences in patterns of communication with mothers and fathers. Mothers are seen by adolescents as more open, more able to listen to problems, willing to understand and accept the adolescent's needs. Adolescents report more communication and higher levels of self-disclosure to their mothers, as well as more conflict with them compared to their fathers. Fathers are seen as more judgmental, less willing to be involved in discussion of feelings and problems. Parent-adolescent communication is also affected by the age and sex of the adolescent. Daughters communicate more with parents than sons, and generally have more positive interactions with their mothers than their fathers. Also, mothers describe their communication with their adolescents as more open than do fathers. Finally, it is noteworthy that there is a well established tendency for adolescents to present a more negative view of the family than do their parents. These different perceptions are likely to be the result of two kinds of biases: the parents' needs to present the family in a good light, and the adolescents' needs to develop a separate identity and to distance themselves from their parents (Noller and Callan 1991).

As regards *conflict,* under certain conditions (especially the form of conflict resolution), it is considered to make a positive contribution to the realignment of the parent-adolescent relationship and to the development of behavioral autonomy (Cooper 1988; Hill and Holmbeck 1986). According to many authors, parent-adolescent conflict is believed to be the highest and behavioral autonomy the lowest during early adolescence, when multiple transitions are occurring—both biological (e.g., puberty) and contextual (e.g., changes from family-like elementary schools to larger middle schools). Late adolescents are viewed as self-governing persons outside the home and conflict with parents is expected to be relatively low (Laursen and Collins 1994). It is in middle adolescence that findings are equivocal, with some researchers reporting high levels of conflict (Smetana 1989) and others reporting that conflict peaks in early adolescence and declines thereafter (Steinberg 1990).

Dowdy and Kliewer (1997) in their United States research on the contribution of dating status to the frequency and intensity of normative conflict and to behavioral autonomy, suggested that social role transitions in addition to age are important when trying to understand conflict patterns and processes across adolescence. They found, for example, that young people currently dating reported more frequent normative conflict with parents than did those not dating; and that females who were dating had more intense conflicts. Salient social transitions like dating appear to change the meaning or importance of normative mundane matters like clothes, or activity with family and friends. They conclude that "rather than being a function of age or grade per se, conflict frequency may differ according to the social developmental task in which parents and adolescents together are adapting."

It also appears important to analyze conflict more analytically, to consider not only the frequency of conflict or the topics around which it occurs, but also to consider the different ways or styles in which it may be expressed, to define the possible outcomes which may occur and to give a picture of the strategies employed in responding to situations which involve conflict. Focusing on these aspects (conflict management and outcomes) might serve to illuminate other aspects of adolescent development, such as adolescent's progress toward autonomy, which are related in some way to the characteristics of adolescent-parent relationships (see Jackson, Cicognani, and Charman 1996)

Gender Differences

Generally speaking, distinct social competencies are expected of boys and girls, especially during preadolescence and adolescence. For boys, the establishment of assertion, especially in the peer group, is of paramount importance for acceptance by both self and others. For girls, establishment of connectedness and communion within the relationships is pre-eminent; they are expected to have communal behaviors, e.g., empathy, sharing, cooperation, and play caregiving (Baumrind 1991; Fuhrman and Holmbeck 1995). Agentic behaviors of boys and communal behaviors of girls are considered gender-normative competencies and sex-typical conduct (Finnegan, Hodges, and Perry 1998). Such conventions appear to allow boys more time to become adults than girls: the moratorium of adolescence is much less obvious for girls than for boys. It appears that society is much more controlling in its demands put on girls.

These ideas are supported by Dekovic, Noom, and Meeus (1997) in their research about the expectations of adolescents and their parents with regard to developmental tasks during adolescence. The authors distinguish:
a) personal tasks (e.g., realizing what one's own strengths and weaknesses are);
b) relational tasks (e.g., having a boy/girlfriend); and
c) social and societal tasks (e.g., having a family and children and taking care of them).

They conclude "gender differences always mean that girls are expected to achieve all these tasks at an earlier age than boys." In respect of parents, gender differences relating to personal and relational tasks were found in mothers only, and those relating to social and societal tasks in both parents.

One explanation may be found in the slower psychological and pubertal development of boys. These differences must be looked at in the context of clearly different life-tasks imposed on boys and girls in the various stages of life. Archer (1996) reports an analysis of ninety-three societies from the ethnographic record by Low (1989): " ... boys are generally taught to be more aggressive, show more fortitude, and to be more self-reliant than are girls. Girls are consistently taught to be more industrious, responsible, obedient, and sexually restrained than are boys." Similar differences are reported by Schlegel and Barry (1991). They analyzed the data of a sample of 186 pre-industrial societies. In the socialization of adolescent girls, compliance is stressed more strongly than in the socialization of boys.

According to these authors, cultural gender differences in adolescence are rooted in the socio-biological necessity of minimizing possibilities for inbreeding. For that reason girls in these pre-industrial societies have more contact and intimacy with their mothers and, it might be argued, they therefore show adult autonomy and behaviors at an earlier age than do boys. Boys in general have more contacts with peers and thus function more outside the family sphere. When girls are allowed to enter the outdoor territory of boys, parents tend to be more restrictive with regard to their daughters than their sons because of the risks of impregnation. Especially when virginity and the economic advantages of marriage (dowry) are important, parents impose strong limitations with regard to the behavioral autonomy of their daughters outside the family home.

While Schlegel and Barry (1991) base their conclusions on their analyses of pre-industrial societies, feminist researchers of the life-world of adolescent girls in today's industrial western societies come to similar conclusions. A short overview of this literature (mostly of studies in the United Kingdom and the Netherlands; see also Wynn & White 1997, who discuss similar evidence from studies in the United States and Australia) is given by De Waal (1989). Girls, and groups of girls tend to move around far less in public spaces than boys. Most of their leisure time is spent indoors. When they do enter public spaces their behavior is more strictly controlled by their parents. De Waal also discusses other strong differences, such as the hierarchical organization of boys' groups versus the more egalitarian organization of groups of girls, the preference of girls for an intimate friendship with another girl while boys mostly go out with other boys in bigger groups, and the double sexual standard used by boys, but these differences are less relevant for this chapter.

Although most studies have focused on gender differences in parenting during infancy and childhood, there are a number of recent studies that do focus on adolescence. For example, Smetana and Asquith (1994) found that families with boys rather than girls employed rules concerning moral issues, whereas families with girls had more rules about personal issues. In addition, Cicognani and Zani (1998) reported studies on parents' perceptions of educational styles and their beliefs about the process of separation/individuation of their adolescent child. Results showed that fathers were more worried about the process of emancipation for female adolescents and they anticipated more difficulties in their future. Fathers' worries induced them to be more restrictive toward their daughters, e.g., in respect of their socializing and the times they were required to return home. In contrast, sons were allowed more freedom of action.

In addition, Cicognani and Zani report that mothers allowed sons more freedom to go out and encounter new experiences, indeed, some of the boys' requests were encouraged and considered to be signs of success in socialization. For daughters, the process of individuation involved more conflict, it was accompanied by problems in communication, by higher control and more restrictive attitudes toward adolescents' requests for more autonomy. This led to difficult negotiations, especially with the emergence of new affective and sexual needs.

As other researchers have shown, it also seems that strong gender differences are related to attitudes to adolescents' sexual experiences. The double standards actually applied by family and society are, by definition, clearly more restrictive for girls than for boys. Parents were likely to respond with greater tolerance to sexual explorations by their sons than to those of their daughters (Rosenthal 1994; Bonini & Zani 1991; Verhofstadt-Denève and Schittekatte 1998).

Other studies have suggested that parents' gender seems to be more relevant than adolescents' gender as a differentiating factor: for example, Marta (1997) in her research on Italian families has shown that mothers play a predominant role in the family and in the life of adolescents, while fathers are less closely involved in the family. Thus, Marta argues, Italian families appear to be "matrifocal," with the mothers over-involved in the rearing of their children and also in the transmission of social norms, while fathers, having abdicated their role as mediator between the private and social realms, find themselves in a no-man's land or else in search of a new role, still to be defined. This study seems to confirm Steinberg's finding (1987) that parents' gender appear to be more significant than adolescent gender in determining the quality of the parent-adolescent relationship, at least during late adolescence (sixteen to nineteen years). No difference emerged between boys and girls in their perceptions about their relationships with their parents, but adolescents do perceive differences in their relationships with their mothers and fathers.

A Cross-national Study on Parent-adolescent Relationships

Aims

We have conducted a study on the construction of adolescence in three European countries (Italy, the Netherlands, and Wales). In particular, two fundamental processes have been examined:

a)   The acquisition of autonomy. We examined "who has the final say' in a list of twenty-one topics. This list concerns more or less daily issues in the lives of adolescents and their parents. We assume that there are age-graded normative expectations with regard to these topics. Expectations about the age at which it is normal that an adolescent decides for him/herself on the topic in question. These expectations guide young people's navigation through adolescence.

b)   The extent to which disagreement/conflict occurs as adolescents seek to gain greater autonomy and independence from their parents. In particular, we investigated the different ways in which conflict is expressed and the possible ways in which it can be solved.

Our specific research questions are: What do adolescents perceive to be normal? What do mothers and fathers perceive to be normal? How do adolescents, fathers and mothers handle conflicts? Is there agreement between these three groups within a culture? Are there cultural differences?

The central questions for this chapter are: Are there differences in the normative perceptions relating to boys and girls? Are there gender differences in the ways in which parent-adolescent conflict is managed?

In respect of normative gender differences, different processes are arguably in operation: First, it could be said that younger generations no longer share the gender differentiated views of their parents. Recent research (Buzzi, Cavalli, and De Lillo 1997) reports that in the last years there has been a change in the young people's opinions toward a more symmetrical view of gender roles. Nevertheless, they are aware of what the societal (and parental) expectations are toward girls and boys. Second, we can therefore hypothesize that the traditional views concerning gender differences still persist among the adults. Finally, we would expect that the gender by generation differences evident in normative expectations would be complemented by age and gender differences in patterns of disagreement between parents and their adolescent children.

Sample and Procedures

Adolescents were recruited from schools in Bologna, Italy; Cardiff, Wales; and in Groningen, the Netherlands. The permission of parents and school authorities was obtained before testing. The sample at the first data collection (in 1993) included adolescents, male and female, of two age groups: thirteen and fifteen years old (for a total of 500 Italian, 397 British and 410 Dutch adolescents). Participants in Bologna and Groningen were contacted again two years later (in 1995), when they were, respectively, fifteen and seventeen years old. Only those subjects who took part in both waves of data collection are considered for the purposes of the longitudinal analyses presented here. Details of the sample of both waves (T1 and T2) are shown in Table 1. On all occasions, testing was carried out at school during class-time, and lasted for approximately forty minutes.

Table 1: Adolescent Sample

	Bologna				Groningen				Cardiff			
	Younger		Older		Younger		Older		Younger		Older	
	T1	T2	T1	T2	T1	T2	T1	T2	T1		T1	
Boys	144	78	97	78	91	65	87	64	101		100	
Girls	129	73	130	112	109	86	123	84	100		96	
Total	273	151	227	190	200	151	210	148	201		196	

Directly after testing, adolescents in Bologna and in Groningen were given envelopes containing test-material for their parents. Each parent received his/her test material in a separate envelope. Parents were specifically asked to complete the material independently of each other and without joint discussion, and to return completed questionnaire in a closed envelope to the researchers. Also a group of Welsh parents (55 fathers and 64 mothers) were asked to complete the questionnaire: they were not related to the adolescent sample, but they had adolescent children of the same age as the Welsh adolescent group. A total number of 422 mothers and 397 fathers in Bologna and 325 mothers and 302 fathers in Groningen returned the questionnaires. The parent groups in Bologna and Groningen were also contacted again in 1995. Details of the longitudinal parents sample are shown in Table 2.

Table 2: Parents Sample

	Fathers							
	Bologna				Groningen			
	Younger		Older		Younger		Older	
	T1	T2	T1	T2	T1	T2	T1	T2
Boys	111	58	64	34	70	50	64	48
Girls	112	56	106	64	72	55	96	62
Total	223	114	170	98	142	105	160	110

	Mothers							
	Bologna				Groningen			
	Younger		Older		Younger		Older	
	T1	T2	T1	T2	T1	T2	T1	T2
Boys	125	65	69	36	72	54	70	55
Girls	117	62	109	68	85	67	98	66
Total	242	127	178	104	157	121	168	121

Note: The number of particpants under T2 are the subjects that participated at T1 as well as at T2. Not included are subjects who participated at T2 but not at T1.

Measures

Data were collected by two different instruments:
The PADM. In order to explore ideas about adolescents' decision-making in the family context a new instrument was developed, the Perspectives on Adolescent Decision Making Questionnaire (PADM) (Bosma et al. 1992). The PADM

includes a comprehensive list of issues of concern within the adolescent-parent relationship. Its aim is to provide issue-specific information on adolescents' and parents' perspectives on who should have the final say, on behaviors that are seen as normal for adolescents of the same age-group, and on whether conflicts arise over decision-making. The version of the PADM used in the first wave of data collection included twenty-one issues which previous studies and pilot research work carried out in the Netherlands and in Italy (Cicognani, Xerri, and Zani 1996) had shown to be important aspects of decisional autonomy during early and middle adolescence. Examples of the issues are the following: "helping with household chores" (Chores), "Time to go to bed" (Bedtime), "how to behave at meal time" (Manners), "where to go when going out" (Going out), "what time to come home at night" (Time in). The full list is presented in Bosma et al. (1996).

Participants were required to answer four question for each issue, using the same format. The questions concerned whether the adolescent decides for him/herself over the issue (Adolescent choice); whether the parents feel the adolescent should or should not ... (Parental feeling); whether there are arguments between parents and adolescent about ... (Arguments); whether it is normal for someone of the adolescent's age to decide for him/herself on ... (Normality). For example:

I decide myself whether I smoke or not	yes	?	no
My parents feel I should not smoke	yes	?	no
I often have arguments with my parents about smoking	yes	?	no
I think it is normal for someone of my age to decide for him/herself about smoking	yes	?	no

Findings concerning the validity of the PADM have been reported elsewhere (Bosma et al. 1996 reported data on a sample of Italian adolescents, and Jackson et al. 1998 reported similar data on a sample of Dutch adolescents). There was a parallel form of PADM for completion by parents.

The version of the PADM used in the second wave of data collection included some slight changes in the types of issues. Some items were excluded, since they were deemed no longer relevant among fifteen and seventeen year old adolescents (e.g., hobbies and sports); others issues were added (future orientation, political participation, and holidays). For the purpose of the present analyses, only the seventeen issues that were tapped at both waves of data collection were considered: chores, bedtime, table manners, language, visits to parents, privacy, smoking, alcohol, sweets, look/style, money, going out, time in at night, choice of friends, sex, church, and homework.

The PADM data can be analyzed in different ways: (1) individual items, (2) the total number of "yes" answers, e.g., in respect of the "is it normal to decide" question and (3) use of constellations across topics (Bosma et al. 1996). When the focus is on the individual items, frequencies can be computed and compared, e.g., which percentage of the fifteen-year old adolescents say that they decide for themselves about smoking, compared to thirteen-year olds. The second way concerns the number of times a subject says "yes" in response to the same type of question across topics, e.g., the question about whether it's normal or not that someone of the subject's age decides for him/herself. In this way it is possible, for example, to compare different groups with regard to the number of topics about which they say they decide for themselves.

A third way to analyze the PADM data concerns the constellations of answers to the four questions per topic. A participant can for example answer "yes" to the question whether he decides for himself about smoking, "yes" to the question whether his parents express negative feelings about smoking, "no" to the question whether he and his parents often argue about smoking and "yes" to the question whether it is normal for boys of his age to decide for themselves about smoking. This "YYNY" constellation can be seen as an indication of a conflict-free compromise between the adolescent's and parent's views on smoking, supported by the view that it is normal that the adolescent decides for himself.

Other constellations which were often used by participants are "norm-supported conflict (YYYY)," "norm-supported autonomy (YNNY)," and "accepted parental authority (NYNN)." Subjects can also be given a score for how often they use each constellation across the topics (Bosma et al. 1996).

The Disagreement Scale. The disagreements questionnaire was based on that developed in the United States by Rands, Levinger, and Mellinger (1981) and Camara and Resnick (1989) for use by adults in connection with their relationships with partners and ex-partners. It was piloted on a British sample of adolescents, concerning their relationships with their parents and subsequently modified. In particular, several items were dropped since they were manifestly relevant only to adult encounters and, following further trials, the terminology was simplified to enable use with young people age eleven and upward. Trials of the questionnaire for use with adults, concerning their relationships with their adolescent children prompted no further changes, so the form of the questionnaire was unchanged for parents. In its original form, the questionnaire was worded into English; it was then translated and back translated into Dutch by both native Dutch and English speakers. The same procedure was followed for the Italian version.

The final form of the questionnaire involves three parts for the description of disagreements between parents and children (see Honess et al. 1997 for details of all three parts). In the first part, the respondent (whether mother, father,or adolescent) describes the other's behavior when there is a disagreement about something which is important to both, e.g., "He gets really wound up and starts shouting" (Response on a four point scale: Not at All (1), Not too Well (2), Fairly Well (3), and Very Well (4) for each question). Second, the respondent describes their own behavior in the same type of situation. The third requires the respondent to think about the *outcomes* of disagreements. Answers are provided on a five point scale (Never (1), Almost Never (2), Once in a While (3), Fairly Often (4), and Very Often (5) for each question. For example, "I end up going along with what he wants."

Gender Differences: Summary of Previous Publications

Some results derived from this cross-sectional and longitudinal data set have been published elsewhere (Bosma et al. 1996; Honess et al. 1997) or are reported in publications in preparation (Jackson et al.; Zani et al.). A short overview of the relevant results from these sources will be presented first. Further results, based on analyses done for this chapter will be presented after that.

In Bosma et al. (1996) the first results with the PADM have been published. These results concern the Italian adolescent sample at Time 1 only. In general the PADM variables are strongly related to age. Fifteen-year-olds say that they decide for themselves on more topics and more often think that it is normal that they decide for themselves than thirteen-year-olds. A gender effect was only found for the incidence of parental feelings, girls reported parental restrictions in more topics than boys did. Clear age differences were also found with regard to the use of constellations. These latter variables, however, did not show any gender differences. In conclusion, the patterns found in this first study with the PADM were highly similar for adolescent boys and girls.

As regards the Disagreement scale, the results of a cross sectional analysis of the responses provided by Cardiff adolescents are reported in Honess et al. (1997). In brief, consistent with expectations, there were clear age and gender differences. Older children reported more aggression, more escalation, and lower intimacy outcomes. Of particular interest was that adolescent girls (valuing both closeness and autonomy) reported higher levels of frustration in outcomes, whereas boys reported relatively more escalation. Overall, mothers were experienced as more compromising and as fostering greater intimacy in comparison to fathers. These results were moderated by family constitution. In particular, whether or not there had been a parental separation in the family. For example, those mothers living with a partner were reported as more confrontative than mothers from non-divorcing families, and adolescents living with mother alone reported more frustration and escalation outcomes.

Zani and Cicognani (1999) analyzed Italian disagreements data, provided by both adolescents (500 subjects, male and female, thirteen and fifteen years) and their parents (393 fathers and 420 mothers). The purpose was to assess similarities and differences in descriptions according to adolescents' age and gender, the parent and the perspective adopted (self vs. other-description). A second purpose was to investigate the relationship between the different styles of conflict and their outcome. Results showed an increase in a more aggressive style, with outcomes of frustration and escalation from thirteen to fifteen years. Parents (especially mothers) describe their relationship with female adolescents as more conflictual. Adolescents describe mothers as more compromising in their style than fathers. Moreover, adolescents are described by all family members as more aggressive. The adoption of a more aggressive style is associated with outcomes of frustration and escalation, whereas a compromising attitude leads to a greater intimacy.

Zani et al. (2000) have analyzed the longitudinal changes in PADM scores in the Groningen and Bologna adolescent samples. The results indicate strong age-related changes in the number of yes-answers across topics. From thirteen years of age to seventeen years of age adolescents report an increase in the number of topics in which they decide for themselves and in which they think it's normal that someone of their own age decides for her/himself. The number of topics in which parents impose limitations and in which there are disagreements decreases. There were no clear gender differences in these longitudinal changes.

Jackson et al. (in preparation) analyzed and compared all of the PADM data (of the adolescent and parent samples) from wave one of the data collection from all three sites in order to explore site, age, and gender differences on the eight main PADM variables (these are described in Bosma et al. 1996): the number of yes-answers for each type of question (adolescent choice, parental feeling, arguments, normality) across the topics, and the use of the four constellations (YYYY, YYNY, YNNY, NYNN), also across topics. A brief overview of the main findings is provided here. For the adolescents, there are strong main effects with regard to site and age on almost all of the dependent variables. In all three sites, younger male and female adolescents have less freedom to decide for themselves than older adolescents. There are only two general sex differences: girls' parents are more likely to be perceived as having feelings about issues (and imposing limitations) and girls are more inclined to use the constellation "norm-supported compromise." All of these findings apply to each of the three sites. The differences between the sites can best be seen as differences in timing: tshe Cardiff adolescents have more freedom to decide at an earlier age than the adolescents from Bologna. Similarly, Bologna adolescents decide earlier than those from Groningen.

Highly similar trends were found for the samples of the mothers and the fathers. Basically there are no sex differences, but clear age differences, and very strong differences between the three sites, in the parents' perceptions of adolescents' decision making. From the perspective of the parents, adolescent decision making follows very similar broad patterns across populations. Both mothers and fathers in all three sites perceive younger boys and girls as having less freedom to decide for themselves than older. They also perceive relatively little conflict with their adolescent children, similar to the adolescent findings, there are strong timing differences between sites in the parents' perceptions. Cardiff adolescents have more freedom to decide at an earlier age than the adolescents from Bologna. Bologna adolescents decide earlier than the adolescents in the Groningen sample. Furthermore, there are strong similarities in the site differences across the three groups (the site differences found among the adolescents have also been found among the samples of mothers and fathers) and the differences between these three groups within sites are mostly similar across sites (the differences between the adolescent and parent samples are similar in each of the three sites).

Jackson et al. (in prep.) interpret this data as evidence for the existence of cultural scripts with regard to adolescent development in decision-making. Within each site, each group uses the same script but gives it its own twist (adolescents of all ages claim more room than parents are prepared to grant); across the three sites these scripts are highly similar, the reported differences are mainly differences in timing. Moreover, what is important for this chapter, is that, according to the parents, these scripts are similar for both sexes. Only the adolescents themselves see gender differences, which was contrary to expectations.

The absence of clear gender differences is surprising in the light of the gender differences reported by other authors (Smetana and Asquith 1994; Steinberg and Silverberg 1986) and the hypotheses presented in the introduction of this chapter. However, it is possible that the relatively global analysis reported earlier may mask gender differences in response to either individual items and/or separate PADM. In fact, this more discrete analysis does lead to important gender differences.

Results

Gender Differences in Normative Beliefs about Autonomous Decisions

The two wave longitudinal results for this analysis has been described above. In the following analysis (Tables 3 to 5), we focused on examining the PADM item: "I think it's normal for someone of my age to decide for him/herself about [topic]." This focus was chosen because it best reflects the age-graded expectations with regard to the topics. These expectations guide young people's navigating through adolescence. Moreover, this type of item correlates strongly with the item of the questionnaire: "I decide myself whether [topic]" (Bosma et al. 1996). The entries in the tables are percentages of yes answers. These percentages are given for boys and girls separately, for the younger group at Time 1 and Time 2, and for the older group at T1 and T2. Chi-square analyses were use to compare the gender differences.

Table 3 concerns the adolescents in the Italian and Dutch samples. Of the seventeen PADM topics that have been used in both waves, nine showed sex differences in one or more of the different age groups. The Italian groups more often reported significant differences than the Dutch groups (thirteen versus seven times).

Table 3: Gender Differences According to the Adolescents
in the Italian and Dutch Samples

	Adolescents							
	Italy				**The Netherland**			
	Younger		**Older**		**Younger**		**Older**	
	Wave 1	**Wave 2**	**Wave 1**	**Wave 2**	**Wave 1**	**Wave 2**	**Wave 1**	**Wave 2**
Chores								
Boys	65.4	69.2	60.3	67.9	40.0	35.4	**42.2**	39.1
Girls	54.8	59.2	61.3	77.7	25.6	25.6	**25.3**	28.6
Bedtime								
Boys	56.4	**70.5**	70.5	**82.1**	17.2	32.3	34.4	79.7
Girls	65.8	**84.9**	74.8	**92.0**	14.0	48.2	38.6	78.6
Visits								
Boys	33.3	52.6	59.0	73.1	64.6	81.3	**73.4**	92.1
Girls	39.7	50.7	62.2	75.9	74.4	89.5	**88.0**	90.5
Privacy								
Boys	76.6	**78.2**	83.3	**78.2**	92.3	96.9	92.2	96.9
Girls	89.0	**90.4**	82.9	**89.3**	90.7	96.5	96.3	100
Smoking								
Boys	30.8	**55.1**	59.0	**71.8**	47.7	83.1	65.6	93.8
Girls	32.9	**71.2**	62.5	**83.9**	43.0	73.3	71.1	86.9
Going Out								
Boys	44.9	**74.0**	43.6	75.6	**53.8**	73.8	**70.3**	90.6
Girls	37.0	**57.5**	36.6	68.8	**32.6**	69.8	**51.2**	84.5
Time In								
Boys	19.2	**35.9**	24.4	46.2	10.8	26.2	**35.9**	**67.2**
Girls	9.6	**17.8**	14.3	40.2	7.0	22.4	**14.3**	**47.6**
Sex								
Boys	**67.5**	79.5	**78.2**	87.0	20.3	67.7	64.1	89.1
Girls	**31.5**	69.9	**63.4**	86.6	24.4	65.5	50.0	86.9
Homework								
Boys	**75.6**	**85.9**	94.8	**87.0**	**61.5**	81.5	82.8	81.0
Girls	**91.8**	**95.9**	94.6	**97.3**	**79.1**	86.0	83.3	81.7

Note: Table entries are percentage yes-answers to the type-4 question per topic ("It is normal for an adolescent to decide for him/herself about...").
Bold-face figures indicate a significant ($p < .05$) gender-difference.

For two topics a difference was found in only one of the eight groups in which gender comparisons have been made. It concerned chores and visits, both for the Dutch fifteen-year olds from the first wave. In the case of chores, the Dutch fifteen-year old boys at T1 more often said that it is normal that a boy of their age should decide for himself than the fifteen-year old Dutch girls (chi-square (1) = 4.69, p <.05). The other Dutch groups and the younger Italian groups showed a similar tendency, but these differences are not statistically significant. With regard to visits, the fifteen-year old Dutch girls at T1 more often said that it is normal for adolescents of their age to decide for themselves (chi-square (1) = 5.08 , p <.05). A similar tendency, though not significant, can be seen for the Dutch adolescents of the younger age groups from wave one and wave two.

For three topics (bedtime, privacy, and smoking) gender differences were found for the older Italian age groups within each cohort. In each case, girls more often said that it is normal for adolescents of their age to decide for themselves (bedtime, fifteen-year olds from the second wave: chi-square (1) = 4.49, p <.05; seventeen-year olds: chi-square (1) = 4.25, p <.05; privacy, fifteen-year olds from the second wave: chi-square (1) = 4.20, p <.05, seventeen-year olds: chi-square (1) = 4.37, p <.05; smoking: fifteen-year olds from the second wave: chi-square (1) = 4.19, p <.05, seventeen-year olds: chi-square (1) = 4.07, p <.05). A similar tendency can be seen for the younger Italian groups in each of the two cohorts, but these differences are not statistically significant. In none of the Dutch groups were significant differences found for these topics, nor is there a tendency comparable to what has been found for the Italian adolescents.

With regard to the topic of sex, gender differences were found for the Italian groups from the first wave, but for none of the Dutch groups, though the Dutch fifteen-year olds from the first wave showed a similar, though not significant difference. In each of the two younger Italian groups, for each cohort, boys more frequently than girls said that it is normal for adolescents of their age to decide for themselves about sex (thirteen-year olds: chi-square (1) = 19.54, p <.001; fifteen-year olds from the first wave: chi-square (1) = 4.76, p <.05). For this topic there seems to be a clear developmental trend in the sense that the gender difference in Italy is big for the thirteen-year olds, while it has completely disappeared in the case of the seventeen-year olds.

The topics "going out" and "time in" also showed higher percentages of boys who see it as normal for adolescents of their age to decide for themselves. This was the case in each group, in Italy as well as in the Netherlands, but these differences were not always significant. In Italy they were significant for the fifteen-year olds from the second wave (going out, chi-square (1) = 4.54, p <.05; time in, chi-square (1) = 6.23, p <.05), while in the Dutch samples differences were found for the thirteen-year olds (going out, chi-square (1) = 6.90, p <.05), the fifteen-year olds from the first wave (going out, chi-square (1) = 5.51, p <.05; time in, chi-square (1) = 9.43, p <.005), and the seventeen-year olds (time in, chi-square (1) = 5.65, p <.05).

Finally, gender differences were found for the topic of homework for three of the Italian and one of the Dutch groups. The significant differences all go in the same direction: Girls more frequently indicated that it is normal for adolescents of their age to decide for themselves about homework. This applies to the thirteen-year olds in Italy (chi-square (1) = 7.11, p <.005) and in the Netherlands (chi-square (1) = 5.59, p <.05), and to the fifteen-year olds from the second wave (chi-square (1) = 4.48, p <.05) and the seventeen-year olds (chi-square (1) = 7.57, p <.005) in Italy.

In five of the seventeen topics, the fathers of boys and girls reported differences (see Table 4). Similar to the perceptions of the adolescents, there are topics where the fathers of girls score higher and topics where the fathers of boys score higher. Another similarity is that the number of differences found in Italy is higher than in the Netherlands (9 versus 3). Generally, the total number of differences is about half of the number found for the adolescent groups.

Table 4: Differences Between Fathers of Boys and Girls
in the Italian and Dutch Samples

	Fathers							
	Italy				The Netherland			
	Younger		Older		Younger		Older	
	Wave 1	Wave 2	Wave 1	Wave 2	Wave 1	Wave 2	Wave 1	Wave 2
Manners								
Boys	**25.0**	43.1	**36.4**	**55.9**	4.1	14.0	8.3	27.1
Girls	**44.6**	52.7	**64.1**	**78.1**	10.9	20.0	16.1	27.4
Going Out								
Boys	22.8	**50.0**	11.8	58.8	24.0	**48.0**	33.3	75.0
Girls	13.0	**25.9**	18.8	48.4	14.5	**24.1**	37.1	67.2
Sex								
Boys	**55.4**	**66.7**	**64.7**	79.4	**28.0**	**48.0**	29.2	50.0
Girls	**21.4**	**45.5**	**28.1**	66.1	**9.1**	**20.0**	27.4	48.4
Church								
Boys	77.2	87.9	**64.7**	91.2	76.0	82.0	81.3	85.4
Girls	87.5	90.9	**87.5**	95.3	61.8	74.5	77.0	85.5
Homework								
Boys	71.9	91.2	82.4	**76.5**	54.0	63.3	52.1	68.8
Girls	80.4	89.1	84.4	**96.9**	49.1	69.1	64.5	72.6

Note: Table entries are percentage yes-answers to the type-4 question per topic ("It is normal for an adolescent to decide for him/herself about...").
Bold-face figures indicate a significant (p < .05) gender-difference.

There are three topics in which the Italian fathers of boys and of girls showed significant differences, but in each case only for one age group. In only one of the corresponding topics (going out) is there also a difference between the Dutch fathers of sons and the fathers of daughters. With regard to "going out," both the Italian (chi-square (1) = 6.85, p <.05) and Dutch fathers (chi-square (1) = 6.48, p <.05) of the fifteen-year old boys in the second wave score much higher than the fathers of the fifteen-year old girls. The fathers more often said that it is normal for fifteen-year old boys of the age of their sons to decide for themselves than do the fathers of fifteen-year old daughters. With regard to church and homework, the fathers of daughters scored higher (church, fifteen-year olds for the first wave, chi-square (1) = 7.10, p <.05; homework, seventeen-year olds, chi-square (1) = 10.09, p <.005). For these age groups and for these two topics Italian fathers of daughters more often said that it is normal for girls of the age of their daughters to decide for themselves.

With regard to manners, the Italian fathers of girls in three of the four age groups scored substantially higher. They more often say that it is normal for a girl of the age of their daughter to decide for herself (fathers of the thirteen-year olds, chi-square (1) = 4.76, p <.05; fathers of the fifteen-year olds from the first wave, chi-square (1) = 6.74, p <.05; fathers of the seventeen-year olds, chi-square (1) = 5.27, p <.05). There is some similar tendency in the data of the Dutch fathers with regard to manners, but none of these differences is statistically significant.

Sex is the only topic where Italian as well as Dutch fathers of sons and of daughters showed differences. These differences were also consistent across the four Italian age groups, although not always significant, and the younger Dutch samples. The older Dutch samples did not show any difference. Fathers of sons far more often said that it is normal for boys of the age of their sons to decide for themselves about sex. This was found for the Italian fathers of the thirteen-year olds (chi-square (1) = 13.63, p <.001), of the fifteen-year olds from the second wave (chi-square (1) = 5.12, p <.05), the fifteen-year olds from the first wave (chi-square (1) = 12.30, p <.001), and for the Dutch fathers of the thirteen-year olds (chi-square = 6.32, p = .021) and the fifteen-year olds from the second wave (chi-square (1) = 9.24, p <.005).

In eight of the seventeen topics, the mothers of boys and girls reported differences (see Table 5). Similar to the perceptions of the adolescents and the fathers, there are topics where the mothers of girls score higher and topics where the mothers of boys score higher. Another similarity with the data of the adolescents and the fathers is that the number of differences found in Italy is higher than in the Netherlands (8 versus 3). Generally, the total number of differences is comparable to the number of differences found in the groups of the fathers and about half of the number found for the adolescent groups.

Table 5: Differences Between Mothers of Boys and Girls
in the Italian and Dutch Samples

	Mothers							
	Italy				The Netherland			
	Younger		Older		Younger		Older	
	Wave 1	Wave 2	Wave 1	Wave 2	Wave 1	Wave 2	Wave 1	Wave 2
Chores								
Boys	**39.3**	61.3	45.7	55.6	16.7	16.7	14.8	29.1
Girls	**61.7**	61.3	50.7	55.2	13.4	13.8	19.7	26.6
Manners								
Boys	**25.4**	51.6	55.6	72.2	14.8	16.7	18.5	27.3
Girls	**43.3**	59.7	65.7	73.5	13.4	20.3	16.7	31.8
Language								
Boys	**20.6**	50.8	41.7	58.3	14.8	24.5	25.9	45.5
Girls	**40.0**	55.7	49.3	66.2	16.4	21.5	28.8	38.5
Privacy								
Boys	56.5	**68.8**	66.7	63.9	77.8	74.1	83.6	78.2
Girls	55.7	**50.8**	55.2	73.1	76.1	71.9	80.3	80.3
Money								
Boys	33.3	61.3	**27.8**	58.3	56.6	60.4	59.3	72.7
Girls	43.5	65.0	**51.5**	55.2	53.7	56.1	51.5	71.2
Going Out								
Boys	15.9	36.5	13.9	58.3	15.1	**37.0**	24.1	**83.6**
Girls	13.3	26.2	10.3	44.8	13.4	**15.4**	21.2	**50.8**
Sex								
Boys	**46.7**	**71.4**	50.0	80.6	18.9	**51.9**	31.5	53.7
Girls	**24.1**	**37.7**	36.8	70.1	12.3	**26.2**	24.2	54.5
Church								
Boys	**71.4**	92.2	80.6	94.4	75.9	83.3	76.4	92.5
Girls	**87.1**	86.9	75.0	88.1	62.1	75.0	77.3	83.3

Note: Table entries are percentage yes-answers to the type-4 question per topic ("It is normal for an adolescent to decide for him/herself about...")
Bold-face figures indicate a significant ($p < .05$) gender-difference.

There are six topics in which a difference was found in only one age group. All of these differences concerned the Italian mothers. The mothers of girls of thirteen years of age more often said that it is normal for girls of the age of their daughters to decide for themselves about chores (chi-square (1) = 6.03, p <.05), manners (chi-square (1) = 4.40, p <.05), language (chi-square (1) = 5.48, p <.05), and church (chi-square (1) = 4.66, p <.05). In the other age groups, the gender differences in these topics were not found. For the Italian mothers, gender only seems to make a difference in these topics for the younger adolescents. With regard to money, the Italian mothers of the fifteen-year old girls from the first wave also more often said that it is normal for girls of the age of their daughters to decide for themselves (chi-square (1) = 5.38, p <.05). The gender difference is reversed in the case of privacy. For this topic more mothers of the fifteen-year old boys from the second wave said that it is normal for boys of the age of their sons to decide for themselves (chi-square (1) = 5.38, p < .05).

Going out and sex are the only topics where mothers of boys and girls showed differences in more than one age group. With regard to going out more mothers of boys said that it is normal for boys of the age of their sons to decide for themselves. This difference is significant in the case of the Dutch mothers of the fifteen-year olds of the second wave (chi-square (1) = 7.33, p < .01) and the seventeen-year olds (chi-square (1) = 14.31, p <.001). There is also a similar tendency in the groups of mothers of the corresponding Italian age groups. This gender difference thus becomes evident when the adolescents grow older.

The differences between mothers of boys and of girls were also very evident in the domain of sex. Similar to going out, more mothers of boys said that it is normal for boys of the age of their sons to decide for themselves. These differences are also rather consistent across age groups, in particular across the younger three groups (Italian mothers of thirteen-year olds, chi-square (1) = 6.53, p <.05; Italian mothers of fifteen-year olds from the second wave, chi-square (1) = 14.23, p <.001; Dutch mothers of fifteen-year olds from the second wave, chi-square (1) = 8.28, p <.005). For this topic the gender difference has more or less disappeared at the age of seventeen.

Gender Differences in Escalation at Disagreement across Countries

In this chapter, we report preliminary analyses of the negative outcomes of disagreements for all respondents—mothers, fathers, and adolescents for both Wave 1 and Wave 2 Dutch and Italian data (see Honess et al. 1997 for a full description of the questionnaire). First, it was important to establish the factor stability of the outcome scales between sites (in this case Italy and Holland) and between respondents (mother, father, and adolescent). Exploratory and confirmatory factor analysis resulted in two stable factors: escalation and intimacy. It is the former that is discussed here, made up of the following eleven items:

1. I end up feeling annoyed or angry
2. I feel as though talking about it was a waste of time
3. I end up feeling hurt
4. He ends up feeling annoyed or angry
5. He feels as though talking about it was a waste of time
6. He ends up feeling hurt
7. Later he uses what I've said against me
8. We start out disagreeing about one thing and end up arguing about lots of things

9. He agrees to change but never does it
10. Later I use what he has said against him
11. Afterward he goes ahead and does what he wants anyway.

Item analysis by respondent and by site on the first occasion of testing (combining thirteen- and fifteen- year olds) gave remarkably stable standardized alpha co-efficients: For Italy, fathers' reports gave alpha = 0.78, adolescents' reports of outcomes with father gave alpha = 0.83, mothers' reports gave alpha = 0.84, and adolescents reports of outcomes with mother gave alpha = 0.82. The corresponding co-efficients for Holland were: 0.83, 0.84, 0.83, and 0.84.

The data were analyzed using the GLM repeated measures procedure of SPSS version 8.0. The design involved two repeated measures: First, respondent (i.e., parent and adolescent—matched within families), second, time (i.e., data collection at times 1 and 2). The between subject factors were age (younger vs. older), gender, and site (Holland vs. Italy).

Consider first, descriptions of escalation outcomes with the father. There were no significant effects involving time of data collection, nor were there significant interaction effects involving respondent. There was, however, a simple main effect involving respondent. Across all sub-groups, children reported more negative outcomes than their fathers: $F_{(1,331)} = 43.35$ p< .001, M score 26.18 vs. M of 24.20. There was, overall, more reported hostility from the Italian respondents in comparison to the Dutch respondents, $F_{(1,331)} = 18.52$, p<.001 (M score 26.20 vs. M of 23.93). There were also age band by site effects, $F_{(1,331)} = 8.43$, p< .005: This stemmed from a difference in Italy *only*. There were powerful increases in reported hostility between age bands on both occasions: From a mean score (for father and adolescent combined) of 24.31 to 28.08 (thirteen to fifteen years old at time 1), and 24.90 to 27.43 (fifteen to seventeen years old at time 2).

We now turn to descriptions of escalation outcomes with the mother. Consistent with the father data, there was, overall, more reported hostility from the Italian respondents in comparison to the Dutch respondents, $F_{(1,355)} = 15.59$, p<.001 (M score 26.13 vs. M of 24.06). From both sites, children reported more negative outcomes in comparison with their mothers: $F_{(1,355)} = 15.31$, p<.001 (M score 25.70 vs. M of 24.39), with the exception of the thirteen year old children where there were no differences. Finally, in contrast to the results with fathers, there were gender differences, $F_{(1,355)} = 5.75$, p<.05: for all sub-groups, both mothers and adolescents reported higher levels of escalation for girls (M score 25.69 vs. M of 24.22).

Conclusions and Discussion

The research presented in this chapter is part of a wider project involving both adolescents and parents in three European countries (i.e., Italy, The Netherlands,

Great Britain). The general aims of the research were to explore adolescent and parental constructions of adolescence and how they affect the development of adolescent autonomy within the family, and to investigate the changing patterns of interaction between adolescents and parents. The research questions addressed in this chapter concern (a) the perception of normative behavior in adolescence according to the adolescents and their parents, and (b) conflict styles and outcomes in parent-adolescent interactions. For both issues we tried to investigate (c) whether there are differences relating to boys and girls, and (d) whether there are cultural differences. We examined opinions about adolescents' decision-making over a list of specific topics (PADM, Bosma et al. 1996) and descriptions of conflict management between parents and adolescents (Disagreement questionnaires, Honess et al. 1997). Participants were adolescents, males and females, of different age-groups (from thirteen to seventeen years of age) and their fathers and mothers, in two time periods.

The PADM data presented here focus on what the adolescent and parent groups think is normal for someone of the age of the adolescent, son or daughter. Of the PADM questions, this one gives the best indication of the instrument's assessment of parents' and adolescents' construction of the nature of adolescence. We assumed that the parents' ideas and expectations about adolescence and adolescent development will guide the way in which they apply their authority and the pace at which they give autonomy. In a similar way, the adolescent's view of adolescence and what is normal for adolescents to decide for themselves is likely to influence their behavior, also in response to the actions of parents (Bosma et al. 1996).

Elsewhere (Jackson et al. in prep.), we have argued that the instrument taps the cultural scripts of normative age-graded expectations with regard to adolescents. Within cultures the PADM responses of groups of adolescents and fathers and mothers show highly similar patterns: a strong age-related increase in the room which is given to adolescents to decide for themselves and a strong increase in yes-answers to the normality question, in combination with a decrease of limitations imposed by parents. Although adolescent and parent groups within one culture seem to refer to similar (maybe even the same) scripts, there are also systematic differences between the adolescent and the parent groups. Each group has its own perspective: Adolescents give themselves more room than the parent groups say they give and parent groups say that they impose less limitations than the adolescents report experiencing. This is entirely consistent with the findings from the Disagreement questionnaire where children generally reported more negative outcomes than either their mothers or their fathers.

These results indicate a strong concordance between parent and adolescent constructions of adolescence, while at the same time showing systematic discrepancies between parents and adolescents which can best be considered as differences in timing (Nurmi 1993). These discrepancies, however, most often do not lead to conflicts.

Finally, gender differences in the PADM scripts have been shown to be almost completely lacking (Bosma et al. 1996). But, as has been said above, this may be due to the kind of variables that has been used so far with this instrument. The global nature of these variables leaves the possibility open that there are undetected gender differences on the level of the individual topics and items. Therefore differences at this level were explored here.

Gender differences were indeed found in the more discrete analysis of topics. For four of the topics, "alcohol," "sweets," "look" and "friends," there are no differences. For seven topics ("chores" in two comparisons, "bedtime" 2, "language" 1, "visits" 1, "smoking" 2, "money" 1, "church" 2) we found only differences in one or two comparisons. However, there is a cluster of topics ("manners" 4, "privacy" 3, "going out" 7, "time in" 3, "sex" 10 and "homework" 5) with more frequent indications for gender differences. In the case of the topics that show gender differences, there is not uniformity in the direction of difference; in some topics (i.e., "going out," "time in") boys have higher scores, whilst in other topics (i.e., "homework," "bedtime") girls have higher scores.

In general, the major cultural difference was that more gender differences were reported by the Italian participants than by the Dutch, but only for the PADM. For the Disagreement scale, we found that for both Holland and Italy, mothers and their adolescent daughters reported higher levels of escalation than the mother and sons. How can we explain this? It appears that Dutch parents see substantially similar trends in the normative expectations regarding the development of autonomy in boys and girls, although the outcomes from any conflict appear to vary between mothers and their male and female children. Nevertheless, it can be noted that the level of autonomy given to the Dutch children is relatively low compared to the Italian peers, and Dutch parents tend to exert more control on their adolescent child. In Italy, it has been widely recognized in other research (Bonini & Zani 1991; Scabini 1995; Venuti & Giusti 1996) that gender is a crucial variable that influences parenting style, especially mothers' beliefs and practices since infancy. Even if it is a process under change, the traditional idea of a woman, considered primarily responsible for the realm of the home, is still persistent, together with parents' more tolerant attitude toward boys' behavior at home. It appears that girls are encouraged to assume responsibility earlier, whereas boys are more "coccolati" (cosseted). The adolescents seem to have internalized these common opinions and models: they recognize the persistence of some differences in the areas considered as "typically" gender oriented. However, girls tend to declare more autonomy for themselves, even in regard to behaviors that could be seen as "transgressive," like smoking.

There were also a number of interesting parent-adolescent differences and in some instances, cohort specific findings. First we focus on the differences for the Italian sample. The adolescents from the second wave reported differences with respect to bedtime, privacy, and smoking, in each case indicating that it is more often normal for the girls to decide for themselves. Only the Italian mothers report gender differences: namely "privacy," but they indicated that it's more often normal for the fifteen-year-old boys to decide for themselves. It is remarkable that the perspectives of the adolescents and mothers with regard to privacy are contrasting. This suggests that the meaning of "privacy" may vary in respects of mothers' constructions of their sons and daughters. A daughter claiming more decisional autonomy on her private affairs may reflect a willingness to defend her intimate territory from what is often perceived as intrusiveness of the mother (see also Bonini & Zani 1991; Cicognani & Zani 1998). In contrast, for mothers, it may be more difficult to admit a zone of "no entry" for them, taking account of an assumed "gender complicity," the desire to be "like a friend." This complicity does not exist with the male child: it is considered normal that he is more autonomous in his private affairs, and also to assume behaviors corresponding to the male/dominant role (e.g., in the sexuality area).

The Italian mothers also saw gender differences for the thirteen-year olds regarding "chores," "manners," "language," and "church." For each of these topics they said that it is normal for girls of the age of their daughters to decide for themselves. But, from the Italian mothers' perspective, this does not apply to the older age groups, when the boys seem to have "caught up" with the girls. In the perspectives of the Italian parents, there is a clear indication of an age by gender interaction in some topics. In these topics, the younger girls seem to be given rather more freedom in comparison to the boys. In the eyes of the fathers, "manners" formed an exception. In this topic, even the seventeen-year-old boys were still given less license.

Similar gender by age interactions in these topics have not been found for the Dutch parents. Indeed, only the Dutch adolescents reported two gender differences for the fifteen-year olds from the first wave, namely with regard to "chores" and "visits," with higher scores for boys in the case of "chores" and higher scores for girls in the case of "visits." These findings for the Dutch adolescents are difficult to interpret, because the parent groups do not report any difference in these or the other topics mentioned by the Italian groups.

The differences between the two cultures in age by gender effects for some topics should be interpreted cautiously. At least one should also note that for "chores," "manners," and "language," the absolute percentages in the Italian groups, in which the mothers see gender differences, are much higher than for the Dutch mothers. So there is a gender difference in favor of the thirteen-year old girls in Italy, but even the percentages for the Italian boys of that age are much higher than in the comparable Dutch groups.

Finally, there is the group of topics which provide a relatively consistent pattern of results across the two cultures: "going out," "time in," "sex," and "homework." For Italy, it was found that the adolescents saw differences in "homework" for the younger age groups, and the seventeen-year olds, with higher scores for the girls. Interestingly, the Italian fathers saw the same difference for the seventeen-year olds, but not for the younger age groups. The Dutch adolescents reported the same difference, but only for the thirteen-year olds. For the other three topics, the scores of the boys were higher. Adolescents in Italy as well as in the Netherlands saw this difference for "time in" for some age groups, but none of the parent groups did. With regard to "going out" and "sex," all the groups reported significant gender differences, although not for every age group. For these topics boys always had higher scores.

In general the findings showed interesting cultural differences in the perception of gender differences, with higher scores for the younger Italian girls as compared to younger Italian boys in topics such as chores, manners, language, private, money, church and homework. Similar differences were not reported by the Dutch samples, but we have to keep in mind that the absolute scores of the Dutch groups were lower for most of these topics. The scores of boys tended to be higher for the topics "time in," "going out," and "sex." This was found for both cultures. We think these findings reflect the general gender differences reported by anthropological and feminist researchers (Archer 1996; Schlegel and Barry 1991; De Waal 1989) who found that girls are given more room in private matters and are more strictly controlled than boys when they enter public spaces. It is normal to grant girls more autonomy inside the family home and boys more autonomy outdoors.

References

Archer, J. (1996). Sex differences in social behavior, *American Psychologist, 51*, 9, 909–917.

Baumrind, D. (1991). Parental styles and adolescent development. In J. Brooks-Gunn, R. Lerner & C.A.Petersen (Eds.) *The encyclopedia of adolescence*, New York, Garland.

Bonini, C., & Zani, B. (1991). (a cura di), *Dire e non dire*. Modelli educativi e comunicazione sulla sessualità nella famiglia con adolescenti, (Parental practices and communication on sexuality in families with adolescents), Milano, Giuffré.

Bosma, H., Jackson, S., Luteijn, E., & Meijer, J. (1992). *Conflicten in perspectief.* Adolescent- en uderperspectieven op conflicten in de adolescentie, Groningen: Department of Psychology.

Bosma, H., Jackson S., Zijsling, D.H., Zani, B., Cicognani, E., Xerri, M.L., Honess, T., & Charman, E. (1996). "Who has the final say? Decisions on adolescent behavior within in the family," *Journal of Adolescence ,19*, 277–291.

Buzzi, C., Cavalli, A., & De Lillo, A. (Eds.) *Giovani verso il Duemila* (Young people towards 2000), Il Mulino, Bologna.

Camara, K. & Resnick, G. (1989) Inter parental conflict and co-operation: *Factors moderating children's post-divorce adjustment.* In E. M. Hetherington & J. Arasteh (Eds.), Divorce, Single Parent and Step-parent Families, New York: Erlbaum.

Cicognani, E., Xerri, M.L., & Zani, B. (1996). "L'acquisizione dell'autonomia decisionale in adolescenza," (The acquisition of decisional autonomy in adolescence) *Scienze dell'Interazione, 3*, 67–87.

Cicognani, E. & Zani, B. (1998). "Parents' educational styles and adolescent autonomy," *European Journal of Psychology of Education, XIII, 4*, 485–502.

Collins, W.A. (1995). *"Relationships and development: family adaptation to individual change,"* in S. Shulman (Ed.) Close relationships and socioemotional development, New York: Ablex.

Collins, W.A. & Russell, G. (1991). "Mother-child and father-child relationship in middle childhood and adolescence: a developmental analysis," *Developmental Review, 11*, 99–136.

Cooper, C. (1988). *The role of conflict in adolescent-parent relationships.* In M.R. Gunnar and W.A.Collins (Eds.) Minnesota symposia on child psychology, Hillsdale: Erlbaum

Dekovic, M., Noom, M., & Meeus, W. (1997). Expectations regarding development during adolescence: parental and adolescent perceptions, *Journal of Youth and Adolescence, 26*, 3, 253–272

De Waal, M. (1989). *Meisjes, een wereld apart* (Girls, a different world). Amsterdam: Boom.

Dowdy, B.B. & Kliewer, W. (1998) Dating, parent-adolescent conflict, and behavioral autonomy, *Journal of Youth and Adolescence, 27, 4*, 473–492

Fuhrman, T. & Holmbeck, G.N. (1995). A contextual-moderator analysis of emotional autnomy and adjustment in adolescence. *Child Development, 66*, 793–811.

Gecas, V. & Seff, M.A. (1990). families and adolescents: A review of the 1980s, *Journal of Marriage and the Family, 52*, 941–958.

Goodnow, J.J. & Collins, W.A. (1990). *Development according to parents: The nature, sources and consequences of parents' ideas*, London: Erlbaum

Grotevant, H.D. & Cooper, C.R. (Eds.) (1983). *Adolescent development in the family*, San Francisco: Jossey-Bass.

Grotevant, H.D. & Cooper, C.R. (1985). Patterns of interaction in family relationships and the development of identity exploration in adolescence. *Child Development, 56*, 415–428.

Hill, J.P. & Holmbeck, G.N. (1986). "Attachment and autonomy during adolescence," *Annals of Child Development, 3*, 145–189.

Holmbeck, G.N. & O'Donnell, K. (1991). *Discrepancies between perceptions of decision making and behavioral autonomy*. In R.L.Paikoff (Ed.) Shared views of the family during adolescence: New directions for child development, San Francisco: Jossey-Bass.

Honess, T. & Charman, L. (1992). *Conflict scales for divorcing and intact parents*, School of Psychology, University of Wales, Cardiff.

Honess, T., Charman, L., Zan,i B., Cicognan,i E., Xerri, M.L., Jackson, S., & Bosma, H. (1997). Conflict between parents and adolescents: variations by family constitution," *British Journal of Developmental Psychology, 15*, 367–385.

Jackson, S., Cicognan,i E. & Charman, L. (1996). "The measurement of conflict in parent-adolescent relationships," in L. Verhofstadt-Denève, I. Kienhorst and C. Braet (Eds.), *Conflict and development in adolescence*, Leiden: DSWO Press.

Jackson, S., Bijstra, J., Oostra, L. & Bosma, H. (1998). Adolescents' perceptions of communication with parents relative to specific aspects of relationships with parents and personal development, *Journal of Adolescence, 21*, 305–322.

Jackson, S. et al. (in preparation). *Progress to personal decision-making in adolescent development*: Studies in three European countries.

Kagitcibasi, C. (1990). Family and socialization in cross-cultural perspective: a model of change. In J.J. Berman (Ed.) *Cross-cultural perspectives*. Nebraska Symposium on Motivation (vol. 37), Lincoln: University of Nebraska Press.

Laursen, B. & Collins, W.A. (1994). Interpersonal conflict during adolescence, *Psychological Bulletin, 115*, 197–209.

Low, B.S. (1989). Cross-cultural patterns in the training of children: An evolutionary perspective, *Journal of Comparative Psychology, 103*, 311–319.

Marta, E. (1997). "Parent-adolescent interactions and psychosocial risk in adolescents: an analysis of communication, support and gender," *Journal of Adolescence, 20*, 473–487.

Montemayor, R. (1983). "Parent and adolescents in conflict: all families some of the time, some families most of the time," *Journal of Early Adolescence, 3*, pp. 83–103.

Noller, P., & Callan, V.S. (1991). *The Adolescent in the family*, London: Routledge.

Nurmi, J.-E. (1993). Adolescent development in the age-graded context: the role of personal beliefs, goals, and strategies in the tackling of developmental tasks and standards. *International Journal of Behavioral Development, 16*, 2, 169–190

Olson, D.H., McCubbin, H.I., Barnes, H.L., Larsen, A.S., Muxen, M.J., Wilson, M.A. (1983). *Families: what makes them work*, Beverly Hills, CA: Sage.

Rands, M., Levinger, G. and Mellinger, G.D. (1981). Patterns of conflict and marital satisfaction, *Journal of Family Issues, 2*, 297–321

Rosenthal, D. (1994). *Gender constructions of adolescent sexuality*, Paper presented at the Biennal meetings of the Society for Research on Adolescence, San Diego.

Scabini, E. (1995). *Psicologia sociale della famiglia*, (Social Psychology of the family), Torino, Boringhieri.

Schlegel, A., & Barry III, H. (1991). *Adolescence. An anthropological inquiry*. New York: The Free Press.

Smetana, J.G. (1988). "Adolescents' and parents' conceptions of parental authority, *Child Development, 59*, 321–335

Smetana, J.G. (1989). "Adolescents' and parents' reasoning about actual family conflict" *Child Development, 60*, 1052–1067.

Smetana, J.G. & Asquith, P. (1994). "Adolescents' and parents' conceptions of parental authority and personal autonomy," *Child Development, 65*, 1147–1162.

Steinberg, L.D. (1987). Recent research on the family at adolescence: The extent and nature of sex differences. *Journal of Youth and Adolescence, 16*, 191–197.

Steinberg, L.D. (1990). "Interdependency in the family: autonomy, conflict and harmony in the parent-adolescent relationship." In. Feldman S.S., Elliot G.R. (Eds.) *At the threshold: the developing adolescent,* Cambridge, MA: Harvard University Press.

Venuti, P. and Giusti, F. (1996). *Madre e padre*. (Mother and father), Firenze:Giunti.

Verhofstadt-Denève, L. and Schittekatte, M. (1998). *Need adolescent boys and girls act "wisely" to grow into "happy" adults?* A tentative answer based on the Flanders longitudinal study, Paper presented at the 6th Biennal Conference of the EARA, Budapest.

Youniss, J. (1983). *Social construction of adolescence by adolescents and parents*. In H.D. Grotevant and C.R. Cooper (Eds.), Adolescent development in the family, San Francisco: Jossey-Bass.

Youniss, J., Smollar J. (1985). *Adolescent relations with mothers, fathers and friends*, Chicago: University of Chicago Press.

Wynn, J. & White, R. (1997). *Rethinking youth*. London: Sage.

Zani, B. & Cicognani, E. (1999). La gestione del conflitto nelle famiglie con adolescenti: le prospettive di genitori e figli, (Conflict management in families with adolescents: the perspectives of parents and children). *Giornale Italiano di Psicologia, 4*, 791–815.

Zani, B. & Cicognani, E., Bosma, H., Zijsling, D. and Jackson, A. (2000). *Developmental changes in decisional autonomy among adolescents: A longitudinal research.*

Part Four

Theoretical Developments in the Research
on Navigating through Adolescence

Adolescents' Self-direction and Self-definition in Age-graded Sociocultural and Interpersonal Contexts

JARI-ERIK NURMI

Introduction

Adolescent development is characterized by two major features. First, during adolescence, individuals are faced with more changes in their developmental environments than is typical of any other phase of the human life-span (Caspi in press). These include a variety of educational transitions and related changes in peer groups, the transition from school to work, and changes in relationships with parents and the opposite sex. Second, partly due to these environmental changes, adolescence is a time for the intensive construction of new thoughts, values, interests, commitments, skills, and self-beliefs (Nurmi 1993). One way to conceptualize the complex nature of adolescent development is to describe it as a process which consists of continuous interactions between young people's thoughts, interests, and beliefs, on the one hand, and their interpersonal, sociocultural and institutional environments, on the other (Magnusson 1985; Rauste-von Wright 1986).

This notion has a number of important consequences. For example, both the adolescent and his or her environment may be expected to play an active role in the development (Lerner 1987). From the individual point of view, it has been suggested that people overall, and adolescents in particular, direct, control and influence their own development as active agents (Brandtstädter 1984; Lerner 1983). However, a much less frequently emphasized idea is that the developmental contexts themselves also often play an active part by encouraging, or sometimes restricting, individual development. For example, a number of significant others, such as parents, peers, and teachers actively encourage and direct the adolescent toward certain developmental patterns. Moreover, age-graded developmental tasks and institutional transitions create a variety of new demands, challenges, and constraints with which adolescents have to learn to deal (Nurmi 1993). What is even more important is that the role of adolescents' interests, beliefs, and skills, and the contextual factors, may change because of mutual and reciprocal influences. For example, development may take quite different directions for the same adolescent in different contexts depending on the environmental options available. In turn, owing to individual differences, adolescent development may be different to different individuals in the same environment.

The aim of this chapter is to describe how adolescents navigate through the second and third decades of their lives. The navigational tools will be described in terms of two processes: self-direction and self-definition. Particular emphasis is given to the conceptualization of the developmental contexts. To fulfill this aim, a short review of the research on developmental environments, in particular the concept of developmental tasks, is first presented. Next, a short overview of the psychological processes that provide a basis for the ways in which adolescents direct their lives and create various self-definitions is given. Then, a theoretical model of adolescent development in age-graded sociocultural environments is summarized. Finally, the role of interpersonal contexts in adolescents' self-direction and self-definition is discussed.

Conceptualizations of the Sociocultural Environment

During the past fifty years various researchers have emphasized the importance of age-related norms, roles, expectations, and beliefs in human development. It has been suggested that these age systems create predictable, socially recognized turning points that provide road maps for human lives and outline life-paths (Hagestad & Neugarten 1985; Valsiner & Lawrence 1997).

Developmental Task

The first concept used to describe age-graded contexts was that of the developmental task introduced by Havighurst (1948). He defined this as "a task which arises at or about a certain period of time in the life of an individual, successful achievement of which leads to his happiness and success with later tasks, while failure leads to unhappiness in the individual, disapproval by the society and difficulty with later tasks" (Havighurst 1948). Havighurst's original conceptualization of the origins of developmental tasks was broad. He saw them as motivated by normative demands, and some were thought to arise mainly from physical maturation, others from personal values and aspirations (Havighurst 1948).

Developmental tasks can be described as follows. (1) They consist of normative expectations and requirements to do or achieve something at a certain age. (2) Even though some key themes of these tasks such as work, human relationships, and ideology are the same across the life-span, different life stages are expected to be characterized by the different patterns of the various developmental tasks. (3) Developmental tasks include expectations about the age and related time range within which some types of behavior, thinking, or transitions should occur. (4) They include beliefs about appropriate behavior and outcomes that are interpreted as a successful way of handling a specific task. Similarly, they can be expected to include beliefs about inappropriate behavior that is evaluated as failure. (5) Developmental tasks also relate to specific role models available in a given culture which provide cues for tackling them in a successful manner. (6) Their influence on individual thinking is often mediated by the behavior of and feedback from other people, including peers, parents, teachers, spouses, and colleagues, who provide direct or indirect cues for what type of behavior is appropriate at certain ages. (7) Developmental tasks, and acting according to them, are closely related to the process of reproduction by which a group, culture, or society generates its typical behavioral patterns from one generation to another. (8) Responding to age-related developmental tasks has been suggested to lead to psychological changes, such as an increase in an individual's competence (Heymans 1994).

Havighurst (1948) also presented a list of developmental tasks for the different stages of the human life-span. According to him, typical developmental tasks for adolescence include achieving mature relationships with peers and forming a sex-role identity, preparing for marriage and family life, achieving emotional independence from parents, and preparing for an economic career, including planning education. Tasks for early adulthood include finding an occupation, selecting a partner and starting a family, rearing children, and finding a congenial social group. Although Western societies have changed substantially during the last few decades, more recent descriptions of developmental tasks are very similar to those of Havighurst (e.g., Cantor, Norem, Niedenthal, Langston, & Brower 1987; Newman & Newman 1975; Strough, Berg, & Sansone 1996).

After Havighurst's work on the developmental task concept, it was not before the mid-70s and early 80s that the next wave of studies on this topic was published. In their popular textbook on life-span psychology, Newman and Newman (1975) used developmental tasks as one of the major concepts to describe human development. Later on, in the 1980s, the concept became popular in Europe, and it was applied in a number of studies related to topics such as adolescents' future-orientation (Nurmi 1987), conceptions of adulthood (Dreher & Oerter 1986), coping (Dittman-Kohli 1986), and leisure activities (Noack 1990).

Social Constraints, Role Transitions and Institutional Careers

In the decades since Havighurst (1948) first introduced the concept of the developmental task, similar types of conceptualizations which also refer to age-graded norms, expectations and roles have arisen. For example, Neugarten, Moore, and Lowe (1965) considered how age norms and social constraints indicate a prescriptive timetable for ordering major life-events. According to them, these sociocultural patterns operate in a society as a system of social controls. On the basis of these normative beliefs, people's behavior at a certain age can be described as "early," "late," or "on time." Two decades later, similar conceptualizations were put forward, such as role transitions (Caspi 1987; Elder 1985) and developmental standards (Caspi 1987). The conceptual differentiation between normative and non-normative life-events suggested by Baltes, Reese, and Lipsitt (1980) also emphasizes the importance of age-graded life-course patterns.

However, most of these conceptualizations have overlooked the fact that age-graded changes in institutional patterns, as well as cultural beliefs and age norms, play an important role in individual development. For example, schooling and educational systems may be described in terms of age-related tracks that strongly influence possible behavior and reasonable decisions at a specific age. These types of changes have been described earlier in terms of institutional careers (Mayer 1986), tracks (Klaczynski & Reese 1991) and action opportunities (Grotevant 1987). The major feature that distinguishes these from developmental tasks and role transitions is that they are based on institutional, organizational, or even legal structures, rather than cultural beliefs.

During adolescence individuals are faced with many institutional transitions, particularly in the domain of education and work. There is, however, a substantial amount of variation in the forms, timing, and sequencing of these transitions across societies (Hurrelmann 1994). For example, in some countries, such as France, children and adolescents from early on face a detailed educational tracking based on school achievement (Motola, Sinisalo, & Guichard 1998), whereas in other societies, such as the Nordic countries, there is no evident tracking before middle adolescence (Nurmi & Siurala 1994). Similarly, the time of entry into the domain of work varies substantially across societies (Hurrelmann 1994; Nurmi, Seginer, & Poole 1995).

So far the discussion has focused on the conceptualizations of age-graded sociocultural environments. Next, I will briefly summarize a variety of theoretical notions concerning the psychological processes by which individuals attempt to deal with such developmental demands (For more detail, see Nurmi 1991, 1993, 1997).

Psychological Basis of Self-direction and Self-definition

The first broader theoretical notion concerns the nature of all psychological processes. It is suggested that, in order to understand any psychological process, its relational nature must be considered (Nuttin 1984). For example, human motives relate not only to the individual's inner needs, but also to certain objectives in the outer world by which they are satisfied (Nuttin 1984). Evidently, the same is true for cognitive schemata and beliefs: they refer to certain objectives in the outer world, or various cultural or interactional patterns. Moreover, Heymans (1994) has defined competence as a coordinated capacity tied to certain environmental potentials. This relational notion also has consequences for the conceptualization of adolescent development: (1) with age, young people become interested in various objectives and events in their socio-cultural age-graded contexts, in particular; (2) they realize their goals by apply-ing competencies which have been developed in a particular historical period in a particular society; and (3) they evaluate their goal attainment on the basis of culturally and historically defined standards (Nurmi 1991, 1993).

There are also several theoretical ideas concerning the nature of psycholog-ical processes that provide a basis for understanding the interaction between the individual's development and his or her sociocultural environment. First, accord-ing to cognitive psychology, people's behavior in different contexts is regulated by forethought, expectations, and competencies which arise from the cognitive schemata and belief systems learned in different situations during earlier life (Bandura 1986; Neisser 1976). Schemata and beliefs concerning life-span devel-opment, the options provided by institutional careers and, finally, those concern-ing oneself, are of key importance in the process of socialization into adulthood. Second, the basic tenet of action theory, and more recent motivation psychology, is that people's behavior in certain environments is directed according to their individual motives, needs, goals, and the different meanings they have attached to the situations in which they are involved (Emmons 1986; Leontjev 1977; Nuttin 1984; Nurmi 1991). These motivational structures differ along a cline of generality, varying from key personal values to specific goals and preferences people have about different action alternatives. Third, it has been emphasized both in cognitive psychology and action theory that when people are faced with new demands and challenges, they need to devise ways of dealing with them, of carrying them out by means of planning, strategic problem solving and coping (Cantor 1990; Markus & Wurf 1987). These efforts then provide a basis for the individual's success in goal attainment and dealing with various situational demands. Fourth, besides aiming at certain future developments, people also try to make sense of and evaluate what has happened to them previously. It has been suggested that unexpected events and goal non-attainments in particular provoke these types of interpretation, described in terms of causal attributions (Weiner 1986).

Finally, in the course of investing effort in dealing with major demands and challenges, people also develop broader self-definitions. This process has been described in terms of identity formation. Young people construct their personal identities in the context of exploring various alternatives for their future adult roles, and ending up making commitments to some of them (Erikson 1959; Marcia 1980). Such explorations, commitments, choices, and related feedback from interpersonal and social environments provide the basis for the individual's identity development.

Adolescent Development in Age-graded Contexts

As discussed earlier, individuals develop by actively directing and controlling their own lives (Brandtstädter 1984; Lerner 1983; Nurmi 1993). In the course of this self-direction process, people also form new self-definitions in terms of self-schemata and self-esteem. This process is described in Figure 1.

Self-direction and Self-definition

The first stage in directing one's own development consists of constructing personal goals, projects, and strivings on the basis of individual motivations developed earlier in life (Nurmi 1989a, 1993). Once people have constructed personal goals, the next major requirement for success in directing their own future life is finding the means to achieve those goals. If a person is facing a familiar situation, this may consist of deciding which set of skills and competencies will be most useful in that situation (Markus & Wurf 1987). However, if the developmental challenges are new, this process can be described in terms of planning, problem-solving, or the construction of cognitive strategies (Cantor 1990; Nurmi 1991, 1993). After making an attempt to realize their personal goals by means of coping, cognitive strategies, and related behavior, people end up at a certain point assessing the extent to which they have succeeded in their efforts (Nurmi 1991). The evaluation of goal achievements, however, is a complex process that includes various psychological phenomena. It has been shown, for example, that

Figure 1: Self-direction and Self-definition Processes

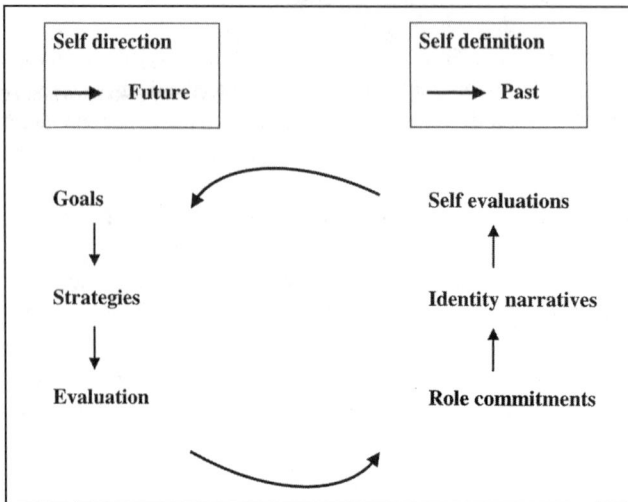

when people are faced with an event, such as goal attainment or non-attainment, they tend to begin exploring its causes (Weiner 1986). Moreover, it has been suggested that people tend to interpret their goal attainments and life events in positive ways: they apply different types of evaluative strategies, such as self-serving attribution bias, for self-protection purposes (Taylor & Brown 1988; Nurmi 1993; Zuckerman 1979).

In the process of directing their lives in terms of constructing goals, trying to find means of realizing them, and evaluating goal attainment, adolescents also learn about themselves, their interests, skills, and achievements (Figure 1). Several processes provide a basis for such self-definitions. First, when, on the basis of their efforts, young people find themselves in new roles and along certain institutional tracks, such as a student in a certain field of vocational education, and subsequently in a certain profession, these then have consequences for their self-identity, i.e., how they think about themselves compared with their peers following other tracks or in other roles. Second, people also create a variety of identity narratives concerning the self-direction process. In other words, they reconstruct a subjective theory of what happened during this process in terms of their original goals, skills, and outcomes. Such identity narratives do not always reflect the history of their self-direction as such, but function as a way of creating a subjective story contributing to their sense of individual self-identity (McAdams 1993). Finally, individuals receive various kinds of feedback in the course of constructing goals, coping strategies and evaluation of behavioral outcomes, all of which provide a basis for a variety of self evaluations concerning their skills and competencies in the relevant life domains (Nurmi 1993).

Although self-direction and self-definition have been described as consecutive sub-stages, starting from goal-setting and ending with self-definitions, they may also be characterized as a system of various feedback loops. For example, self-schemata and self-esteem influence individual motives, personal goals, and strategy construction: low self-esteem might be expected to lead to the motivation to protect oneself in future situations against failure, and therefore to set lower-level goals. This may then lead to the use of different self-protection strategies, such as self-handicapping (Jones & Berglas 1978) or a failure-trap strategy (Nurmi, Salmela-Aro, & Ruotsalainen 1994). Moreover, the evaluation of goal attainments, together with the related causal explorations, may also influence the anticipation of future outcomes, and subsequent goal-setting and strategy construction.

Overall, the self-direction and self-definition processes might be assumed to be the major processes responsible for changes in personality across time. Self-direction relates to the changes in the ways in which individuals deal with the challenges of their developmental environments, whereas self-definition leads to changes in how people perceive themselves.

Self-direction in Age-graded Contexts

The self-direction and self-definition processes takes place in a complex age-graded developmental context, which is described in Figure 2. The model consists of two components: (1) the age-graded sociocultural context is described in terms of developmental tasks (Havighurst 1948), action opportunities (Grotevant 1987) provided by institutional settings (Mayer 1986), and finally, the standards for age-appropriate behavior (Nurmi 1993). (2) On the individual level, the process is described in terms of setting personal goals, constructing the means for their realization, evaluating success in goal attainment, and constructing subsequent self-definitions. Since this process has been described in detail earlier (Nurmi 1991, 1993, 1997), it is only summarized here.

Figure 2: Self-direction and Self-definition in a Life-span Context

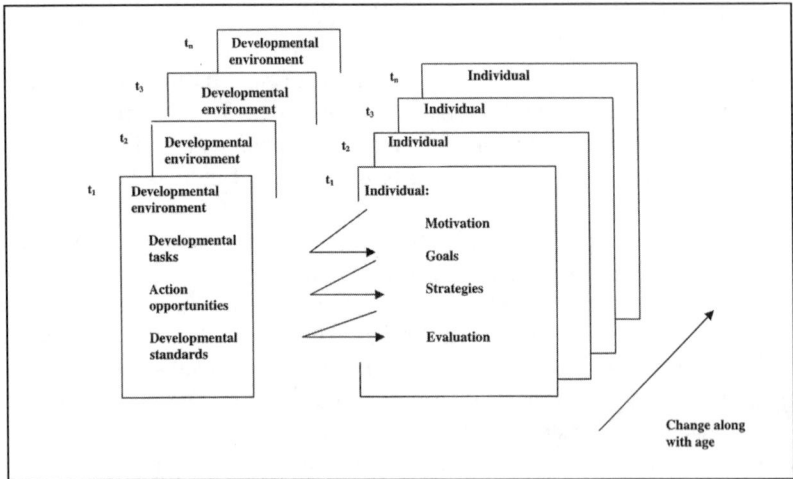

t_n	Developmental environment
t_3	Developmental environment
t_2	Developmental environment
t_1	Developmental environment

Developmental tasks

Action opportunities

Developmental standards

t_n	Individual
t_3	Individual
t_2	Individual
t_1	Individual:

Motivation

Goals

Strategies

Evaluation

Change along with age

First, constructing personal goals that will enhance future development requires the assessment of individual motives against different normative expectations and beliefs about future options (Nurmi 1989a, 1993). Thus, a variety of social age systems, such as age-graded developmental tasks and role transitions, are assumed to play an important role in constructing personal goals because they provide information about the options available in the future by which those personal goals can be attained (Dannefer 1984; Nurmi 1991; 1993). It has also been shown that adolescents' and young adults' personal goals at different stages of their lives reflect the major developmental tasks of this age phase (Cross & Markus 1991; Nurmi 1991, 1992). Interestingly, these have also been shown to be relatively similar across different cultures (Nurmi 1991; Nurmi, Poole, & Kalakoski 1994).

Once people have constructed personal goals, the next major requirement for success in directing their own future life is finding the means to achieve them. One important aspect of this planning and strategy construction is the consideration of options provided by the institutional environment (Nurmi 1991: See Figure 2). It has been suggested, for example, that educational and vocational planning is influenced by different types of educational careers and vocational transitions (Osipow 1983). Different contextual opportunities may also play an important role in the planning of other domains of life, such as interpersonal relationships.

It might also be assumed that cultural beliefs about the life-span development may play some role in the ways in which adolescents evaluate their success in dealing with age-graded demands. A variety of cultural beliefs concerning appropriate ways of handling a certain developmental demand or transition may provide a basis for the extent to which and the ways in which adolescents evaluate their success in goal attainment. There are, for example, cultural beliefs concerning the appropriate forms and age for initiating close relationships with the opposite sex; such cultural standards then influence how adolescents think and feel about themselves. Interestingly, it has also been found that the extent to which young adults are satisfied with or happy about themselves is associated with the actualization of their educational and occupational plans (Kuusinen, Hietala, & Mustapää 1994).

Changing Developmental Context

So far I have discussed the ways in which adolescents direct their lives when faced with a certain set of developmental tasks, standards, and action opportunities. However, one feature typical of adolescence is that such normative and institutional demands change rapidly with age. To complement the theoretical model, an additional dimension consisting of the subsequent stages of adolescents' development, in terms of changing developmental tasks, institutional opportunities, and developmental standards along with age (t_1, t_2 ... t_n), is introduced in Figure 2. This dimension consists of changing age-graded environments, and the development of individual goals, strategy construction, evaluational strategies, and self-definitions, at different temporal stages of adolescence.

This extension of the original model suggests that there are at least three types of developmental issues related to changing sociocultural environments. First, developmental tasks, role transitions, institutional careers, and developmental standards vary from one stage of adolescence to another (t_1 ... t_n). This means, in fact, that not only individuals, but also their sociocultural and institutional environments change with age in a way that might even be described as development. For example, the developmental demands concerning the domain of education change substantially from early to late adolescence in terms of investment of the time, autonomous decision making, amount of school work, etc.

The second developmental feature of sociocultural environments is that the ways adolescents solve different developmental tasks, and the types of decisions and commitments they make in the related life domains, orient them toward different future institutional tracks and developmental environments. This tracking then influences the sociocultural environments they face later on in life. These types of developmental patterns have been described earlier in terms of irreversible transitions (Petersen, Crouter, & Wilson 1988). For example, the choice of school track typically influences the individual's future options in the educational domain. Similarly, earlier behavior and commitments, such as teenage pregnancy or marriage, will have a crucial impact on the individual's normative demands and action opportunities in the future (Petersen et al. 1988). Partly related to this, being early or late in solving age-graded developmental tasks influences later developmental environments, the former by creating new developmental challenges and the latter by emphasizing the need to continue the work related to earlier normative demands.

The third issue related to the changing sociocultural context is that the ways in which adolescents reconstruct their goals, strategies, and self-definitions as a consequence of their success in dealing with certain age-graded developmental tasks and demands provide a basis for the ways in which they deal with the demands and challenges of similar kinds of future situations. For example, the level of success experienced in working with certain personal goals might be expected to either encourage or discourage people in working with a set of similar goals in the future (Salmela-Aro in this volume). Moreover, adolescents' success in dealing with a particular challenge, and the ways in which this influences their strategies, have consequences for the kinds of strategies they use later on in life (Eronen in this volume). Finally, the self-definitions people have constructed during previous stages of their lives in terms of self-schemata and self-esteem not only influence their self-definitions at the next stage, but also the kinds of goals and strategies they construct (Nurmi 1993).

Self-direction in Interpersonal Contexts

Although the emphasis so far has been on individuals, the adolescent's self-direction process is in most cases embedded in various interpersonal settings. A typical example of these are adolescent-parent dyads and peer groups. These interpersonal settings are important for adolescents' self-direction and self-definition processes in two ways. First, it might be assumed that negotiations with significant others and their social support, for example, provide a basis for the ways in which adolescents direct their lives and how they evaluate themselves. Second, the adolescent's life is embedded in many ways to the development of significant others, such as parents and peers. This co-development of individual life-paths also creates new challenges for the adolescent during various stages of his or her life.

Self-direction as Interpersonal Negotiation

There has been increasing evidence that a substantial amount of goal and strategy construction takes place in interpersonal settings. For example, Malmberg (in this volume) showed recently that adolescents report a substantial amount of future planning not only when they are alone but also together with friends, peers, and parents. Moreover, Berg (1998) showed recently that many of the individual's personal goals are shared with significant others, such as parents and friends. This interpersonal aspect of self-direction and self-definition processes is described in Figure 3.

One major interpersonal context that plays an important role in adolescents'

Figure 3: Self-direction as Interpersonal Negotiation

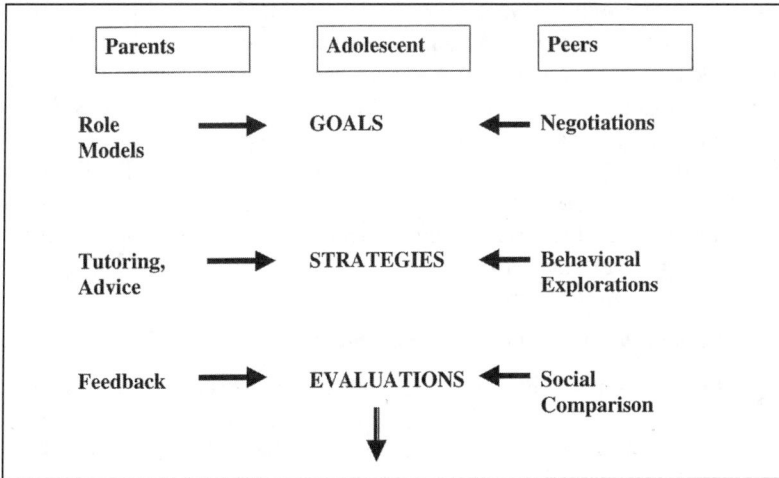

self-direction is their home and parents (Grotevant & Cooper 1986). First, it might be assumed that parents serve as important role models, at least for some of the adolescents when they make decisions and construct goals related to their future, such as future education, career, and family. For example, a positive family climate and parents' marital happiness have been shown to actively encourage adolescents to plan their own future family life (Niemi 1988). Moreover, parents expectations also have been shown to be associated with their children's educational aspirations (Seginer 1983). Second, parents are also an important source of tutoring and advice when adolescents are trying to figure out how to reach their future goals. For example, adolescents have been shown to report home and parents as the most important source for future-related information gathering and planning (Malmberg in this volume). Similarly, Dreher and Oerter (1986) found that adolescents frequently mentioned support from their parents as helpful to their ability to cope with major developmental tasks. Third, parents might also be assumed to play an important role when adolescents evaluate their success in their goal attainment, and, in particular, in how this is reflected in their self-definition. Discussions between parents and adolescent offspring about his or her school achievement are quite frequent in many families.

Peers and friends also play an important role in the ways in which adolescents create their future. First, the construction of personal goals is likely to be influenced by discussions and negotiations with peers. For example, Malmberg (in this volume) showed that adolescents evaluate fellow students and friends as an important source of future-related information. Second, behavioral exploration in the peer group might be assumed to play a particularly important role in the decisions and commitments adolescents make in the interpersonal domains of life (Marcia 1980). Meeus (1993) found that social support by friends in educational settings stimulated the development of adolescents' occupational identity. Finally, peer groups provide a natural environment for the evaluation of goal attainment in terms of social comparisons and related discussions. Such social comparisons might be assumed to play an important role in the ways in which adolescents evaluate their competencies to deal with the various demands of their developmental environments, such as those at school and in peer groups. Such evaluation will then have important consequences for the adolescent self-concept (Nurmi 1993).

Co-development in Sociocultural Environments

The interpersonal context in which adolescents are living not only contributes to the key processes of their self-direction, such as goal and strategy construction, but also creates new developmental demands for them: the demands and challenges which young people face originate in many cases from the events faced by their parents. Such interlinked developments have been described earlier in terms of co-development (Brandtstädter, Krampen, & Heil 1986), interwoven lives (Hagestad & Neugarten 1985) and interlocking trajectories (Elder 1985). Some of these co-developmental processes are described in Figure 4 in more abstract terms, using the model described earlier.

The major, although not the only, context for the individual's co-develop-

Figure 4: Self-direction in the context of co-development

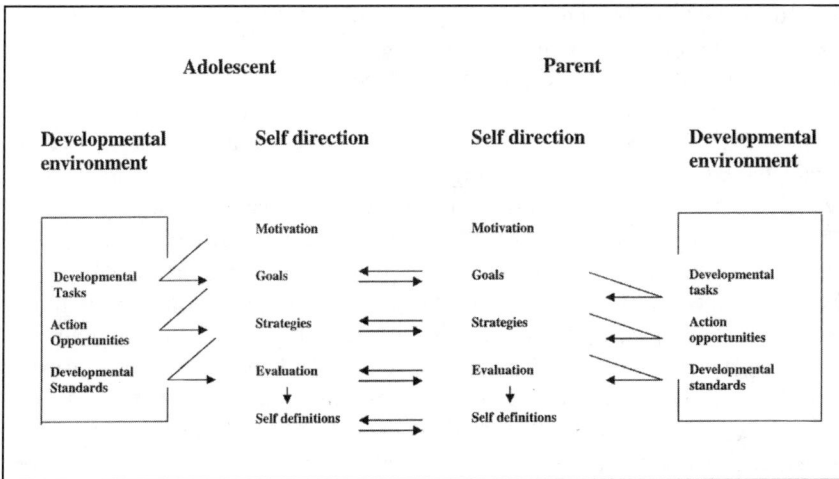

	Adolescent		Parent	
Developmental environment	**Self direction**	**Self direction**	**Developmental environment**	

ment is the family. The co-development of the adolescent and his or her parents means that the former's goal-setting is affected not only by the developmental tasks of his or her own sociocultural environments, but also by the developmental tasks and role transitions of significant others, and the ways they handle their normative demands. For example, a number of life-events and transitions faced by the parents, such as career transitions and related household moves, provide new challenges and transitions for the adolescents living with them. On the other hand, a number of the transitions parents face during middle-age are in fact determined by the transitions of their children's lives during their late adolescence and early adulthood, such as the "empty nest" syndrome and becoming a grandparent (Hagestad & Neugarten 1985). Similarly, many of the developmental tasks and institutional transitions faced by an adolescent form new normative challenges for his or her parents. For example, the adolescent's entrance into high school or college is not only a challenge for him or her, but creates new demands for the parents as well, such as a helping out financially and entering into negotiations with the adolescent about new rules and privileges. In some cases, the developmental demands faced by the adolescent and his or her parents may even be in conflict, requiring joint problem-solving. It is also to be expected that the evaluation of one's success at a certain period of life sometimes includes the necessity of taking into account of other people's achievements. For example, poor school achievement on the part of the adolescent may lead the adult to view him/herself negatively as a parent.

Final Remarks About Social Age Systems

There are, however, a few considerations concerning adolescents' age-graded sociocultural contexts that I would like to raise before concluding the chapter. First, the major idea behind the model presented was that normative age systems occur in certain normative and orderly progressions. However, there has been some discussion about the extent to which people's lives overall, and adolescents' lives in particular, really follow these types of normative age systems. For example, Rindfuss, Swicegood, and Rosenfeld (1987) presented results based on data gathered in the 1970s suggesting that over half of men and women in high school had sequences of transitions inconsistent with what is often assumed to be the "normal" pattern. There was, for example, frequent "in and out activities" not usually considered in life-course analysis, such as being a homemaker or at work, and later on returning to education. Although this notion may be problematic in some of the life-span theories, it fits with the model presented here: earlier decisions and efforts of tackling developmental tasks cause an increasing amount of differentiation in the sociocultural and institutional settings people face across time. In any case, deviations from "normative developmental patterns," and their consequences for later development in particular, constitute the most interesting research questions.

My second point is that there is no doubt that the age systems adolescents face, even the major stages of adolescence, vary across historical time (Hurrelmann 1989; Kohli & Meyer 1986), cultures (Nurmi, Seginer, & Poole 1995), and social class (Zepelin, Sills, Heath 1986–1987). For instance, the whole process of socialization during adolescence in the form of formal and extended education is relatively new from the historical point of view (Hurrelmann 1989). This diversity of age-graded developmental environments has also been shown to be reflected in the ways in which adolescents' direct their lives in terms of constructing personal goals (Nurmi 1991; Nurmi, Seginer, & Poole 1995).

It has also been suggested recently that there is a movement toward an age-irrelevant society (Neugarten & Neugarten 1987). The findings seemed to show, however, that even though some age norms have become less limiting within the past decades, there is still a persisting consensus on age-based timetables, particularly for the most critical role transitions such as schooling, career, parenthood, and marriage (Zepelin et al. 1986–1987). It might be suggested that adolescence, in particular, is a life period that is still strongly regulated by various age systems, developmental demands, and institutional transitions. Even given the evident changes in modern societies, such as the complexity of educational and from-school-to-work transitions, the model presented provides a heuristic tool for understanding individual development and creating hypotheses for research. Although there may be more diversity in the age-graded transitions adolescents face, related demands and opportunity structures still provide a basis for the ways in which individuals construct and reconstruct their goals and various means to attain them.

It has also been typical in the developmental task framework, as in a number of other life-span theories, to apply certain normative, or even moral, arguments to emphasize the importance of such tasks during adolescence and young adulthood. I would like to take a more non-normative position here. Instead of defining the achievement of age-graded developmental tasks as a definite abstract norm, I would prefer to express their importance in adolescent development and cultural reproduction in functional terms. In order to adapt to the society and to be positively evaluated by other people, an adolescent needs to complete the successive normative tasks in it, otherwise his or her chances of living in that society will be limited in various respects. Similarly, cultures and societies cannot function and survive if young people are not socialized according to the major normative patterns. The major benefit of this approach is that it provides tools for understanding that age-graded sociocultural environments may vary across cultures and historical periods. Moreover, there may exist subcultures in which the menu of normative tasks differs substantially from those of society at large, although they will still be functional in that particular context.

A further interesting issue is how sociocultural age systems begin to play the important role in individual development suggested in the model. The answer may be quite simple. Age as well as gender can reasonably be expected to be one of the key social constructs by which children begin to differentiate and make sense of their environments from the outset of their development: people of different age vary according to their physical size, strength, and power. If age becomes the key construct by which children interpret their social environment, it is easy to understand why it has such a powerful role in later development. This is often complemented by age-related argumentation early in family settings: children are often told "Because of your age, you cannot, you should, you may try, or you are allowed" to do something. Later on, school, as one of the major institutions shaping people's later lives, is based on strict age stratification.

Conclusions

This chapter focused on discussing a theoretical model describing the ways in which young people navigate through their adolescence. The navigational tools were conceptualized in terms of two processes: self-direction and self-definition. Moreover, the changing developmental environments were described as alternative routes through which the adolescent could navigate into adulthood. The conceptualization of adolescents' age-graded developmental contexts was complemented by discussing two further topics. First, a life-span framework was used to emphasize the importance of age-graded changes in the developmental tasks and institutional opportunities that exists during adolescence. It was further suggested that adolescents' ways of dealing with previous demands and challenges create differences in the future developmental demands and environmental options they will face in the future. Second, the notion that individual development is often embedded in various interpersonal contexts, and also influenced by them, was discussed. Particular emphasis was given to parents and peers. The chapter focused on the discussion of theoretical issues. However, the applicability of the model in different research fields, such as adolescents' future orientation (Nurmi 1991, 1992), overall development (Nurmi 1993), mental health (Nurmi 1997), and cross-cultural differences in adolescents thinking (Nurmi et al. 1995), has been discussed previously.

The theoretical ideas discussed in this chapter might be assumed to provide a basis for more thorough understanding of several issues in adolescent psychology. First, the majority of research on adolescence has been carried out in the United States and Western Europe. Because researchers typically aim at finding major principles of adolescent development, there is a tendency to over-generalize the findings to all individuals living in the second decade of their lives in a variety of contexts. Because adolescents are investigated in relatively homogenous institutional and cultural settings, some of these findings, which may in fact reflect the particular characteristics of such settings, are interpreted as general psychological laws (Kalakoski & Nurmi 1998). The only way, in fact, to test whether some of the major findings are context-specific would be to carry out the studies simultaneously in different cultures and societies.

Second, there is an increasing amount of evidence to support some of the key ideas presented in this chapter. For example, the self-direction process that adolescents undertake, such as goal construction and identity exploration and related commitments (Nurmi 1991, 1993), seem not only to be influenced by cultural differences in age-graded developmental environments (Nurmi et al. 1995) and forthcoming transitions (Kalakoski & Nurmi 1998), but seems also to direct individuals' future life-paths (Salmela-Aro & Nurmi 1997). Moreover, young people's success in dealing with the major age-graded transitions, such as the transition from school to work, have been found to be reflected in the ways they reconstruct their subsequent goals: the major function of goal reconstruction seems to be adaptation to the current life situation (Nurmi & Salmela-Aro in press). This means that adolescents not only face different kinds of lifepaths, but also that their success in dealing with such diversity is reflected in the ways in which they direct their lives later on. Understanding the key mechanisms of such differences can be assumed to increase understanding not only of adolescent development overall, but also the variety of problem behaviors that today's adolescents face in different developmental contexts.

References

Baltes, P. B., Reese, H. W., & Lippsitt, L. P. (1980). Life-span developmental psychology. *Annual Review of Psychology, 31,* 65–100.

Bandura, A. (1986). *Social foundation of thought and action.* Englewood Cliffs, NJ: Prentice-Hall.

Berg, C. (1998). *The contextual-model for goals.* A paper presented at the XVth Biennial Meeting of the ISSBD, Bern, Switzerland, July, 1998.

Brandtstädter, J. (1984). Personal and social control over development: Some implications of an action perspective in life-span psychology. In P. B. Baltes & O. G. Brim (Eds.), *Life-span development and behaviour* (Vol. 6, pp. 2–28). New York: Academic Press.

Brandstädter, J., Krampen, G., & Heil, F. E. (1986). Personal control and emotional evaluation of development in partnership relations during adulthood. In M. M. Baltes & P. B. Baltes (Eds.). *The psychology of control and aging* (pp. 265–296). Hillsdale, NJ: Erlbaum.

Cantor, N., Norem, J., Niedenthal, P., Langston, C., & Brower, A. (1987). Life-tasks self-concept ideals, and cognitive strategies in a life transition. *Journal of Personality and Social Psychology, 53,* 1178–1191.

Cantor, N. (1990). From thought to behavior: "Having" and "doing" in the study of personality and cognition. *American Psychologist, 45,* 735–750.

Caspi, A. (1987). Personality in the life-course. *Journal of Personality and Social Psychology, 53,* 1203–1213.

Caspi, A. (in press). Social selection, social causation and developmental pathways: Empirical strategies for better understanding how individuals and environments are linked across the life course. In L. Pulkkinen & A. Caspi (Eds.), *Successful development.*

Cross, S. & Markus, H. (1991). Possible selves across the life span. *Human Development, 34,* 230–255.

Dannefer, D. (1984). Adult development and social theory: A paradigmatic reappraisal. *American Sociological Review, 49,* 100–116.

Dittman-Kohli, F. (1986). Problem identification and definition as important aspects of adolescents' coping with normative life-tasks. In R. K. Silbereisen, K. Eyferth, & G. Rudinger (Eds.). *Development as action in context,* pp. 19–38. Berlin: Springer-Verlag.

Dreher, E. & Oerter, R. (1986). Children's and adolescents' conceptions of adulthood: The changing view of a crucial developmental task. In R. K. Silbereisen, K. Eyferth, & G. Rudinger (Eds.), *Development as action in context. Problem behavior and normal youth development* (pp. 109–120). Berlin: Springer-Verlag.

Erikson, E.H. (1959). *Identity and the life cycle.* New York: International Universitits Press.

Elder, G. H. Jr. (1985). Perspectives on the life course. In G. H. Elder, Jr. (Ed.), *Life course dynamics* (pp.23–49). Ithaca, N.Y.: Cornell University Press.

Emmons, R. A. (1986). Personal Strivings: An approach to personality and subjective well-being. *Journal of Personality and Social Psychology, 51*, 1058–1068.

Grotevant, H. D. (1987). Toward a process model of identity formation. *Journal of Adolescent Research, 2*, 203–222.

Grotevant, H. D. & Cooper, C. R. (1986). Individuation in family relationships. A perspective on individual differences in the development of identity and role-taking skill in adolescence. *Human Development, 29*, 82–100.

Hagestad, G. O. & Neugarten, B. L. (1985). Age and the life course. In R.H. Binstock & E. Shanas (Eds.), *Handbook of aging and the social sciences* (pp. 35–61). New York: Van Nostrand Reinhold.

Havighurst, R. J. (1948/1974). *Developmental tasks and education* (3rd ed.). New York: McKay. (Original work published 1948).

Heymans, P. G. (1994). Developmental tasks: A cultural analysis of human development. In J. J. F. ter Laak, P. G. Heymans, & A. I. Podol'skij (Eds.), *Developmental tasks: Towards a cultural analysis of human development* (pp. 3–34). The Netherlands: Kluwer Academic Publishers.

Hurrelmann, K. (1989). The social world of adolescents: A sociological perspective. In K. Hurrelmann, & U. Engel (Eds.), *The social world of adolescents* (pp. 3–26). Berlin: Walter de Gruyter.

Hurrelmann, K. 1994 (Ed.). *International Handbook of Adolescence*. Westport: Greenwood Press.

Jones, E. E. & Berglas, S. (1978). Control of attributions about the self through self-handicapping: The appeal of alcohol and the rate of underachievement. *Personality and Social Psychology Bulletin, 4*, 200–206.

Kalakoski, V. & Nurmi, J.-E. (1998). Identity and educational transitions: Age differences in adolescent exploration and commitment related to education, occupation and family. *Journal of Research on Adolescence, 8*, 29–47.

Klaczynski, P. A. & Reese, H. W. (1991). Educational trajectory and "action orientation": Grade and track differences. *Journal of Youth and Adolescence, 20*, 441–462.

Kohli, M. & Meyer, J. W. (1986). Social structure and social construction of life stages. *Human Development, 29*, 145–149.

Kuusinen, J., Hietala, R., & Mustapää, O. (1994). *Nuorten aikuisten onnellisuus, elämään tyytyväisyys ja kehityksen hallinta* (Young adults' happiness, life satisfaction and control beliefs). A poster presented at the Psykologia 94 Congress, August 1994, Jyväskylä, Finland.

Leontjev, A. N. (1977). *Toiminta, tietoisuus, persoonallisuus* (Action, cognition, and personality). Helsinki: Kansankulttuuri.

Lerner, R. M. (1983). A "goodness of fit" model of person—context interaction. In D. Magnusson, & V. L. Allen (Eds.), *Human development: An interactional perspective* (279–294). New York: Academic Press.

Lerner, R. M. (1987). A life-span perspective for early adolescence. In R. M. Lerner, & T. T. Foch (Eds.), *Biological-psychosocial interactions in early adolescence* (pp. 9–34). Hillsdale, N. J.: Lawrence Erlbaum Associates.

Magnusson, D. (1985). Implications of an interactional paradigm for research on human development. *International Journal of Behavioural Development, 8,* 115–137.

Marcia, J. E. (1980). Identity in adolescence. In J. Adelson (Ed.), *Handbook of adolescent psychology.* New York: Wiley.

Markus, H. & Wurf, E. (1987). The dynamic self-concept: A social psychological perspective. *Annual Review of Psychology, 38,* 299–337.

Mayer, K. U. (1986). Structural constraints on the life course. *Human Development, 29,* 163–170.

McAdams, D. P. (1993). *The stories we live by: Personal myths and the making of the self.* New York: W. Morrow.

Meeus, W. (1993). Occupational identity development, school performance, and social support in adolescence: Findings of a Dutch study. *Adolescence, 28,* 809–818.

Motola, M., Sinisalo, P., & Guichard, J. (1998). Social habitus and future plans. A comparison of adolescent future projects in Finland and France. In J.-E. Nurmi (Ed.), *Adolescents, Cultures and Conflicts. Growing up in contempory Europe* (pp. 43–73). New York: Garland Publishing Inc.

Neisser, U. (1976). *Cognition and reality. Principles and implications of cognitive psychology.* San Fransisco: Freeman.

Neugarten, B. L. & Neugarten, D. A. (1987, May).The changing meanings of age. *Psychology Today,* 29–33.

Neugarten, B. L., Moore, J.W., & Lowe, J. C. (1965). Age norms, age constants, and adult socialisation. *American Journal of Sociology, 70,* 710–717.

Newman, B. M. & Newman, P. R. (1975). *Development through life. A psychosocial approach.* Homewood, NJ: The Dorsey Press.

Niemi, P. (1988). Adolescents and the family: Images and experiences of family life in Finland. *Annales Universitatis Turkuensis,* B, 181. Turku: University of Turku.

Noack, P. (1990). *Jugendentwicklung im Kontext. Zum aktiven Umgangmit sozialen Entwicklungsaufgaben in der Freizeit.* München: Psychologie Verlags Union.

Nurmi, J.-E. (1987). Age, sex, social class, and quality of family interaction as determinants of adolescents' future orientation: A developmental task interpretation. *Adolescence, 22,* 977–991.

Nurmi, J.-E. (1989a). Adolescents' orientation to the future: Development of interests and plans, and related attributions and affects, in the life-span context. *Commentationes Scientiarum Socialium, 39.* Helsinki: The Finnish Society for Sciences and Letters.

Nurmi, J.-E. (1991). How do adolescents see their future? A review of the development of future orientation and planning. *Developmental Review, 11,* 1–59.

Nurmi, J-E. (1992). Age differences in adult life goals, concerns, and their temporal extension: A life course approach to future-oriented motivation. *International Journal of Behavioral Development, 15*, 487–508.

Nurmi, J.-E. (1993). Adolescent development in an age-graded context: The role of personal beliefs, goals, and strategies in the tackling of developmental tasks and standards. *International Journal of Behavioral Development, 16*, 169-189.

Nurmi, J.-E. (1997). Self-definition and mental health during adolescence and young adulthood. In J. Schulenberg, J. L. Maggs & K. Hurrelmann (Eds.). *Health risks and developmental transitions during adolescence* (pp. 395-419). Cambridge: Cambridge University Press.

Nurmi, J.-E., Poole, M. E., & Kalakoski, V. (1994). Age differences in adolescent future-oriented goals, concerns, and related temporal extension in different sociocultural contexts. *Journal of Youth and Adolescence, 23*, 471-487.

Nurmi, J.-E. & Salmela-Aro, K. (in press). Goal construction, reconstruction and depressive symptomatology in a life-span context: The transition from school to work. *Journal of Personality*.

Nurmi, J.-E., Salmela-Aro, K., & Ruotsalainen, H. (1994). Cognitive and attributional strategies among unemployed young adults: A case of the failure-trap strategy. *European Journal of Personality, 8*, 135-148.

Nurmi, J.-E., Seginer, R., & Poole, M. E. (1995). Searching for the future in different environments: A comparison of Australian, Finnish, and Israeli adolescents' future orientations, explorations and commitments. In M. Hofer, J. Youniss & P. Noack (Eds.), *Psychological responses to social change: Human development in changing environments*.

Nurmi, J.-E. & Siurala, L. (1994). Finland. In K. Hurrelmann (Ed.). *International Handbook of Adolescence*. Westport: Greenwood Press.

Nuttin, J. R. (1984). *Motivation, planning, and action. A relational theory of behavior dynamics*. Hillsdale, NJ: Lawrence Erlbaum Associates.

Osipow, S. H. (1983). *Theories of career development*. Englewood Cliffs, NJ: Prentice-Hall.

Petersen, A. C., Crouter, A. C., & Wilson, J. (1988). Heterosexual behavior and sexuality among normal young adolescents. In M. D. Levine, & E. R. McAnarney (Eds.), *Early Adolescent Transitions* (123-137). Lexington, MA: Lexington Books.

Rauste-von Wright, M. (1986). On personality and educational psychology. *Human Development, 29*, 328-340.

Rindfuss, R. R., Swicegood, C. G., & Rosenfeld, R. A. (1987). Disorder in the life course: How common and does it matter? *American Sociological Review, 52*, 785-801.

Salmela-Aro, K. & Nurmi, J.-E. (1997). Goal contents, well-being and life context during transition to university: A longitudinal study. *International Journal of Behavioral Development, 20*, 471-491.

Seginer, R. (1983). Parents, educational expectations and childrens' academic achieve-ments: A literature review. *Merrill-Palmer Quarterly, 29*, 1-23.

Strough, J., Berg, C. A., & Sansone, C. (1996) Goals for solving everyday problems across the life span: Age and gender differences in the salience of interpersonal con-cerns. *Developmental Psychology, 32*, 1106-1115.

Taylor, S. E. & Brown, J. D. (1988). Illusion and well-being: A social psychological per-spective on mental health. *Psychological Bulletin, 103*, 193-210.

Valsiner, J. & Lawrence, J. A. (1997). Human development in culture across the life span. In J. W. Berry, P. R. Dasen, & T. S. Saraswathi (Eds.), *Handbook of Cross-Cultural Psychology.* (Vol. 2, pp. 70-106). Boston, MA: Allyn & Bacon.

Weiner, B. (1986). *An attributional theory of motivation and emotion.* New York: Springer-Verlag.

Zepelin, H., Sills, R. A., & Heath, M. W. (1986-87). Is age becoming irrelevant? An exploratory study of perceived age norms. *International Journal of Aging and Human Development, 24*, 241-256.

CHAPTER 10

A Dynamic Systems Approach to Identity Formation: Theoretical Background and Methodological Possibilities

E. SASKIA KUNNEN, HARKE A. BOSMA, AND
PAUL L. C. VAN GEERT

Introduction

This chapter focuses on demonstrating how dynamic systems theory provides a useful way of conceptualizing the development of identity in adolescence. We also aim to show how our conceptualizations of identity development can be simulated with spreadsheet models. Such simulations can best be seen as "thought experiments" that give insight into the validity of these conceptualizations. Thus, the mathematical modeling of developmental processes offers a tool that can be used to explore the implications of the way the process of identity development is conceptualized.

"Identity" is a broad term. In her book on identity development in adolescence, Kroger (1996) discusses a range of theories that she considers relevant to identity in adolescence. We begin with a brief review of her discussion; we will then add a number of elements that we also need to take into consideration in discussing a concrete conceptual model of identity development. A central element is the idea that adolescents themselves play an active role in their own development. They do so by the way they make meaning of what happens to them. Their way of meaning-making determines their preferences, goals, choices they make, and their conflicts and actions. We call this element "self-direction," which, in our view, plays a central role in identity development in adolescence and adulthood.

In this perspective, development is a complex process. First, it implies that we should see development as the development of a person-in-context. We should not perceive adolescent and context as two separate entities that can be assessed independently. Rather, person and context define each other in a dynamic, interactive way. Goals, needs, challenges, conflicts, and important events are not objectively given, but are only goals, needs, challenges, conflicts, and important events when the person perceives them as such.

Second, there probably exist complex and mutual relationships between the variables involved. Adolescents' way of making meaning determines which events are important to them, in which conflicts they engage, and what their goals and challenges look like. However, meaning-making is in turn affected by experience, which is at least partly determined by the kind of preferences and choices people make. Conflicts in particular are seen as the motor behind developmental changes in meaning-making. Consequently, we see development as an iterative process in which the state at time t+1 strongly depends on the state at t. Moreover, the often non-linear relationships between the variables involved pose specific demands on our conceptualizations and research methods. We shall try to show how Dynamic Systems Theory complies with these demands.

Essentials of Identity Development in Adolescence and Beyond
Erikson's Theory of Identity

Erik Erikson is normally accredited with first raising "identity" as an important issue in adolescent and life-span developmental psychology. Although his first studies on identity are more than half a century old, they still form a very useful introduction to any discussion of identity development.

Erikson has defined "a sense of identity" as "a sense of personal sameness and historical continuity" (1968, p.17), " ... [which] ... is based on two simultaneous observations: the perception of the selfsameness and continuity of one's existence in time and space and the perception of the fact that others recognize one's sameness and continuity" (1968, p.50). In his definition Erikson emphasizes two important things. First, he speaks of "a sense of identity." In this way he gives identity a psychological, experiential meaning and thus steers free of the centuries-old philosophical discussion of what "identity" means and whether there is something like "an identity." Second, he links the perception of one's sameness and continuity to the recognition of that sameness and continuity by others. Thus, he emphasizes that identity not only refers to the continuity of oneself, but also one's continuity in the perception of others. In this way a sense of identity refers to a subjective perspective; the subjective experience of a person's core aspects as well as to an objective perspective in the form of the social recognition of these very same core aspects. Thus, to the combination of some very personal, and some very social, contextual process. This is also the reason why Bosma et al. (1994) had conceptualized identity as a person-context relationship.

Identity as a person-context relationship concerns the question of whether there is a fit ("an identity") between essential characteristics of the individual and their continuity in time on the one hand, and the recognition of the sameness and continuity of these characteristics in the individual's context, on the other. This fit involves a dynamic relationship between individual change and the change of contexts over time and from situation to situation. In the tuning process—the process of maintaining a fit—both the context and the person play an important role. They actively "negotiate" which identity characteristics are relevant. With regard to "identity," person and context thus mutually define each other, seek to achieve "identity" in the sense of a person-context fit.

In many situations, this negotiation process remains implicit (e.g., when I work in the garden, buy a bagel, cycle to work). In other situations (e.g., personal relationships, work), this negotiation process can be an active and conscious process in which person and context try to achieve agreement on the relevant identifiers (one's identity as a friend, partner, colleague, psychologist, etc.). There are multiple possibilities for failing to achieve an agreement in such identity processes. One well-known example is the discrepancy between the way a person sees her/himself and how others see that person. In addition, individuals can also feel strong discrepancies between their identity in their personal relationships and their identity at work. (For a taxonomy of discrepancies that can lead to identity problems, see Van der Werff 1990; Van Halen 2001)

Kroger (1989, 1996) in her review of identity theories in developmental psychology, has also strongly emphasized the relationship between self and other, i.e. the relationship between person and context. Her perspective is based on the common and central features of a number of ego- and cognitive psychological approaches of identity in adolescence (Erikson, Blos, Kohlberg, Loevinger, and Kegan). According to Kroger (1989, p. 5–6), "despite usage of different concepts, a further basic commonality seems present as we look across these developmental approaches to the essence of identity. Identity invariably gets defined (at various stages of the life cycle) as a balance between that which is taken to be self and that considered to be other".

Recent Theories of Identity

With regard to the issue of identity, adolescence has a special status in life-span developmental psychology. The adolescent reaches the adult reproductive status as a result of physiological, psycho-sexual, and cognitive changes which interact with changes in the societal expectations regarding the adolescent person. For example, it is expected that adolescents will prepare themselves for the labor market and choose an occupation, start to function as autonomous persons who no longer depend on their parents, begin to take a position of their own in matters of religion and politics, etc. All these expectations can be subsumed under the label "the adolescent curriculum." Because of all these personal and contextual changes, the identifications built up in childhood are inadequate to guide the person's functioning as an adult. The process of identity formation in adolescence implies an active selection and rejection of these childhood identifications in the light of the adolescent's interests, talents, and values, and the chances and options offered by the society (the societal affordances, see Jackson 1995). In this way adolescents begin to direct their own lives and development. Identity development, thus, begins in childhood with (the more passive) processes of identification and introjection. Adolescents begin to build their own identity by actively selecting and discarding earlier identifications in the light of the demands and affordances of the society. In adulthood, every change in the person or the context potentially demands a renegotiation of the identity achieved in adolescence. Identity formation, thus, is a life-long process.

The element of actively making identity choices is central in Marcia's identity status model. This is the empirical approach to identity in adolescence and adulthood that is most often used (Marcia et al. 1993). The identity statuses are "modes of dealing with the identity issue characteristic of late adolescents" (Marcia 1980, p. 161), and they form an extension of Erikson's bipolar description of the outcome of the identity crisis in adolescence (identity versus identity diffusion). According to the identity status model, by the end of adolescence, adolescents have either actively made identity choices and in this way have solved the normative identity crisis (Achievement), have not made such choices (and end up in a state of Identity Diffusion), are still actively exploring identity choices (Moratorium), or have never experienced an exploratory period (Foreclosure).

Marcia sees commitments in important domains of life as the behavioral indications of a sense of identity. Commitments (identity choices) play a central role in the status model. In terms of the perspective presented here one can also see them as the (more or less temporary) crystalizations of the fit between person and context. This may become evident from the following citation of Bourne (1978): "Commitments can of course be of many kinds—vocational, avocational, social, marital, ideological, ethical. From an outside observer's point of view, an individual's commitments would include the domains in which he appears most engaged or involved. From the individual's own point of view his commitments are the matters which he characteristically cares about most or values. *From either point of view, these commitments have a social significance and at the same time provide the individual with a definition of himself*" (p. 227; italics added). In other words, the mutual dependency of subjectively and objectively being identifiable in different contexts is central to the concept of "commitment." Commitments, thus, form a kind of fit between person and context, give a person a psychosocial self-definition, and, as such, play a central role in identity processes. To quote Bourne again: "By my commitments I shall know myself and be known to others" (1978, p. 234). The dynamics of sameness and change in an individual's commitments can therefore offer a promising empirical starting point for the study of the dynamics of identity and of the course of the identity formation process in adolescence and adulthood.

The identity status model, however, is not very suitable for the study of the process of identity development (Bosma 1992; Côté & Levine 1988; Grotevant 1987; Meeus 1996; Van Hoof 1998; Waterman 1982). It has its descriptive use (Waterman 1982), but empirical research shows that any conceivable change from one status to another can actually occur (Goossens 1995; Meeus 1996;

Waterman 1982). Thus, we even observe changes from the Achievement to the Foreclosure status (Marcia 1976), a change that would be impossible if Marcia's theory were true. Moreover, the status approach gives hardly any clue what factors might explain why some individuals move from one status to another (e.g., from Foreclosure into Moratorium) while other individuals remain in the same status for a long time (e.g., Diffusion).

A different conceptualization of identity development, although related to Marcia's approach, is offered by Raphael and Xelowski (1980), who suggest three types of developmental trajectories. The first is an "open" trajectory of adolescents who commit themselves but whose commitments can also change because of new circumstances. The second is a "closed" trajectory of individuals whose commitments do not change. The third is a "diffuse" trajectory of individuals who, despite changes, do not change in their diffused style of approaching identity issues. Berzonsky and colleagues (1990, 1994, 1996) have adopted this approach to identity development and focused on person-related factors that could explain the stable inter-individual differences in developmental trajectories. Basically, they see these differences in terms of a preference for either assimilation or accommodation, or a balance between these. A preference for accommodation means that people are open to new information and can change their commitments. Individuals with a preference for assimilation have a strong tendency to perceive and interpret events in such a way that they support their commitments so that there is no need to change these. Individuals with a diffuse orientation either do not commit themselves or have fluctuating and opportunistic commitments. Differences in developmental pathways can thus be explained on the basis of different ways of dealing with new information and new demands (Bosma & Kunnen, 2001, give a much more detailed discussion of the factors involved in stable inter-individual differences in development).

Identity in Context

Marcia is not the only author to emphasize that adolescents begin to actively direct their lives and development in the process of exploring identity choices. Nurmi (1991, 1993) gives another well-elaborated model with self-direction at its core. This model comprises three components. The first is the socio-cultural context with elements such as developmental tasks, role transitions, career possibilities, and norms for age-adequate behaviors. The second component consists of personal beliefs such as life-span expectations, contextual knowledge, and ideas about successful behaviors. The third component comprises elements of life planning such as values and needs, personal goals, plan strategies, behavioral choices, goal evaluation, and self-concept. The interaction between person and context factors, thus, is central to the model. In the process of life-planning, adolescents choose personal goals on the basis of age-related developmental tasks, make plans and choose behaviors to reach these goals, and evaluate whether these goals have been reached. Successful planning cycles have positive effects on the self-concept, on the new goals that can be set, and on the course of further development. Negative evaluations will steer the individual's development in a different direction. In this way adolescents and adults direct their own lives.

Nurmi's model is very cognitively oriented. Adolescents are assumed to oversee their situation clearly, to know how to set and reach their goals, to be able to make good plans and behave accordingly and to evaluate their achievements realistically. In principle, these assertions are true. Although adolescents have the cognitive resources to see and know what they want and what they are doing (Mann, Harmoni, & Power 1989), they do not always act rationally and life hardly ever proceeds smoothly and according to plans. Life is messy; emotions and chance factors also play a role. For this reason Kunnen and Bosma (1996, 2000) have argued that the person's experience should be taken as the starting point when looking at self-direction. By experience they mean the whole mix of emotions and cognitions a person has with regard to any particular situation, or, in the terms suggested by Kegan (1994), how they give meaning to that situation.

It is assumed that the relations between the different aspects of a person's experience are not linear and causal, but can be better understood as a complex dynamic system of factors (perceptions, thoughts, associations, feelings with regard to the situation), each of which derives its meaning from the system as a whole (Van Geert 1994). The development of the individual is determined by this complex of mutually interacting factors. It cannot be predicted on the basis of one or some of the components of the system (Nowak & Vallacher 1998). We think that adolescents make choices on the basis of how they experience themselves and their situation and, in this way, direct their own life and development.

Toward a General Formal Model of Change

A dynamic systems model provides highly generalized descriptions and formal explanations of the structure of change and development. Depending on the characteristics of the topic under study, different types of dynamic systems models can be constructed. By using examples of simple, general models, we will show how specific properties of a particular topic of interest can be translated into properties of a dynamic systems model. The behavior of these simple and formal models can be easily visualized as interesting patterns and trajectories. It shows, for example, that simple models may generate irregular behavior and uneven trajectories. These models may thus help in explaining observed individual developmental trajectories that could not be explained by more traditional approaches.

Dynamic systems models—in whatever field or domain of inquiry—have two general properties. First, they specify events and phenomena in a geometric space that consists of all the variables necessary to specify a particular system, including, and probably also most importantly, time. Second, they conceptualize events or phenomena as the results of partially open (or partially closed) systems. A dynamic system typically consists of a few variables or components that interact with one another and that are also engaged in some form of interaction with an environment. In principle, the characteristic features of the patterns or processes are produced by the transactions among the variables in the system, not by the inputs coming from the environment. For instance, a coupled support-competition dynamics leads to an oscillating pattern. The oscillations stem from the asymmetric interaction of the variables (one is competitive, the other supportive) and not from an oscillating input of energy or information from the environment. It is in this sense that all dynamic systems can be said to be self-organizing.

Let us begin with the geometric aspect of dynamic systems modeling and apply this to our current topic, the development of identity and the influences of the environment on the one hand and of self-direction on the other. It is assumed that identity development and whatever relevant environmental factors are determined or defined by a multitude of properties or variables. That is, in order to describe or specify identity and its development, a great number of different variables and aspects are involved. For the present purpose of building a dynamic systems model, we need not worry about the exact nature and number of those variables or properties. It is sufficient to say that they constitute an abstract geometric space, specified by as many dimensions as there are variables needed to describe identity in all its different forms and appearances. In this descriptive space, different regions or ranges, located at different points in the space, represent different forms of identity or identity statuses. We may also assume that this space contains some geometric origin, that is, a point where the values of all the variables involved are near zero. That is, the origin specifies a point where none of the properties are present that characterize the identity forms or statuses discerned in some particular model. This point or origin determines, by definition, a theoretical initial state of identity development. It is important to note that, for the time being, we do not have to specify the empirical properties of this origin or of the identity states or statuses that populate our abstract geometric space.

The simplest possible model of identity development in this space concerns the transition from the origin—the theoretical initial state—to a particular identity state or status. For the time being, we need only be concerned with the distance between the origin—the initial state—and the goal—the identity state at issue. By reducing the problem to one of bridging a distance, we have of course simplified the issue enormously. This simplification, however, is one of the characteristic features of a dynamic systems approach to a problem.

Let us see how we can arrive at a simple model describing how a goal state of identity may be reached starting from an initial state. The simplest assumption is that the developing system covers a fixed distance per unit time, the distance A. This is, after all, the basic assumption of linear regression models that explain development or change as a function of time. Hence, if the distance to be covered is represented by Dmax and the current distance from the goal state is represented as Dt, or D in general, we may represent this simple linear model as follows:

$$\Delta D/\Delta t = A \qquad\qquad\qquad\qquad\qquad\qquad \text{eq. 1}$$

for ΔD= difference in D in a time interval Δ t

This could be a model based on the assumption that progress is simply a matter of external influences, for instance teaching or modeling. The magnitude of the modeling or teaching effort is best represented by a constant, hence A (or by a stochastic function with a constant mean and standard deviation). The magnitude of A depends on how "attractive" the goal state is, i.e. how much force it exerts upon the person. We have argued, however, that external events are mediated and defined by the person's own point of view. Thus, a more psychologically valid way of expressing this force of attraction is by referring to the subject's interest in the goal state, or the degree to which the goal state corresponds with the person's personality traits or with the salience of that goal state in the person's environment.

According to this model, a person would progress toward a specific identity state by covering a constant distance per unit time, depending on the level of external stimulation, teaching or modeling that this particular identity state exerts upon the person. For instance, the identity state at issue is represented in the form of personal models (that is, in the form of other persons who demonstrate the identity state), of models offered through education and teaching and so forth. Note that we can already make this model more complicated by assuming that there is not merely one identity state that exerts a certain attraction upon the person, but possibly two or more. If that is the case, we need to specify how those two or more distances (from the person's current state to the two or more attractive, potential states) are related in our abstract geometric space. This degree of relationship is conceptually similar to the notion of shared variance in variables specified across samples or populations. However, we shall not go further into this more complicated version of the model here but rather proceed with a further elaboration of the single distance case.

The simple linear model can easily be extended by a second assumption, namely that it is probable that the distance covered per unit time *decreases* as the person approaches the goal state. There exist several reasons why this could easily be so. For instance, as the person approaches the goal it becomes increasingly more difficult to find models or examples that help one further approach the goal state. Or, as the person approaches the goal state, the person's motivation to invest more effort in achieving the goal state diminishes, since he or she is already in the vicinity of the goal state anyhow. The simplest way to express this notion is to modify the constant of increase A by a function that diminishes as D approaches D_{max}. This function is the simple dimensionless function $(D_{max} - D) / D_{max}$, which approaches 0 [zero] as D approaches D_{max} and is maximal when D is equal to about 0 [zero], i.e. when the system is at the initial state. Our modified model then becomes:

$$\Delta D/t\Delta = A \ (D_{max} - D) / D_{max} \qquad\qquad \text{eq. 2}$$

By the same logic, this model can be extended by assuming that there is not only one but several goal states.

Since this is supposed to be a very general model, we should also assume that there are factors that make it *easier to cover the distance to the goal state the closer one approaches the goal state*. For instance, as one approaches the goal state, the requirements and exigencies of that goal state become progressively clearer, which makes it easier for the person to comply with them. How could this assumption be added to the current model? One solution would be to make A change by a function whose value becomes increasingly bigger as the distance from the goal state becomes increasingly smaller. An obvious candidate for such a function is the inverse of the function that decreases as it approaches the goal state, namely:

$$\Delta D/\Delta t = A \ D_{max} / (D_{max} - D) \qquad\qquad \text{eq. 3}$$

This function has a major disadvantage: that it approaches infinity as the distance from the goal state approaches zero. It would be much more natural to assume that A increases to some maximum as the distance from the goal state becomes zero (that is, when the goal state has been reached). The simplest way to express this condition is by making A dependent on the value of the distance covered, D:

$$\Delta D/\Delta t = A \ D \qquad\qquad \text{eq. 4}$$

We can now easily combine the two general assumptions that have been made so far. The first is that A (the distance covered per unit time) decreases as D (the distance already covered) increases; the second is that A increases as D decreases. The two assumptions have been expressed in the form of equations 2 and 4, which can now be combined:

$$\Delta D / \Delta t = A \, D \, (D_{max} - D) \, / \, D_{max} \qquad\qquad \text{eq. 5}$$

or, written in another way:

$$Dt+1 = Dt * (1+A) - A * D_t^2 / D_{max} \qquad\qquad \text{eq. 5b}$$

This is nothing but the standard logistic growth function that can be used to describe a significant variety of processes of change, growth, and development. In Section 4, the equation will be employed in its so-called difference form (as in equation 3.5b). That is, it will be assumed that Δt's can be conceived of as discrete stretches of time, for instance the amount of time required for a psychological event to take place. Note also that this equation functions like a general default option. If other assumptions apply, it can be easily adapted (such adaptations exceed the scope of the present chapter, however).

Now that we have a general model of how some goal states can be reached from an initial state, we can proceed with more complicated theoretical assumptions to transform the model into one that specifies the major aspects of a theory of identity development.

Let us start by recapitulating the major assumptions from the previous section: firstly, that there exist several goal states, in the form of distinct identity states or statuses. We shall, therefore, have to reflect on how the idea of various goal states can be represented in terms of the dynamic formalisms set out above. The second assumption is that the growth toward any of the goal states is mediated by both subjective, i.e., person-oriented, aspects and by objective, i.e., environment-oriented aspects.

The subjective aspects concern the subject's preferences with regard to specific identity states. A central feature of those preferences is that the choices that have already been made, that is, the identity state at which the subject is aiming, strongly affect the future choices. In other words, the process is characterized by a positive feedback function, amplifying the existing tendencies to move in a particular identity state direction. Note, however, that there also exist various other forces that can eventually counteract the influence of the positive feedback force and drive the system in some other direction than was originally chosen.

The objective aspects consist of events and experiences that eventually change the degree of attractiveness of the available identity states or statuses. A social role model, e.g., a friend who has made a definite choice for a specific political viewpoint, can act as an experience that helps a person overcome his or her doubts concerning political and ethical preferences. However, the value and therefore the effect of an experience, do not solely depend on the objective properties of the experienced event. Here we arrive at another major assumption from the preceding section: that the value and the meaning of an experienced event greatly depend upon the person's internal value and meaning systems.

A Dynamic Systems Model of Commitment Development

Having discussed basic theoretical assumptions relating to the development of identity, and secondly, the general characteristics of dynamic systems models, we shall now show in detail how we can translate specific assumptions concerning the development of identity into the mathematical equations of a quantitative dynamic systems model. The model to be presented describes the changes of two competing commitments over time as a function of (1) the sequence of (positive and negative) events that influence commitments and (2) the adolescent's individual tendency to accommodate or assimilate. To present a complete model would be beyond the scope of this chapter. Our intention is rather to show and discuss how to translate theoretical issues into specific equations and how we can relate the outcomes of the simulations to empirical findings and theoretical issues. Specifically, we shall investigate the effects of systematic manipulations of the following two variables: the individual's tendency to assimilate or accommodate, and the specific patterning of positive and negative events.

A first step in the process of building the model is to define the relevant variables and the relations between them, and to bring them together in a flow chart model (Nowak & Vallacher 1998). The next step is to translate the flow chart model into a mathematical dynamic systems model. This part in the building of a dynamic systems model forces the researcher to be very explicit about assumptions concerning the developmental process under study. The available literature is often insufficiently detailed or explicit enough for concrete decisions that have to be made in order to specify the relationships between the variables in the flow chart model into mathematical functions. However, we can test assumptions about these relationships with simulations to see if they do make sense. In this sense, the simulations are thought-experiments which offer a direct test of the validity of such new assumptions.

Defining the Variables and Their Relationships

In the model that follows, we focus on the development of specific commitments in a particular domain, i.e., jobs and education. Adolescents have many possibilities open to them in choosing commitments, but in most situations, only one of these can be chosen. Thus, different potential commitments compete with each other. Take for example an adolescent who is in doubt whether to follow her parent's wishes, or to study art; or whether to take a job and earn money, or go to university and study medicine. We will model the development of two of such competing commitments, C and A.

The development and selection of one of the competing commitments are not purely internal psychological processes. It is most likely that adolescents will be involved in all kinds of situations that are relevant to this choice process. In part, they may be deliberately looking for these situations: discussions with parents, friends, reading information about the study, talking with an employment manager, etc., but unplanned events can also be important. For example, a movie with a heroic physician, a meeting with a now working schoolfriend who owns a car, a cousin who failed in her studies, etc.

We can assume that each situation which is relevant to one of the commitments as one iteration in the developmental process. In an iteration, the interaction between the present state of the commitment and the event results in an "outcome." The outcome either strengthens or weakens the developing commitment. Figure 1 shows this schematically.

It was argued above that the meaning of an external event and its outcome are not inherent to the event itself, but depend on the interaction between the event and internal conditions (person factors). On the basis of theories of identity development (Kroger 1996), we can make several assumptions concerning this interaction.

First, the effect of an event will depend on the actual strength of the commitment. If the commitment is very weak, there is little at stake for the person,

Figure 1: The Development of Two Competing Commitments in a Scheme

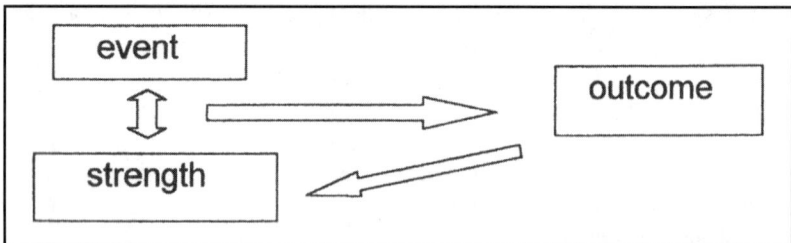

and events will have only a small chance to affect the commitment. In the situation where the commitment is already very strong, events will also have only a minor effect on the commitment (since there is little left to change). Secondly, because both commitments compete for the same resources, they will negatively affect each other. Because only one commitment can be chosen, a high degree of support for one commitment will be at the cost of the other. Thirdly, the stable inter-individual differences in preference for assimilation or accommodation, discussed in the second section, will affect the growth of commitments. Assimilation means that the person tries to fit new events into the existing system. Assimilation can be seen as a tendency to perceive and interpret events such that they support one's actual commitments. During the development of new commitments, it might mean a stronger tendency to stick to the strongest commitment and to pay less attention to alternatives. Figure 2 shows in a flow chart how these three factors interact with the external event.

Figure 2: The Interaction of Factors in the Development of New Commitments

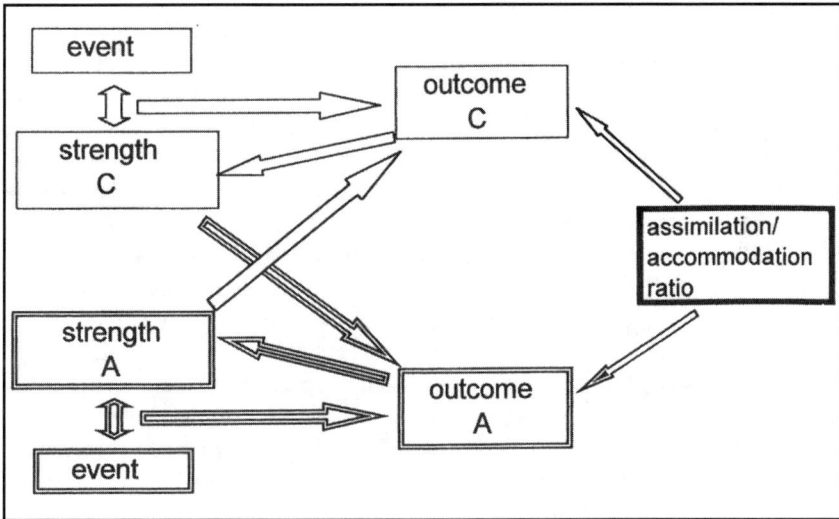

Defining the Mathematical Equations

As a next step, we should translate this verbal description, presented in the flow chart, into an equation. Because we assumed two commitments, we need an equation for each commitment. The basic equation we shall use is the logistic growth equation as explained in the previous section. ,

$$C_{t+1} = C_t * (1 + r) - r * C_t^2 / C_{max} \qquad \text{eq. 6}$$
$$A_{t+1} = A_t * (1 + r) - r * A_t^2 / A_{max} \qquad \text{eq. 7}$$

Here, C_t = the commitment at time t; A_t = the alternative commitment at time t; r = the growth factor that determines the growth or decline of each commitment, the effect of r on the commitment depends on the value of the commitment; C_{max}, A_{max} = the maximum stable value that the commitment can reach. In this equation, the maximum stable value has been set to "1" and thus can be omitted.

If we compute the respective values of C and A iteratively for, say, a thousand steps, we get a time series of values for the strength of commitments of both C and A. (Such computations can easily be done with a spreadsheet program.) These series represent simulations of the developmental trajectories of the strength of C and A. The outcome of each interaction between person and event - one for each iteration — will differ, depending on the situation. The "r"s in the equations represent the outcome of this interaction. We will now specify the r on the basis of the discussion above.

First, r should include the external component of the event. These events can be negative or positive. Whether they are negative or positive is not systematically related to the development of identity as described in the model. Because negative and positive events occur more or less at random, they can be represented by randomly chosen numbers. In each iteration, a random number is generated that represents the external components of the event. The selection of the range and the distribution of the random numbers should be based on assumptions concerning the occurrence of the external events. The range should cover positive and negative numbers. Because we assume some positive attractiveness of the commitments, we choose a range that is slightly biased: the probability that an event is positive is slightly higher than the probability that it is negative. We also assume that events have more or less impact, for instance depending on how salient they are to the person. The differential impact can be represented mathematically by the size of the numbers, with larger numbers having more impact. Since they represent the occurrence of actual events, we shall also have to determine the distribution of the numbers. Do we expect more and less powerful events to be equally distributed, or do we expect that, for example, less powerful events will be more frequent? In our model we chose, for the sake of simplicity, an equal distribution.

Next, we have to determine how this event, represented by the random number, interacts with the other factors. We begin with the effect of the competing commitment. What will be the effect of a more or less strong alternative commitment on the growth of the commitment under study? We assume that the presence of a strong competing commitment will negatively affect the meaning of events that supports its competitor. These events will be interpreted rather less positive if the competing commitment becomes stronger. In order to specify mathematically the reduction of the effect size of an event, we subtract a small number from the numerical value that corresponds with the event at issue. The magnitude of this number will be determined by the strength of the competing commitment (with more strongly competing commitments corresponding with larger subtractors).

Finally, we have to include the individual's preference for assimilation or for accommodation. We described assimilation above as a tendency to stick to the dominant commitment, at the cost of alternatives. This tendency can be translated into an equation by calculating the difference in strength between both commitments. A strong tendency to assimilate enhances the positive impact of events for the strongest commitment, and reduces the positive impact for the weaker commitment.

Summarizing, the "r" in equation 6 and 7 consists of an external component (a random factor), a negative factor determined by the value of the competing commitment, and a factor representing the assimilation tendency. This factor depends on the difference between the values of both commitments. A random number represents the external component, which is called the "random" in the equation. This number is selected from an evenly distributed range that covers both negative and positive numbers but is slightly skewed to the positive side. From this number a factor is subtracted that consists of the value of the strength of the competing commitment: random - A_t. Finally, the tendency to assimilate is presented by a factor depending on the difference in strength between both commitments: $C_t - A_t$.

We now have to determine how these three components of "r" are to be combined. Different mathematical operations have different types of effect. If we multiply the competing factor, the random number and the assimilation factor, the consequence will be that the width of the random range changes. That is, events will have a stronger impact if the factor is higher. If we add the competing factor and the random number, the effect will be a shift of the range, either to the positive or to the negative side. Thus, a more positive factor will give more positive and less negative events. The latter option, addition, seems most realistic.

We can integrate all arguments together now in equations 8 and 9:

$$C_{t+1} = C_t * (1 + z*(s*(C_t - A_t)+ \text{random} - x*A_t)) - (z*(s*(C_t - A_t) + \text{random} - x*A_t))* C_t^2 \qquad \text{eq. 8}$$

$$A_{t+1} = A_t * (1 + z*(s*(A_t - C_t) + \text{random} - x*C_t)) - (z*(s*(A_t - C_t) + \text{random} - x*C_t)) * A_t^2 \qquad \text{eq. 9}$$

Where C_t = the commitment at time t; A_t = the alternative commitment at time t; z = parameter that regulates the range of the total r (0.5); s = parameter that regulates the relative impact of the difference between both strengths. This parameter thus represents the tendency to assimilate (0 - 0.1); x = parameter that regulates the relative impact of the strength of the competing commitment (0.02); "random" is a randomly chosen number in an evenly distributed range.[1]

In the equations, several parameters are added (z, s, x), which have a scaling function: they regulate the relative impact of one factor compared to the others. The meaning of the value of these parameters is basically mathematical. They adjust the different ranges of the different factors to each other. The actual sizes of those ranges are mathematical artifacts. What matters, in relation to the theory simulated by the equations, is the proportionality between the various ranges. This proportionality is specified by the scaling parameters. In the model presented above, the regulating parameters in the equations of both commitments are the same. This need not be so, of course. It may well be that one commitment is more strongly supported by the environment, or that one commitment has higher intrinsic attractiveness than the other one. These differences should be expressed in differences in parameter values, but we assume here that the two commitments are comparable in every aspect.

Given the function of the scaling parameters, we may conclude that variations in their values have a psychological meaning. For example, the parameter x regulates the relative impact of the value of the competing commitment. We can imagine that sometimes commitments are more competitive than at other times. For instance, the adolescent mentioned above might find a way to enter university and to find an additional job in which he can make money, and in this way reduce the competition between both commitments. An example of very strongly competing commitments would be the case of an adolescent who entertains doubts about staying in the fundamentalist-religious group of her parents allegiance. Here, even thinking or talking about other commitments will strongly compete with the current commitment. Thus, variations in competition between the commitments can be translated into the model by modifying the value of parameter x. In the same way, variations in the seriousness and valence (positive or negative) of the events can be simulated by modifying the range of the random numbers.

We now have a mathematical model that can be used to study the developmental effects of systematic manipulations of the parameters and/or changes in initial values of the main variables. Since it is a model that proceeds by discrete steps, it can easily be implemented in the form of a spreadsheet model (Excel, Quattro Pro, Lotus). The effect of parameter manipulations can be investigated by running several simulations and by comparing their results. In the next two subsections we consider the effects of changes in the tendency to assimilate or accommodate and the effects of the patterning of positive and negative events.

The Effects of Differences in the Tendency to Assimilate or Accommodate

In the equations 8 and 9, parameter "s" regulates the relative impact of the strongest commitment. In an earlier section, we stated that a stronger preference for assimilation would manifest itself in a stronger preference for the dominant commitment. Thus, the value of s represents the tendency of an individual to assimilate. This implies that variations in this parameter should show differences in the simulated development of commitment that resemble the real differences between people who have a more and less strong tendency to assimilate. Figure 3 shows three pairs of simulations generated by the model.

The top pair gives the results of two simulations with the same, high value for parameter s, drawn from a set of simulations typical of high s-values. They show that the strength of one commitment rises rapidly to a maximum value, while the strength of the other commitment remains very low and decreases to zero. Although this happens in all the simulations with this value for s, it can take more or less time (iterations) before the dominant commitment rapidly rises to its maximum value.

In addition to the assimilation parameter, the random numbers (representing

Figure 3: Results of Simulations with Different Tendencies to Assimilate.

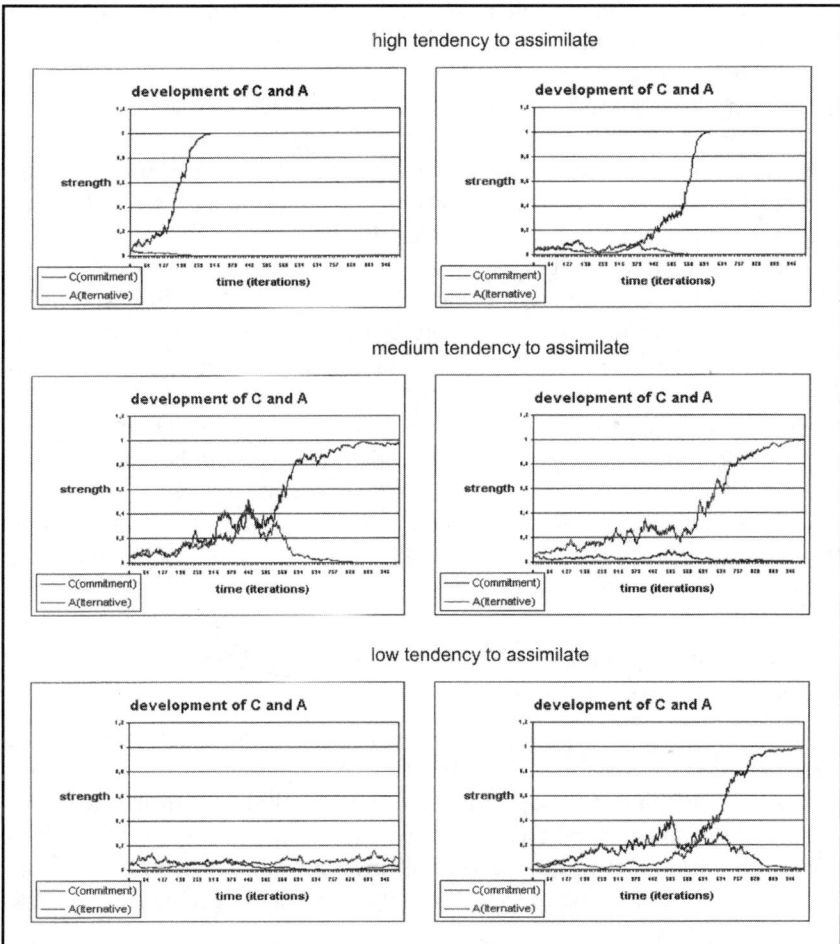

randomly distributed experiences) also affect the course of a trajectory. The differences within each pair are due to these random factors. A high tendency to assimilate thus leads to trajectories in which a confrontation with alternatives more or less quickly leads to a progressive strengthening of one commitment. This is also what the literature suggests about individuals characterized by the Foreclosure status (see for example Marcia et al. 1993).

A medium tendency to assimilate has a different effect. The middle row of pictures, especially the left picture in this row, suggests a different type of trajectory. Here we see that C and A both gain in strength. For a while, both commitments are moderately strong. We can interpret this as a period during which both alternatives are explored. One could call this a moratorium period. Then C begins to grow in strength and the strength of A diminishes. The exploratory period is over and a clear choice between alternatives has been reached. The right-hand picture of the middle row shows a rather similar picture. Again, the difference between both is completely due to chance factors.

The bottom row of pictures in Figure 3 shows some typical results of simulations with a low tendency to assimilate. The tendency to assimilate is represented in the model by a preference for the strongest commitment. A low tendency to assimilate means that the preference for the strongest commitment disappears: both the strongest and the weakest commitments are treated in the same way. The parameter value "s" is zero. Our simulations show that in most cases, no commitments develop. The picture on the left shows a typical example. This looks like a diffuse trajectory. However, in some cases, depending on a lucky "choice" of the random numbers that are generated, we find results that resemble a moratorium-achieved trajectory (as can be seen in the picture on the right). The psychological meaning of lucky random numbers is that there is relatively strong and consistent support for one commitment. However, the bias could also become negative so that there is a systematic preference for the weakest commitment. This represents an attitude in which the alternative that is not chosen looks more attractive afterward: the grass is always greener on the other side of the fence. In simulations with such a negative parameter value, no commitments develop at all.

The Effects of the Patterning of Positive and Negative Events: Developmental Versus Firm Foreclosures

Kroger (1995) distinguishes two types of foreclosure: firm and developmental (see also Archer & Waterman 1990). Whereas developmental foreclosures develop into moratorium and achievement later, firm foreclosures remain foreclosed. Our aim is to simulate these two types of trajectories. To do this, we have to specify our assumptions about the mechanisms behind these two types and translate them into equations. Developmentally foreclosed individuals resemble moratorium ones with regard to their intrapsychic structure, e.g., the separation-individuation dimensions. Kroger (1995) does not elaborate the factors and mechanisms that may cause the difference in status between these two groups with comparable intrapsychic characteristics.

Parameter s represents the tendency to assimilate. We have shown that the model generates foreclosed trajectories when this parameter has a high value. The trajectories generated with this value for s remain foreclosed and probably resemble the firm foreclosures, but what about the developmental foreclosures? They do not differ from moratorium subjects in terms of intrapsychic structure and thus our parameter s should be the same as in moratorium-achieved trajectories. We hypothesized that developmental foreclosure may be caused by a lack of challenge of one's commitments. As long as the events in the adolescent's life support the chosen commitment and as long as there are only few events that show the attraction of another commitment, there is no need to explore.

In Kroger's study, the developmental foreclosed subjects did show development later, i.e., after two years at university. This is in line with Waterman's (1993) account, in which he argued that the university as a context challenges one's commitments, especially in the later years at college. In these later years, students are confronted with the demands and contents of the study and career they have chosen. Meeus (1996), however, presented evidence indicating that it is not the university, but the high school context of several years earlier that can induce more identity change.

These contrasting findings pose no problem for the simulations because the increase in challenges is important, not its timing. The mechanism behind the developmental foreclosure could be a temporary lack of challenge of the dominant commitments followed by a confrontation with strong challenges. In order to simulate such trajectories, we manipulated the range and valence of the random numbers in our model (while using the moratorium/achievement value for parameter s). During the first part of the trajectory, we gave events supporting the dominant commitment C a positive bias, and events affecting the alternative A a negative bias. This represents a period in which little challenges occur to the dominant commitment.

The top pictures of Figure 4 show that this indeed resulted in a rapid growth to maximum strength of one of the commitments, resembling the first part of the foreclosed trajectory presented in the left picture of the top row of Figure 3.

In the middle of the trajectory, we induced a period of crisis in the simulations by reversing the bias. Thus, the dominant commitments were then challenged strongly and there was strong support for the exploration of alternatives. After this simulated crisis period, the parameters affecting the events were again set to the standard values they had in the simulations shown in Figure 3. As can be seen in the two upper pictures of Figure 4, the crisis results in a period of

Figure 4: Simulations of Patterns of Events Resulting in
Developmental Foreclosure. The two upper pictures have
a Moderate Tendency to Assimilate, the Lowest a high Tendency.

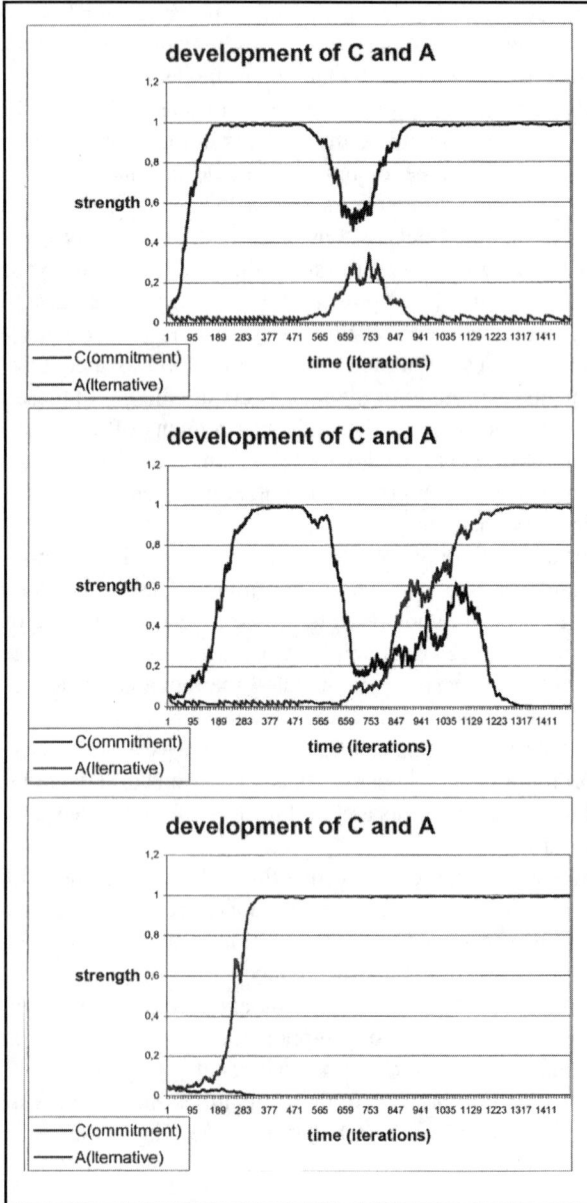

moratorium and finally an achievement pattern comparable to the pictures in the middle row of Figure 3. The same pattern of biased events did not have any effect if the tendency to assimilate (parameter s) was set high. This is shown in the lower picture of Figure 4. Only one picture is given for these conditions, since the simulations invariably led to this kind of trajectory.

Discussion and Conclusions

Our dynamic systems model generates trajectories that fit in with theoretical notions and empirical findings about identity development. It can be concluded that the assumptions built into the spreadsheet model therefore make sense. Of course, there is much remaining to be explained about the simulations. In this chapter, however, we wanted to focus on the application of dynamic systems thinking to identity development and the model presented here primarily served illustrative purposes.

A dynamic systems approach offers new ways of conceptualizing and understanding stability and change in identity development. It fits in well with recent developmental theories that stress the mutual interaction between person and context for example. A dynamic systems model describes theoretical assumptions concerning mutual and non-linear relations between different components of a system and shows how characteristics of the person-context interaction on a microscopic level (of one iteration) cause changes on a macroscopic level (the trajectories).

A mathematical model necessitates and allows for far more specific questions and assumptions than a theory or a conceptual model can ever do (Nowak & Vallacher 1998). For instance, we had to specify in one of our examples the different mechanisms of developmental and firm foreclosures in a detailed way. For the developmental foreclosure trajectory, we had to specify exactly what type of sequence of events could cause such a trajectory. By means of the mathematical model, theoretical assumptions can be translated into very specific hypotheses, which can then be tested in computer simulations.

Of course, verification in computer simulations is only a first step in the validation process; the simulations help to specify and evaluate the plausibility of theoretical ideas and thus restrict the number of alternative hypotheses that have to be put to the empirical test. For example, we could use longitudinal studies to test our assumptions about firm and developmental foreclosure events, which proved to be plausible in the simulations. We would then expect for adolescents with a moderate tendency to assimilate that a confirming pattern of events should result in a foreclosed trajectory more often than a challenging pattern. For adolescents with a strong tendency to assimilate we would not expect such differentiation.

The confirmation of hypotheses by the simulations with the mathematical model will provide us with evidence for the plausibility of the model and its underlying theoretical assumptions. We should realize that verbal models alone do not allow us to arrive at predictions beyond a few steps in the developmental process. The point is that the wealth of—often mutual—relationships discerned by those models prevents us from verbally anticipating the intended effect of those relationships beyond a very short time window. We need a "mechanical" device in order to infer the results of the developmental mechanisms. Such a device takes the form of a simple computer program—a spreadsheet model— that allows us to run numerical experiments with various types of—psychologi- cally plausible—conditions. For instance, our very simple model has shown under which circumstances (the type of sequence of events) an individual ten- dency to assimilate may result in a foreclosed, diffused, or achieved identity tra- jectory.

One major advance in building mathematical models is, that it forces researchers to be very explicit about their assumptions concerning the develop- mental mechanisms and processes. Although these assumptions underlie the the- ories, they often remain hidden. By exposing them, and comparing the simula- tions with the expected trajectories, these assumptions can be tested and chal- lenged. As for the development of commitments, a well-accepted and explicit assumption is that differences in the tendency to assimilate are important. In our model, we represented the strength of this tendency as a bias in the interpretation of events. The stronger the bias, the more events were seen as supporting one's existing preferred commitment. In our simulations, the effects of differences in the tendency to assimilate accorded with theoretical expectations and empirical findings: higher assimilation results in more foreclosed trajectories. However, alternative representations of the assimilation tendency are possible. The simu- lations of models including these alternative representations could be compared with those presented here. Moreover, further research could be carried out to test different representations of the tendency to assimilate more directly.

In the literature, different types of foreclosure and diffusion (Archer & Waterman 1990; Kroger 1995; Marcia 1989) have been described. To model firm and developmental foreclosure, we had to specify the assumed mechanisms behind these two types of foreclosure in a more detailed way than theory had previously done. The simulations showed that a foreclosed trajectory may be ini- tiated by different mechanisms, and the mechanism that we called "develop- mental foreclosed" (a lower tendency to assimilate in combination with a tem- porary lack of challenge, followed by a strong confrontation with challenges) does result in a moratorium and achievement status later in life.

In a comparable way Marcia (1989) distinguished developmental diffusion from "firm" diffusion. He has distinguished four types of identity diffusion. "Diffusion" can be applied to the borderline personality, but, according to

Marcia, this personality would be described more accurately by "self-fragmentation." Another type of pathological diffusion is the kind of disturbed identity which Erikson called identity diffusion ("disturbed diffusion"). A second type of diffusion is called "carefree diffusion." This type of diffusion concerns socially skilled individuals who, nevertheless, are unable to commit themselves. They suffer from the same "inner emptiness" (Marcia 1989, p.292) as the disturbed diffusions. Both types can be seen as "firm" diffusions. The other two types of diffusion are not characterized by a fundamental incapability for lasting commitments. The "culturally adaptive diffusions" occur in situations in which making firm commitments is non-adaptive (e.g., trying to achieve strong occupational commitments in times of economic hardship). Culturally adaptive diffusions probably develop into achievement when their environment encourages commitment and provides alternatives. The "developmental diffusions," according to Marcia (1989), are similar to persons in the achievement status in personality structure and values, but they deliberately and temporarily postpone commitments.

Our simulations suggest that the chance of diffused trajectories increases when the tendency to assimilate is lower. In situations with a negative bias, that is, a bias for the commitment not chosen, no commitments develop at all. These simulations could represent a firm diffusion. "Developmental diffusions" do not differ from people in the achievement status. Thus, they should have a medium tendency to assimilate. Typically for them is that for some reason they are not in situations that ask them for developing commitments. In the model, this could be represented by reducing the values (= importance) of the events. In our simulations, a reduction of the range of event values does indeed result in a sharp increase of diffused trajectories. In the previous section we mentioned the psychological mechanism that underlies the negative parameter value: it represents a tendency to feel attracted to the alternatives that were not chosen. If one has a girlfriend, one longs for freedom and breaks the relation, but then one longs for intimacy and starts to look for a new relationship. Literature does not—as far as we know—describe these or other mechanisms underlying diffusion. We see the mechanism described here as a hypothesis that could be tested in empirical research.

The model presented here contains only a few variables, as compared with the detailed list of components as formulated for example in Nurmi's model (1991, 1993). Nevertheless, our model covers the most relevant interactions. The variables in the model integrate the specific variables into a few broad mechanisms (see also Nowak & Vallacher 1998; van Geert 1994). Of course, in validating the model it might turn out that some important aspects are still missing and need to be added.

In this way, building a model and simulating development involves a close interplay between formulating theoretical hypotheses, translating them into equations, checking the simulated trajectories against theoretical expectations and empirical knowledge, and adjusting and elaborating the model. We also could compare competing theoretical notions, by translating them into different mathematical models, and comparing the simulated outcomes.

A common objection to this type of model building is that many arbitrary choices have to be made and that the numbers of parameters allow the researcher to simulate almost every thinkable trajectory. It would be beyond the scope of this chapter to discuss these objections in any detail, but we wish to mention just one point. In the approach described here, theory dictates the kind of model we can build. Changing a model in order to generate "better" trajectories is defensible only if there are good theoretical reasons to add or omit a parameter or to adjust a mathematical relationship. Given the model, the possibility of manipulating the model's behavior by the choice of right parameters is considerably more restricted than is often thought. For a more thorough discussion of this topic we refer to Van Geert (1998) and Olthof, Kunnen, & Boom (2000).

The whole process of model building is a continuous interchange between formulating equations, and checking resulting trajectories against theoretical notions and empirical knowledge concerning commitment development (Nowak & Vallacher 1998). A final test of the model should consist of validating simulated trajectories against empirical data. However, for this we need a different type of data than is currently available. Although specific kinds of group data could help in validating the model, the best way to verify the dynamics of the developmental process empirically would be to gather time series of data of the relevant variables for different individuals (here the valence and impact of events and the strength of commitments). Although there are now more calls for intensive longitudinal and individual data (Magai & McFadden 1995), these are still scarce and collecting such data will require new types of research programs. The collection of such data is time-consuming and difficult. In the model described here for example, regularly measuring the strength of commitments is not only required but also possible (e.g., Bosma 1992). Frequently repeated measurements run the risk that the procedure affects the data. Observational data, or simple diary and free report data could diminish this risk. It is more difficult to gather reliable time series of events. In the model, each event includes a discrete external component, the random number. In real life the valence and strength of events can be assessed only by means of the person's experience and we cannot separate the "random number" component from the interpretation component. Assessment of events can thus only be extrapolated from the individual's experience. Consequently, it will be hard to come to an assessment of the external component of events.

Self-direction in identity development involves a complex interaction between adolescent and context, and characteristics of both determine the characteristics of the developmental trajectory. Because of this complexity, the dynamic systems approach, although not the easiest road to take, has much to offer in the study of self-direction.

References

Archer, S.L. & Waterman, A.S. (1990). Varieties of identity diffusions and foreclosures: An exploration of subcategories of the identity statuses. *Journal of Adolescent Research, 5*, 96-111.

Berzonsky, M.D. (1990). Self-construction over the life span: A process perspective on identity formation. In: G.J. Neimeyer & R.A. Neimeyer (Eds.), *Advances in Personal Construct Psychology* (vol. 1, pp. 155-186). Greenwich, CT: JAI Press.

Berzonsky, M.D., (1994). Self-identity: The relationship between process and content. *Journal of Research in Personality, 28*, 453-460.

Berzonsky, M.D. & Ferrari, J.R. (1996). Identity orientation and decisional strategies. *Personality and Individual Differences, 20*, 597-606.

Bosma, H.A. (1992). *Identity in adolescence: Managing commitments.* In: G.R. Adams, T.P. Gullotta & R. Montemayor, (Eds.), *Adolescent identity formation* (pp. 91-121). Newbury Park: Sage.

Bosma, H.A., Graafsma, T.L.G., Grotevant, H.D., and D.J.de Levita (1994). *Identity and development: an interdisciplinary approach.* Thousand Oaks, CA: Sage Publications.

Bosma, H.A. & Kunnen, E.S. (2001). Determinants and mechanisms in identity development. A review and synthesis. *Developmental Review*, 39–66.

Bourne, E. (1978). The state of research on ego-identity: a review and appraisal. Part I and Part II. *Journal of Youth and Adolescence, 7*, 223-252, 371-392.

Côté, J.E. & Levine, C. (1988). A critical examination of the ego identity status paradigm. *Developmental Review, 8*, 147-184.

Erikson, E.H. (1968). *Identity, youth and crisis.* New York: Norton.

Goossens, L. (1995). *Identity status development and students' perception of the university environment: a cohort-sequential study.* In A. Oosterwegel & R.Wicklund (Eds.), *The self in European and North American culture: development and processes* (pp 19-32). Dordrecht: Kluwer.

Grotevant, H.D. (1987). Toward a process model of identity formation. *Journal of Adolescent Research, 2*, 203-222.

Jackson, A.E. (1995). *Adolescent identity development and social context: Toward an integrative perspective.* In Oosterwegel & Wicklund (Eds.), The self in European and North American culture: development and processes (pp 33-44). Dordrecht: Kluwer.

Kegan, R. (1994). *In over our heads.* Cambridge: Harvard University Press.

Kroger, J. (1989) *Identity in adolescence. The balance between self and other.* London: Routledge.

Kroger, J. (1995). The differentiation of "firm" and "developmental" foreclosure statuses: a longitudinal study. *Journal of Adolescent Research, 10*, 317-337.

Kroger, J. (1996). *Identity in adolescence. The balance between self and other.* London: Routledge.

Kunnen, E. S. & Bosma, H. A. (1996). Adolescent conflict and the development of mean-ing making. In L.Verhofstadt-Denève, I. Kienhorst & C. Braet (Eds.), *Conflict and development in adolescence* (pp. 61-74). Leiden: DSWO Press.

Kunnen, E. S. & Bosma, H. A. (2000). The development of meaning making: a dynamic systems approach. *New Ideas in Psychology, 18*, 57-82.

Magai, C. Z. & McFadden, S. H. (1995). *The role of emotions in social and personality development. History, theory and research.* New York: Plenum Press.

Mann, L., Harmoni, R., & Power, C. (1989). Adolescent decision-making: the develop-ment of competence. *Journal of Adolescence, 12*, 265-278.

Marcia, J.E. (1976). Identity six years after: A follow-up study. *Journal of Youth and Adolescence, 5*, 145-160.

Marcia, J.E. (1980). Identity in adolescence. In: J. Adelson (Ed.), *Handbook of adolescent psychology* (pp. 159-187). New York: Wiley.

Marcia, J.E. (1989). *Identity Diffusion differentiated.* In M.A. Luszez & T. Nettelbeck (Eds.), *Psychological development: Perspectives across the life-span* (pp. 289-294). Amsterdam: North-Holland Elsevier Science.

Marcia, J.E., Waterman, A.S., Matteson, D.R., Archer, S.L. & Orlofsky, J.L. (1993). *Ego identity. A handbook for psychosocial research.* New York: Springer Verlag.

Meeus, W. (1996). Studies on identity development in adolescence: An overview of research and some new data. *Journal of Youth and Adolescence, 25*, 269-298.

Nowak, A. & Vallacher, R.R. (1998). *Dynamical social psychology.* New York: Guilford Press.

Nurmi, J-E. (1991). How do adolescents see their future? A review of the development of future orientation and planning. *Developmental Review, 11*, 1-59.

Nurmi, J-E. (1993). Adolescent development in an age-graded context: The role of per-sonal beliefs, goals and strategies in tackling of developmental tasks and standards. *International Journal of Behavioral Development, 16*, 169-189.

Olthof, T., Kunnen, E.S. & Boom, J. (2000). Simulating mother-child interaction: Exploring two varieties of a non-linear dynamic system approach. *Infant and Child Development, 9*, 33-60.

Raphael, D. & Xelowski, H.G. (1980). Identity status in high school students: Critique and a revised paradigm. *Journal of Youth and Adolescence, 9*, 383-389.

Van Geert, P.L.L. (1994). *Dynamic systems of development. Change between complexity and chaos.* New York: Harvester Wheatsheaf.

Van Geert, P. L. C. (1998). A dynamic systems model of basic developmental mecha-nisms: Piaget, Vygotksy, and beyond. *Psychological Review, 105*, 634-677.

Van Halen, C.P.M. (2001) *The uncertainties of self and identity. Experiencing self-defini-tion problems over the lifespan.* University of Groningen, NL: doctoral dissertation.

Van Hoof, A. (1998). *Identity formation in adolescence: Structural integration and guid-ing influences.* University of Utrecht, NL: doctoral dissertation.

Van der Werff, J.J. (1990). Individual problems of self-definition: An overview, and a view. *International Journal of Behavioral Development. 8*, 445-471.

Waterman, A.S. (1982). Identity development from adolescence to adulthood: An extension of theory and a review of research. *Developmental Psychology, 18*, 341-358.

Waterman, A.S. (1993). Developmental perspectives on identity formation: From adolescence to adulthood. In J.E. Marcia, A.S. Waterman, D.R. Matteson, S.L. Archer, & J.L.Orlofsky (Eds.), *Ego identity: A handbook for psychosocial research* (pp. 42-68). New York: Springer Verlag.

Notes

1. To rebuild the model, additional technical information is necessary. The model can be downloaded from: http://www.xs4all.nl/~sajama/models1.htm. On request, this information will be send by email: sajama@xs4all.nl

CHAPTER 11

Adolescents' Scholastic Field, Identity Frames, and Future Projects

JEAN GUICHARD

Introduction: Structures, Interactions, Self-Direction and Future Plans

How are the future plans of adolescents created? Such a question is typical of our century (though by no means exclusive to it), i.e., for the time in history when emphasis is placed upon the individual (Häyrynen 1995, "die Gesellschaft der Individuen," Elias 1987), vocational choice (Parsons 1909) and "self-concern" (le Souci de soi, Foucault 1984).

Many theoretical models have been suggested in the past hundred years in attempts to provide answers to this question. Some of these theories are general, focused on the development of individuals and of their "subjectivity" (e.g., James, 1890; Freud 1917, 1963; Jung 1926, 1960; Mead 1934; Wallon 1934; Cattell 1950; Kelly 1955; Rogers 1961; Erikson 1968; Bandura 1977. "Subjectivity" is used here as a rag-bag word referring to everything covered by the concepts, each in their own theoretical way, of "ego," "self," person," identity," basic personality structure," "habitus, etc.). Other theories, often derived from earlier work, take into consideration essentially the development of individual vocations and occupational choices (e.g.: Ginzberg, Ginsburg, Axelrad & Herma 1951; Roe 1956; Super 1957, 1984; Gysbers & Moore 1973; Krumboltz 1977; Gottfredson 1981; Law 1981; Huteau 1982; Vondracek, Lerner & Schulenberg 1986; Nurmi 1991).

Whether concerning the development of "subjectivity" or limited to the question of personal and occupational "vocations," these theories lead on to various discussions, one of which is essential. This is the question of the stability or malleability of "subjectivity": does an individual *retain the same personal identity, gradually evolve* throughout life or, even more malleable, does *subjectivity vary according to contexts* by which the individual is confronted?

Without going into the fundamental considerations specific to each notion, it is evident that *approaches that put weight to the individual's past at the same time emphasize the relative stability of their subjectivity*. This applies to psychoanalysts. They emphasize the role of the conscious and unconscious desires of parents. It also applies to more sociological perspectives: the "basic personality structure" of Abraham Kardiner or the "habitus" of Pierre Bourdieu designate stable constituents of subjectivity. The same goes for certain approaches to the self. This stability does not mean immutability. However, stability does imply "resistance to change".

Most psycho-social approaches and some psychological notions are, on the contrary, focused on the dynamics of subjectivity. The basic idea is that events which individuals experience (and some which they anticipate) lead to restructuration of their subjectivity: the structure and self-conception of the individual changes.

Currently dominant trends surmise a *dynamic conception of identity processes*, though it seems impossible to analyze this dynamic without taking into account the relative stability of the structures of social relations. It is within these structures of varying degrees of stability that individuals enter for certain social games according to the interactions to which they are exposed. In other words, not only *structures* but also *interactions* must be taken into account in order to understand the dynamics of identity constructions. It is the role of these two aspects in the development of the future projects of adolescents which is examined here.

This examination first concerns the role of the structure of scholastic organization in the creation of the future goals of young people. The school has taken on a major role in the socialization of young people in developed countries in the twentieth century. The fields and habitus theory of Pierre Bourdieu (1984) leads to the following hypothesis: attendance of a scholastic system (organized in a certain way) by adolescents leads to the formation in their minds of a system of representations of themselves, of others, of training, and of occupations, organized according to the basic dimensions structuring the system, as perceived by adolescents from the position they occupy in this organization.

However, this analysis leaves two questions unclear. These are, first, analysis of mediations via which these "objective" structures become mental structures and, second, the problem of integration into a relatively unified system of representative "constructs" generated by the various experiences to which young people are exposed. Adolescents are not only pupils, they also live outside school. What cognitive dimensions do they construct as the result of these different categories of activities? How do they combine together? What are the inherent processes of their integration?

Two hypotheses are offered in answer to these questions. The first is derived from the concepts of symbolic interactionism (Mead 1934; Becker 1963) and of dialogic pragmatic philosophy (Bakhtin 1981; Jacques 1979). It suggests that all interactions and interlocutions play an essential role in the construction and integration of representative dimensions, which both constitute adolescents' subjectivity and determine the creation of their future representations. Indeed, as Nurmi noted, identity and future representations combine in a dialectic relation: "the ways in which adolescents direct their life have consequences for their self-definition (identity construction), which further direct their subsequent self-direction."(Nurmi 1997).

The second of these hypotheses arises from a bringing together of sociological models (Dubar 1992, 1998a, 1998b) and the concept of frame (Minski 1975; Barsalou 1992) as developed in artificial intelligence. This hypothesis leads to the conception of subjectivity as a (relatively) unified and structured system of substitutable "identity forms" in which individuals construct and represent themselves and others. These identity forms are developed from "identity" cognitive frames, i.e. structured patterns relating to categories of people determined by social organization.

This model of frames and vicarious identity forms enables the integration of different approaches relative to "construction of self" and "identity strategies," analysis of the complex processes involved in the creation of future goals in adolescence and questioning of pertinent guidance activities involving today's youths.

Scholastic Field and Future Projects

In developed societies, school is a basic structure in the socialization of young people. It is an organization, a system, or—to use the terminology of Pierre Bourdieu—a field, i.e. *"a collection of social objects having relations of hierarchy and opposition with each other"* (Doise 1990, p.125). Scholastic field is characterized in particular by the "salience" of its organization: its various streams have precise relations between them; and rules governing its function.

The component streams of a scholastic field generally differ in terms of prestige: some enable the continuation of longer studies in socially esteemed areas, while others quickly lead to "active life" or to unemployment. In France, educational tracks that are highly valued today are those which emphasize pure sciences, mathematics or classical humanities: *the degree of abstraction of studies determines their value at school* (or to use Bourdieu's terminology, determines the specific gravity of the scholastic field). *Streams differ also according to the types of pupils* who have chosen them (or have been selected in them): some streams are mixed according to gender and/or social groups, whereas others tend to attract either boys or girls, young people from advantaged or disadvantaged backgrounds, etc.

Marked differences certainly exist between scholastic systems, concerning how systematically they are organized. All scholastic systems nevertheless function according to rules, some of which are explicit. Others are less clear in the eyes of those concerned—teachers, pupils, and parents—who nevertheless heed them. This leads to statements such as "it seems to me that such and such a stream would suit this boy." In Bourdieu's terminology, this indicates that his habitus—i.e., his ways of judging and being—is perceived as being similar to that ordinarily encountered in the stream concerned. It has hence been possible to show the prevalence of a "dominant cultural habitus," i.e. adolescents' relative homogeneity of cultural activities, leisure, and interests in a given scholastic stream (Guichard, Devos et al. 1994a; Guichard 1996).

Such an organization of socialization *defines the fundamental dimensions in which adolescents learn to perceive themselves.* School can hence be described as a *structured mirror* offering adolescents a *certain reflection of themselves* in *which they recognize themselves in a given way.* Seen this way, this structured mirror often becomes a structuring mirror (Guichard 1993, 1996). Thus, the *main dimension* organizing vision of self in this mirror is that of *excellence as scholastically produced and defined.*

Many studies have demonstrated the fundamental role of success or of scholastic failure in the construction of a certain self image. For example, Gilly, Lacour and Meyer (1972) introduced a powerful devaluation mechanism—related to scholastic failure—of own and social images of intelligence, perseverance and attentiveness. Pupils who do poorly at school consider themselves (own self image) to be less intelligent, less persevering and less attentive than those who succeed in class. They also feel that others (social self images) judge them in the same way. In addition, Gilly et al. found evidence in these low achieving pupils of disharmony between their own self image and their social self images: they feel that others judge them even more negatively—such as "very dull"—than they judge themselves, e.g., "dull".

Research carried out by sociologists who have looked at the question of the adaptation of young underachievers leaving school (Dubar 1987; Nizet and Hiernaux 1984; Laks 1983) lead to same conclusions. They showed that these adolescents frequently constructed self images of *"men of no quality."* Such studies validate the broad lines of Gottfredson's hypothesis (1981) according to which *at school, adolescents learn to determine the upper limits of the social positions to which they can reasonably aspire.*

This basic dimension of scholastic excellence is not the only one involved in the organization of the scholastic system as a structured mirror. As has already been said, a scholastic system, is always a *system of classification of scholastic disciplines* going hand in hand with a *system of distribution of individuals.* This has cognitive consequences: adolescents plunged into a given scholastic system learn in it (implicitly, based upon the organization of a system), first, that certain disciplines tend to go together and that they differ from others, and, second, that these categories of disciplines tend to correspond to types of pupils. For example, in the French scholastic system, pupils learn that modern languages and French tend to go together. They also note that these literary disciplines contrast with scientific disciplines. At the same time, they see that "literary" is concretely associated with "feminine" and "scientific" with "masculine".

Once these objective systems of classification of knowledge and of individuals become cognitive schemes, they play a fundamental role on the representation of the task "making choices for its own future." This was shown at the end of the 1970s by Kokosowski (1983). He noted that future representations of French secondary school pupils formed two sub-schemes. The first refers to the pupil's current scholastic situation. Depending on it, adolescents either appreciate or don't appreciate the school stream in which they are engaged; they feel that they are either strong or weak; they consider themselves doing well, average, or poorly in various subjects, etc. The second sub-scheme covers, first, constructs enabling the evaluation of higher educational streams (long or short, masculine or feminine, including certain subjects or not, easy or difficult, etc.), and, second, dimensions allowing the representation of occupations (Is it a sedentary or a mobile job ? Is it relational or office ? Is it conception or execution ?). These dimensions are indeed derived from the present school situation. The current scholastic self vision is hence the determinant in representation of the future.

It has been shown more recently that *not all the pupils do represent occupations in the same way,* and this is connected to the position they occupy in the scholastic system. Notable differences exist in the perception of occupational structure according to the gender of pupils, their study stream (Guichard, & Cassar 1998) and also, probably, their social and scholastic trajectory (Guichard, Devos, et al. 1994a and 1994b; Guichard 1996). For example, a boy working for a scientific "baccalauréat" (science related grade) tends to describe doctors and engineers in the same way and to clearly differentiate them from occupations involving helping others. A girl working for a medico-social "baccalauréat" (health service grade) tends, on the contrary, to perceive the occupations of doctor, nurse, and schoolteacher as being similar, and to differentiate them from engineer.

These findings are contradictory to Gottfredson's (1981) hypothesis of a single cognitive map of occupations: although all adolescents emphasize the dimensions "prestige" and "masculinity-feminity" in their evaluation of occupations (as postulated by Gottfredson), this does not imply that they refer to a single cognitive map describing the occupational structure. On the contrary, the structure of relations between occupations appears to be determined by the position occupied by the adolescent in the educational system.

Consequently, it looks as if *the scholastic system provides a basis for shaping not only the self image of pupils but also the way in which they project themselves into the future.* The scholastic self-reflection formed in the structured mirror is hence a powerful stimulant to the "creation of vocations."

But how and when do pupils recognize themselves in this reflection? How do they internalize this self-image offered by school? How does the structured mirror become a structuring mirror? Or, as was asked by Sartre (1952, p.56) about Jean Genet: how and when does the person to whom one says: "I see you as a thief," then say to himself "I'll become the thief that you see in me".

Social Cosmos, Interactions, Dialogue, and Subjectivity

Structural Homologies

Pierre Bourdieu's model provides a useful approach to the understanding of this self-recognition. According to his theory, highly differentiated societies are made up of a collection of "relatively autonomous social microcosms" (Bourdieu & Wacquant 1992, p. 73), i.e., of fields, of which the scholastic system is a proto-type example. Relations between the elements of a field are always "evaluative"; but what determines value (the *"specific gravity"*) in a given field is different to the one in an other. For example, "the artistic field, religious field or economic field obey different logics" (Bourdieu, and Wacquant 1992, p. 73). These fields are nevertheless organized in an analogous manner: relations between positions of individuals in these fields are generally homologous.

To educate an individual is to plunge him/her into a plurality of fields. This immersion is necessarily located at a given point in each field. This has a major consequence: *individuals learn to perceive the entire field, i.e., the elements making it up, and the relations of its elements, from the individual's viewpoint.* This viewpoint of the field which is produced from experiences—practices — related to this particular position in the field, is a constituent of the habitus of the individual. For example, an individual who, as a child, went to see with his/her parents many exhibitions of contemporary art may have built in his/her mind a system of classification of paintings that values all forms of abstractionism. Hence, for such an individual, one of the fundamental dimensions of evaluation in this field of art would be: how much any work renews the way the material is worked? S/he would then tend to organize all the works of art (and also the people interested in them) particularly along this dimension (and would make a clear distinction between the "pompous" painting of the end of the ninteeth century—seen as common or vulgar—and impressionism, seen as an important step towards abstractionism). Another individual, whose experiences in this field were completely different from the previous one, may have built in his/her mind a completely different system of classification of paintings. For him/her, one fundamental question to judge any work could be: how well is nature depicted? In such a case, all the kinds of paintings of the end of the ninteeth century would be seen as relatively similar and totally different from works by Poliakoff, Pollock, Rothko, etc. (which probably would be rejected as: "stains, that a child could do").

Habitus consists of a *certain number of schemes of perception, assessment, and action* which continue to provide guidance in the individual's representations, judgments and acts long after the period of its creation. Social position in each field is therefore fundamental: it determines the nature of learning experiences, which themselves lead to the creation of systems of classification and perception (and practices).

This model raises the hypothesis according to which *the more similar are the positions occupied by adolescents in the various fields they are involved, the more they will immediately recognize themselves in the scholastic self-reflection.* Hence the middle-class boy, living in a middle class area, good pupil in a scientific stream, will be ready to see himself as being endowed with abstract intelligence. Reciprocally, a girl of modest origins, living in a working class suburb, having difficulty working for an administrative diploma, can easily see herself as tending more to have good practical sense. The situation is more complex in cases of positional disharmony[1]. Taking as a background the findings of Howard Becker (1963 1985) in the constitution of deviant identities, it can nevertheless be suggested that *interactions with others then play a fundamental role.* In a more directly dialogic perspective, it can even be postulated that "I" is defined, redefined, and constructed via the mediation of *discussion with others. Dialogic interaction would then play a fundamental role in the construction of self.* In the dialogic interaction with others, "I" recognize myself and hence construct myself.

Relational Transaction and Biographic Transaction

In his approach to identity construction, Claude Dubar (1992 1998a) draws a distinction between two types of process: a biographic transaction and a relational transaction. The *biographic* (or subjective) *transaction* consists of *relating inherited identities and targeted identities,* of "the projection of possible futures in continuity or break with a reconstituted past (trajectory)" (Dubar 1992, p. 520). *The relational* (or objective) *transaction* is a process *of relating attributed or proposed identities and assumed or incorporated identities.* It involves "ensuring recognition or not by institutional partners of the legitimacy of one's expectations, taking into account goals and means ("policy") of the institution" (Dubar 1992, p. 520). "The biographic, temporal and "subjective" dimension brings into play the continuity of social origins and the direction of individual trajectories; the purpose of the relational, spatial and "objective" dimension is the recognition of claimed positions and the success of structural policies. Interconnected by necessity, the two transactions are in an interaction relation: the outcome of each depends upon the other" (Dubar 1992 p. 521). The biographic transaction could hence be said *diachronic* and the relational transaction to be *synchronic.* Identity construction would hence be the fruit of a *double transaction*: a negotiation relative to institutional identity offer and an intimate deliberation (1998b).

This model can be translated into the language of the self psychology. The relational transaction refers to the problem of *articulation between social images of self and own images of self.* The biographic transaction designates the question of *links between past self, current self, and possible self.* Two major differences nevertheless lead to a distinction between the self psychology and Dubar's model. Dubar emphasizes the role of social labeling and of what he calls identity offer, i.e., proposed identities in which individuals can recognize themselves or not. This labeling and this offer are one of the origins of *identity forms*. These forms, in which individuals identify themselves at least momentarily, are defined as *"unstable products of these biographic and relational transactions in a context of powerful instigations to change"* (Dubar 1998b, p. 100). Dubar also emphasizes the role of *"narrative,"* the role of argumentation about self, in the genesis of these identity forms.

This interesting model of Dubar needs to be more precisely defined for the psychologist. In particular, the role of narrative in the construction of self and the notion of identity form must be analyzed and clarified.

Forms of Interlocutions and Identity Forms

A narrative is always intended for someone. This can be an actual other. This other person can also be an internalized other: another within oneself. The narrative is for others. In every instance, the narrative refers to a dialogue: it is what the individual intends to say to the person to whom s/he is talking. The narrative presupposes somebody else who is addressed in answer to a question, an assertion, a sign, etc. Dialogic interaction is the very principle of narrative.

This other (empirical actual or imaginary) to whom the individual addresses him/herself depends upon current or past interactions. S/he enters into dialogue with a person—or s/he constructs this narrative for people—with whom s/he has or has had certain relations. The community interactions evoked by Bill Law (1981) or the micro-systems of Vondracek et al. (1986) hence appear to play crucial roles in the construction of self. It can be surmised that *during these actual or imaginary dialogic interactions*—or during these narratives—*a given possible self appears to the individual as a probable self while other possible selves become improbable.*

Dialogic interaction is certainly not the only factor involved in this move from a possible self to a probable self: the actual experiences of individuals (and notably their activities, successes and failures, encounters, etc.), combined with the way in which they are represented, play a major role. It may, however, be surmised that in order to internalize these experiences and representations as their own, individuals must tell themselves (or others) about them, interaction with others then playing an essential role.

The distinction drawn by Dubar between synchronic process and diachronic process is heuristic. However, the biographic (diachronic) transaction cannot be analyzed as a simple intimate deliberation. This very deliberation is dialogic in essence. It can be postulated that is precisely the recounting of self for others that enables *this move from identity offer to self-identification in this specific identity form.* As noted by Francis Jacques (1979, p. 384) in an ontological perspective: "In fact the question is not so much to know whether the "me" is defined only in relation to another, but to know whether the relation with the other really helps in defining oneself (...). 'You,' is the other as its enters 'me' in a community of communication (...). The first philosophical fact is that of exchanged speech circulating between themselves in their created space." "Each hears him/herself in the other, just as the other speaks in him/herself," stresses Jacques (1979, p. 385).

But Bakhtin (1981) would add, *this other speaking within us, speaks in determined forms.* These voices (to use Bakhtin's terminology) of others in us use national languages. They are made up of *types of social speech* (e.g., occupational jargon) and *sorts of speech* (e.g., table conversation). My voice—i.e., my uttered statement, for that intention, with this tone and that accent—is based upon the appropriation ("ventriloquism") of the voices of other people in other contexts. "The word in language is half someone else's. It becomes 'one's own' only when the speaker populates it with his own intention, his own accent, when he appropriates the word, adapting it to his own semantic and expressive intention. Prior to this moment of appropriation, the word does not exist in a neutral and impersonal language (it is not, after all, out of a dictionary that the speaker gets its words!), but rather it exists in other people's mouths, in other people's contexts, serving other people's intentions; it is from there that one must take the word and make it one's own." (Bakhtin 1981, pp. 293–294, cited by Wertsch 1990, p. 117).

Our own language is thus constructed in the social forms of speech, in what could be called, to use the terminology of Schank and Abelson (1977) "scripts" but scripts varying according to the social contexts frequented by the individual. It therefore seems possible to propose the following conclusive hypothesis: *socially determined forms of interlocutions* (see Erving Goffman 1974) *seem to be an essential factor in the construction of self in a determined identity form* (i.e., in the appropriation of a given identity offer).

In adolescence, these forms of interactions and interlocutions—notably with pairs—could play an essential role in the trials of identity forms which some authors consider to be characteristic of this period (see adolescence as psychosocial moratorium of Erikson, and the period of tentative choices of Ginzberg et al. 1951). It is possible, for example, that the "inner voices" produced in each participant by the types of socialized speech used by a group of young rappers create the image of a dynamic, impulsive, or even violent personality. By the appropriation of this "voice," during these interlocutions, via ventriloquism of this voice, adolescents could construct themselves in this determined identity form of "rapper." (In a way, this comes down to the idea of learning by imitation; but what is imitated is the "voice," i.e., language, tone, intention, type of social speech, and sort of speech of others).

Frames and vicarious identity forms

The concept of "identity form" is ambiguous to the psychologist. This terminology suggests the existence of underlying and relatively integrated dimensions. But what are these dimensions? How are they integrated? How to conceive the relative instability of the identity which the concept of identity form attempts to grasp? These various questions lead to an essential query for the psychologist: what is the nature of the mental representations involved?

In psychology, the concept semantically closest to that of form is that of *frame*. This was defined by Minsky in 1975, in the field of artificial intelligence. *Frame designates a mental pattern relative to the structure of a familiar situation or object.* This mental structure incorporates slots which have generally some default values (Barsalou 1992, p. 160). For example, the *"room"* frame incorporates the features *"walls," "floor," "ceiling," "door,"* and *"window."* These features have defined relations with each other. According to this cognitive perspective, our mind is made up notably of a system of frames. To understand information or a situation or recognize an object is to determine the frame or configuration of frames which best enable it to be grasped.

Identity frames

The cognitive frame is not a representation immediately present in consciousness. It is a structure which enables individuals to immediately grasp an "object" (actual, social, a situation, etc.) in the world around them. The following definition can be proposed in this context: an *identity frame is a structured (cognitive) scheme relative to the main characteristics of individuals belonging to one of the categories of people which our social experience leads us to identify.* Examples include: woman, catholic, gay, Ford worker, football team supporter, Scorpio star sign, truck driver, German, immigrant, etc. The particular characteristics which the identity frame takes into account are: physical traits, "psychological" traits (character, temperament, skills, etc.), ways of presenting oneself, of behaving, interacting, speaking, acting, etc. Some of these characteristics have defined relations with each other: for example, certain factors are immediately perceptible while others depend upon the interior nature of the person, and perceptible factors may be indicative of character traits.

The identity frames system

Identity frames are cognitive (not immediately conscious) representations enabling the situation of others and the situation of oneself in relation to others. Some of these frames are more general than others, or are formed earlier, or more central, or more universal, perhaps; some are prestigious, some designate minorities, some refer to stigmatized social groups, etc. Identity frames form a system in the mind of those using them as representation. The *identity frames system designates the structured entity of relations between identity frames*, in the mind of a socially situated individual. These relations may be *inclusions, exclusions*, or *complementarities*. They often involve *evaluations*, notably in terms of *prestige* and *legitimacy*.

The identity frames system is the substratum of representation of the structure of relations between social categories ("social groups" of all types) as organized in the mind of an individual objectively and subjectively situated in his or her "social cosmos." It is the identity frames system which organizes the vision of relations between "social groups" of an individual. The identity frames system is the *identity offer in our mind*.

Identity forms

The identity frames system is a structure of structures underlying the representation of self and of others and the construction of self. In such a perspective, *identity form is a conscious representation of self (or of a determined other) according to the structure of a defined identity frame.*

Results of research on identity and groups, however, lead to a distinction between identity forms and subjective identity forms. These do not simply involve an activation in working memory of identity frames in which individuals would recognize themselves. Whereas some stereotyped dimensions can enable the representation of others in a defined identity frame, *subjective identity form is a veritable construction of self in an identity frame*, bringing into play the phenomenon of "identisation" (individuation) (Tap 1980), of "primus inter pares" (first among equals) (Codol 1975) and of "subjectivisation" (Foucault 1983 1994–IV). From a cognitive standpoint, this means that individuals assign particular values to certain slots of the frame when they construct themselves in a form corresponding to this frame.

The Construction of Vocational Identity Forms in Adolescence

One of the "developmental tasks" (Havighurst 1953) which our societies demand of adolescents is that they construct representations of self in certain subjective identity forms corresponding to jobs "which would suit them." In the early 50s, Ginzberg et al. (1951) described the stages in this process as they were able to observe in American boys from a privileged background. More recently, Dumora (1990) observed the evolution of the construction of such vocational identity forms in adolescents from various social backgrounds, aged between eleven and sixteen, whom she monitored for four years. She identified four phases in this construction.

The first is a *tautological link* between self and a given occupation. It is not so much the job, as the person doing it which arouses the dreams of the pre-adolescent. This link is described as "tautological" insofar as there is no argument as its basis: no characteristic, of the job incumbent nor job, is mentioned. A girl who "sees herself" as a model hence says: "model? (laughs) ... well (laughs) I don't know, I like that, it's like this ... when you like something, it's because it's what you enjoy ..." (Dumora 1990, p. 113).

The second phase is that of a "*metaphoric projection*": between the individual and the person doing the job, there is transfer of an entity to the other, without possible recognition of shared characteristics, hence of a descriptive category, of a feature linking the current status of the one with the anticipation of the other. Syncretically, there is a single edifice, with the subject identifying themself with the person or character: 'oh, it's because I would really enjoy that, I just dream about it, ... I can already imagine myself ... just as if it was now ... as if I was already there ... I can imagine myself with lots of animals around me to keep me busy.'" (Dumora 1990, p. 115).

This is followed by the time of a "*metonymic projection.*" "Projection because it refers to a character or known person, but with the beginnings already of separation from the character so as to retain only qualities or characteristics, and metonymic because there is (...) an intersection between the various characteristics of the subject and the various characteristics of the professional." For example, a girl about fifteen years old says "secretary, there like Mrs. M. at school, it's because you have files, the telephone to answer, people to see... since I enjoy contact with others ... me, I'm quite an obsessional type (...) but that doesn't make me difficult on the telephone ... , (...) so" (Dumora 1990, pp.115–116). This is certainly still a projection ("like Mrs. M."), but descriptors relative to actions seen are now brought into correspondence with the qualities perceived as being necessary for the job.

The final phase in the construction of these vocational identity forms consists of "*tensional comparisons.*" Reference to the person doing the job is no longer necessary: "The metonymic process no longer functions by reference to an individual mentioned but already to the impersonal image of a professional (...). The subject sheds identificatory investment, to opt for the cognitive construction of the professional image and hence put it at a distance. A girl about fiftenn years old hesitating between doctor and teacher argues as follows: 'since I like contacts, talking to younger or older people, and I also like long and difficult studies preferably (laughter) ... not short things ... since I want to succeed in life, it's important ... oh, it's difficult to say ... (...) I am hesitating because I want a good job but I want to do studies well ... for example medicine (...) that's a job which I would enjoy ... the job and not the studies ...'" (Dumora 1990, p. 117).

Progress from tautological links to tensional comparisons is hence "a cognitive detachment of identification by the designation of resemblance, then by a classification of categories emerging from this identification support, and finally by logical implication" (Dumora 1990, p. 117). These observations cover the description of creation, in adolescents at school, of relational transaction processes—reported by Dubar (1992)—relative to the anticipation of vocational subjective identity forms.

The second process described by Dumora is an equivalent, in the school field, of Dubar's (1992) biographic transactions. This involves a *"probabilistic reflection"* consisting of "a subjective calculation in which the subject takes the measure between the space of possibles and the space of probables" (Dumora 1990, p. 118). Dumora notes that from entry to leaving junior high school, this reflection evolves "from prediction (positive or negative quasi-absolute certainty), to conjecture (uncertainty) and finally to a reasoned and ordered strategy of possibles" (Dumora 1990, p. 118).

Vicariance of Identity Forms

While vocational subjective identity forms play an important role in the construction of self, they are nevertheless not the only identity forms in which subjects construct themselves.

The construction of self (in any particular subjective identity form) depends upon the relatively stable characteristics of the person (recognizing themself according to these dimensions of those particular identity frames) and contexts of actualization of self. It seems necessary to return to the analyses of Michel Foucault (extending old debates in psychology, notably between Thorndike and Eysenck). Foucault (1984 1994–IV, p. 719) states that the subject "is not a substance. It is a form, and *this form is not always the same.* You do not have with yourself the same type of relation when you take yourself to be a political subject who is going to vote or when you seek to fulfill your desires in a sexual relation. *There are doubtless relations and interferences between these different forms of the subject, but the same type of subject is not present.* In each instance, *one plays, one establishes different forms of relation with oneself"*.

The notion of "vicarious processes" suggested by Reuchlin (1978 1997) leads to proposition of the hypothesis of a *vicariance of identity forms.* In a given context, the subject constitutes him/herself in a *particular identity form* (e.g., supporter of "Paris-Saint Germain" football club). This construction of self in this identity context would be in an identity *form characteristic of the individual* concerned: *a subjective identity form* (where the slots of the frame have their own specific values). In another context, this same individual could construct him/herself in another subjective identity form (e.g., "Ford worker"). This process would involve *variations in the construction of a given subjective identity form related to the context of actualization.* The "specific" value assigned to one or other slot of the frame would be subject to certain variations. For example, the "behavior" characteristic of the "Paris-Saint-Germain supporter" identity frame could take the specific value "violent to others" in a given individual. This value would be that of the behavior "slot" of its *subjective identity form*. This, in the context of a particular match, could lead to self constitution in an *actualized subjective identity form* of a verbally violent individual, and in another, a physically violent individual.

Identity Forms System and Subjectivity

This vicariance of identity forms does not lead to disappearance of the unity of the individual. Feelings of being the same and that others are the same are very strong. These two types of representation are based upon the unity of the identity frames system. The feeling of being the same is based upon the feeling that the different personal identity forms in which we identify ourselves go together, that they are all mine. They form for individuals the subjective *system of their* (subjective) *identity forms. Subjectivity is hence the unified and structure system of the identity forms in which individuals construct and represent themselves.* This is the conscious representation of relations between subjective identity forms. This representation can obviously evolve. It is also sensitive to social contexts: in a very structured social organization, in which social relations between individuals are at one and the same time simple, clear and salient, the feeling of being the same, of always being identical to oneself, is much stronger than in a society where individuals may construct themselves in different identity frames.

Scope of The Frames and Vicarious Identity Forms Model

The advantage of the model just described in terms of its broad lines is to enable *integration of different current approaches of "subjectivity" in cognitive psychology and in sociology.* The concepts of identity frames and forms, and vicariance identity forms system allows one to relate the problematics of psychosocial identity, self-schemata, implicit theories of personality, the "ego ecology of identity words," identity strategies, etc. Being unable to examine all these problematics here, only two of them will be considered: those of "self-schemata," and of "identity strategies." These approaches appear to be particularly pertinent in analysis of the construction of future projects of adolescents.

The *"identity frames"* in which individuals construct themselves in a certain form echo *self-schemata* of the self psychology. This notion of identity frames nevertheless adds not only cognitive (concerning the structure of these schemata) but social considerations. In the self psychology, "social" is generally limited to taking into account local interactions with others, as if they took place in a social vacuum, independently of local structures (i.e., fields) as well as of the social cosmos. In the model proposed here, the central dimensions of self involve the representation of the structure of relations between groups of individuals.

This model of the vicariance of identity forms also enables analysis of identity changes and strategies. These can be conceived as being notably determined by contextualized actualizations of identity forms. The subjective identity form of an individual in a given identity frame would be the product of the different contextualized actualizations in this form. These actualizations would be the source of its evolution. Inter-individual interactions would hence play a major role, leading to "day by day adjustments, brought about according to variations in situations and their consequences—i.e., finalities expressed by social actors—and their resources" (Taboada-Leonetti 1990).

The role of socially esteemed identity frames in these individual (and inter-individual) strategies cannot be ignored. They can be considered to be at the *origin of forms of idealized self and of forms of possible selves*: these forms being related to certain social insertions (to positions) in determined social contexts (in fields).

In contrast to the canonic model of identity strategies (Camilleri et al. 1990), the considerations of Michel Foucault concerning power and "*governmentality*" are actually taken into account in the model presented here. It is known that Foucault (1988) considers "*technologies of the self*" to be techniques of power. They designate "*procedures which are proposed or prescribed to individuals to determine their identity, maintain it or transform it* according to a number of ends, by virtue of relations of mastery of self over self or knowledge of self by self" (Foucault 1981 1994–IV, p. 213). In Foucault's conception, *subjectivity forms* in which individuals recognize themselves are the product of strategic relations of power between groups or between individuals, with, as their consequence, the government of each individual through his/her relations to others. The maintenance of social order requires the recognition—by each—of self and of others in these forms. In other words, questions of the identity of individuals or of the anticipation of self in "possible selves" are not of a strictly personal or inter-individual nature. They involve, in essence, social organization as a whole and the power relations which ensure its cohesion.

Identity Forms and Adolescent Goals

Only the undertaking of a systematic program of empirical studies would enable validation of the frames and vicarious identity forms model. This could involve identification of the various identity frames in which, for example, secondary school pupils constitute themselves in defined identity forms. It would also look at the structure of each of these frames and the system which they form. It would also need to confirm the role of inter-individual interactions in the construction of self in certain identity forms.

Although such a research program is as yet only at the stage of a preliminary outline, various empirical studies can be considered as providing indirect confirmation of some of the hypotheses proposed. Three will be mentioned. Two concern the role of effective interactions in the construction of self. The third more precisely concerns identity strategies.

Interactions and Subjectivity

The question of the role of interactions in the formation of a self image was considered in particular by Meyer in 1986-1987 in a new look at the work cited earlier of Gilly, Lacour and Meyer (1972). The fundamental intention in 1986 was the same as that of 1972: to describe the link between scholastic results and the way adolescents perceive themselves. However, on this second occasion, mediating variables were taken into account. These include the interest shown by the family in the adolescent's school work. Such an interest involves family dialogue about school work. The results showed that good pupils had a more positive scholastic self image than the weak. However, this image was also more positive, among both good and weak pupils, when parents discuss these matters. Such a result is of capital importance from a pedagogic standpoint: it is known that self image as a good or weak pupil is not merely a product of scholastic results. This image plays a role in the production of school performance: it produces a certain cognitive function (Monteil 1988 1990).

Dialogue and Self Image

Another research project (Guichard & Falbierski 1994; Guichard & Dosnon 1999) more directly manifests the role of dialogue interactions in the formation of certain self images. This research was also inspired, in part, from the problematic of Gilly, Lacour, and Meyer. The participants were young people (mean age: seventeen) leaving school having failed, unemployed, and in precarious social conditions. Two equivalent groups (experimental and control) of twelve young people were created. Each answered at a five week interval two questionnaires (using Likert's scales in particular) concerning their own and social self images, skills, representations of occupations, etc.

During the five weeks, the experimental group participated in a Careers Education program (DAPPI, see Guichard 1989, 1992) lasting four half-days. The objectives of such sessions were as follows: to help these adolescents to enhance their self image and overcome—when applicable—their feelings of desperation, to lead them to establish a link between personal skills and vocational qualifications and to discover ways of acquiring skills other than by learning at school.

DAPPI educational method is based upon two basic principles: the avoidance of cognitively costly transfer operations and encouragement of verbal exchanges. In order to meet the first of these requirements, the DAPPI program limits itself strictly to the question of vocational choice. Material has been constructed on the basis of interviews with employees doing jobs accessible to the youngsters in question. In order to enhance exchanges and dialogue, DAPPI consists of several game exercises, where the aim is to reach a satisfactory solution by coming to an agreement with one's peers. Participants often find themselves in situations analogous to those of socio-cognitive conflicts: they have to negotiate to reach an agreement.

DAPPI consists of three basic stages. During each of them, participants are divided into sub-groups of three. The first is aimed at leading participants to discover that their vision of occupations is limited and simplified. Each group of three participants is given a pack of about sixty cards, showing the description of a task forming part of an occupation. For example: "I reserve the director's airline tickets. I also telephone to make his appointments." The adolescents are told how these cards have been written following interviews with professionals who described everything they do during their working days. Participants (1) have to discover how many occupations are covered by the sixty cards they are holding and (2) to reconstitute these occupations, i.e., to reconstruct the descriptions of the working days of each of these job incumbents.

Packs distributed to each group are actually based upon interviews with three job incumbents. Following this first game, participants generally reach the following three main conclusions: (1) a job covers far more activities than they had imagined, (2) different jobs include identical activities and (3) certain positions, which they thought they knew, are very different from the image they had had of them.

The second stage is intended to lead the youngsters (1) to focus on the link between personal skills and vocational qualifications and (2) to discover various means for the acquisition or development of skills. The same small groups of three youngsters are given a new pack of about fifty cards. Each card describes an experience (positive or negative) which, in the eyes of a job incumbent, has played a role in his or her vocational career. These experiences are reported by the same three professionals whose job the adolescents discovered during the first game. They must now reconstitute the life itineraries of each of them. Following this second game, participants often draw two conclusions: (1) most trajectories are non-linear and there is not always a link between diplomas and jobs done, and (2) skills are acquired during various life experiences: collective responsibilities, training schemes, little jobs, leisure activities, sports, etc.

The third stage involves the transfer to self of findings discovered during the two previous stages. It consists itself of three phases. First, each participation chooses, with the help of the others, vocational activities—tasks—which he or she would like to find in their future job. The aim is to force the adolescent to enter into a process of thought about their vocational future, not in terms of jobs (so as to avoid difficulties related to the stereotyped nature of their representation), but based upon the activities they would like to find in any future job. Each participant then makes a sort of personal "evaluation," based upon an inventory of their skills, knowledge, strong points, etc. Each then defines a plan of personal activities to be taken up in order to acquire or develop the skills required in vocational activities which interest them. Interactions with the other two members of the small group are essential at this point. It is they who actually suggest these activities to the adolescent concerned.

The results of this study are clear-cut. Descriptions of self of youngsters in the experimental group were much more positive in the second questionnaire than in the first one (there was no notable variation in the control group). As an example, results related to two questions taken from Gilly, Lacour, and Meyer (1972) will be presented. (For presentation of all findings, see Guichard & Falbierski 1994).

The adolescent was confronted with a series of descriptors (social openness, intelligence, memory, frankness, independence, perseverance, politeness, quickness, organization, beauty, strength, experience, enthusiasm, and foresight). S/He was first ("own self-image") asked what score s/he would give to each of them (scores ranging from 1: *I am not at all like that* to 7: *that's just like me*). S/He was then ("social self-images") to say what scores s/he imagined his/her co-participants, the educator, etc., would give him/her on the same grading system.

Table 1 ("own self-image") clearly shows the increase in mean scores assigned by participants. This progression affected above all those descriptors referring to *social qualities* (social openness, foresight, experience, frankness, politeness, etc.).

The greatest change concerned the social self-image "educator," i.e., the scores which the adolescent imagined that the educator would give him/her.

Table 1: "The way that I am."
"Own self-image." Overall Mean Scores

	Assessment	
Group	First	Second
Experimental	4.58	5.22
Control	4.78	4.63

Note: To help in reading this table: 4.58 = mean scores assigned by D.A.P.P.I. course participants, to all descriptors, at the time of the first questionnaire.

(Table 2). They increased by more than one point on average in the experimental group, while there was no change in the control group.

The model sketched here suggests the following interpretation of these observations: variations seen in the experimental group could reflect changes—

Table 2: "The way that I imagine the educator sees me."
"Social self-image educator." Overall Mean Scores

	Assessment	
Group	First	Second
Experimental	3.96	4.99
Control	4.36	4.35

Note: To help in reading this table: 4.58 = mean scores assigned by D.A.P.P.I. course participants, to all descriptors, at the time of the first questionnaire.

in the personal identity form of each—resulting from the dialogue-based activities of the program. Unfortunately, the experimental device did not offer the possibility of confirming whether these changes were durable: several questions would have been needed to ensure the stability of these variations. (It may be mentioned that the methodology used presupposed that individuals perceived themselves in the identity frame imposed upon them by the questionnaire).

Anticipated Identity Forms

The studies of Paul Willis (1977 1978) in the Midlands in the late seventies appear to be fully consistent with the conceptual frame proposed here. Willis observed the transition from school to active life of adolescents—underachievers—whose fathers worked in the heavy metal industry. He depicted ways of being, talking, interacting with others, values, certain social representations, etc., of these youngsters and their fathers. This led Willis to describe to what he calls, on the one hand, a counter-school culture, and on the other hand, a shop-floor culture. These two cultures proved to be very similar. For example, on the shop-floor, the fathers of these adolescents distributed tasks among them without paying attention to the instructions of their supervisors. Similarly, at school, the youngsters organized disturbances aimed at disorganizing timetables. On the shop-floor, as at school, the representation of self and of others was structured according to a fundamental opposition between "us" ("lads," "those in on things," forming part of the group) and "them" ("ears'holes," "those who want to succeed," the others).

Willis' main conclusion is that the counter-school culture provides adolescents with active preparation for entry into the world of the shop-floor. It can be considered as showing processes of construction of self in a *current identity form anticipating a probable and esteemed personal identity form.* These processes could be as follows. The organization of production and work in the steel industry determined a powerful identity frame enabling steelworkers to develop a representation of themselves in powerfully structured personal identity forms, particularly stable and esteemed in their eyes. Via family stories about shop-floor life, the sons of these steelworkers developed very precise self-representations in this identity frame.

The counter-school culture also seems to be a sort of game in which youngsters learn in anticipation their ways of doing, being, talking, etc., making up the personal identity form which will be theirs a few months later in the "steelworker" identity frame. It can therefore be considered that these games of the counter-school culture are collective *identity strategies* (Camilleri et al. 1990). They lead these adolescents to anticipate a social position which will be theirs several years later. Actively constructing themselves in these particular identity forms, these youngsters—in agreement with Foucault's hypothesis—accept their lot: they participate in the maintenance of the structure of power relations between social groups.

Conclusion: Adolescence, Subjectivity, and Society

Previously presented findings and hypotheses can be summarized as three propositions. The first concerns the weight of scholastic organization in the construction of some dimensions of self-images of adolescents, dimensions which are fundamental in the formation of their future goals. This organization structures in particular the way in which the task—"making choices about my future"—is represented. The second stresses the role of interactions and dialogues with others in the construction of adolescents' self-images and goals. It emphasizes that these interactions and dialogues take place in social contexts and frames (in the sense of Erving Goffman). The third proposition considers that any society determines an "identity offer" which is organized in a person's mind in the form of a system of identity (cognitive) frames. In a given context and at a given time, an individual constructs him/herself in a determined subjective identity form. Hence these identity forms appear to be susceptible to vicariance.

This model corresponds to a conception of relatively malleable subjectivity. More precisely, the "stability" or "malleability" of self depend fundamentally upon the development of the particular society (the degree of diversification of identity offer varies according to societies), the degree of integration of the various domains of the social cosmos (and, hence, of different identity frames) and the variety of contextualized interactions in which the subject becomes involved.

In our complex (and democratic) societies, where different fields have their "own logic," adolescence (and also young adulthood) are phases during which young people try out transitory identity forms. These experiments enable them to hasten the construction of their subjective systems of identity forms (the evolution of which is often slower afterwards). Transitory formations and the diversity of juvenile subcultures would hence provide the means for this construction. There are two known dangers which, according to Erikson and Marcia, then threaten the adolescent: identity confusion and forclosure. In the model sketched here, the first designates inability to recognize oneself in a stable manner in a subjective system of identity forms. The second refers to incarceration in a few identity forms, incarceration which may be related to family pressures or due to more directly political events (such as inter-ethnic conflicts).

These considerations certainly have consequences with regard to vocational guidance methods. They lead to definition of a first line of demarcation between them. The aim of some of these methods is to *lead adolescents to stabilize themselves in a determined identity form*. Others may *persue the opposite aim.*

Counseling activities aimed at helping the client to reach a decision belong to the first type of intervention technique. Reaching a decision implies accepting to construct oneself in one or several determined identity forms. It implies to make progressively this (or these) form(s) into one (or some) subjective identity forms(s) ("this is how I see myself in the future").

Counseling activities aimed at helping clients to commit to a transition process pursue the opposite objective. This may involve helping the person to "renounce" certain identity forms: this is often what is meant by the expression "developing flexibility." Some interventions are aimed at helping each adolescent to construct a subjective system which is at one and the same time rich, diversified, and articulated. "Exploration" is encouraged. This was the aim of the European "grand tour" of affluent young men in the eighteenth and nineteenth centuries. Today, it is one of the aims of methods such as DAPPI (see Guichard & Dosnon 1999).

However, the ends of an activity are always defined in terms of certain values. This is why a second line of demarcation differentiates guidance methods: is their final goal to *preserve or, on the contrary, to transform the structure of social relations*? These two lines of demarcation appear to be relatively independent. This is why methods in the area of helping the career development of adolescents can be presented in the form of a graphic which contrast them according to these two dimensions (see figure 1).

Figure 1 represents a notion that in the areas of careers education or vocational guidance, the objective of certain activities may be to help adolescents to diversify their identity forms system. For example, they encourage involvement in exploration activities. Other activities may pursue the opposing objective: leading the client to stabilize in a vocational identity form with the aim of following a defined career path. This first dimension (right versus left) is independent of a second one (up versus down). It draws a distinction between methods according to whether their objective (implicit or explicit) is to transform the structure of social relations (e.g., by defining priority actions) or retaining it (e.g., by merely meeting the demands of a clientele). Activities which can be considered to be characteristic of the two closest poles are mentioned at the four corners of the figure. For example, the proposed development of flexibility (down versus left) refers to diversification between identity forms, while generally falling within a perspective of maintenance of the structure of social relations.

Figure 1: Ends of Vocational Guidance Methods

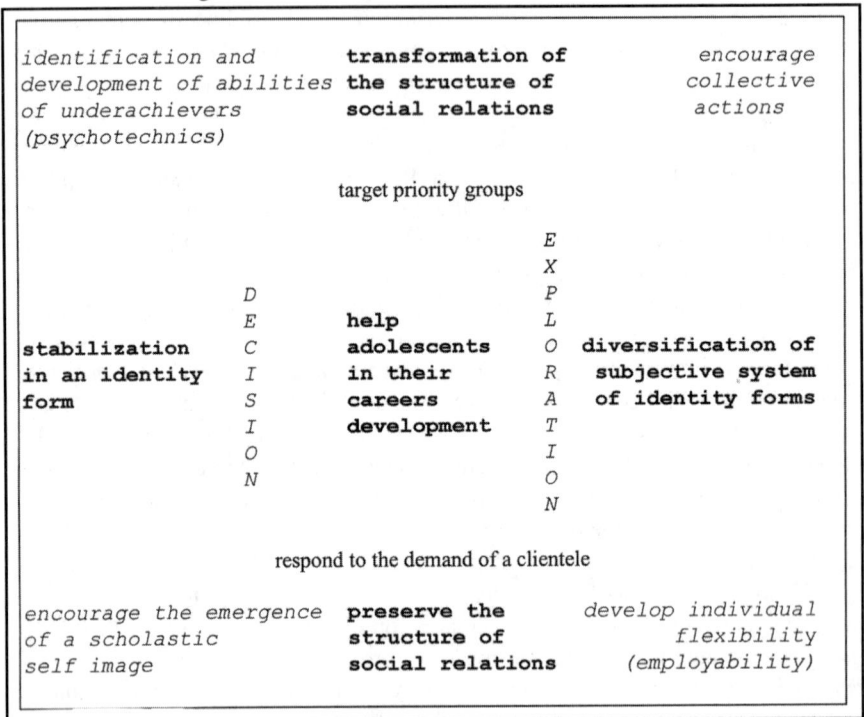

identification and development of abilities of underachievers (psychotechnics)	**transformation of the structure of social relations**	*encourage collective actions*
	target priority groups	
		E X P
		L
stabilization in an identity form	D E C I S I O N	help adolescents in their careers development	O R A T I O N	**diversification of subjective system of identity forms**
	respond to the demand of a clientele	
encourage the emergence of a scholastic self image	**preserve the structure of social relations**	*develop individual flexibility (employability)*

The distinction between identity "frames" and "forms" seems to allow an integration of the different approaches of the "subject" and his/her "subjectivity" as they were described in the human sciences during the twentieth century. The identity frames are cognitive schemata. They form a system that constitutes a mental representation of social structure and social categories in our society. One can assume that adolescence is an important time in the formation of this system of cognitive frames, which—very likely—evolves much more slowly in the following periods of life. A subjective identity form constitutes a self creation and representation based on the structure of a given identity frame. In complex societies, any individual "creates" her/himself in different forms according to the context and interactions in which s/he is involved. For this reason, her/him subjectivity may appear as relatively malleable. Such a model increases certainly the complexity of adolescent's vocational counseling. It's main aim cannot only be to help the client find the activities that fit best to the person that he or she is. The aim is also to help her/him to discover and build the subjective system of identity forms in which s/he intends to construct her/himself. As these identity forms refer to social categories (via the cognitive system of identity frames), this is not only a problem of personal development. It raises the question of the society that we want to develop.

References

Bakhtin, M. M. (1981). *The dialogic imagination* (M. Holquist ed.). Austin: University of Texas Press.

Bandura, A. (1977). *Social Learning theory*. Englewood Cliffs, NJ: Prentice-Hall.

Barsalou, L. (1992). *Cognitive Psychology: an overview for cognitive scientists.* Hillsdale, NJ: Lawrence Erlbaum Associates.

Becker, H. S. (1963). *Outsiders*. The free Press of Glencoe: Macmillan Publishing. French translation (1985). Paris: Editions A.M. Métailié.

Bourdieu, P. (1984). *Distinction: A Social Critique of the Judgment of Taste.* Cambridge MA: Harvard University Press.

Bourdieu, P., & Wacquant, L. (1992). *An Invitation to Reflexive Sociology.* Chicago,IL: The University of Chicago Press.

Bruner, J. S., Tagiuri, R. (1954). The perception of people. In Lindsey, G. (ed.): *Handbook of social psychology.* (vol. 2). Cambridge, MA: Addison-Wesley.

Camilleri, C. et al. (1990). *Les stratégies identitaires*. Paris: PUF.

Cattell, R.-B. (1950). *Personality: a systematic, theoretical, and factual study.* New-York: McGraw Hill.

Codol, J.-P. (1975). On the so-called "superior conformity of the self" behaviour: twenty experimental investigations. *European Journal of Social Psychology, 5*, 390, 457–501.

Doise, W. (1990). Les représentations sociales. In R. Ghiglione, Cl. Bonnet & J.-F. Richard (Eds): *Traité de psychologie cognitive* (tome 3, pp. 111–172). Paris: Dunod.

Dubar, Cl. (Ed.) (1987). *L'autre jeunesse*. Lille: PUL.

Dubar, C. (1992). Formes identitaires et socialisation professionnelle. *Revue Française de Sociologie, 33*, 505–530.

Dubar, C. (1996). La sociologie du travail face à la qualification et à la compétence. *Sociologie du Travail, 2*, 179–193.

Dubar, C. (1998a). *La socialisation. Construction des identités sociales et profession-nelles* (2ème édition revue). Paris: Armand Colin.

Dubar, C. (1998b). Identité professionnelle et récits d'insertion. Pour une approche socio-sémantique des constructions identitaires. *L'Orientation Scolaire et Professionnelle, 27*, 1, 95–104.

Dumora, B. (1990). La dynamique vocationnelle chez l'adolescent de collège: continuité et rupture. *L'Orientation Scolaire et Professionnelle 19*, 2, 111–127.

Elias, N. (1987). *Die Gesellschaft der Individuen*. Francfort/Main: Suhrkamp Verlag.

Elias, N. (1991). *La société des individus*. Paris: Arthème Fayard.

Erikson, E. (1968). *Identity: Youth and crisis*. New York: Norton.

Foucault, M. (1984). *Le souci de soi* (Histoire de la sexualité, tome 3). Paris: Gallimard.

Foucault, M. (1984). L'éthique du souci de soi comme pratique de la liberté. *Concordia. Revista internacional de filosofia, 6*, 99–116. Repris dans: M. Foucault (1994). *Dits et écrits, volume 4*, 708–729.

Foucault, M. (1988). Technologies of the self. In P.-H Hutton, H. Gutman & L.-H. Martin (Eds.), *Technologies of the Self: a seminar with Michel Foucault* (pp. 16–49). Anherst: the University of Massachusetts Press. (French translation (1994), Dits et écrits, tome IV, pp. 783–813).

Foucault, M. (1994). *Dits et écrits*, 4 volumes. Paris: Gallimard.

Freud, S. (1917). Introductory lectures on Psychonalysys. In Standard Edition (1963, Vol. 15 & 16). London: Hogarth.

Gilly, M., Lacour, M., & Meyer, R. (1972). Image propre, images sociales et statut scolaire: étude comparative chez des élèves de CM2. *Bulletin de Psychologie, 25*, 792–806.

Ginzberg, E., Ginsburg, S., Axelrad, S., & Herma, J., (1951). *Occupational choice: an approach to a general theory*. New York: Columbia University Press.

Goffman, E. (1974). *Les rites d'interaction*. Paris: Editions de Minuit.

Gottfredson, L.S. (1981). Circumscription and compromise: A developmental theory of occupational aspirations. *Journal of Counseling Psychology Monograph, 28*, 6, 545–579.

Guichard, J. (1989). Career education in France: new objectives and new methods. *British Journal of Guidance and Counselling, 17*, 166–178.

Guichard, J. (1992). Comparative evaluation of several educational methods used in orientation: tools, results and methodological problems. *European Journal of Psychology of Education, 7*, 73–90.

Guichard, J. (1993). *L'école et les représentations d'avenir des adolescents*. Paris: PUF.

Guichard, J. (1996). Cultural habitus, school experiences and the formation of future intentions in adolescence. *Revista Portuguesa de Psychologia, 31*, 9–36.

Guichard, J. (1998). Conceptions de la qualification professionnelle, organisation scolaire et pratiques en orientation. *Cahiers Binet-Simon*, n° 656, 117–139.

Guichard, J. Devos, P., Bernard, H., Chevalier, G., Devaux, M., Faure, A., Jellab, M., & Vanesse, V. (1994a). Diversité et similarité des représentations professionnelles d'adolescents scolarisés dans des formations différentes. *L'Orientation Scolaire et Professionnelle, 23*, 409–437.

Guichard, J. Devos, P., Bernard, H., Chevalier, G., Devaux, M., Faure, A., Jellab, M., & Vanesse, V. (1994b). Habitus culturels des adolescents et schèmes représentatifs des professions. *L'Orientation Scolaire et Professionnelle, 23*, 439–464.

Guichard, J. & Falbierski, E. (1994). Compétences et projets: mots vides ou concepts pertinents pour l'insertion des jeunes en difficulté ? *Carriérologie, 5*, 131–157.

Guichard, J. & Cassar, O. (1998). Social fields, habitus, and cognitive schemes. Study stream and the categorisation of occupations. *Revue Internationale de Psychologie Sociale, 11*, 123–145.

Guichard, J., & Dosnon, O. (2000). Cognitive and social relevance of psycho-pedagogical methods in guidance. *Journal of Career Development, 26,* 161–173.

Gysbers, N.C. & Moore, E.J. (1973). *Life career development: A model.* Columbia: University of Missouri.

Havighurst, R.J. (1953). *Human development and education.* White Plains, NY: Longman.

Häyrynen, Y.P. (1995). Le concept de soi: un bien personnel, une norme ou une entité légitime ? *L'Orientation Scolaire et Professionnelle, 24,* 1, 5–17.

Hogg, M. A., & Abrams, D. (1988 1992). *Social Identifications.* London: Routledge.

Holland, J.L. (1973). *Making vocational choices: a theory of careers.* Englewoods Cliffs, NJ: Prentice-Hall.

Huteau, M. (1982). Les mécanismes psychologiques de l'évolution des attitudes et des préférences vis-à-vis des activités professionnelles. *L'Orientation Scolaire et Professionnelle, 11,* 107–125.

Jacques, F. (1979). *Dialogiques, recherches logiques sur le dialogue.* Paris: PUF.

James, W. (1890). *Principles of Psychology.* New York: Holt.

Jung, C.G. (1926). The structure and dynamics of the psyche. In *Collected works* (1960, Vol. 8). Princeton, NJ: Princeton University Press.

Kelly, G.A. (1955). *The psychology of personal constructs.* New York: Norton.

Kokosowski, A. (1983). Déterminants socio-scolaires, rationalisations et orientation des lycéens et étudiants. In A. Kokosowski (Ed.), *Les lycéens face à l'enseignement supérieur.* Issy-Les-Moulineaux: EAP, 127–170.

Krumboltz, J.-D. (1979). A social learning theory of career decision making. In A.-M. Mitchell, G.-B. Jones, and J.-D. Krumboltz (Ed.): *Social learning and career decision making.* Cranston, RI: The Carroll Press.

Laks, B. (1983). Langage et pratiques sociales, étude sociolinguistique d'un groupe d'adolescents. *Actes de la Recherche en Sciences Sociales, 46,* 73–97.

Law, B. (1981). Community Interaction: a "Mid-Range Focus for Theories of Career Development in Young Adults." *British Journal of Guidance and Counselling, 9* 142–158.

Law, B. (1996). A Career learning theory. In A.-G. Watts, B. Law, J. Killeen, J.-M. Kidd, & R. Hawthorn (Eds.), *Rethinking Careers Education and Guidance, Theory, Policy and Practice* (pp. 46–71). London: Routledge.

Mead, G.H. (1934). *Mind, self and society.* Chicago, IL: University of Chicago Press.

Meyer, R. (1986–1987). Image de soi et statut scolaire. Influence des déterminants familiaux et scolaires chez des élèves du cours moyen. *Bulletin de Psychologie, 49,* 933–942.

Minsky, M. (1975). A framework for representing knowledge. In P.-H. Winston (Ed.), *The Psychology of Computer Vision.* New York: MacGraw-Hill.

Monteil, J-.M. (1988). Comparaison sociale. Stratégies individuelles et médiations socio-cognitives. Un effet de différenciations comportementales dans le champ scolaire. *European Journal of Psychology of Education, 3*, 3–18.

Monteil, J-.M. (1990). *Eduquer et former: perspectives psycho-sociales*. Grenoble: Presses de l'Université de Grenoble.

Motola, M., Sinisalo, P., & Guichard, J. (1998). Social habitus and future plans—A comparison of adolescent future-projects in Finland and France. In J.-E. Nurmi (Ed.), *Adolescence, culture and conflicts: growing up in contemporary Europe* (pp. 43–73). New York: Garland Publishing.

Nizet, J. & Hiernaux J.-P. (1984). *Violence et ennui*. Paris: PUF.

Nurmi, J.-E. (1991). How do adolescents see their future ? A review of the development of future orientation and planning. *Developmental Review, 11*, 1–59.

Nurmi, J.-E. (1997). Self definition and mental health during adolescence and young adulthood. In J. Schulenberg, J. Maggs, and K. Hurrelmann (Eds), *Health risks and developmental trajectories during adolescence* (pp. 395–419). Cambridge, MA: Harvard University Press.

Parsons, F. (1909). *Choosing a vocation*. Boston: Houghton Mifflin.

Reuchlin, M. (1978). Processus vicariants et différences individuelles. *Journal de psychologie normale et pathologique, 75*, 138–145.

Reuchlin, M. (1997). *La Psychologie différentielle*. (nouvelle édition entièrement refondue). Paris: PUF, Le Psychologue.

Rogers, C.-R. (1961). *On becoming a person: a therapist's wiew of psychotherapy*. Boston: Houghton Miflin.

Roe, A. (1956). *The Psychology of Occupations*. New York: Wiley.

Sartre, J. P. (1952). *Saint Genet, comédien et martyr*. Paris: Gallimard.

Schank, R. C. & Abelson, R. P. (1977). *Scripts, plans, goals and understanding*. Hillsdale, NJ: Lawrence Erlbaum.

Schank, R. C. (1995). De la mémoire humaine à la mémoire artificielle. *La Recherche, 26*, 273, 150–155.

Super, D.-E. (1957). *The Psychology of Careers: an Introduction to Vocational Development*. New York: Harper.

Super, D.-E. (1984). Career and life development. In D. Brown, L. Brooks, et al. (Eds.), *Career and life development* (pp. 1992–234). San Francisco, CA: Jossey-Bass.

Taboada-Leonetti, I. (1990). Stratégies identitaires et minorités: le point de vue du sociologue. In C. Camilleri, et al., *Les stratégies identitaires* (pp. 43–83). Paris: PUF.

Tajfel, H. (Ed.) (1982). *Social Identity and Intergroup Relations*. Cambridge: Cambridge University Press.

Tap, P. (Ed.) (1980). *Identité individuelle et personnalisation*. Toulouse: Privat.

Touraine, A. (1955). La qualification du travail: histoire d'une notion. *Journal de psychologie normale et pathologique, 13*, 27–76.

Turner, J.-C. (1985). Social categorisation and the self concept: a social cognitive theory of group behaviour. In E.-J. Lawler (Ed.): *Advances in Group Processes: Theory and Research* (vol. 2). Greenwich, CT: JAI press.

Vondracek, F.-W., Lerner, & R.-M., Schulenberg J.-E. (1986). *Career development: a life span developmental approach.* Hillsdale, NJ: Lawrence Erlbaum.

Wallon, H. (1934). *Les origines du caractère chez l'enfant. Les préludes du sentiment de personnalité.* Paris: Presses Universitaires de France.

Wertsch, L.-V. (1990). The voice of rationality in a sociocultural approach to mind. In L.-C Moll (Ed.): *Vygotsky and Education. Instructional Implications and Applications of Sociohistorical Psychology.* New York: Cambridge University Press.

Willis, P. (1977). *Learning to labour: How Working-Class Kids Get Working-Class Jobs.* New York: Columbia University Press.

Willis, P. (1978). L'école des ouvriers. *Actes de la Recherche en Sciences Sociales, 24,* 50–61.

Zavalloni, M., & Louis-Guérin, C. (1984). *Identité sociale et introduction à l'égo-écologie.* Montréal: P.U.M.

Notes

1. Disharmony of positions in different fields marks representations of occupations. The study mentioned earlier (Guichard et al. 1994) evaluated in particular the "cognitive maps" of occupations of certain adolescents in contrasting positions in different fields (e.g.: secondary school pupils in a prestigious stream, but with "popular" cultural habits, distinguishing them from the great majority of their co-pupils, or apprentice mechanics whose "distinguished" cultural habits differentiate them from other apprentices). Such individuals are very much in the minority. It is therefore difficult to draw firm conclusions from these findings. Nevertheless, the cognitive maps of occupations of these adolescents invariably differ from those of their companions. For example, secondary school pupils with a privileged position in the scholastic system but with popular cultural habits represent prestigious occupations in the way of youngsters with popular tastes (differentiating them from their class companions) while they perceive less prestigious occupations in the same way as their companions.

CHAPTER 12

Conclusions and Future Perspectives
JARI-ERIK NURMI

The aim of this book was to increase our understanding of the ways in which individuals navigate through adolescence in a variety of sociocultural and interpersonal contexts. In its chapters, European researchers on adolescent development presented data concerning the tools adolescents deploy during this transition. A number of conceptualizations, such adolescents' values, personal goals, future-planning, occupational explorations, decision making, identity commitments, and identity frames were introduced and examined. A further emphasis was on co-navigation through adolescence. To investigate this, adolescents were asked, for example, with whom they typically plan their future, what the major sources of their future-related knowledge are, and the kinds of issues they are allowed to decide by themselves. Moreover, parents were asked how they think about their adolescent children's future. The last three chapters discussed the theoretical and methodological advances in recent European research on navigating through adolescence. These consisted of an introduction to a model in which adolescent development in age-graded developmental and interpersonal contexts was described in terms of the processes of self-direction and self-definition; a discussion of the mechanisms by which socioeconomic background, related cultural ways of speaking, and institutional environments influence adolescents' identity development; and an introduction to a dynamic system theory approach as an alternative way of testing some of the assumptions about adolescent development.

Navigating Through Adolescence

Navigation through adolescence was described as a complex and multifaceted process which has a variety of consequences for a young person's present and future life; which is preceded by a number of antecedents in the adolescent's previous life; which forms a variety of cumulative cycles across time; and which includes many interactive patterns with significant others. Some of the results reported might be summarized as follows.

The Role of Values, Goals and Strategies

One major assumption in several chapters was that the kinds of values, personal goals, identity explorations, and cognitive-motivational strategies adolescents have constructed previously play an important role in the ways in which they navigate through adolescence. Such assumption was explicitly stated by Stattin and Kerr, Salmela-Aro, Eronen, Malmerg, Kracke and Schmitt-Rodermund, and Nurmi.

For example, Stattin and Kerr argued that values may be important because they function as an organizing principle for how adolescents feel, think, behave, and relate to others. A similar role was suggested for personal goals in the chapters written by Salmela-Aro and by Nurmi. The results presented in the volume provided also support this notion.

Stattin and Kerr's results showed that adolescents with self-focused values reported more away-from-home activities, hanging around with peers, less regular activities at home, and poorer parent and teacher relationships compared with those with other-focused values. They were also more engaged in norm-breaking behaviors and showed poorer school adjustment than the young people with other-focused values. Adding to this picture, Salmela-Aro's findings suggested that the kinds of personal goals young people reported when faced with the transition from school to work were associated with their well-being: those whose personal goals concerned either interpersonal issues, or work and family, showed higher well-being than those whose goals focused on self-related and property-related topics.

Interestingly, both Stattin and Kerr, and Salmela-Aro, made a distinction between self-focused goals on the one hand and other-focused goals on the other. Both also found that self-focused goals tend to lead to non-adaptive developmental patterns and low well-being, whereas other-focused goals, or those related to interpersonal and normative issues, lead to adaptive patterns and high well-being. Stattin and Kerr sought the explanation for this result in the major principles of socialization: Many of the basic values that parents try to instill in their children deal with the concern for the good of others. Along somewhat similar lines of thinking, Salmela-Aro suggested that personal goals which concern interpersonal relationships, family and work are associated with high well-being, because they focus on dealing with the major age-graded developmental tasks, and help adolescents to adapt successfully to a particular life-period, whereas focus on self-related, existential issues lead to low well-being, because they do not contribute such adaptive efforts.

The results reported by Eronen also revealed that the kinds of cognitive-motivational strategies young people deploy play an important role in their success in dealing with the demands they face in their developmental environments. For example, young people who deployed a defensive, pessimistic achievement strategy seemed to show high academic achievement, whereas those who deployed a self-handicapping strategy showed low achievement. Moreover, the deployment of a planning-oriented social strategy seemed to lead to success in initiating close relationships and a low level of feelings of loneliness, whereas the use of a social avoidance strategy lead to the opposite pattern.

Cumulating Cycles

One major argument raised in several chapters was that the kinds of personal goals, cognitive-motivational strategies, and identity explorations and commitments adolescents construct to deal with a variety of demands they face in their developmental environments, and the outcomes of these efforts, form cumulative cycles.

On the one hand, adolescents' success in dealing with previous demands provide a basis for the kinds of personal goals and strategies their construct later on. For example, the findings reported by Salmela-Aro showed that young adults' previous commitments are reflected in the kind of goal patterns they show later on: those who had previous family commitments reported goals that concerned family- and work-related topics. Similarly, Eronen showed that young people's success in dealing with the demands of a particular life domain influence the kinds of strategies they later deploy. For example, low academic satisfaction seemed to increase the use of dysfunctional achievement strategies, such as self-handicapping, whereas high academic achievement led to the deployment of adaptive strategies. Moreover, success in initiating peer relationships was found to increase the use of a planning-oriented social strategy, whereas problems in interpersonal relationships led to the use of a social-avoidance strategy.

On the other hand, the kinds of personal values, goals, cognitive-motivational strategies, and identity explorations reported by adolescents were found to influence their success in dealing with particular developmental challenges. For example, the findings reported by Salmela-Aro showed that those young people who showed an interest in work and family were more successful in finding a job after graduation from school than other participants. In turn, individuals who were interested in social relationships were less likely to be successful in terms of finding a job after graduation.

Eronen reported findings according to which the kinds of achievement strategies young people deployed contributed to their success in dealing with academic demands: the use of adaptive strategies, characterized by optimism and task-focused goals and behaviors, led to high academic achievement, whereas the use of maladaptive strategies typified by failure expectations and active avoidance, increased the likelihood of low achievement. Similarly, the deployment of adaptive social strategies, such as a planning-oriented strategy, seemed to lead to success in initiating close relationships and a low level of feelings of loneliness, whereas the use of a social avoidance strategy was associated with an opposite pattern. A somewhat similar pattern was reported by Kracke and Schmitt-Rodermund in the context of searching for information about future careers and work. According to their results, a low level of occupational exploration predicted subsequent uncertainty about occupational plans. This may be assumed to be associated with a low level of related information, which they also found to be associated with a low rather than high level of occupational exploration.

Overall, these results emphasized the importance of investigating the developmental dynamics of the processes involved in navigating through adolescence in terms of cumulative, either positive or negative, cycles. One interesting methodological tool for formulating hypotheses for such research is the dynamic systems theory approach introduced by Kunnen, Bosma, and van Geert. According to them, the dynamic systems theory offers new ways of conceptualizing and understanding stability and change in adolescent development. It describes the theoretical assumptions concerning mutual and non-linear relationships between different components of a system and shows how particular characteristics of person-context interaction induce changes in individuals' developmental trajectories. In other words, by constructing a model to describe a particular developing system, identifying the key variables, and defining the mathematical formulas governing their relationships, it is possible to test the kinds of systemic properties such a model will show across time.

The Role of the Family

One major contribution made in this volume to the present literature is that the ways in which adolescents direct their lives in terms of goal-construction, future-planning, and identity explorations should be described as a co-navigation through adolescence rather than a purely individual adventure. For example, the findings reported by Malmberg showed that adolescents reported nearly as much as future-planning in the home environment together with their parents as they did when alone. Moreover, when adolescents were asked about the most important sources of future-related information, one of the most often mentioned source was home and parents.

The results of Lanz, Rosnati, Marta, and Scabini showed that parents' views about their children's future resembles in many ways the views of the adolescents themselves. First, parents were optimistic about their adolescent children's future, as were the adolescents. Second, parents hopes for their children's future concerned the key age-graded developmental tasks of adolescence and young adulthood, such as future occupation, family, and education, which was in accordance with adolescents' views. Parents also expected that their hopes concerning their adolescents' future would be actualized at about the same time as the latter expected them to be actualized, reflecting the normative life-span development. These results are important because they show that parents view their adolescents' future much as the adolescents do: both expect it to consist of efforts dealing with the major developmental demands and role transitions demanded in the process of becoming an adult. The results reported by Zani, Bosma, Zijsling, and Honess provide a somewhat similar view of the relationship between parents' and their adolescent children's views about the major issues surrounding family decision making: adolescents and their parents, overall, perceived the norms related to a variety of issues concerning autonomy in similar ways. Although there were also discrepancies in their views, they seem to mainly concern the timing of autonomous decision making.

Lanz et al. found also that the family relationships were influential for adolescents' future-orientation: openness of communication in the family was associated with young people's beliefs in personal control regarding their own future. Similarly, Kracke and Schmitt-Rodermund found that child-centered parenting, such as parental openness and an authoritative style, was an important determinant of adolescents' exploration concerning their future occupation and career. It may be, however, that adolescents' ways of directing their lives also influence their relationships with their parents. The results of Stattin and Kerr, for example, showed that adolescents with self-focused values seemed to have more away-from-home activities, poorer parent-relationships, and to be less involved in regular activities at home than those with other-focused values.

Role of Peers and Friends

The findings reported in this volume showed that not only parents but also peers were involved in co-navigation through adolescence. For example, Malmberg's findings revealed that adolescents considered their peer groups an important context for planning the future. Moreover, school friends and other peers were reported to be important sources of future-related information exceeding, for example, the role of school.

Interestingly, the kinds of navigational tools adolescents reported in terms of values, personal goals and cognitive-motivational strategies seem also to have important consequences for their peer relationships. For example, Stattin and Kerr's findings revealed that adolescents with self-focused values were more involved in a variety of peer activities but less in regular activities at home than those who reported other-focused values. Such involvement in peer activities may also explain why they showed a higher level of norm breaking behavior and a lower level of school adjustment. Similarly, Salmela-Aro's results showed that, although young people who were interested in interpersonal relationships showed higher well-being than those whose goals focused on other kinds of topic, they were less likely to be successful in terms of finding a job after graduation. Overall, these findings suggest that, although adolescents' focus on interpersonal and peer relationship may be personally satisfying and associated with high well-being, such activities may lead to risks in dealing successfully with other developmental challenges, such as those related to education and occupation.

The Role of Sociocultural and Institutional Contexts

Two chapters emphasized the importance of sociocultural and institutional contexts for the ways is which individuals navigate through adolescence. Nurmi suggested that a variety of demands and opportunities available in the age-graded developmental environment adolescents face during this particular age phase play an important role in their development because such age-graded demands and opportunities provide a basis for the formulation of realistic personal goals, the construction of adaptive plans and strategies, and also a framework for the evaluation of individual success in dealing with them. He also reviewed a number of studies showing that cross-national and cross-cultural differences in such age-graded sociocultural environments are reflected in the kinds of future-oriented goals and identity explorations adolescents report.

Similarly, Guichard suggested that school is one major agent of socialization that provides a basis for the ways in which adolescents learn to perceive themselves. For example, school achievement and related feedback provides long lasting consequences for an adolescent's self-concept. Such self-identities are then also reflected in young peoples' future projects, particularly the ways in which they see their future career. Moreover, other culturally-defined processes, such as interactions and dialogues with others, provide a basis for the ways in which adolescents contruct their self-identities and future goals.

Perspectives for Future Research

Overall, the findings reported here showed that the kinds of values, personal goals, identity explorations, and cognitive and motivational strategies adolescents have play an important role in the ways in which they navigate into adulthood; that these navigational tools and individuals' success in dealing with the major developmental demands and challenges form a variety of cumulative cycles; and that this process takes place in the context of many interpersonal relationships, such as parents and peers, and that it is influenced by a variety of sociocultural and institutional transitions. Overall, these findings have a number of implications for future adolescent research.

First, there exists a variety of theoretical frameworks, and related conceptualizations which have been applied in the research on how individuals navigate through adolescence. Although such diversity of theoretical conceptualizations may contribute to innovative research on adolescent development, there is an evident need to integrate some of these overlapping conceptualizations, or at least to discuss their relations.

Second, despite the substantial amount of research on the ways in which young people navigate through adolescence from the individual point of view, only a few studies have investigated the role of parents, and peers in particular, in this process. Consequently, further studies focusing on the ways in which family and parents are involved in adolescents' navigation into adulthood in terms of family discussion, negations, role modeling, and tutoring, on the one hand, and the role that peers and friends may have in this process in terms of discussions and social comparisons, on the other, are needed.

Third, it was suggested in many chapters that the kinds of values, personal goals, and identity explorations and commitments adolescents have reflect in a variety of ways the age-graded developmental and institutional transitions they face, and even the changing demands and challenges across such transitions. Because there is a substantial amount of variation in the timing and sequencing of such transitions across societies and cultures, for example in Europe, cross-cultural comparisons of the ways in which adolescents navigate through adolescence would be particularly helpful in efforts to understand the key mechanisms of adolescent development. One important requirement of such research, however, is to include societies that systematically differ according to the timing, sequencing, and available trajectories of major developmental transitions, and to plan research along such differences.

Fourth, although some of the studies reported in this volume used a longitudinal procedure to investigate adolescent development, they admitted to some limitations, too. Only a few studies used a full cross-lagged longitudinal procedure; most of them focused on a limited period of adolescence only; and none of them included an intensive follow up of the development of navigational tools, by conducting measurements every half year for example. Consequently, there are at least three methodological approaches open to future studies on the ways in which individuals navigate through adolescence. The first and the most traditional approach would be to develop an extensive cross-lagged longitudinal study across the years of adolescence. By expanding, such a study with cross-cultural comparisons would provide a possibility not only to test the generality of the key developmental mechanisms across different contexts but also to examine the impacts of the diversity of environments on adolescent development. The second line of research would be to investigate adolescents' development across certain "critical transitions," such as that from junior to senior high school, from school to work, and starting a family. Although such short-term cross-lagged longitudinal studies would focus only on a limited time-period, they could provide important information on adolescent development for two major reasons: they allow intensive data gathering, for example across a few months rather than years, which then enables examination of the developmental dynamics of the years of adolescence; and such studies would make it possible to investigate adolescents in a situation in which the timing of the major transitions is similar for all participants. The third line of future research could include an intensive investigation of the individual adolescent's trajectories across time. Such a time-series approach was also suggested by Kunnen, Bosma, and van Geert as a complementary way of investigating developing systems across time.

Practical Implications and Interventions

Several practical implications for and interventions to promote adolescents' success in dealing with the transition into adulthood were introduced. Such interventions were typically described in relation to major developmental contexts, such as families, schools, communities, and institutions.

The majority of the suggestions focused on what might be done in schools. For example, Stattin and Kerr suggested that adolescents' values should be explicitly included in designing future intervention programs in schools. As discussed by Salmela-Aro, such interventions may include efforts to promote adolescents' beliefs in the value of the future, to encourage them to focus on personal goals relating to the major challenges and demands they face during this age-period, and to help them to focus on how to construct efficient means toward attaining their goals. Kracke and Schmitt-Rodermund emphasized that schools may do more to stimulate adolescents' career exploration. For example, teachers should stimulate such activities, paying particular attention to those young people, who are less prepared for such exploration because of their personality factors or family background.

In her chapter on cognitive-motivational strategies, Eronen made many suggestions about how to promote adolescents' use of adaptive achievement strategies at school. According to her, the typical approach of simply encouraging adolescents in the achievement of good grades is problematic, because it may increase the likelihood of arriving at negative self-appraisals, and because it does not enhance his or her striving to learn. Alternative procedures in academic settings may include efforts to create a supportive atmosphere in which failures are seen as a natural part of the learning process; to increase the importance of individual feedback after learning rather than focusing on individual differences in grades; and the use of group learning, which encourages students to participate and commit themselves to learning activities rather than to compete with each other.

Another related context concerns adolescents' peer groups, because peer relations are initiated to a considerable extent in school settings. If adolescents are provided with interventions for their social skills and the strategies they deploy in interpersonal settings, the school environment is a natural choice. Eronen suggested several possibilities for intervention in adolescents' problems in the interpersonal domain, such as efforts to encourage individuals' motivation to engage in social interaction and to help them to construct adaptive strategies to deal with such challenges rather than focusing on threatening information. As possible techniques for such an effort, she introduced the ideas of adaptive self-talk, re-attribution therapy, and the integration of individuals showing problems with those who behave in an adaptive manner.

In several chapters, for example in those written by Lanz, Rosnati, Marta, and Scabini; Zani, Bosma, Zijsling, and Honess; and Malmberg, the role of the family was emphasized as an important agent in the effort to promote adolescents' navigation into adulthood. According to Kracke and Schmitt-Rodermund, for example, parents should be encouraged to stimulate their adolescent children's career exploration. This may include, on the one hand, helping adolescents to become more aware of their abilities and interests, and, on the other, introducing them a wide range of possible future options. Parents may even try to practice such activities early on during late childhood and early adolescence.

One additional institution that was discussed as a possible context for helping adolescents to deal with the key developmental challenges they face is vocational counseling. Depending on the society, such counseling may be done as part of the school system or take place in vocational counseling agencies. For example, Salmela-Aro suggested that personal goals may serve as a direct focus in such occupational counseling. Such efforts may enhance adolescents' well-being by helping them to identify positive life goals which reflect the major age-graded normative tasks and demands, by expanding the information at their disposal about future opportunities, and by providing tutoring and support for goal construction and attainment.

Similarly, Guichard discussed the possibilities and methods of providing vocational guidance. He suggested that the main aim of counseling cannot only be to help the client to find a job that best suits his or her personal characteristics, but rather to help the adolescent to discover and build up an identity that will provide him/herself with the possibility of finding new career prospects. This process may include either helping the adolescent to identify a variety of future career possibilities, or helping them to stabilize or commit themselves to one of the alternatives.

Navigation through adolescence was conceptualized in several chapters as a kind of cumulative, either positive or negative, cycle. On the one hand, adolescents' success in dealing with the variety of challenges, demands and transitions they face in academic, interpersonal, and institutional settings provide the basis for the kinds of navigational tools they deploy later on in life. On the other, the kinds of tools they deploy in turn provide a basis for their success in navigating through adolescence into major adult roles. Such a notion of adolescent development as cumulative or self-perpetuating cycles also has important practical implications, because it suggests that cumulative negative cycles should be interrupted whenever the first signs of this kind of development are visible, before it escalates to other life domains and negative self-definitions.

Contributors

Harke A. Bosma is a senior lecturer of adolescent psychology at the University of Groningen. He has authored several articles and books on identity in adolescence. His most recent book (with Saskia E. Kunnen as co-editor) is *Identity and Emotion: Development through self-organization* (Cambridge University Press, 2001).

Sanna Eronen earned her Ph. D. at University of Helsinki, and works presently as a researcher in a Centre of Educational Assessment, at the University of Helsinki. She has written many articles about social strategies, interpersonal behavior and well-being of adolescents and young adults.

Paul van Geert is a professor of developmental psychology at the University of Groningen, the Netherlands. His major interest lies in dynamic systems models of developmental processes. He published various articles on this topic and a book *Dynamic systems of development* (1994).

Jean Guichard is a professor of psychology. He is the director of the National Institute for the Study of Work and Vocational Guidance (INETOP-CNAM) in Paris (France). He has published many papers and books on the development of identity and future plans in adolescence. His most recent book (in collaboration with Michel Huteau) is *Psychologie de l'orienation* Paris (Dunod).

Terry M. Honess is a reader in psychology at City University, London. He has two broad areas of research interest: Adolescent adjustment, with particular reference to family conflict, and with an increasing interest in adolescent coping in especially difficult environments; and Juror and jury decision making, with particular reference to pre-trial publicity and juror competence.

Margaret Kerr earned her Ph. D. at Cornell University, U.S.A., and is now an associate professor of psychology at Örebro University in Sweden. Her research deals with risk and protective factors in adolescent development and across the lifespan. Her published work includes studies on shyness and inhibition, parenting processes such as monitoring, and delinquency.

Baerbel Kracke is a researcher at the Department of Work and Organizational Psychology at the University of Jena. She works in the fields of relationship development in families with adolescents, youths' career exploration, and the integration of family and work.

Saskia Kunnen works as a researcher at the University of Utrecht, the Netherlands. Her publications concern development of identity in adolescents and adults, and the application of dynamic systems methods in the field of developmental psychology. Recently she published, with Harke Bosma, the book *Identity and emotion: development through self-organization* (Cambridge University Press).

Margherita Lanz is a researcher in social psychology at the Catholic University of Milan. She is author of numerous articles concerning families with adolescents and young adults, future orientation. Her most recent book is *Cognizioni sociali e relazioni familiari.* [Social cognition and family relationship]. Milan: Franco Angeli.

Lars-Erik Malmberg, is a researcher at the Department of Teacher Education in Vasa, Åbo Akademi University, Finland. His research interests are educational psychology, future-orientation, cross-cultural studies and quantitative methods.

Elena Marta is an associate professor in social psychology at the Catholic University of Milan. She is author of numerous articles concerning families with adolescents and young adults, young adults volunteers. Her most recent book is *Cognizioni sociali e relazioni familiari.* [Social cognition and family relationship]. Milan: Franco Angeli.

Jari-Erik Nurmi is Chair Professor at the Department of Psychology, University of Jyväskylä. He is an author of numerous articles and edited books on adolescent development, personal goals and motivation, coping strategies, and life-span development. One of his particular interest during the past years has been modeling development across critical life-span transitions.

Rosa Rosnati is a researcher in social psychology at the Catholic University of Milan. She is author of numerous articles concerning adoptive families, families with adolescents and educational and occupational expectations, families with young children. Her most recent book is *Il patto adottivo. L'adozione internazionale di fronte alla sfida dell'adolescenza* [The adoptive pact. Intercountry adoption in front of the adolescent challenge]. Milan: Franco Angeli.

Katariina Salmela-Aro is now acting as a professor in the Department of Psychology at the University of Jyväskylä in Finland. Her main interest concerns the meaning of personal goals in different life transitions and well-being. She received her Ph. D. from the University of Helsinki and spent her post-doctoral year in the Max-Planck Institute for Human Development in Berlin, Germany.

Eugenia Scabini is a professor in family social psychology at the Catholic University of Milan. She is author of numerous articles concerning families with adolescents and young adults. Her most recent book is *Il Famigliare. Legami, simboli e transizioni* [The familiar. Bonds, symbols and transitions], Milan: Raffaello Cortina.

Eva Schmitt-Rodermund is an assistant professor for developmental psychology at the University of Jena. Her areas of interest include career development, problem behavior, the timing of adolescent development, and puberty. Her most recent research project relates to the development of entrepreneurship in adolescents.

Håkan Stattin is a professor of psychology at Örebro University, Sweden. His research publications deal with the developmental background of antisocial behavior; crime prevention; "healthy functioning" and protective factors; the role of pubertal maturation in adolescent development; and parent-child interactions and communication. He is the leader of the longitudinal project the Solna study, a birth-to-maturity study, and he is involved in several other Swedish longitudinal programs.

Bruna Zani is a professor of social psychology at the University of Bologna, Italy. She is member of the Executive Committee of EARA since 1998 and of the Social Psychology Division of the Italian Association of Psychology since 1999. She is the director of the Ph.D. program in Social and Developmental Psychology of the University of Bologna. She is the author of several books and articles on social and community psychology. Her most recent book is *Psicologia della salute* (Health Psychology), Bologna: Il Mulino, 2000.

Djurre H. Zijsling graduated in developmental psychology at the University of Groningen. Since then he has participated in several large research projects with a major responsibility for data management and analysis.

Index